Post-Imperial Brecht

Post-Imperial Brecht challenges prevailing views of Brecht's theatre and politics. Most political theatre critics place Brecht between West and East in the Cold War, and a few have recently explored Brecht's impact as a Northern writer on the global South. Loren Kruger is the first to argue that Brecht's impact as a political dramatist, director and theoretical writer makes full sense only when seen in a post-imperial framework that links the East/West axis between US capitalism and Soviet communism with the North/South axis of post-colonial resistance to imperialism. This framework highlights Brecht's arguments with theorists like Benjamin, Bloch, and Lukács. It also shows surprising connections between socialist East Germany, where Brecht's 1950s projects impressed the emerging Heiner Müller, and apartheid-era South Africa, where Brecht's work appeared on the apartheid as well as anti-apartheid stage. Brecht also shaped the work of South Africa's Athol Fugard, whose work reappeared in state and dissident theatres in East Germany. The book concludes with a reflection on Brechtian aspects of South Africa's Truth and Reconciliation Commission and introduces new more precise translations of key Brechtian terms.

LOREN KRUGER is a graduate of the University of Cape Town, South Africa, and Cornell University, and teaches the history and theory of drama and other cultural forms at the University of Chicago. She is the author of *The National Stage* (1992) and *The Drama of South Africa* (1999), and the editor of *Lights and Shadows: The Autobiography of Leontine Sagan* (1996), and of South African special issues of *Theatre Journal* and *Theatre Research International.*

CAMBRIDGE STUDIES IN MODERN THEATRE

Series editor

David Bradby, *Royal Holloway, University of London*

Advisory board

Martin Banham, *University of Leeds*

Jacky Bratton, *Royal Holloway, University of London*

Tracy Davis, *Northwestern University*

Sir Richard Eyre

Michael Robinson, *University of East Anglia*

Sheila Stowell, *University of Birmingham*

Volumes for Cambridge Studies in Modern Theatre explore the political, social and cultural functions of theatre while also paying careful attention to detailed performance analysis. The focus of the series is on political approaches to the modern theatre with attention also being paid to theatres of earlier periods and their influence on contemporary drama. Topics in the series are chosen to investigate this relationship and include both playwrights (their aims and intentions set against the effects of their work) and process (with emphasis on rehearsal and production methods, the political structure within theatre companies and their choice of audiences or performance venues). Further topics will include devised theatre, agitprop, community theatre, para-theatre and performance art. In all cases the series will be alive to the special cultural and political factors operating in the theatres examined.

Books published

Brian Crow with Chris Banfield, *An Introduction to Post-Colonial Theatre*

Maria DiCenzo, *The Politics of Alternative Theatre in Britain, 1968–1990: the Case of 7:84 (Scotland)*

Jo Riley, *Chinese Theatre and the Actor in Performance*

Jonathan Kalb, *The Theatre of Heiner Müller*

Richard Boon and Jane Plastow, eds., *Theatre Matters: Performance and Culture on the World Stage*

Claude Schumacher, ed., *Staging the Holocaust: the Shoah in Drama and Performance*

Philip Roberts, *The Royal Court Theatre and the Modern Stage*

Nicholas Grene, *The Politics of Irish Drama: Plays in Context from Boucicault to Friel*

Anatoly Smeliansky, *The Russian Theatre after Stalin*

Clive Barker and Maggie B. Gale, eds., *British Theater between the Wars, 1918–1939*

Michael Patterson, *Strategies of Political Theatre: Post-War British Playwrights*

Elaine Aston, *Feminist Views on the English Stage: Women Playwrights, 1990–2000*

Gabriele Griffin, *Contemporary Black and Asian Women Playwrights in Britain*

Loren Kruger, *Post-Imperial Brecht: Politics and Performance, East and South*

Post-Imperial Brecht

Politics and Performance, East and South

Loren Kruger
University of Chicago

CAMBRIDGE
UNIVERSITY PRESS

PUBLISHED BY THE PRESS SYNDICATE OF THE UNIVERSITY OF CAMBRIDGE
The Pitt Building, Trumpington Street, Cambridge, United Kingdom

CAMBRIDGE UNIVERSITY PRESS
The Edinburgh Building, Cambridge, CB2 2RU, UK
40 West 20th Street, New York, NY 10011–4211, USA
477 Williamstown Road, Port Melbourne, VIC 3207, Australia
Ruiz de Alarcón 13, 28014 Madrid, Spain
Dock House, The Waterfront, Cape Town 8001, South Africa

http://www.cambridge.org

First published 2004

Printed in the United Kingdom at the University Press, Cambridge

Typefaces Trump Mediaeval 9.25/14 pt. and Schadow BT   *System* LaTeX 2$_\varepsilon$ [TB]

Library of Congress Cataloguing in Publication data
Kruger, Loren.
Post-imperial Brecht : politics and performance, east and south / Loren Kruger.
   p.   cm. – (Cambridge studies in modern theatre)
Includes bibliographical references and index.
ISBN 0 521 81708 0
1. Brecht, Bertolt, 1898–1956 – Criticism and interpretation.   2. Brecht, Bertolt,
1898–1956 – Political and social views.   3. Brecht, Bertolt, 1898–1956 –
appreciation – South Africa.   I. Title.   II. Series.
PT2603.R397Z74446   2004
832'.912 – dc22   2003069750

ISBN 0 521 81708 0 hardback

Contents

Illustrations

Jacket: Arthur Molepo in Junction Avenue Theatre Company's *Love, Crime and Johannesburg* (1999). Photograph by Ruphin Coudyzer. FPPSA; *www.ruphin.com*

Chapter 2:

Fig. 1: Regine Lutz and Ekkehart Schall in *Katzgraben* (Berlin, 1953) by Erwin Strittmatter; adapted and directed by Brecht. Photograph reprinted with permission from the Stiftung Akademie der Künste Bertolt Brecht Archive (SAdK/BBA). *68*

Fig. 2: "The New Household": Lutz as Elli, Günter Gnass as her father Kleinschmidt and Angelika Hurwicz as her mother in *Katzgraben*. Photograph reprinted with permission from the SAdK/BBA. *78*

Fig. 3: "Studiere ihn tot": Lutz and Hurwicz in *Katzgraben*. Photograph reprinted with permission from the SAdK/BBA. *79*

Fig. 4: "The Model Worker's Burden": Dieter Montag in *Der Lohndrücker* (1956) by Heiner Müller, adapted and directed by the author (Berlin 1988). Photograph by Sybille Bergemann; Stiftung Akademie der Künste: courtesy of the Theaterdokumentation. *125*

Fig. 5: Visions of abundance and the HO queen in *Der Lohndrücker* (1988). Photograph by Sybille Bergemann; courtesy of the SAdK: TD. *127*

vi

Acknowledgments

This book has its origins in a hunch that personal experience of cultural and political life in Germany and South Africa could be grounded in historical connections that are compelling as well as surprising. Its evolution has followed a characteristically comparative literary path between languages, discourses, and cultures, but owes its substance to the study of theatre, a subject still often marginalized in the fields of comparative and other literatures.

On this route between cultures and, specifically, between Berlin and various points in South Africa, I have been supported by many people and institutions. In South Africa, my debts to the people named in the preface to my last book, *The Drama of South Africa*, are renewed with this one, especially to Ann Torlesse at the National English Literary Museum. In addition, Heidi Grunebaum, Yazir Henry, and their comrades at the Direct Action Centre for Peace and Democracy in Cape Town offered unparalleled insight into the personal and political ramifications of truth, reconciliation, and their antagonists in post-apartheid society. Also in Cape Town, Mark Fleischman provided me with an opportunity to revise my thoughts in formal and informal presentation on current South African theatre; Tony Parr and Gay Morris added to the conversation. In Johannesburg Malcolm Purkey reminded me of the eclectic history of Brecht in South Africa; Carole Archibald of the Witwatersrand University Historical Papers Library helped me document the Garment Workers' Union's political theatre before Brecht; and Patricia Watson Shariff raised questions about the limits of theatre in a cultural field shaped increasingly by new media.

My research in Berlin was funded in part by the German Academic Exchange Service (DAAD) and an Andrew Mellon Foundation

ix

Acknowledgments

grant administered by the University of Chicago, and enriched by the resources of the Berlin City Museum (Berliner Stadtmuseum), the Bertolt Brecht Archive, the Archive of the Academy of Arts (Akademie der Künste) and the theatres in Berlin and beyond. Thanks are due to the director and staff of the Brecht Archive, Erdmut Wizisla, Elke Pfeil, Helga Streidt, and Ute Kohl; Frederike Biron at the Berliner Ensemble; Lothar Schirmer at the Berliner Stadtmuseum; Heike Solisiak at the Volksbühne; Kerstin Walter at the Hans-Otto Theater Potsdam; and above all to Peter Ullrich of the Academy's Theatre Documentation department, whose support of this project with textual and visual material went well beyond the routine obligations of the archivist. Interviews and correspondence with Freya Klier, Eckhardt Becker, and especially Rolf Winkelgrund, director of several East German premieres of plays by Athol Fugard, enhanced my understanding of the East German stage, as did exchanges with Joachim Fiebach and Kurt Goldstein. Also in Berlin, Erika Fischer-Lichte offered valuable recommendations; Marija Erceg sought out essential sources, and Gaby Dietze, Dorothea Dornhof, Wilhelm Werthern, and Brian Currid contributed conversation and culinary pleasures.

Among many colleagues at various institutions, I am grateful above all to the International Brecht Society, which has provided numerous occasions in stimulating places for exchanging ideas about Brecht and the Brechtian legacy, as well as key interlocutors for this project, especially Marc Silberman, Darko Suvin, John Rouse, Hans-Thies Lehmann, Katrin Sieg, and Patricia Ann Simpson. Thanks are due also to organizers and participants at conferences that offered stimulating exchange: to Russell Berman, Leslie Adelson, and others reflecting on globalization and German studies at Stanford University, to David Bathrick, Frank and Therese Hörnigk, and others discussing Heiner Müller at Cornell University, and to Peggy Pietsche and others reviewing East Germany's hidden race relations in Berlin. In Chicago for the short as well as long term, several colleagues and friends have enriched my work on this project: Hunter Bivens, Dipesh Chakrabarty, Lisa Fittko, Michael Geyer, David Graver, Miriam Hansen, Julia Hell (University of Michigan), Warren Leming, Sem Sutter, Robert von Hallberg, and above all Katie Trumpener (now at Yale University).

Acknowledgments

Portions of this research have appeared in earlier versions in the following journals: *Brecht Yearbook* 17 (1992) and 23 (1998); *Theatre Journal* 46 (1994); *Rethinking Marxism* 7 (1994) and 11 (1999); *Modern Drama* 43 (2000); *Theatre Research International* 27 (2002), and *Modern Philology* 100 (2003). Thanks are due to the publishers and especially to the editors: Marc Silberman, John Rouse, David Ruccio, Carole Biewener, W. B. Worthen, Richard Paul Knowles, Brian Singleton, Katie Trumpener, and Joshua Scodel. At Cambridge University Press, commissioning editor Victoria Cooper supported the project from the outset, and series editor David Bradby offered timely advice to speed the manuscript through final revisions. Responsibility for errors or eccentricities in the published book remains mine.

Abbreviations

AdK   Akademie der Künste, Berlin, including
                Theaterdokumentation (GDR Theatre
                Documentation; TD), Athol Fugard, and Heiner
                Müller collections
ANC   African National Congress, South Africa (1912–);
                underground 1964–90
BE   Berliner Ensemble
BBA   Bertolt Brecht Archive, Berlin
Brecht, *Werke* Bertolt Brecht, *Werke: Berliner und Frankfurter
                Ausgabe* in 30 vols. (Frankfurt: Suhrkamp, 1988–)
BoT   *Brecht on Theatre*, ed. and trans. John Willett
                (1964; New York: Hill and Wang, 1992)
BOSS   Bureau of State Security, South Africa (1964–77);
                succeeded by the State Security Council (until
                1990s)
BPT   Bantu Peoples' Theatre (1937–9); later the African
                National Theatre (1940–1)
CPSA   Communist Party of South Africa (1919–50)
CWLP   Culture and Working Life Project, South Africa
                (1980s)
DSM   *Diagnostic and Statistical Manual of Mental
                Disorders*, 4th edn (Washington: American
                Psychiatric Association, 1994)
DWCL   Durban Workers Culture Local, South Africa
                (1980s)
FDJ   Freie Deutsche Jugend (Free German Youth):
                SED-affiliated German youth organization

Abbreviations

FRG	Federal Republic of Germany (West), 1949 (Ger.: Bundesrepublik Deutschland or BRD)
GDR	German Democratic Republic (East), 1949–90 (Ger.: Deutsche Demokratische Republik or DDR)
GWU	Garment Workers' Union, South Africa
HfÖ	Hochschule für Ökonomie (GDR): College of Economics
HRV	Human Rights Violations Committee of the Truth and Reconciliation Commission, South Africa
HUAC	House UnAmerican Activities Committee, USA (1938–75)
IU/LL	Indiana University Lilly Library; includes Athol Fugard collection
JATC	Junction Avenue Theatre Company, *At the Junction: Four Plays by the Junction Avenue Theatre Company*, ed. Martin Orkin (Johannesburg: Witwatersrand University Press, 1995)
JPL/STC	Johannesburg Public Library: Strange Theatre Collection
KPD	Kommunistische Partei Deutschlands or German Communist Party (1919–33; 1945–6)
MK	UmKhonto we Sizwe or Spear of the Nation (1964–94): guerrilla arm of the ANC
NELM	National English Literary Museum, Grahamstown, South Africa
NSDAP	Nationalsozialistische Deutsche Arbeiterpartei or Nazi Party (1924–45)
PACT	Performing Arts Council of the Transvaal, South Africa (1963–98)
PTSD	Post-traumatic stress disorder
SABTU	South African Black Theatre Union (1969–73)
SACP	South African Communist Party (underground 1950–90; legal from 1990)

SED	Sozialistische Einheitspartei Deutschlands or Socialist Unity Party, ruling party of GDR
SPD	Sozialistische Partei Deutschlands or Socialist Party; absorbed in the GDR by the SED in 1946
Stasi	Ministerium für Staatssicherheit or Ministry for State Security (GDR, 1951–90)
STC/JPL	Strange Theatre Collection, Johannesburg Public Library
Steinweg	Brecht, *Die Massnahme*, ed. Reiner Steinweg
TRC	Truth and Reconciliation Commission, South Africa (1996–2000)
UCT	University of Cape Town
UW/WC	University of the Witwatersrand William Cullen Library: includes Garment Workers' Union (GWU), South African Institute of Race Relations (SAIRR) collections, Lewis Sowdon's "Red Rand", and other materials

Introduction

At the height of the Cold War, in August 1961, as the Berlin Wall realized in concrete the ideological, political and economic barriers that
already separated Eastern from Western Europe, the "communist"
from the "free" or "imperialist-capitalist" world (depending on point
of view), Bertolt Brecht figured alternately as hero and villain of the
political melodrama unfolding in its shadow. In articles published
in the West German magazine *Der Monat*, which was funded, like
its English equivalent *Encounter*, by the CIA-sponsored Committee
for Cultural Freedom, Brecht was cast as equal to the "immediate
threat of the Red Army." Anti-communist ideologues charged him
with delusional attachment to Communism; even the critical theorist T. W. Adorno accused him of "glorifying the Party," or, more
subtly, of "oversimplifying" artistic form in favor of political content.[1] In the other camp in the German Democratic Republic (GDR)
or East Germany, the ruling Socialist Unity Party (SED) was stirred

---

[1] The equation of Brecht and the Red Army is Friedrich Tolberg's: "Soll
man Brecht im Westen spielen?", *Der Monat* 14, no. 159 (1962), 56–62;
reiterated by respondents in "Soll man Brecht spielen? Antworten an
Friedrich Tolberg," *Der Monat* 14, no. 161 (1962), 57–64. The case for
Brecht's delusional attachment to Communism was made by Herbert
Lüthy in "Vom armen BB," *Der Monat* 4, no. 44 (May 1952), 115–44,
reprinted in *Encounter*. The claim was reiterated, with an effort to
separate Brecht's artistry from his politics, by Martin Esslin in *Bertolt
Brecht: A Choice of Evils* (London: Methuen, 1962). For the more
subtle critique of Brecht's assault on the autonomy of art, see
T[heodor] W[iesengrund] Adorno, "Engagement" (1962) in *Noten zur
Literatur* (Frankfurt: Suhrkamp, 1980), trans. as "Commitment" in
Aesthetics and Politics: Debates between Brecht, Lukacs, Brecht,

by campaigns in the West to boycott Brecht to abandon its Stalinist denunciation of his experiments as "alien to the people" to attempt after Brecht's death in 1956 to claim him and even his most experimental form, the *Lehrstück* or learning play for worker-players, as its own. Even though it had criticized Brecht while he lived, the SED used Brecht posthumously as the guarantor of the party's legitimacy as the true inheritor of the anti-fascist and anti-imperialist tradition of the German left.[2] On the basis of this claim, the SED continued until the late 1980s to cast Brecht as a "fighter against capitalist exploitation" whose work contributed to "mobilizing reason in the struggle against irrationalism, imperialism, and SDI [the United States's Strategic Defense Initiative]."[3]

In claiming Brecht as the representative of the anti-fascist legacy of the 1920s, the SED sought to shore up its own inheritance

Benjamin, Adorno (London: Verso, 1977). Although he rejects Esslin's psychodrama of the deluded artist ("Engagement," 419; "Commitment", 185), Adorno accuses Brecht of "unmediated glorification of the Party" ("Engagement" 415; "Commitment" 182) and reiterates the Cold War dichotomy between artistic autonomy and political instrumentalization, as the title of the original radio broadcast, "Engagement oder Autonomie von Kunst" (Radio Bremen, March 1962) attests. For analysis of the "crusade against Brecht," see André Müller, *Kreuzzug gegen Brecht. Die Kampagne in der Bundesrepublik 1961/62* (Darmstadt: Progressverlag, 1963); for comment in English, see John Willett, "The Changing Role of Politics," *Brecht in Context*, 2nd edn (London: Methuen, 1998), 193–238.

[2] For the attack on Brecht's alleged formalism, see Walter Ulbricht (general secretary of the SED), "Der Kampf gegen den Formalismus in der Kunst und Literatur. Für eine fortschrittliche deutsche Kultur" (1951), in *Dokumente zur Kunst-, Literatur- und Kulturpolitik der SED*, ed. Elimar Schubbe (Stuttgart: Seewald, 1972), 178–86, here 182; for the recovery of the anti-fascist *Lehrstück* for the GDR, see Ulbricht, "Der Weg zur Sicherung des Friedens und zur Erhöhung der materiellen und kulturellen Bedingungen des Volkes" (1959), in *Dokumente*, 540–6.

[3] Hans Joachim Hoffmann (GDR Culture Minister), Address on Brecht's ninetieth birthday, 10 February 1988, in the GDR Theatre Union journal *Theater der Zeit* (April 1988), 6–9. The initials SDI were in the original.

2

of the German Communist Party (KPD)'s opposition both to residual imperialism left over from the Reich under Kaiser Wilhelm in the army and police of the Weimar Republic and the ruling Socialist Party (SPD), and to the rise of the National Socialist Workers Party or Nazi Party (NSDAP).[4] The SED claimed to have cleared away Nazi remnants through systematic denazification, while blaming the Western Federal Republic of Germany (FRG) for failing to prosecute Nazi war criminals and for retaining symbols like the imperial *Deutschlandlied* ("Deutschland, Deutschland, über alles") as the national anthem.[5] Especially at a time when the GDR was recognized officially only by the Soviet Union and its Eastern European allies, but not by the

---

4 "Communist" (with a capital letter) and "communist" (with a small letter) are used respectively to refer to party membership and to the broader affiliation of leftists such as Brecht not only with anti-fascist politics but also with the social and cultural community afforded by the movement. Antonia Grunenberg, in *Antifaschismus – ein deutscher Mythos* (Hamburg: Rowohlt, 1993), 22, notes that the Communist International defined "fascism" in 1924 broadly as the "instrument of war used by the bourgeoisie against the proletariat" and thus lumped together the fascist regime of Italy with bourgeois democracies including Weimar Germany. The KPD promoted radical socialist redistribution rather than the gradualist program of the ruling SPD, which the KPD viewed as a betrayal, especially when SPD police banned KPD activities. This sense of betrayal shaped KPD hostility to the SPD as "social fascists," as well as later SED attacks on the persistence of Nazi personnel and habits in the post-war FRG. For an English-language discussion of this legacy, see Eric Weitz, *Creating German Communism, 1890–1990* (Princeton University Press, 1997).

5 For the political implications of the *Deutschlandlied* as against the new GDR anthem, *Auferstanden aus Ruinen* ("Arisen from the Ruins"; music: Hanns Eisler; lyrics: Johannes R. Becher), see Maos Azaryahu, *Vom Wilhelmplatz zum Thälmannplatz: Politische Symbole im öffentlichen Leben der DDR* (Tel Aviv: Institut für deutsche Geschichte, 1991), 102–7; for the SED's representation of the GDR, through the hammer, circle and engineer's compass on the flag, as a peaceful country as against alleged Western militarism symbolized by the Prussian eagle, see Azaryahu's comments on the SED's use of these symbols, including images of the hammer smashing the eagle (112–13).

FRG, which granted automatic citizenship to refugees from the GDR, every test of legitimacy took on global proportions.[6]

Brecht was not ideally suited to the role of anti-fascist mascot since his political actions were not always consistent with his stated convictions. His plays, prose, and drama exposed the contradictions of capitalist society and bourgeois mores, yet his personal relations with his family and (especially female) collaborators have been described as exploitative. Moreover, his creative appropriation of found material contrasts with his vigilant defense of intellectual property. Although anti-communist commentators from the House Un-American Activities Commitee (HUAC) through Martin Esslin to John Fuegi have used these inconsistencies as the basis for a cold-war melodrama in which Brecht appears as a Stalinist or, more recently, sexist demon, the influence of Brecht and his collaborators – writers like Elizabeth Hauptmann, Margarete Steffin, Günter Weisenborn, Lion Feuchtwanger; designers like Caspar Neher, John Heartfield, Teo Otto, Karl von Appen; composers like Kurt Weill, Paul Hindemith, Hanns Eisler, Paul Dessau; photographer Ruth Berlau, and actors Helene Weigel (also his wife), Ernst Busch, Carola Neher, Erwin Geschonneck, Renate Lutz, Käthe Reichel, and others – remains unparalleled. While the work of these collaborators should be acknowledged, Brecht was both catalyst and director, without whom this extraordinary output would not have been possible.[7]

[6] As Hans-Siegfried Lamm and Siegfried Kupper note, in *DDR und Dritte Welt* (Munich: Oldenberg, 1976), 270–1, the GDR began trading with third world countries like Egypt and India in the 1950s but the diplomatic recognition of the GDR was hampered by competition from the FRG under its Hallstein Doctrine of a single German nation (53–63).

[7] Esslin, *Bertolt Brecht: A Choice of Evils*, and John Fuegi, *Brecht and Company* (New York: Grove Press, 1994). Despite its enthusiastic reception by the Western media, Fuegi's argument that Brecht's collaborators were exploited (1994) is not new; similar arguments have been advanced by German writers from Peter Weiss, in *Aesthetik der Widerstand* (Frankfurt a.M.: Suhrkamp, 1971), at once a novel and a treatise on the politics of art, to Fritz Raddatz, "Bertolt Brecht," in his *Männerängste in der Kunst* (Reinbek: Rowohlt, 1993), and the subject

Although he moved from an anarchic anti-bourgeois attitude in the early 1920s to an affiliation by the late 1920s with Communists such as film maker Slatan Dudow and composer Hanns Eisler, with whom he produced the controversial *Lehrstück*/chorale *Die Massnahme* (Measures Taken, or The Expedient, 1930) and the film *Kuhle Wampe, oder Wem gehört die Welt?* (Kuhle Wampe, or to whom does the world belong?, 1932), Brecht was never a Communist Party member. Conversely, although he spent the Second World War in the United States, his commitments were leftist enough to provoke HUAC's investigation in 1947 and the subsequent refusal of visas for travel to West Germany under US control. Brecht received support for his theatre in East Germany but he expressed private reservations about SED policy, especially after the workers' uprising on 17 June 1953 challenged the party's claim to lead a "workers' and peasants' state."[8] The SED's attempt to subordinate Brecht and the legacy of experimental leftist performance (pioneered by KPD members like Eisler and Busch, who returned to the GDR, or director Erwin Piscator, who went to West Berlin) to Soviet norms of orthodox "socialist realism" promulgated by Stalin's Minister of Propaganda, Andrei Zhdanov, remained at best incomplete. The contradictory claims of this orthodoxy were to be undermined by critical heirs of Brecht, especially Heiner Müller, whose work from the 1950s to his death in 1995 invoked the legacy of the Weimar left to challenge the SED's exclusive

has since received serious critical treatment from Sabine Kebir, *Ich fragte nicht nach meinem Anteil: Elisabeth Hauptmanns Arbeit mit Brecht* (Berlin: Aufbau, 1997) and *Ein akzeptabler Mann?*, 2nd edn (Berlin: Aufbau, 1998), and Paula Hanssen, *Elisabeth Hauptmann: Brecht's Silent Collaborator* (Bern: Peter Lang, 1995), among others.

[8] Brecht's letter to Ulbricht included a reflection on the workers" "revolutionary impatience" as well as his own support for the SED. Only the latter sentiment was published in the SED journal *Neues Deutschland* (see Werner Hecht, *Brecht-Chronik 1898–1956* (Frankfurt a.M: Suhrkamp, 1997)). Privately, Brecht noted that "17 June has estranged existence itself": see Brecht, *Werke: Große kommentierte Ausgabe* (Frankfurt a.M.: Suhrkamp, 1988–98), 27: 346 (hereafter *Werke*).

claim to represent anti-fascism and anti-imperialism in Germany and beyond.

Far from the Berlin Wall but still caught up in the Cold War melodrama, the newly declared Republic of South Africa attempted after its abrupt departure from the British Commonwealth in May 1961 to establish its credentials as a "young country" representing "Western civilization" on the African frontier. Among other institutions borrowed from Europe, the Afrikaner Nationalist government founded and subsidized Performing Arts Councils to display its Western aspirations. Although Brecht had been boycotted in West Germany – a key model for South African cultural policy – *The Caucasian Chalk Circle* opened in 1963, the inaugural year of the Performing Arts Council of the Transvaal (PACT), albeit without Brecht's controversial prologue of 1951, in which Soviet peasants discuss land redistribution. Alongside Shakespeare and patriotic Afrikaans drama, this production appeared as evidence of the "European" aspirations of white South Africa as a loyal ally of the West in the battle against Communism, which had been banned in South Africa in 1950.[9] In contrast, in 1964, the not-yet-famous playwright Athol Fugard staged a South African interpretation of the play with the Serpent Players, a group of black performers with whom he went on to create theatre that deployed Brechtian techniques in the critical representation of South African reality, from *The Coat* (1966) to *Sizwe Banzi is Dead* and *The Island* (1972).

South African engagement with international anti-fascist culture began well before Fugard, however. Over the course of the 1920s and 1930s the Communist Party of South Africa (CPSA) became the

[9] For South Africa's aspirations to "Western civilization" in the arts, see *Performing Arts in South Africa: Cultural Aspirations of a Young Country* (Pretoria: Dept of Information, 1969), 1. The Afrikaner National Party, which ruled South Africa from 1948 to 1994, passed the Suppression of Communism Act in 1950, which suppressed not only the Communist Party, but also persons deemed, in the broadest terms, to further the interests of communism worldwide. The program for PACT's production of *The Caucasian Chalk Circle* (STC/JPL) indicates that the performance began with scene 2 in the Abashvili palace.

most integrated political organization in the country and supported anti-fascist cultural activism, albeit on a much smaller scale than the communist and socialist movements encountered by Brecht in Berlin. To be sure, Fugard and the Serpent Players stimulated the growth of anti-apartheid theatre that drew on Brecht's example to produce the distinctively South African genre of the workshopped testimonial play, from Workshop '71's *Survival* (1976) to the collective creations of the Market Theatre, such as *Born in the RSA* (1985), and the Junction Avenue Theatre Company, best known for *Sophiatown* (1986). But, two generations before the leftist revival of the 1970s and one generation before the National Party banned the CPSA and any remotely related organization in the 1950s, associations with implicit or explicit socialist programs, from the CPSA through the socialist but non-communist Garment Workers' Union to the African National Theatre, promoted anti-segregationist and anti-fascist cultural, political, and social programs from the 1920s to the 1940s.[10] In forms from May Day parades and agit-prop skits on picket lines to formal performances of written drama for mixed (union/non-union, black/white) audiences, cultural production addressed not only the travails of local actors but also, as the Bantu Peoples' Theatre put it in 1940, "economic disintegration, the breakdown of tribal economy, and the impoverishment

---

[10] From its transformation from a white labor party in 1919 to a black-majority party by the late 1920s until its banning in 1950, the Communist Party of South Africa (CPSA) was the most integrated political organization in the country. The role of party intellectuals and union organizers in the broader liberation movement has been noted not only by the CPSA and its successor, the underground South African Communist Party (SACP; 1950–94), but also by independent leftists. For the party line, see *South African Communists Speak: Documents from the History of the South African Communist Party, 1915–1980* (London: Inkululeko Publications, 1981); for comments by a critical former member, see Edward Roux, *Time Longer than Rope: A History of the Black Man's Struggle for Freedom in South Africa* (Madison: University of Wisconsin Press, 1964), and by members of the party in exile, Stephen Ellis and Tsepo Sechaba, *Comrades against Apartheid: The ANC and the South African Communist Party in Exile* (London: James Curry, 1992).

of Europeans, the massing of classes in their trade unions and employer organizations," as well as the "emotional complications of race and colour."[11] Personal and institutional links between South African activists and international socialist movements were forged, for instance, by CPSA members in Moscow from the 1920s, and by visitors to South Africa, such as André van Gyseghem, author of a book on Soviet theatre and animator of local events such as the Bantu Peoples' Theatre's adaptation of Eugene O'Neill's *Hairy Ape*, or by emigrés such as Kurt Joachim Baum, whose Johannesburg Art Theatre influenced unionist Guy Routh. Over and above these links, the iconographic and performance forms of international socialism, from the Red Flag to the raised fist whose origin historian Eric Weitz traces to the KPD in 1926 and the agit-prop performance honed by workers' groups not only in the Soviet Union and Germany, but across the world from the United States to Japan, permeated South African activism in this period, until the banning of the CPSA in 1950, and of most other mass organizations including the African National Congress (ANC) in the early 1960s, drove this legacy underground. From the 1970s, with the revival of mass opposition to apartheid, this legacy resurfaced in the form of anti-apartheid performance as well as of posters and publications of the movement.[12]

The juxtaposition of these different inheritances of international socialism in performance – the official anti-fascism of the GDR as against the anti-apartheid activism of the outlawed CPSA and ANC and internal opposition to apartheid – might seem tendentious, were it not for the concrete historical links between the GDR and liberation

[11] Bantu Peoples' Theatre, *Drama Festival Program* (25–27 July 1940), 10 (STC/JPL).
[12] Weitz, *Creating German Communism*, 3; André van Gyseghem, *Theatre in Soviet Russia* (London: Faber and Faber, 1939). The international links can be seen in the "solidarity messages" from workers' theatre groups in Japan and Australia, as well in Europe, in *Workers Theatre* magazine, edited by German emigré and director of the New York Proletbuehne, John Bonn (New York Public Library; Performing Arts Division).

movements like the ANC and SACP. Building on ties with the Soviet Union, which dated back to individual CPSA members studying in Moscow in the mid-1920s and the Communist International's (Comintern's) promotion of a "native republic" for South Africa, the SED set up a Solidarity Committee in 1960.[13] In keeping with its memorialization of former Nazi concentration camps on GDR territory as sites commemorating the "victims of fascism . . . in *many countries*" (my emphasis), the SED promoted a foreign policy of "solidarity and support [*solidarische Unterstützung*] for the . . . liberation movements against imperialism, colonialism and neocolonialism" in Asia, Africa, and Latin America.[14] In the early 1970s, Western governments treated the ANC and SACP as little more than communist outlaws. Before the Basic Treaty between West and East Germany in December 1972 paved the way for the admission of both German states to the United Nations, the SACP and ANC delegations came to East Berlin in May to set up diplomatic missions-in-exile. This occasion, and GDR support for Southern African liberation movements more broadly, gave the government an international stage for proclaiming not merely solidarity with third world liberation, but also an "organic" link between the socialist tradition of international anti-fascism and the struggle against racism. Even though the very different experience of solidarity among exiles and solidarity among

---

[13] The GDR pursued trade, educational, and cultural exchanges with newly independent third world countries and liberation movements as a means to greater international recognition; see Lamm and Kupper, *DDR und Dritte Welt* and, in English, Gareth M. Winthrow, *The Foreign Policy of the GDR in Africa* (Cambridge University Press, 1990). On the international dimension of commemorating the "victims of fascism," see Azaryahu, *Vom Wilhelmplatz zum Thälmannplatz*, 188–97; on the link between proletarian internationalism and anti-racism, see the speech by Herman Axen (SED Central Committee Secretary) at the special anti-apartheid session of the United Nations in Berlin, 25 May 1974, *Dokumente zur Außenpolitik der DDR: 1974* (Berlin: Staastverlag der DDR, 1978), 1020–8; here 1022.

[14] Gerhard Hahn *et al.*, *Außenpolitik der DDR–für Sozialismus und Frieden* (Berlin: Staatsverlag der DDR, 1974), 139.

grassroots activists at home has led to tensions in post-apartheid South Africa, many ANC and SACP members bear witness to this link as they continue to speak the language of socialist solidarity.[15] On the cultural front, GDR solidarity took the form of guest appearances of troupes from socialist countries from Cuba to Angola, and publication, in English and other languages alongside German, of the writings of exiles banned in their home countries.

More surprisingly perhaps, this solidarity also included staging in translation the works of non-communist non-exiles such as Fugard. An admirer of Brecht, Fugard was an avowed liberal rather than a socialist. His plays spoke to GDR audiences interested not only in solidarity with the oppressed majority in South Africa, but also in the local resonances of his depiction of dissidence and oppression in the most intimate as well as the public sphere. The scale and intensity of racialized brutality perpetrated by the apartheid state far exceeded the oppressive measures of the SED, and this should alert readers against premature generalizations about undifferentiated "totalitarianism", popularized more by ideologues' manipulations of Hannah Arendt's influential concept to fit the hardened polarizations of the Cold War than by her cogent analysis, in *The Origins of Totalitarianism*, of the dangerously unstable totalitarian *movements* unleashed by Hitler and Stalin a generation earlier.[16] Nonetheless, the impact of Fugard in the

[15] On the ANC delegation's visit to Berlin and subsequent domicile in the GDR, see the SED communiqué in *Dokumente der Sozialistische Einheitspartei Deutschland: Beschlüße und Erklärungen des Zentralkomitees sowie seines Politbüros und seines Sekretariats* (Berlin: Dietzverlag, 1977), 14: 234–37; on the training of cadres, see Francis Meli (Ph.D. from Leipzig's Karl-Marx University), *History of the African National Congress: South Africa Belongs to Us* (Bloomington: Indiana University Press, 1989), and Ellis and Sechaba, *Comrades against Apartheid*, 88.

[16] See Hannah Arendt, *Origins of Totalitarianism*, 2nd edn (New York: World Publishing Company, 1958), especially part three. For critical commentary on the limits of the totalitarian concept and of the presumed equation of Nazi and Stalinist tyranny, see Ian Kershaw and Moshe Lewin, eds., *Stalinism and Nazism: Dictatorships in Comparison* (Cambridge University Press, 1994).

GDR highlighted points of comparison between the infiltration, disinformation and detention operations of East German and South African institutions of surveillance, respectively the Ministry of State Security or Stasi and the Bureau of State Security (BOSS) and its successors, in two otherwise differently oppressive societies, and the capacity of theatre in each environment to constitute as a virtual public sphere the rehearsal of a potential alternative rather than a merely substitute form of public life.[17]

In post-unification Germany, Fugard's work has continued to lend itself in adaptation to dramatizing race relations in the officially unified but still practically divided country. While superficial parallels or glib assertions about global struggles for freedom from oppression, of the sort all too prominent in Western and Northern self-congratulation after the fall of the Wall and of apartheid, should be treated with appropriate disdain, these points of comparison nonetheless offer an illuminating rubric for seeing anew hitherto unseen links between the East/West axis of Cold War and its legacy and the North/South axis of first and third world relations and their troubled

[17] Jürgen Habermas's conception of the public sphere (or rather the sphere of *Öffentlichkeit*, the quality of public-ness), as a condition of communication or representation free from coercion or pressure from the state, as developed in his *Structural Transformation of the Public Sphere*, trans. Thomas Burger (1962; Cambridge, MA: MIT Press, 1989), took on poignant resonance in the movements working for free civil society in both Eastern Europe and South Africa in the 1970s and 1980s. In the wake of new capitalist exploitation, encouraged in many cases by post-communist states' or parties' refusal to intervene on behalf of the disadvantaged, citizens in both regions have registered scepticism about premature equations of free speech with free trade. On the potential of theatre to constitute an alternative rather than a merely substitute or fake public sphere in South Africa, see Loren Kruger, *The Drama of South Africa: Plays, Pageants and Publics since 1910* (London: Routledge, 1999), 9–13, and in the GDR, "'Wir treten aus unseren Rollen heraus': Theatre Intellectuals and Public Spheres," in Michael Geyer, ed., *The Power of Intellectuals in Contemporary Germany* (Chicago: University of Chicago Press, 2002), 183–211.

future. Remapping these two axes in the same plane will in turn provide a framework for investigating the impact of Brecht and associated cultural practices in a post-imperial world. But before we can do so, we need first to establish the value of this category *post-imperial*, against other contenders, above all "post-colonial."

When and what was post-imperial?

The entwined strands of cultural and political history sketched here offer a starting point for investigating nodes of intersection and entanglement between the ideological (hence capitalized) coordinates of North and South, East and West, under the aegis of *post-imperial Brechts*. Naming Brecht in the plural highlights his various, even contradictory roles: the anti-capitalist and anti-fascist dissident of the 1920s, the critical but loyal representative of the officially anti-fascist state of the 1950s, and, in his afterlife, the exemplary figure of progressive anti-fascism in a country suppressing dissidence. This ensemble would also include political cultural practices, especially theatre, which deploy techniques we have come to associate with Brecht, even though, as was the case with internationalist socialist theatre from Canada to Japan and including South Africa from the 1930s to the 1950s, these practices did not bear his name. Calling the configuration of Cold War, third world liberation movements, Brecht, the GDR, and South Africa "post-imperial" may seem odd to those who see the term as a synonym for "post-colonial" and who might therefore expect from "post-colonial Brecht" a worthy but peripheral supplement to the metropolitan center of Brecht's career, against which "Brecht in South Africa" would be an afterthought to the main (European) business. "Post-imperial" may also puzzle readers who habitually associate "empire" with Britain and the North, and "post-imperial" therefore with the "post-colonial" condition of former British colonies in the South, rather than with the debates invoked here, in the Cold War battles between West and East after the collapse of the Third Reich and in the shadow of the rivalry between the American and the Soviet imperia. Using the terms "empire" and "imperial" to refer to the overland expansion of German states from Prussia in the eighteenth century to the Second Reich in the nineteenth, and the Third and most notorious Reich in the twentieth, and to the ideological and economic power of the Soviet Union and the United States, as against the more familiar overseas expansion of Britain (or France or Portugal), may seem counter-intuitive to English speakers, but no less a thinker than Hannah Arendt makes these connections. Imperialism occupies the whole of the second part of *The Origins of Totalitarianism,* commanding as much attention as the subjects of its better-known first and third parts, on anti-Semitism and totalitarianism respectively. Although Arendt does not herself use the term "post-imperial," she expands the terrain of imperialism to include the land-based expansion of the Second and Third Reichs as well as the domination in their respective spheres maintained by the Soviet Union and the United States, and thus allows for the conceptualization of a post-imperial world that brings together the East/West axis polarized by the Soviet Union and the United States and the North/South axis usually understood to mark the movement of colonization and decolonization.

The rubric "post-imperial Brechts" highlights the theatrical, theoretical and political connections among Brecht, the GDR and South Africa, even where Brecht functions retrospectively as a powerful *absent presence* – as in early political theatre in South Africa or, via more recent international influences such as Augusto Boal, in theatre "of the oppressed" and theatre for development – in the Southern African region. The culture of international socialism and related debates about the political function of art, which deeply influenced Brecht and fellow leftists in the 1920s and 1930s – from now famous theorists, such as Walter Benjamin or Georg Lukács, to less known but significant theatre practitioners, such as John Bonn in New York and Kurt Baum in Johannesburg – re-emerged, albeit more ambiguously, in the protestations of third world solidarity by GDR state *and* dissidents in the 1970s and 1980s. It still continues to inform theatre for development projects the world over, especially in post-apartheid South Africa, where the leftist language and practices inherited from the international socialist tradition continue to resonate more forcefully than metropolitan readers commonly realize.

The relocation of Brecht and his legacy South and East provides a way of seeing "post-imperial Brecht" as something more than just another supplement to a supposed original genius who remains, even in post-unification commentary published up to Brecht's centenary in 1998, Western and European.[18] The relationship between Brecht and South Africa remains *asymmetrical* but this very asymmetry invites us to re-examine not only the influence of a "European" Brecht on the third world, but also the impact of the third world on "Europe" as an idea as well as a geographical entity. The acknowledgment of this asymmetry draws on an appeal made as early as 1922 by CPSA member Sydney Bunting for "solidarity despite inequality" between white and black, Europe and Africa.[19] It also highlights the anti-imperialist moment in the project that historian Dipesh Chakrabarty calls "provincializing Europe."[20] The final part of

---

[18] Peter Thomson, ed., *The Cambridge Companion to Brecht* (Cambridge University Press, 1994) focuses on the canonical plays in Europe and North America; Siegfried Mews, ed., *A Bertolt Brecht Reference Companion* (Westport: Greenwood Press, 1997) includes essays on "Brecht in Asia" and "Brecht in Latin America" as well as articles on Brecht's *Lehrstücke* and on his prose; Stephen Giles and Rodney Livingstone, eds., *Bertolt Brecht: Centenary Essays* (Amsterdam: Rodopi, 1998), offers three essays on Brecht's GDR period, but only on links to the canonical figures Anna Seghers and Christa Wolf. The essays in Walter Delabar and Jörg Döring, eds., *Bertolt Brecht (1898–1956)* (Berlin: Weidler, 1998) focus primarily on classic Brecht texts or on comparing Brecht with other canonical Western European authors; "*Und mein Werk ist der Abgesang des Jahrtausends*": 22 *Versuche eine Arbeit zu beschreiben*, compiled by Erdmut Wizisla (Berlin: Akademie der Künste, 1998), by contrast, provides new insights into Brecht's reading matter, including Trotsky and other heterodox marxists.

[19] S. P. Bunting, "The 'Colonial Labour' Front" (1922), in Allison Drew, ed., *South Africa's Radical Tradition: A Documentary History*, 2 vols. (Cape Town: University of Cape Town Press, 1996), 1: 51–4.

[20] Chakrabarty, *Provincializing Europe: Postcolonial Thought and Historical Difference* (Princeton University Press, 2000), 7: "Historicism enabled European domination of the world in the nineteenth century. . . . [it] is what made modernity or capitalism look

---

my title, "Politics and Performance, East and South", pinpoints this critique of European priority. Brecht's legacy should not be mapped only on a West/East or only on a North/South axis, but rather understood within a field of multilateral lines of force, so as to show the intersections of the Cold War axis – between West and East, capitalism and communism, and charges of imperialism on both sides – in the same plane as the post-colonial axis – between affluent North and impoverished South, between metropolitan or imperial centers and (post)-colonial margins. In this schema, East and South, the site of performance of Brecht and related theatre in the GDR and South Africa, provide a critical perspective on the usually dominant viewpoints of West and North, the sites of canonical interpretation. East and South function each as the synecdoche of a familiar geographical and ideological pair, marking both points of reference but inverting the usual order of their representation. This inversion highlights the historical subordination of East to West, South to North, and the critique of that history, but should be construed not as a mere inversion of dominance, which would simply mirror the imperial idea with the local response, but rather as a challenge to the notion of a clear-cut separation of concepts or practices along these axes.

The shape of this book

Brecht's negotiation of irreducibly complex relationships between the forms and functions of cultural, especially theatrical, production brought him up against the SED demand for orthodoxy in the short term, but has ensured the ongoing influence of his example half a century after his death. What is not always clear to those who read only the English-language versions of his work, however, is the crucial contribution of Brecht's institutional engagements, not only with orthodox and heterodox communism through the twentieth century,

> not simply global but rather as something that became global *over time*, by originating in one place, Europe, and then spreading outside it. This 'first in Europe, then elsewhere' structure of global historical time is historicist; different non-Western nationalisms would later produce local versions of the same narrative, replacing 'Europe' by some locally constructed center."

but also with the dissident institutions and more informal groups criticizing an allegedly "actually existing socialist state" from a realistically socialist point of view. It is this particular experience of defending pluralist socialism against a monopolistic socialist party at the
historic moment of post-imperialism, rather than a generalized marxist attitude, that enabled Brecht to refine the theoretical as well as
the political point of his key terms, estrangement and realism, and
their critical relation, and to argue convincingly that estrangement
was under the circumstances the most realistic method. An understanding of the institutional and socio-historical context is thus necessary if we are to fully understand Brecht's theory, the actual and
potential operation of his method, and the modification of that operation by this and other quite different contexts, from the subsidized
regional theatres of the United States to picket lines in apartheid South
Africa. Only with this understanding can we avoid the habit, all too
prevalent in the Anglo-American world, of treating Brecht's method
as a timeless set of tools that can be applied to anything from political
theatre to advertising. In order to deepen our sense of the historical
contexts of theory and practice, the first chapter proposes a political
history of theatre and theory. This chapter highlights not only the
intense political pressures – in the era of totalitarian movements and
critical resistance to them from around 1920 to 1950 – on Brecht and
his contemporaries in and alongside international socialist associations, from political leaders like Rosa Luxemburg to dissidents like
Karl Korsch and committed cultural activists and Communist Party
members like Ernst Busch and Hanns Eisler. It also demonstrates the
largely unacknowledged impact of Brecht's *theoretical* as well as practical thinking on terms and categories usually associated with writers
more thoroughly canonized as theorists, such as Georg Lukács, Walter
Benjamin, and Theodor Adorno.

Juxtaposing Brecht's legacy with the differential development
of international socialist cultures allows us to bring together several projects which, despite their apparent differences, belong together
under the rubric of "post-imperial Brecht," of an Eastern and Southern critique of Brecht's canonization in the affluent capitalist North
and West. Chapters two, three and four examine Brecht's uneasy if

not downright contradictory position as sanctioned dissident in his last few years in the GDR, and the consequence of this ambiguity for the political and cultural impact of theatre intellectuals for the rest of that state's history. At issue in this cluster of chapters is a clear understanding of the limits of intellectual dissent and the temptations of complicity with power, whether the official socialist state or the power of capital in the new Berlin, capital of Germany, the most powerful state in Europe. Chapters two and three reassess Brecht's legacy in the GDR, whose leaders claimed to inherit the mantle of international socialism and anti-imperialism, and the impact of these debates and the Cold War context on the work of Brecht and his most influential successor and critic, Heiner Müller, and the directors who shaped their reception in the GDR. Chapter four explores the marketing of this legacy as a consumable spectacle in, as well as persistent resistance to, this commodification in the as yet un-unified margins of greater Germany.

This frame also allows us to see how the promotion of the South African playwright Athol Fugard in the GDR complicates the legacy of political theatre in general and of Brecht in particular, and to consider not only the impact of the North on the South, of Brecht and other leftist theatre practitioners on theatre in Southern Africa, but also the reverse: the role that third world liberation played in the legitimation of the *second* world (concretely: the practice and propaganda of third world solidarity in state policy and self-definition of the GDR against its main rival, West Germany) in addition to dissident leftists in the West. The second cluster of chapters outlines the history and future of political performance in South Africa as an exemplary site for investigating both the power and the limits of the legacy of Brecht and of "Brecht power," the political and cultural legitimacy carried by the name of Brecht even in the absence of his actual influence. Chapter five begins with the emergence in South Africa of a leftist political theatre without Brecht and the resolutely *apolitical* theatrical use of his name and reputation, in order to highlight the complexity of more obvious instances of Brechtian theatre, and also considers the limits of Brecht's urban and European practices and his presumptions about racial typing, in contexts that are unevenly urban and mostly not European. Chapter six uses the curious itinerary of Fugard in the GDR to turn a critical lens on Germany, particularly on the solidarity pretensions of the allegedly "actually existing socialist state" but also on the anti-imperialist pretensions of West German intellectuals, who routinely forgot their country's colonial atrocities, even as they claimed to lead the anti-apartheid crusade. Finally, chapter seven explores the limits of a Brechtian theatre of instruction in a post-apartheid South Africa in the wake of the Truth and Reconciliation Commission, where the traumatic testimony of survivors and, perhaps surprisingly, of perpetrators as well threatens to elude the sense-making tools of the Enlightenment tradition to which Brecht ultimately belongs and thus to test the long-standing conviction at the heart of this book: that performance and politics can create a resonant and effective field of force capable not only of interpreting the world but of changing it.

1 The political history of theatre and theory: Brecht and his contemporaries

Reinforced by readily available editions of his work in German and other major European languages, Brecht's status as a theorist in Europe has yet to be matched in English-speaking circles. Hampered by very selective translation, by performance cultures hostile to critical reflection (let alone to "theory") and by political cultures that have historically marginalized if not utterly demonized the left, Brecht in English remains somewhat of an oxymoron. These obstacles to the reception of Brecht hamper even further any understanding of the impact of international socialism not only on the evolution of Brecht's practice and theory, but also on the intersecting political and cultural formations that brought him in contact and conflict with contemporaries, from Georg Lukács through Walter Benjamin to Theodor Adorno. Furthermore, the influence of Brecht as a theorist on these other better-known theorists, which can be easily tracked in the German originals, remains invisible, even incredible, to many English-only readers.

Since this problem is above all a problem of translation, we can further the understanding of Brecht's evolving techniques of theatre and theory and of his influence on his contemporaries if we deploy new translations that show these links more clearly and thus recontextualize these techniques within and against the institutions and formations that informed them.[1] Key terms, from *episch* (narrative rather

[1] Raymond Williams, in *The Sociology of Culture* 2nd edn (Chicago: University of Chicago Press, 1995), 35, distinguishes between institutions – formal social entities from the education system and the political party to systems of patronage and subsidy – and formations,

than epic) theatre and the *Lehrstück* in the 1920s, to *Verfremdung* (estrangement or *dis-illusion* but *not* alienation) and the reconfiguration of realism in the direction of *eingreifendes Denken* (interventionist thinking) and a militant interpretation of the popular in the 1930s and 1940s, emerge out of attempts by Brecht, his associates such as Eisler, Piscator, and Benjamin, and his antagonists, especially Lukács, to develop cultural practices and supporting institutions that would be understood as marxist – in other words, as contributing to the critical representation and radically democratic transformation of a society in turmoil.[2] These terms and their political implications proved later to be provocative, not only for avowed anti-communists such as the members of HUAC but also for ambivalently critical theorists such as Theodor Adorno, once a Jewish leftist in anti-fascist exile, later a West German professor of critical theory publishing in explicitly anti-communist papers. As my revisionist retranslation suggests, tracing competing translations and interpretations of key terms can pinpoint moments of crisis and of critique in the turbulent first half of the twentieth century, which later post-imperial accounts use as touchstones for their own self-definition. It can also highlight crucial gaps in present-day interpretations and canonizations of Brecht in English-language environments throughout the world. In order to understand

informal associations of cultural producers, from the relatively formalized (such as a school of poets) to the informal and transient activist performance troupes made up of non-professional worker-players (rather than the leisured bourgeois implied by "amateur"). For distinctions among professionals, amateurs, and worker-players in the institution of theatre, see Loren Kruger, *The National Stage: Theatre and Cultural Legitimation in England, France, and America* (Chicago: University of Chicago Press, 1992).

[2] Brecht's engagement with socialist institutions began with his work with the director Piscator (1927), his collaboration with the composer Eisler and his attendance of lectures by the heterodox marxist Karl Korsch (1928); they bore fruit in the series of *Lehrstücke*, from the *Badener Lehrstück vom Einverständnis* (1928) to *Die Massnahme* (1930) and the film *Kuhle Wampe* (1932); see Werner Hecht, *Brecht Chronik, 1898–1956* (Frankfurt a.M.: Suhrkamp, 1997), 223–346, and John Willett, *Brecht in Context*, 2nd edn (London: Methuen, 1998).

the terms and troubles of this translation, however, we need to look more closely at Brecht in the environments that produced him as a leftist cultural practitioner: Berlin at two crucially turbulent moments, the last half decade of the Weimar Republic of Germany (1927–33), and the first decade of post-war East Germany (1946–56).

Anti-imperialism and the *Lehrstück*: Brecht's pedagogy of the oppressed

Bearing in mind both the historical grounding of critique and the critical deconstruction of history, we can see in the evolution of Brecht's theatre the history of the interaction of political and cultural practices, from party organization and disorganization to the representation and contestation of political commitments in music, art, and film, as well as Brecht's chosen field of theatre, and thus also of the *theoretical* importance of the shaping historical contexts, from the anti-capitalist culture of the late Weimar years to the conditions of exile and fragile unity in an anti-fascist Popular Front in the 1930s. If, as I suggested in the introduction, the post-Second World War configuration of East/West and North/South tensions can be seen as post-imperial, the ferment in inter-war Europe might be described as *inter-* as well as anti-imperial, in that it took place in a precarious place and time between movements and polities with imperial reach: between the fall of older dynastic empires – especially those centuries-old rivals, the Austro-Hungarian, Romanov and Ottoman Empires – and the much younger *Kaiserreich* of Imperial Germany, which lasted only from 1871 to 1918, and the rise of the modern expansionist tyrannies Nazism and Stalinism, which remain yoked together in the popular imagination under the influential but controversial term "totalitarianism." In the inter-imperial period, especially before Hitler won the election of 1933 and before Stalin consolidated power in the Soviet Union, many leftists in the Weimar Republic saw the "socialist" in the ruling Socialist Party as a "figleaf for the decent veiling of counter-revolutionary policy" that included war credits in the First World War, support for British imperial troops fighting the Red Army in the Soviet civil war, and the violent suppression of the radical socialist revolution in Germany – to use the words of KPD founder Rosa Luxemburg, whose murder in 1919 by soldiers supposedly escorting her to prison went unpunished by the SPD.[3] By contrast, the Nazis projected an "opportunistic copy of socialism" to compete with the KPD for the votes of labor and the unemployed, as the heterodox marxist Ernst Bloch put it after Hitler's failed putsch in 1924. To combat imperial nostalgia as well as rising nationalist feeling, socialists and communists had, in his view, to recruit genuine "tribunes of the people" through cultural as well as political activity.[4] The institutions and formations hosting this meeting between culture and politics ranged from official party organizations through music and theatre groups with informal affiliations to collectives, whether large, such as the Arbeitertheaterbund Deutschlands (ATBD: German Workers Theatre

[3] On the First World War as a conflict between imperial powers backed by industrial capitalists at the expense of worker-soldiers, see Rosa Luxemburg, "Die Krise der Sozialdemokratie" (a.k.a the "Junius Pamphlet", 1915), in *Gesammelte Werke* (Berlin/GDR: Dietz, 1974), 4: 49–150, excerpted in English in Luxemburg, *Selected Political Writings*, ed. Dick Howard (New York: Monthly Review Press, 1971), 322–51; on the "socialist figleaf" over SPD attacks on radical socialists, "Unser Program und die politische Situation" (speech at the founding convention of the KPD, December 1918), 4: 488–512; here: 499; excerpted in *Selected Political Writings*, 377–408.

[4] Ernst Bloch, "Hitler's Force [or Power]" (1924), in *The Weimar Republic Sourcebook*, ed. Anton Kaes, Martin Jay, and Edward Dimendberg (Berkeley: University of California Press, 1994), 147–9. Despite considerable differences between them, Bloch shared with Luxemburg a common leftist disappointment in an SPD compromised by its association with German imperialism. After the Nazis came to power but before Communists understood the regime's staying power, Wilhelm Reich, psychoanalyst and heterdox marxist, reiterated the claim that the KPD lost the working class to the Nazis when they dismissed the emotional appeal of Nazi rhetoric as mere false consciousness. See Reich, "What is Class Consciousness?" (1934), in *Sex-Pol: Essays, 1929–1934*, ed. Lee Baxandall (New York: Random House, 1972). Even if hindsight encourages us to see the KPD representation of the SPD as "social fascists" as mere Soviet propaganda, we should not forget that workers and the unemployed experienced the SPD as the force behind police brutality towards them, as did leftist activists and youth, whether KPD members or not.

Association), or small, such as the brief but influential collaboration among Brecht, Eisler, and Dudow, who created *Measures Taken* and *Kuhle Wampe*.[5]

Marxism was for Brecht a practical matter. Taking his cue from contradictions and conflict in Berlin in the late 1920s, especially the historic irony of a ruling Socialist Party repeatedly quashing Communist agitation, he grounded his investigation on Marx's eleventh thesis on Feuerbach: "The philosophers have sought to *interpret* the world in various ways; the point, however, is to *change* it."[6] While Brecht certainly studied the marxist classics (Marx, Engels, Lenin, Luxemburg), mediated by the heterodox Karl Korsch, Wilhelm Reich, and other teachers at the Marxistische Arbeiterschule (MASCH or Marxist Workers' School), his interest expressed itself not as unshakable conviction, but rather as a means of contributing to the transformation of society by representing contradictions between ideology and material social relations.[7] As a theatre practitioner bent on

---

[5] For socialist performance culture produced by worker-players and professionals, see Ludwig Hoffmann, ed. *Theater der Kollektive: Proletarisch-revolutionäres Berufstheater in Deutschland: 1928–33: Stücke, Dokumente, Studien* (Berlin/GDR: Henschel, 1980), 2 vols., and *Deutsches Arbeitertheater: 1918–33* (Munich: Rogner and Bernhard, 1973), 2 vols. In English, see *Weimar Republic Sourcebook*, esp. sec. 9: "Forging a Proletarian Culture," and sec. 21: "Theater, Politics, and the Public Sphere." Richard Bodek, *Proletarian Performance in Weimar Berlin: Agitprop, Chorus, and Brecht* (Columbia, SC: Camden House, 1997), 81, cites police reports and the KPD paper *Die Rote Fahne* concurring in estimates of two to three hundred groups by 1929.

[6] Karl Marx, "Eleven Theses on Feuerbach," *The Marx-Engels Reader*, ed. Robert Tucker (New York: Norton, 1977), 145.

[7] Klaus Völker, "Erinnerungsbild und eine Salve Zukunft: Bertolt Brechts Lehrstück 'Die Massnahme,'" in *Massnehmen: Kontroverse, Perspektive, Praxis: Brecht/Eislers Lehrstück Die Massnahme* (Berlin: Theater der Zeit, 1999), 15–22; here: 15. During the 1920s MASCH rented public schools in working-class districts for evening classes, moving to private homes when the SPD banned its classes from schools in 1931; see Martin Bienert, *Mit Brecht durch Berlin: ein literarischer Reiseführer* (Frankfurt a.M.: Insel, 1998), 71–6. Karl

radical social transformation, Brecht strove to change not only the forms but also the institutions of theatre. Although he collaborated with Piscator on the latter's innovative multi-media stagings of critical or satirical drama, such as *The Good Soldier Schweyk* (1927), Brecht argued in essays on the "primacy of the institution" (*Apparat*) that these expensive spectacles might have renewed theatrical form but were not socially revolutionary. In his view, the high cost of Piscator's productions in central, state-of-the-art theatres made them dependent on the generosity of wealthy patrons and thus maintained the capitalist institutional and social status quo even if the target audience was proletarian.[8] Brecht's most polemical pamphlet contrasting "epic" (or "narrative") and "dramatic" theatre was published in the *Versuche* of 1930, first in a life-long series of "essays" both creative and critical, but developed during work with Kurt Weill on the "new opera" *Mahagonny* (1927). This document appears emphatically to favor particular forms, sober narrative rather than (melo)drama,

Korsch (1886–1961) was a KPD member until his expulsion for "revisionism" in 1926. His *Marxism and Philosophy* (1923) revised orthodox presumptions about "scientific socialism" that the SPD inherited from Engels. Korsch argued that Marx's early work was indebted to the speculative philosophy of Hegel and to the utopian socialists and that even his later political economy was enhanced by the subjective and activist dimensions of his thought: see Patrick Goode, "Karl Korsch," in *A Dictionary of Marxist Thought*, ed. Tom Bottomore (Cambridge, MA: Harvard University Press, 1983), 263–4. Brecht's correspondence with Korsch reflects his serious but nonetheless sceptical engagement with party orthodoxy; in a letter written in exile in January 1934, Brecht agrees with Korsch's argument that participatory democracy is not merely a lever to launch the proletariat but an essential part of socialism, without which tyranny arises; letter no. 533, *Werke* 27: 404–7.

[8] Brecht, "Piscatortheater" (1927), and "Primat des Apparats" (1928), *Werke* 21: 197–8, 225–7. Brecht's comments on theatre, film, and radio develop a sociologically rich conception of institution that brings together the realms of artistic form, electronic and other technologies, audience formation, and the economic basis of the enterprise, rendered in English by "institution" rather than the narrowly technical "apparatus."

montage rather than plot development, and to encourage in the spectator reason as opposed to feeling, analysis of as opposed to absorption in the action (*Werke* 24: 78–9).[9] However, the often forgotten introduction to this polemic reminds readers that formal innovation is not "free" or autonomous but rather a product of social institutions; only those innovations that "challenge the social function of the institution," usually "an evening's entertainment," are potentially revolutionary (*Werke* 21: 73; *BoT* 34).

Brecht's attention to the institutions of culture, as well as his insistence that even the most hermetic modern art could not be devoid of social function even if its function was to project an aura of functionlessness, shaped his changing responses to established genres, from spoken to musical theatre, as well as to new media like radio and film, but also led him to invent new forms and formations that could create new publics and social agents. Working with flexible formations of like-minded friends intersecting with rather than fully inhabiting mass institutions like the KPD, Brecht undertook to develop theatre as an experimental method, as a means for learning and teaching, for militant action as well as for play. A key vessel for this experimentation was the *Lehrstück*, the learning play, in which all those present should be actors rather than spectators. The goal of Brecht and his associates was to forge a link between "die große und die kleine Pädagogik" (pedagogics great and small), linking the small-scale learning of performing action to the larger project of understanding and changing conflicts between ruling and oppressed classes and between social being and political consciousness. This plan to abolish the "system of player and spectator" and make a "statesman" out of every spectator (*Werke* 21: 396) echoes the utopian notion offered by Marx and reiterated by Lenin of the "withering away" of the state with the transformation of passive subjects into active citizens. It anticipates by half a century Augusto Boal's project of transforming the spectator into a spect-actor

[9] The essay "Notes on the Opera 'Rise and Fall of the City of Mahagonny'" and a fraction of Brecht's critical output appear in John Willett's edition of *Brecht on Theater* (1963; New York: Hill and Wang, 1992), 37–8; hereafter *BoT*.

and social actor, and with it his mentor Paolo Freire's "pedagogy of the oppressed," the practice of conscientization through "problem-*posing* education" that develops informal expertise from below against the formal imposition of instruction from above.[10]

The resonances of this education of the oppressed from below have been considerable, especially in the third world, but Brecht was more immediately confronted with the legacy of the Soviet Revolution of 1917. In particular, he had to tackle Lenin's equivocal vision, in "State and Revolution," of a state made up of armed workers whose authority is ideally disseminated throughout the population rather than concentrated in the hands of a few.[11] As Lenin's praise for direct democracy in principle was complicated in practice by his claim for the pressing need for central control, so Brecht's conception of the participant audience emerges in negotiation with party discipline.[12] His

---

[10] Paolo Freire, *Pedagogy of the Oppressed*, trans. M. B. Ramos (Harmondsworth: Penguin, 1974), esp. 49–59; Augusto Boal, *Theatre of the Oppressed*, trans. Charles McBride and Maria-Odilia Leal McBride (New York: Urizen, 1979) and *Games for Actors and Non-Actors*, trans. Adrian Jackson (London: Routledge, 1992).

[11] Lenin [Vladimir Ilyich Ulyanov], "State and Revolution" (1917), in *The Lenin Anthology*, ed. Richard Tucker (New York: Norton, 1985), 380 and "Can the Bolsheviks Retain Power?" (1917), ibid., 405; Freire, *Pedagogy of the Oppressed*, 47–59.

[12] The authoritarian streak in Brecht's pedagogics should not erase the utopian moment in the *Lehrstücke* as a mode of participatory theatre, but we ought nonetheless to acknowledge the historical limitations as well as historical potential of this practice. For the comments of Brecht and his collaborators in this period, see *Brechts Modell der Lehrstücke: Zeugnisse, Diskussion, Erfahrungen* (Frankfurt a.M.: Suhrkamp, 1976), ed. Reiner Steinweg, whose pioneering analysis of the *Lehrstück* as utopian practice, *Das Lehrstück: Brechts Theorie einer ästhetisch-politischen Erziehung* (Stuttgart: J. B. Metzler and Carl Ernst Poeschel, 1972), shaped the West German New Left reappropriation of Brecht; for discussion in English, see Karl-Heinz Schoeps, "Brecht's *Lehrstücke*," in *A Bertolt Brecht Reference Companion*, ed. Siegfried Mews (Westport: Greenwood, 1997) and Roswitha Mueller, *Bertolt Brecht and the Theory of the Media* (Lincoln: University of Nebraska Press, 1989), esp. 23–43.

reiteration of the Leninist phrase "discipline, the foundation of free-dom" (*Werke* 24: 88) appears to mean freedom to act *as if* all citizens were also active party leaders; the injunction shines with the radiance of radical utopian democracy while at the same time invoking the shadow of party discipline as authoritarian control.[13] This tension between democracy and discipline is encapsulated in the very term *Lehrstück*: it invites the translation "teaching play," but Brecht introduced the concept to English-speaking readers with the translation "learning play," highlighting its experimental and, as Raymond Williams would later gloss Brecht, its *subjunctive* along with its didactic character.[14]

Brecht's *Lehrstücke*, from *Der Jasager und der Neinsager* (two plays: He Who Says Yes; He Who Says No) to *Die Massnahme* (both 1930), to *Die Mutter* (The Mother, 1931) and the unfinished *Fatzer* project (1926–56), play out this tension between discipline and free-dom in representations of critical action and decision that deploy narrative performance in which actors show their characters rather than fully embody them. This technique, which Brecht would later call "transposition to the third person . . . to make possible critical dis-tance" (22: 644; *BoT* 138) should be understood as narrative as opposed not only to melo- or overly dramatic, but also to "epic" representa-tion, the usual but overly lofty translation of *episch*. These plays and other contemporary work, especially *Kuhle Wampe*, also carry anti-imperialist themes, such as the Soviet activists organizing in China in *Massnahme*; the links drawn between Fatzer and his comrade desert-ers from the First World War on the one hand, and the anti-imperialist

[13] Lenin, "State and Revolution," 369.
[14] Brecht's discussion of the experimental character of the *Lehrstück* appeared in the article "The German Drama – Pre-Hitler," *The New York Times*, 24 November 1935; trans. Eva Goldbeck in collaboration with Brecht; reproduced in English in *Werke* 22: 939–44. The German text appeared only in 1967 (*Werke* 22: 164–8). Williams's reflections on the subjunctive action of socially critical fictions and the indicative action that its producers hope to provoke in political practice appear in "Brecht and Beyond," in *Politics and Letters. Interviews with New Left Review* (London: New Left Books), 219–24.

activity of Lenin behind the lines on the other; the Russian Pelegea Vlassova and "the Vlassovas of other nations" as the key scene-title in *Die Mutter* has it; or the debate between young communists and older bourgeois about poverty and world coffee prices at the close of *Kuhle Wampe*. But it is the dramaturgical structure and institutional location and occasion of performance, not merely new forms, that make of this material the tools of anti-imperialist performance whose legacy has been the post-imperial theatre as well as the pedagogy of the oppressed. *Der Jasager*, based on Arthur Waley's English translation (with German adaptation by Brecht's collaborator Elisabeth Hauptmann) of the Japanese fable by Taniko about a boy who agrees to his own sacrifice for the greater good of travelers on a difficult journey, was performed by and for students at the Karl Marx School in working-class Neukölln. Brecht responded to the critical comments of students and teachers by writing *Der Neinsager* as a counter-*Lehrstück* (*Werke* 24: 92–4; 484).

Borrowing from *Der Jasager*, but not *Der Neinsager*, *Die Massnahme* began with am abstract parabolic conflict between yes and no to personal sacrifice in the name of a common good, but inserted it into a play with choral music (by Eisler) in which four Soviet Communists report to the Party (or Control Choir) on the endangerment of their attempts secretly to organize local workers in China for long-term struggle by immediate and public expressions of sympathy by an inexperienced comrade. The four activists propose and finally take measures – or resort to an "expedient" – to eliminate the errors by eliminating the person who committed them; the comrade himself submits willingly to his own death.[15] Although performed

---

[15] Steinweg's edition, *Die Massnahme: Kritische Ausgabe mit einer Spielanleitung* (Frankfurt: Suhrkamp, 1972), hereafter cited as "Steinweg," includes the earliest extant version (A1, 1930), the first published versions in *Versuche* (A2, 1930 and A3, 1931), a fragment of a revision prepared for an unpublished Moscow edition (A4, 1936) and a further revision published in London by Malik Verlag in 1938 and reprinted under Elisabeth Hauptmann's direction in the *Gesammelte Werke* of 1967, as well as commentary from the creators and their critics (A5). The 1988–98 *Werke* reprints only the first two published

for an audience and thus at one remove from Brecht's proposed abolition of the "system of player and audience," the two performances in Berlin (December 1930 at the Philharmonie and January 1931 at Max Reinhardt's Großes Schauspielhaus) reached a public composed largely of party subscribers and critics. The production, directed by Brecht and Slatan Dudow, included three choirs of non-professional workers, political kin to the audience, with professional actors and Brecht associates Busch, Helene Weigel, and Alexander Granach, and romantic tenor Anton Maria Topitz playing the four activists, who in turn represented their absent comrade. All except the tenor wore half-masks to foreground their roles as members of a collective rather than individualized characters. This representation of the collective was, however, complicated by the breakdown of some choral speeches and songs into statements by single actors in turn and by the contrast to the activists' austerity presented by the tenor. The tenor's performance drew on operatic conventions of heightened expression, while his coiffed hair and operatic make-up constituted a mask of sorts, and, with his equally sentimental rendering of the capitalist trader in scene 5, sharpened the mise en scène's estrangement of his portrayal of the comrade's emotion.[16] The scale and the institutional prestige of

versions (1930 and 1931). Despite Brecht's use of the term "expedient" in "The German Theatre Before Hitler," 944 and Eisler's reiteration of this translation in his testimony to HUAC (see US Congress House of Representatives, *Hearings Regarding Hanns Eisler: Hearings before the Committee on Un-American Activities, House of Representatives, Eightieth Congress, First Session. Public Law 601 (Section 121, Subsection Q (2))* (Washington, Govt. Printing Office, 1947), 14), the translation appended to the HUAC hearing renders *Die Massnahme* as *The Rule* (193–208). Eric Bentley published his translation of A2 with the title "The Measures Taken," in *The Jewish Wife and Other Short Plays*, trans. Bentley (New York: Grove, 1965). Subsequent citations of the play refer to Steinweg's numbered versions and to Bentley's translation, modified where necessary.

[16] For the masks, see the photographs in *Brecht: Versuche 9: Die Massnahme, Lehrstück: Das Exemplar eines Kritikers von der Uraufführung am 13.12.1930*, ed. Reinhard Krüger (Berlin: Weidler, 2001), esp. 117. Using archival evidence, Krüger argues (94–107) that

the venue, the Berlin Philharmonie, might have made the premiere too spectacular an occasion (a *Schau-* rather than a *Lehrstück*) to function in the analytical manner of an experiment among comrades; Brecht's program notes acknowledged that this performance was something of an "exhibition" (*Ausstellung*), despite the questionnaire encouraging audiences to evaluate the expedient (*Werke* 24: 96). Nonetheless, the questions – do you believe that this sort of performance has political instructional value for the audience? For the performers? Against what aspect of the expedient would you have political objections? Do you think that the form of our performance is appropriate for its political goal? Could you suggest other forms? – provoked debate not only among critics but among performers who took the play into labor halls and other multi-purpose venues.

The debate about the role of the Party, the expedients it might have endorsed, and the tension in their execution between discipline and betrayal echo through the work of Brecht and his successors in the GDR, with more force than one might expect from a play that disappeared from the repertoire after three years and reappeared only intermittently – and only in the West – from the 1970s. In order to understand the citation and critique of moments in this play in later East German work, even in its official absence, we need to look at the performance text published in the *Versuche* series in 1930, as well as subsequent revisions. Brecht's revision of the text between performances and over the next decade took account of private and published responses, especially those by leftists, to rework the tension between teaching and learning, discipline and experiment.

The first scene, called "The Writings [*Schriften*] of the Classics" in the first two versions including the first performance version (A2), dramatizes conflict between the four activists bringing from Moscow

the critic in question was probably the conservative and later pro-Nazi music critic Paul Fechter. Despite his political objections to the piece, Fechter's notes on this copy confirm the contrast suggested by the images between the highly emotional and highly artificial performance of the tenor, and the deliberately prosaic rendering of emotion by the other speakers.

the "writings of the classics, the ABC of Communism . . . to the
oppressed, class consciousness and to the class conscious revolutionary experience" (A2, Steinweg 9; Bentley 79) and a young Chinese comrade whose disappointment that the Soviets brought no material help
is juxtaposed with but not resolved by his decision to join them: "I
will abandon my position that was too difficult for two . . . and go with
you. Marching forward, spreading the communist classics and world
revolution" (ibid.). The control choir's song that follows this scene,
"In Praise of the USSR," likewise depicts a revolutionary situation
full of contradiction, in which

> Schon beredete die Welt / Unser Unglück /
> Aber noch saß an unserem / Kargen Tisch
> Aller Unterdrückten Hoffnungen die . . .
> Das Wissen belehrte / Hinter zerfallenen Tür / . . . die Gäste.
> Wenn die Türen zerfallen / sitzen wir noch weiter sichtbar . . .
> Unermüdlich beratend / Die Geschicke der Welt.
>
> (A2; Steinweg 39–40)

> Already the world was / Debating our misery
> But still seated at our / Spare table
> Was the hope of all oppressed, who
> Taught knowledge to guests behind a broken door. . . .
> When the doors break down / We are still to be seen . . .
> Tirelessly advising / The fate of the world.
>
> (Bentley 79–80; trans. modified)

This sense of contradiction and of the fallibility and vulnerability of the USSR in its revolutionary years is muffled in revisions
which emphasize the infallibility of the Party, first with the change
from the "writings of the classics" to the "teachings" (A3 and A5) and,
in the 1967 version, the shift from comradely "advising [*beratend*]"
to paternalistic "taking care of [*betreuend*]."

Despite this movement towards Party authority, the revisions
do not produce an unambiguous defence of the Party or the activists
who decide that, although it is "a fearsome thing to kill," they must

eliminate their comrade. In scene 6, entitled "Rebellion against the Teachings" (A2) and later simply "Betrayal" (A3, A5), the young comrade asserts, moved by the vision of his "own two eyes," that "misery cannot wait," and calls for immediate action. The activists respond not in Party unison but in individual voices: Weigel speaks the initial "Praise of the Party" that has "a thousand eyes" against the comrade's two, presenting in matter-of-fact prose the claim that "the individual can be wiped out / But the Party cannot be wiped out" (A2 57; Bentley 100). When the young comrade insists that his "heart beats for the revolution" and that the revolution is now, in the spontaneous uprising of the unemployed not in the classics (which he threatens to shred) Granach speaks the activists' counter-argument: "Do not shred them [*zerreiße sie nicht*] . . . your revolution is quickly made, lasts one day / and is strangled the morning after /our revolution begins tomorrow / triumphs and changes the world / your revolution stops when you stop / when you have stopped /our revolution marches on" (A2 58; Bentley 101; trans. modified).[17] This assertion that the revolution depends on the masses' long-term commitment that may include the destruction of individuals is endorsed by the massive voice of the control chorus reiterating the praise of the Party which, unlike the individual, cannot be destroyed. Nonetheless, the scene does not conclude with a simple triumph of Party doctrine over individual sentiment, even though the control choir reiterates the "Praise of the Party."

The shifts in the following combative dialogue are not unambiguous, even though the comrade's voice in the tenor role is matched by the terse chorus of the three activists:

YOUNG COMRADE: The sight of injustice drove me into the ranks of the fighters. Here is injustice.

THREE AGITATORS: Be quiet! [*Schweig!*]

YOUNG COMRADE: Here is oppression. I am for freedom!

THREE AGITATORS: Be quiet! You are betraying us!

[17] Krüger (ibid., 144, 145), reproduces Fechter's annotations indicating Weigel's and Granach's parts here. Subsequent references in the text are to Krüger.

YOUNG COMRADE: I have seen too much I shall therefore
go before them / As what I am and
state what is.
(A2 59; Bentley 101–2; trans. mod.)

In the revised version published in 1931, the following exchange
comes between the agitators' accusation of betrayal and the comrade's
assertion of personal revelation:

YOUNG COMRADE: I cannot be quiet, for I am right
THREE AGITATORS: Whether you are right or wrong, if you
speak, we are lost! Be quiet!
(A3, Steinweg 91; trans. LK)

and then returns to the comrade's statement of intent and the exposure, as the activists, represented in the 1930 performance by the sole
woman, Weigel, see it:

THREE AGITATORS: And we saw him and in the twilight
Saw his naked face / Human, open,
guileless / He had torn up his mask.
(A2 59; A3 91; Bentley 102; Krüger 147)

This moment of compassion, highlighted by Weigel's contralto, is juxtaposed with the hostile reaction against the foreigners provoked by
the young comrade's exposure, the unruly crowds waiting for guidance from the activists who flee with the comrade they have knocked
unconscious, as reported by Granach; but the tension between compassion, even pathos, and matter-of-fact report is not resolved. Far
from consolidating the authority of the Party, the 1931 addition
"whether you are right or wrong, be quiet!" focuses attention on the
expediency rather than the legitimacy of the measures taken, and
leaves the meaning of the "betrayal" moving in both directions.

In the final scenes, in which the measures are taken and the
expedient executed, the revisions may tend in the direction of Party
discipline, but the performance text (A2) remains conflicted. The
subtitles of the A2 final scenes – sc. 7, "Final Pursuit [or Persecu-
tion, *Verfolgung*] and Analysis" and sc. 8, "Interment" (Steinweg 59,

62; Bentley 103, 106; trans. mod.) – carry the note of pathos and urgency from the confrontation between the control chorus repeatedly demanding to know the "measures to be taken" and the activists' deflecting response "Wait a moment / It is easy to know what is right / Far from the shooting" (Steinweg 62; Bentley 103), through a difficult consensus (in Brecht's key political term *Einverständnis*, lit. "into understanding") between activists who admit, in Weigel's voice, that *"it is a fearsome thing to kill"* (italics in original) while asserting that "only with force can this *killing* / World be changed" (A2 63; Bentley 107; trans. mod; Krüger 150; italics LK) and the young comrade who requests and receives help from the activists who bear him in their arms before shooting him and throwing him into a hot lime pit. The chorus's final reiteration of consensus, using the abstract language from the opening ABC of Communism, "to the oppressed, class consciousness and to the class conscious revolutionary experience," may defuse this pathos, but its echo remains. The revision of 1931 shortens the last exchange among activists and thus pares down the pathos in the image of the young comrade's head resting on his fellows' arms, but the closing consensus chorus is supplemented by the italicized line "Only when taught by reality, can we / Change reality" (A3, Steinweg 96), which brakes if it does not divert the abstract tautology of the chorale.

The abstract language of the play, and its depiction of the young comrade's death has allowed later readers to add their own content to the play, while paying insufficient attention to the crucial performance elements outlined above. The immediate response of KPD members was conflicted: neither praise nor criticism on the left fell neatly into a party line. One anonymous contributor to the KPD organ *Die Rote Fahne* (Red Flag) called it "revolutionary" while another complained that the play "presented a barely plausible extreme case."[18] The latter was probably Alfred Kurella, who dismissed this "attempt with not quite suitable means" as abstract and

---

[18] "Die Massnahme: Revolutionäres Lehrstück von Brecht und Eisler," (*Die Rote Fahne*, 16 December 1930) v. "Hat die Massnahme Lehrwert?" (24 December), in Steinweg 336–8 and 341–3; the latter was signed "D", probably for "Durus," pen-name of Alfred Kurella,

idealist, even though he allowed that the action of the play could illuminate actual crises in recent KPD history such as the uprising of 1923 and its betrayal by a hostile SPD state.[19] Cemented by his post-war position as secretary for culture in the SED's Central Committee, Kurella's dismissal would become the orthodox Stalinist line and by extension the SED justification for dissolving the SPD in 1946 as a delayed response to the betrayal of the KPD by the SPD in 1919; but the most notorious reading would come from the other side in the Cold War. Former communist Ruth Fischer argued as a friendly witness to HUAC in 1947 that Brecht's drama endorsed the Soviet Communist Party's elimination of its own most loyal members in the Moscow show trials in 1935 and subsequently, even though the play was performed in 1930 for members of a German Communist Party under threat by an anti-Communist state and disappeared from view until brought before HUAC.[20] HUAC's reading of the young comrade's fate, "murdered by his comrades because it was in the best interest of the Communist Party," marked subsequent readings, even by Brecht promoter Eric Bentley. By translating "Da doch nur mit Gewalt diese *tötende* / Welt zu ändern ist" as "Since only by force can this *dying*

who later revised his criticism to praise the *institutional* achievement of the performance as the appropriation of a bourgeois space like the Philharmonie and as the sign of the growing appeal of communism even to sons of the bourgeoisie like Brecht (30 January 1930; Steinweg 365–6).

[19] Kurella, "Ein Versuch mit nicht ganz tauglichen Mitteln," *Literatur der Weltrevolution* (Moscow, 1931), in Steinweg 378–93; trans. Eric Bentley as "What Was he Killed For?" in *The Jewish Wife and Other Short Plays*, 161–72. For the KPD uprising and its legacy, see Weitz, *Creating German Communism*, 160–232.

[20] Ruth Fischer asserted, in *Stalin and German Communism: A Study in the Origins of the State Party* (Cambridge, MA: Harvard University Press, 1948), 752, that the 1930 play "portrayed the annihilation of the party opposition" and thus constituted a "prediction" of the Moscow trials of 1935 onwards. This assertion was the key element in her denunciation of Brecht and her former brother-in-law Hanns Eisler to HUAC; see *Thirty Years of Treason: Excerpts from Hearings before the House Committee on UnAmerican Activities*, ed. Eric Bentley (New York: Viking, 1971), 59–72.

[rather than *killing*] world be changed" (italics LK), Bentley missed the opportunity to highlight Brecht's representation of revolutionary violence as a legitimate *response* to state violence and betrayal rather than murder or malicious homicide, and thus the chance to highlight the allusion to the immediate history of the SPD's violent repression of protests by workers and the unemployed, as well as the longer history of state violence against mass movements for redistribution and democratization and, as Brecht put it to HUAC, the "feelings and ideas of the German workers who fought against Hitler."[21] More recent critics, led by Adorno, have argued that the very abstractness of the drama removes it from the arena of direct political impact and makes of the text, despite Brecht's explicit commitments, an autonomous work of art, in which the "estrangement [*Verfremdung*] of the unmediated appearance of events" constitutes an artistic distance from those events rather than a "practical proximity" and that the very "correction of form by social and political externality, the obliteration of ornament in the service of functionality [*Zweckmässigkeit*]" contributes to the autonomy of the work (418–19; 185, trans. mod.).[22]

[21] The reading of the comrade's willing death as murder was Congressman John Stripling's. Brecht responded by attempting to argue that conditions in late Weimar Germany encouraged revolutionary art; see US Congress House of Representatives, *Hearings Regarding Communist Infiltration of the Motion Picture Industry: Hearings Before the Committee on Un-American Activities, House of Representatives, Eightieth Congress, First Session. Public Law 601 (Section 121, Subsection Q (2))* (Washington, Govt. Printing Office, 1947), 495–6. Bentley's edition of this exchange, *Thirty Years of Treason*, 210–11, smooths out the dialogue and cuts Brecht's strategic pauses as well as his asides to translator David Baumgardt, heard in the recording; for the latter, note Bertolt Brecht, *Werke: Eine Auswahl* (20 CDS) (Berlin: BMG, 1997), v.1.

[22] T. W. Adorno, "Engagement" (1962), in *Noten zur Literatur* (Frankfurt a.M.: Suhrkamp, 1980), 418, trans. "Commitment," in *Aesthetics and Politics: Debates between Brecht, Lukacs, Brecht, Benjamin, Adorno* (London: Verso, 1977), 185. Adorno's elaboration of a paradox by which Brecht's most engaged production becomes his most autonomous work

Brecht's and Eisler's conception of *Die Massnahme* as an experiment certainly includes the estrangement of immediate events, such as the actual struggle of the KPD against the SPD police. This conception was critically engaged by proponents of the productive links between the transformation of theatrical and musical form and that of society. The musicologist Hans Stuckenschmidt, who offered a nuanced case for the pedagogical and musical power of Eisler's setting and Brecht's script, arguing that together they dramatized the tension between revolutionary precepts and the actual difficulty of making revolution in a state in which the ruling socialist party suppressed social transformation and a coalition of bourgeois nations blocked its dissemination to anti-imperialist movements beyond Europe.[23] Although Brecht worried that the location of the premiere in the Philharmonie turned the play into a mere exhibition, subsequent performances by worker-players in industrial centers from the Western Ruhr to Eastern Saxony-Anhalt – areas associated with the violent suppression of worker rebellion – were marked by police disruption as well as intense participant discussion, which gave the action in the house an urgently political rather than exhibitionist character and suggested that the "correction of form by social and political externality" was, *contra* Adorno, part of the meaning of the text in performance and that the play "teaches through being performed not through being seen" (*Werke* 22: 351). After violent suppression of political opposition, the Nazi regime cut short plans for at least four revivals in 1933, *Die Massnahme* lost the vital contact with informed participants that Brecht considered fundamental to the meaning as well as the impact of the *Lehrstück* (Steinweg 469). With this connection severed by exile and the world war against fascism, and later by the Cold War in general and by HUAC's treatment of the play as Stalinist propaganda in

is the inspiration and core thesis of *Die Massnahme* in Susanne
Winnacker's doctoral dissertation, *"Wer immer es ist, den ihr hier
sucht, ich bin es nicht": Zur Dramaturgie der Abwesenheit in Bertolt
Brechts Lehrstück, "Die Massnahme"* (Frankfurt: Peter Lang, 1997).
[23] Hans Stuckenschmidt, "Politische Musik," *Der Aufbruch* (1931), in
Steinweg, 341–8.

particular, Brecht remained reluctant even after Stalin's death to allow revivals of this play. In a 1956 letter, a few months before his death, he argued that performance for a disengaged audience could draw forth merely "moral effects."[24] Brecht was undoubtedly also responding to the ambivalent reception of the *Lehrstück* in the GDR in the 1950s, in the context of SED support for orthodox Soviet "socialist realism," and to his memory of debates about *Die Massnahme* in 1931.

Despite these constraints, Brecht's prediction of and resistance to the transformation of the *Lehrstück* into a *Schaustück*, of the experiment into a spectacle or, worse, into a commodity, may well be borne out in the spectacular revival of *Die Massnahme* by the Berliner Ensemble in 1997, in anticipation of Brecht's centenary in February 1998. Chapter one analyses the historical and critical coordinates of Brecht's evolving theory of theatre and politics and thus the grounds for his key theoretical terms. Brecht's negotiation of cultural policy in the "actually socialist" SED state forms the groundwork of chapter two, on post-imperial Brecht and his successor Heiner Müller in the Cold War context. The resonance of Brecht's *Lehrstück* and institution theory in the GDR, specifically in Müller's radio version of Brecht's asocial *Lehrstück* fragments in the *Fatzer* project, informs chapter three, and the ironies of Brecht commodified in unified Germany is the subject of chapter four. The links between Brecht's critical spectator and Boal's spect-actor are explored in chapter five, on Brecht in South Africa, and chapter six, on the South African playwright Athol Fugard in the GDR. Chapter seven, on performance and the South African Truth and Reconciliation Commission, examines the limits of an Enlightenment theatre project, Brechtian or otherwise, in circumstances where telling the truth may prolong trauma rather than set the speakers free. Before embarking on these topics, however, we should look at the collisions between Brecht and Soviet cultural policy in the 1930s, especially Brecht's debates with the primary defender of this policy, Georg Lukács, whose pronouncements from Moscow provoked essays from Brecht, writing in Western European and later in

---

[24] Brecht, Letter to Paul Patera of the Chamber Theatre in Uppsala, Sweden, 21 April 1956; Steinweg 258.

American exile, on the contested concepts of socialism, realism and modernism.

The verisimilitude of *Verfremdung*: Brecht's search for a modern realistic socialism

Once the Nazi regime had forced leftists of all stripes into exile, arguments about the politics of form lost their dialectic connection to political practice in the streets and in the theatres, and became linked instead to the attempt to create a Popular Front against fascism. Although it inspired contributions from progressive writers worldwide, culminating in an International Writers' Congress in Paris in 1935, in which Brecht participated, this anti-fascist Popular Front was also, by way of the Moscow-based Comintern, entangled with the ideology and intrigues of Soviet policy encapsulated in the doctrine of socialist realism. In Andrei Zhdanov's paradigmatic speech to the Soviet Writers Congress in 1934, socialist realism was defined not only by ideological function – "educating the masses in the spirit of socialism" and promoting the "achievements of socialism and the socialist individual in the present and future" – but also by its ahistorical attribution of realism to the narrative coherence, ideological totality, and satisfying closure of the nineteenth-century novel of bourgeois life and its twentieth-century successors.[25] Zhdanov dismissed the work of modernists as decadent and pathological, in terms that came close to the Nazi defamation of expressionist and other modernist art staged in the notorious exhibition of *entartete Kunst* (degenerate art) in 1937.[26] This exhibition provoked among Germans in exile the "expressionism

[25] A. A. Zhdanov, "Soviet Literature. The Richest in Ideas, the Most Advanced Literature," in *Problems in Soviet Literature. Reports and Speeches of the First Soviet Writers Congress*, ed. H. G. Scott (1935; rpt Westport: Hyperion Press, 1981), 17, 21.

[26] Ernst Bloch and Hanns Eisler make this point in "Avantgarde-Kunst und Volksfront" (Avant-Garde and Popular Front, 1937) and "Die Kunst zu erben" (The Art to Inherit, 1938), both published in the Prague exile paper *Die neue Weltbühne*; rpt in *Zur Tradition der deutschen sozialistischen Literatur: eine Auswahl von Dokumenten* (Berlin/GDR: Aufbau, 1979) 2: 401–15, a collection of essays which represents the SED take on the socialist inheritance, which in the more flexible

debate" between those like Brecht and Eisler who argued for modernist experimentation as the most appropriate, indeed the most *realistic*, engagement with a society in turmoil and those, led by Lukács, who claimed in his signature essay, "Es geht um den Realismus" (Realism is at Stake) (1938), that this experimentation was morally as well as politically decadent and that only the narrative depiction of social totality, perfected in the nineteenth-century novel from Balzac to Tolstoy, constituted realist representation.[27] In the paranoid environment of the "Moscow group" of German Stalinists, exiles close to Brecht including Carola Neher, who had starred in the *Threepenny*

1970s could accommodate Brecht, Bloch and other modernists to a greater degree than in the Stalinist 1950s. "Die Kunst zu erben" was reprinted earlier in the West German collection *Die Expressionismusdebatte: Materialien zu einer marxistischen Realismuskonzeption*, ed. Hans-Jürgen Schmitt (Frankfurt: Suhrkamp, 1973), which witnesses to the revival of the Weimar left by West German intellectuals after 1968.

[27] Lukács's attack on modernism as decadence took its most emphatic form in "Es geht um den Realismus," in *Das Wort* (1938); rpt in *Die Expressionismusdebatte*, 180–230 and *Zur Tradition der deutschen sozialistischen Literatur* 2: 513–64. Lukács was responding to Bloch and Eisler's essay on "the art to inherit" as well as to Bloch, "Diskussion über Expressionismus," in *Das Wort* 6 (1938). Only Bloch, "Discussing Expressionism" and Lukács, "Realism in the Balance" appear in English in *Aesthetics and Politics*, which represents a narrower view of Lukács and his antagonists, Bloch, Brecht, Adorno, and Benjamin, as pioneers of the Western New Left; this translation muffles the rhetorical urgency of Lukács's title, rendered more accurately as "Realism is at Stake." The essay provoked several rebuttals by Brecht: "Kleine Berichtigung" (A Little Correction), "Volkstümlichkeit und Realismus" (On the Popular and the Realistic) and "Die Essays von Georg Lukács," *Werke* 22: 402–14, 456–8. Published in Moscow, *Das Wort* carried Brecht's name and those of the Moscow-based Erpenbeck, Kurella, and Willi Bredel as editors, but this did not ensure publication of Brecht's essays; see commentary in *Werke* 22: 1026–31; 1046–7. Despite his influence on *Das Wort*, Lukács was not its editor but, as Brecht reminded Erpenbeck (*Werke* 22: 1028), editor of the Comintern journal, *International Literature*, published in English, German, and other European languages.

Opera, and Ernst Ottwalt, who had collaborated on *Kuhle Wampe*, found not refuge from Hitler but a secret court in which they were condemned as "enemy aliens" by Lukács and his allies, including Kurella, Erpenbeck and Johannes R. Becher, later prominent figures in GDR cultural politics.[28] The stakes in these debates, to rephrase Lukács, thus involved not merely literary realism but also the real lives of the participants.

Brecht's disagreement with the Stalinist orthodoxy led him to refine in the 1930s and 1940s what would become the key term of his theatre, *Verfremdung*. Even before he coined the term, Brecht had argued for "estrangement" (*Befremdung*) as a mode of "realism" shaped, as he argued in the dark days of 1934 in "Five Difficulties in Writing the Truth," by "cunning" as well as "art" and "good judgment" (*Werke* 22: 74–88), rather than by adherence to classical form. The debates that shaped these terms had already begun in the Weimar years, when Lukács defended in "Reportage or Portrayal" and "Tendency or Partisanship" (published in *Die Linkskurve*, 1932) the artistic as well as political rightness of omniscient narrative and rounded portrayal (*Gestaltung*), as against the arguments of Eisler and Bloch for the appropriateness of montage, interruption and other new techniques for representing modernity and for bringing together avant-garde and Popular Front; and when Brecht argued – especially in *Der Dreigroschenprozeß* (*The Threepenny Lawsuit*; about the commodification of his anti-capitalist *Threepenny Opera* by the film industry) that debates about form needed to be grounded in the knowledge that even apparently autonomous art is shaped by institutions, and in projects for the refunctioning (*Umfunktionierung*) of those institutions (film, radio, theatre, publication) in the interests of

---

[28] For the abandonment of heterodox German leftists by their orthodox compatriots in Moscow, see Lukács, Becher, Friedrich Wolf, and others, *Die Säuberung: Stenogram einer geschlossenen Parteiversammlung*, ed. Reinhard Müller (Hamburg: Rowohlt, 1991). The "Moscow group" returned with Red Army backing in 1945 to dominate the GDR; the most compelling chronicler of this group remains a former member and later defector, Wolfgang Leonhard, *Die Revolution entläßt ihre Kinder* (Cologne: Kiepenheuer and Witsch, 1990).

revolutionary actors and audiences.[29] The debates took on a sharper tone under exile conditions; Brecht and other heterodox marxists lost a solid institutional base from which to challenge the orthodox Stalinist line. While Lukács's *Linkskurve* essays and his 1936 paper "Narrate or Describe" showed a virtuoso analysis of narrative form, the basic argument of "Realism in the Balance" reiterated Zhdanov in its condemnation of the "so-called avant-garde . . . from Naturalism to Surrealism" as an abandonment of "the objective mirroring of reality [*objektive Wirklichkeitswiederspiegelung*] and the artistic battle [*Ring*] to shape the rich diversity and unity of [artistic] mediations" (trans. mod.).[30]

Brecht's first essay on the concept of *Verfremdung* (1936) predates Lukács's most polemical attempt to dismiss modernist innovation as mere formalism while himself promoting a particular historical form, the novel on the model of Balzac and Tolstoy, as the only means of "objectively mirroring" reality. Nonetheless, *Verfremdung*, accurately translated not as "alienation" but rather as estrangement or *dis-illusion*, established the groundwork for Brecht's critique of Lukács. Brecht attacked especially Lukács's denial that new forms might be better able than old ones to represent new social formations, and proposed instead a more compelling and more practical theory

---

[29] Lukács, "Tendenz oder Parteilichkeit" and "Reportage oder Gestaltung: Kritische Bemerkungen anläßlich des Romans von Ernst Ottwalt" (1932); rpt in *Zur Tradition der deutschen sozialistischen Literatur* 1: 479–93; 499–523, with Ottwalt's rebuttal, "'Tatsachenroman' und Formexperiment: eine Entgegnung an Georg Lukács," 1: 524–33. Lukács's essays appear in English in his *Essays on Realism*, ed. Rodney Livingstone, trans. David Fernbach (Cambridge, MA: MIT Press, 1982). For the full text of Brecht's *Dreigroschenprozeß* (1932), see *Werke* 21: 448–514; *The Threepenny Lawsuit*, in *Brecht on Film and Radio*, ed. and trans. Marc Silberman (London: Methuen, 2000).

[30] Lukács, "Es geht um den Realismus," in *Die Expressionismusdebatte*, 203, 211; "Realism in the Balance", *Aesthetics and Politics*, 37, 43. See also Lukács, "Erzählen oder Beschreiben", *Internationale Literatur* (1936), rpt in *Zur Tradition der deutschen sozialistischen Literatur* 2: 331–99.

of realism.[31] Unlike e*strange*ment, "dis-illusion" may not translate the *fremd* in *Verfremdung*, but it captures Brecht's affinity with the modern enlightenment project; undoing theatrical illusion and the apparent self-evidence of ideology or superstition recalls Max Weber's idea of the "de-enchantment" [*Entzauberung*] of the world. Brechtian dis-illusion goes further to encourage the audience to see the contradictions between ideology and actual social conflict and thus to change the world off- as well as on-stage. "Alienation," by contrast, translates the Hegelian/Marxian *Entfremdung*, which characterizes the dispossessed subject of slavery or proletarianization rather than the critical observer of Brecht's theatre; hence his argument, in notes on "epic theatre and alienation" and "dialectics and dis-illusion," that dis-illusion (*Verfremdung*) constitutes a return from alienation (*Entfremdung*) to understanding (*Werke* 22: 211–12; 401–2). The pedagogical emphasis in Brecht's theatre "for instruction" and "for pleasure" (22: 106–18; *BoT* 69–77) also distinguishes his understanding of "shock" (*Erschütterung*), in the sense of the thought-provoking surprise of the contradictory element in the apparently self-evident everyday experience of ideology (22: 110; *BoT* 71), from Benjamin's. Even though Benjamin admired Brecht's analytical theatre, his sense of the progressive implications of shock effects was influenced more by psychoanalysis and its surrealist interpretation – from the unconscious *mémoire involontaire* he found, via Bergson, Proust, and Breton, in

[31] Brecht's first use of the term is in "Verfremdungseffekte in der chinesischen Schauspielkunst," *Werke* 22: 200–10. The first English version was "The Fourth Wall of China: An Essay on the Effects of *Disillusion* in Chinese Acting" (italics LK), trans. Eric Walter White in *Life and Letters Today* (1936, rpt Brecht, *Werke* 22: 960–68). Apart from the whimsical reference to the Wall of China, this title captures better than the standard translation by Willett, "Alienation Effects in Chinese Acting" (*BoT* 91–9) Brecht's emphasis on the de-enchantment of the theatre in the service of critique. On the epistemological difference between these terms, see Ernst Bloch, "*Entfremdung, Verfremdung*: Alienation, Estrangement," in *Brecht*, ed. Erika Munk (New York: Bantam, 1972) and Reinhold Grimm, "Alienation in Context: On the Theory and Practice of Brechtian Theater," in *A Bertolt Brecht Reference Companion*, ed. Mews, 35–46.

Charles Baudelaire's prose poems on city life to the more sociological notion, borrowed in part from the film critic Siegfried Kracauer, of distraction (*Zerstreuung*).[32] Where distraction was for Kracauer a way of describing the leisure habits of white-collar workers as an "improvised response" to the "uncontrolled anarchy of our world," for Benjamin it was a more mysterious mode of modern apperception: an index of the possible transformation not only of audience response but of society through a "mobilization of the masses" that tended to the "inadvertent" rather than organized.[33] Although Brecht allowed that disillusion effects should include unpredictable play and astonishment

[32] Kracauer, "Kult der Zerstreuung," in *Ornament der Masse* (Frankfurt a.M.: Suhrkamp), 311–17; here: 316; trans. Thomas Y. Levin, "Cult of Distraction", in *Mass Ornament* (Cambridge, MA: Harvard University Press, 1995), 323–8; here: 327. On shock effects in Baudelaire's prose poems, see Benjamin, "Über einige Motive bei Baudelaire," in *Gesammelte Schriften*, ed. Rolf Tiedemann (Frankfurt a.M.: Suhrkamp, 1980), 2: 605–53; trans. Harry Zohn, "On Some Motifs in Baudelaire," in *Illuminations* (New York: Schocken, 1969), 155–200.

[33] Benjamin began writing on Brecht in 1929, but published only reviews of Brecht's *Die Mutter* (Berlin 1932) and *Furcht und Elend im Dritten Reich* (in *Die neue Weltbühne*, 1938). His essays on epic theatre and the aesthetics of production appeared posthumously; see Benjamin, *Gesammelte Schriften* 5: 511–39, and, in partial English translation, *Understanding Brecht* (London: New Left Books, 1980). As Steve Giles shows in *Bertolt Brecht and Critical Theory* (Bern: Peter Lang, 1997), Brecht's influence on Benjamin marks not only the latter's essays on theatre but also, by way of the institution theory in Brecht's *Dreigroschenprozeß*, Benjamin's most cited essay, "On the Work of Art in the Age of its Technical Reproducibility". The 1935 draft and 1936 publication of "Das Kunstwerk im Zeitalter seiner technischen Reproduzierbarkeit" are in his *Gesammelte Schriften* 2: 435–508; notes 3: 982–1271; a third version between them (preferred by Benjamin) is in vol. 7: 350–84; notes, 661–90. The English version, "The Work of Art in the Age of Mechanical Reproduction," in *Illuminations*, as the inaccurate title reveals, is based on the French translation of the published text. The key sentences, translated here from Benjamin's preferred version, read: "The distraction offered by art secretly/inadvertently [*unter der Hand*] registers the extent to which new tasks can be solved by new modes of perception. . . . Art will

to allow for new insights that could emerge only from unpredicted surprise, his was an art dedicated to a goal: the realistic and illuminating representation of social conflict, including conflicting representation, made possible the understanding necessary to change that reality.

Brecht's commitment to the goal of social transformation or, indeed, to any goal that might override the autonomy of art would later provoke sharp rebuke from Adorno. At his most polemical, in the radio essay on "Commitment or the Autonomy of Art" (1962), Adorno accuses Brecht of the "unmediated glorification of the Party" in *Die Massnahme*.³⁴ In a more sophisticated mode, he argues that Brecht oversimplifies the complexity of economic crises, such as the stock market crash in *St Joan of the Stockyards*, or the machinery of tyranny and "the true horror of fascism" in *The Resistable Rise of Arturo Ui*, in order to make these complex problems fit into the limited form of the parable play (417–18; 183–4). Invoking Brecht's own commitment to ideological clarity, Adorno charges Brecht with "political naivete," even with "bad politics" (417; 183) and goes on to generalize that "political untruth contaminates aesthetic form" (420; 186). Yet even as he criticizes Brecht for subjecting art too aggressively to an "agitational goal" ("agitatorischer Zweck"; 417; 184; trans. mod.), Adorno finds in Brecht's drama, even in the *Lehrstück*, an expression of the autonomy and the complexity of artistic form. But Adorno's central paradox – that the "correction of form by social and political externality, the obliteration of ornament in the service of functionality [*Zweckmässigkeit*]" contributes to the autonomy of the work (418–19; 185, trans. mod) – as well as his blunter claim that Brecht's "artistic simplification" leads to the "falsification" of objective reality (419; 185) depend themselves on a simplified reading of Brecht's experimental staging of conflict as a univocal didactic text, "preaching to the saved [sic]."

---

intervene in the most difficult and most important [task] to the degree that it can mobilize the masses" (7: 381).
³⁴ Adorno, "Engagement," in *Noten zur Literatur*, 415; trans. "Commitment" in *Aesthetics and Politics*, 182; subsequent references in the body of the text.

Although he never lived to read it, Brecht might have responded to Adorno's claim that the militantly functional *Lehrstück* becomes more artistic, autonomous and therefore, in Adorno's schema, functionless the more it strips itself of visible artistry, with the reminder that the *Lehrstück* was conceived as an experimental form, rather than the didactic form that Adorno takes it to be. Even if, as Adorno charges, the engaged work of art, whether *Die Massnahme* or Picasso's *Guernica*, never "won over anyone" for the cause (418; 184), the work can, as Picasso is alleged to have responded, say "no" (424; 190). But limiting the social function of the work to its negative formal resistance to repressive reality, which would become the signature theme of Adorno's *Aesthetic Theory* (1969), was for Brecht a concession to idealism. For all his attention to art and to play, theatre and other writing was for Brecht an instrument – albeit a delicate one, with all its difficulties – to "write the truth," to enlighten readers and audiences, and so to give them means to understand and change the world. Nor did the dichotomy between autonomy and instrumentalization detract from his recognition that the institutional context, no less than the apparently immutable form of the work of art, shapes the function or the functionlessness of that work *as* art or instrument or both. Rather he sought to overcome this dichotomy between autonomy and instrumentalization by arguing as a practitioner against the theorists, in a journal note against Lukács (*Werke* 26: 321), that art can take its appropriate form only in *production*, whose engagement with dynamic social conditions cannot be restricted by a priori prescription of fixed forms.

In this emphasis on the primacy of production over theory, and thus of experiment over prescription in the realm of social as well as artistic transformation, Brecht charged the proponents of both prescriptive extremes with formalism. He maintained, in his essay on "the formalist character of the theory of realism" (1938), that Lukács's prescription of a particular novelistic form as the appropriate vehicle for critical and socialist realism was the more formalist in its fixed attachment than the modernists' attempts to develop, through experiment, a form capable of representing a modern reality more complex than the nineteenth-century world, and argued instead that "literature cannot be forbidden to employ new skills" if they prove useful in representing the new world realistically (*Werke* 22: 437–45).[35] In "The Popular and the Realistic" (*Werke* 22: 405–15; *BoT* 107–15), Brecht challenged the attempts of Moscow Group member Fritz Erpenbeck to use the category of the popular, or, more precisely, the *volkstümlich* or "of the people (as unadulterated race)" in a manner that, despite Erpenbeck's protests, recalled Nazi promotions of an allegedly pure German culture against allegedly degenerate international modernism.[36] Instead of a racial notion of the folk, Brecht argued for a dynamic conception of the popular that "refers to a people that not only participate fully in the process of development but are taking it over" and thus "represents the most progressive section of the people" while also making sense to the others (408; 108; trans. mod.). He likewise advocated a flexibly realistic writing practice, arguing that realism, in the form of the novel, could not be simply "expropriated" from the bourgeoisie like an intact factory of cultural production but rather that writers ought to "make lively use of all means, old and new, tried

---

[35] Brecht's "The Formalist Character of the Theory of Realism" appears in abbreviated form in *Aesthetics and Politics*, 70–6, with "Remarks on an Essay [by Georg Lukács]," 76–9, but these represent a fraction of his writings on the expressionism debate and on the "breadth and variety of the realist way of writing" in *Werke* 22: 417–65. This last essay, "Weite and Vielfält der realistischen Schreibweise" (*Werke* 22: 423–33) was published as one of Brecht's *Versuche* (London: Malik, 1938) after futile correspondence with *Das Wort* (*Werke* 22: 1031–40). In a letter to Bredel in July 1938, Brecht argued that *Das Wort* was run by a "small clique apparently led by Lukács and [Julius] Hay" engaged in attacking everything that "does not fit into this ideal form, derived from the bourgeois novel of the last century" (28: 106, letter no. 844).

[36] Fritz Erpenbeck, "Volkstümlichkeit," *Das Wort* 7 (1938); rpt in *Zur Tradition der deutschen sozialistischen Literatur* 2: 600–9. Brecht's posthumously published response has since influenced a wide range of English-speaking progressives, from Raymond Williams and Stuart Hall in Britain to the San Francisco Mime Troupe's former director, Ronnie Davis.

and untried, deriving from art and from other sources, in order to put reality in the hands of living people in a way in which it can be mastered" and that they ought to respond, as he did in working on the *Lehrstücke*, to worker audiences and potential players (408, 410/109; 110).

Brecht's recognition of the institutional and social as well as formal stakes in this struggle distinguished his commitment also from those of his friends, in particular from the attachment of the avowed modernists Bloch, Eisler, and Benjamin to exclusively modernist forms. In insisting that the transformation of society through theatre and other cultural practices required the transformation of the institutions of production and reception over and above formal innovation, Brecht differed from his allies in the expressionism debate who treated techniques like the interruption and estrangement of actors in performance, or conceptual montage in the cinema, as *in themselves* revolutionary acts – as well as from his antagonist Lukács, who had in common with Benjamin the idea that particular artistic techniques carried an immanent politics, even if he praised quite different forms. Brecht's willingness to combine modern techniques of dis-illusion and montage with the refunctioning of old forms for progressive ends in new institutional contexts, even historically conservative forms such as the *Volksstück* or "folk comedy," would prove key in his critical negotiation with orthodox socialist realism in its post-war GDR reincarnation.

Illusory solutions to real problems? The politics of socialist realism

In the first turbulent decade or so of the GDR (1949–61), from the post-war period of scarcity and turmoil, and the uncertain founding of separate and unequal German states, to the temporary stability enforced by the Berlin Wall in 1961, debates about the obligation of art to represent the new society and to create an anti-fascist citizenry out of a population corrupted by the Nazis probed the contradiction between utopian socialism and actually existing resignation. The status of the SED state as sole legatee of socialist anti-fascism, as against a West Germany where former Nazis remained in key positions, was sustained not only by the Soviet Army and the Moscow group of exiles flying in under the Soviet banner, but also by socialist exiles who had spent the war in the West rather than the East, such as Brecht or Anna Seghers, first chair of the Writers Union. Despite the SED's consolidation of power, critical intellectuals like Brecht, who returned with misgivings about Soviet policy, argued that socialism demanded not affirmative slogans but engagement with the ongoing struggle to establish a modern but non-capitalist society. The difficulty posed by the lag between the promise of prosperity and the experience of scarcity was exacerbated by refugees from the former German territories in Poland and Czechoslovakia (up to three million, more than a fifth of the total East German population), Soviet appropriation of industrial infrastructure as reparations (until 1954), and staggering emigration to the West (over two and a half million until 1961), only worsened by the SED's zealous application of Soviet-style centralized power and production.[37]

Despite an early debate about a distinctly "German" *Sonderweg* (exceptional route) to socialist democracy, the SED's claim on power became increasingly monopolistic and at the same time more dependent on the Soviet Union, especially after the Paris Treaty of 1952 drew the Federal Republic of [West] Germany (FRG) into a security alliance with Western Europe.[38] Soviet and GDR reaction to this

---

[37] For the refugee figures, see Dietrich Staritz, *Geschichte der DDR*, 2nd edn (Frankfurt a.M.: Suhrkamp. 1996), 67; for emigration and its impact on GDR demography, see Hermann Weber, *Geschichte der DDR*, 2nd edn (Munich: Deutscher Taschenbuchverlag, 1999), 123–222; here: 220.

[38] Anton Ackermann called for diverse forms of art in "Marxistische Kulturpolitik" at the first Cultural Congress of the SED (8 May 1948, the anniversary of VE Day and, for the SED, of the defeat of fascism in Germany), before the declaration of an independent state. See *Dokumente zur Kunst-, Literatur-, und Kulturpolitik der SED*, ed. Elimar Schubbe (Stuttgart: Seewald, 1972), 84–90. On the impact of the Paris Treaty on SED policy, especially the acceleration of production that triggered the 1953 rebellion, see historian Rolf Söckigt (document no. 2) in *Es hat alles keinen Zweck, der Spitzbart muss weg: Der 17. Juni 1953*, ed. Armin Friedrich and Thomas Friedrich (Berlin: Paetec,

treaty as "imperialist" led to the militarization of the GDR with the consolidation and expansion of the Stasi, the fortification of the East/West German border (1953), the founding of the Volksarmee (1955), and the SED program for "building socialism" by accelerating heavy industrial production at the expense of consumer goods.[39] At moments of crisis, the workers' rebellion against this acceleration in June 1953, the Soviet invasion of Hungary in 1956, the erection of the Berlin Wall in 1961, and again at the Eleventh Plenum of the Central Committee in 1965, the SED cracked down on dissenters, especially on avowed socialist intellectuals, for alleged "counter-revolutionary agitation" and demanded loyalty to the actual state over and above any utopian socialist goals.[40] The SED sentenced vocal dissidents to political prisons but, in comparison with major upheavals in Hungary and Poland, it secured relative compliance (if not always loyalty) from the majority by guaranteeing the needs, including greater access to education and training, of the formerly underprivileged, especially women and workers, and by rewarding those citizens who joined the party and party-loyal organizations, from the Free German Youth (FDJ) to the Free German Union Federation (FDGB) to the unions of writers, and theatre and other artists, with work, consumer, and travel privileges.[41] Although technically not the only party, the SED constituted a

1992), 11–12. In 1955 the FRG joined NATO, while the GDR joined the Warsaw Pact.

[39] For the SED program for "building socialism" (*Aufbau des Sozialismus*) see "Second SED Party Conference (June 1952)" (document no.1) in Friedrich, ed., *Es hat alles keinen Zweck*, 6–10; the decree accelerating production, "Notice on the Decision to Raise Production Quotas [*Arbeitsnormen*]" (28 May 1953) is document no. 4, 14–19 (hereafter: "Production Quotas").

[40] The trials in 1957 that convicted philosopher Wolfgang Harich and editor Walter Janka of "counter-revolutionary agitation" were remarkable for their hysterical treatment of loyal critique as a threat to national security. See Janka, *Schwierigkeiten mit der Wahrheit* (Reinbek: Rowohlt, 1990), and Harich, *Keine Schwierigkeiten mit der Wahrheit: Zur nationalkommunistischen Opposition 1956 in der DDR* (Berlin: Dietz, 1993).

[41] For expanded educational opportunities for workers and women in the GDR, see Weber, *Geschichte der DDR*, 242–5; for the limits of this

Parteidiktatur, which is best translated as a "dictatorial [single] party state" rather than as "dictatorship," since the latter term suggests the dominance of a charismatic individual dictator rather than the ruling bureaucracy in place here. As such, the SED was able to regulate if not entirely suppress dissent by alternating the disbursement and the withholding of privileges or welfare according to a logic that remained opaque to those on the receiving end but deterred most from overt opposition.[42]

The debates about socialist realism in the GDR were thus in a primary way political; that is, they engaged directly with the question of the legitimacy of the self-declared German socialist state. The authority of the GDR as a bulwark against capitalist encroachment was invoked to grant official status to the "great tradition" of the novel from Balzac to Gorky and to denounce formal experimentation as a national security risk that would "lead to the uprooting of national culture, the destruction of national consciousness, and . . . support for the war policies of American imperialism."[43] The SED's use of

transformation, see Dagmar Langenhan and Sabine Ross, "The Socialist Glass Ceiling: Limits to Female Careers," and Dorothee Wierling, "The Hitler Youth Generation in the GDR," in *Dictatorship as Experience: Towards a Socio-Cultural History of the GDR*, ed. Konrad Jarausch, trans. Eve Duffy (Oxford: Berghahn, 1999), 177–91, 307–24.

[42] For analysis of the political form of the SED state and the social forms of the GDR, see Jarausch, "Beyond Uniformity: The Challenge of Historicizing the GDR" and "Care and Coercion: The GDR as Welfare Dictatorship," ibid., 3–16, 47–71, and Weber, *Geschichte der DDR*, 169–222. Though the GDR was not literally a one-party state, the SED dominated all political and economic institutions after forcibly uniting the historically larger SPD with the local remnants of the smaller KPD. Of the minority "block" parties, the Christian Democratic Union (CDU) and Liberal Democrats (LDPD) were survivals from the Weimar Republic, while the National Democrats (NDPD) and the Farmers Party (DBD) were created by the SED in the early years of the republic to appeal to constituencies, nationalists and farmers, who were unlikely to favor any socialist party.

[43] Ulbricht, "Der Kampf gegen den Formalismus in der Kunst und Literatur," *Dokumente*, 180.

socialist realism as a weapon in this war, and its denunciation of formal experimentation as the hallmark of the class enemy, drew not only on Zhdanov's symptomatic reading of experimental form as the sign of Western decadence, but also on the intellectual authority of Lukács, whose assault on the "so-called avant-garde" was by 1949 canonical. In the 1950s, when Brecht was back in Berlin directing the new Berliner Ensemble, influential SED critics, led by Brecht's old rival Fritz Erpenbeck, continued to denounce Brecht's methods of estrangement and gestic action and his critique of theatrical empathy as "volksfremde Dekadenz" ("decadence alien to the people").[44] Brecht, so this argument went, alienated the great tradition of the European novel and its dramatic analogues in Stanislavsky and, locally, in Friedrich Wolf by favoring "negative criticism" rather than "revolutionary romanticism," in Gorky's sense of the portrayal of the present in the foreglow of the utopian future.[45] Despite the SED's ostentatious commemoration of martyrs in the anti-fascist struggle, including the memorialization of the critical socialist Rosa Luxemburg in the square that housed the historically socialist theatre, the Volksbühne, the party's treatment of Brecht's dissidence remained paternalistic.

Especially after the uprising on 17 June 1953, in which Berlin workers in the key construction sector rebelled against accelerated production quotas or "norms," the SED enjoined artists to celebrate the achievements of socialism in the GDR and so offset the ideological damage done by the uprising. But, even before the crisis years of 1953 and 1956, SED secretary general Walter Ulbricht reiterated Zhdanov's instrumental definition of socialist realism as a tool "to re-educate working people in the spirit of socialism" in the face of alleged threats from Western "capitalism and imperialism."[46]

---

[44] Fritz Erpenbeck, "Formalismus und Dekadenz," *Dokumente*, 109–13. As editor of the Theatre Association journal, *Theater der Zeit*, Erpenbeck was well placed to attack Brecht.

[45] Maxim Gorky, "On Socialist Realism," in *Socialist Realism in Literature and Art* (Moscow: Progress Publishers, 1971), 32–8 and Achim Wolter, "Die internationale Bedeutung des sozialistischen Realismus," *Dokumente*, 210.

[46] Ulbricht, "Der Kampf gegen den Formalismus," *Dokumente*, 178.

Claiming the mantle of socialist victory rather than fascist defeat in the Second World War, while tarring West Germany and its American ally with the brush of fascism and imperialism, Ulbricht inveighed against the alleged hostility to a "just war" in Brecht's anti-war cantata, *Der Verhör des Lukullus* (The Trial of Lucullus). The cantata, in which a dead Roman war hero is tried by an otherworldly court for crimes against humanity, opened before a restricted public at the Staatsoper in March 1951. Attacking Brecht's alleged lack of an anti-fascist sense of history, Ulbricht's article nonetheless acknowledged disparities between state endorsement of an anti-fascist past and a communist future, on the one hand, and the passivity of the population in the face of a harsh present, on the other. A more subtle attack acknowledged the historical merits of *Verfremdung* and other techniques of anti-capitalist theatre but argued that they were out of place in a society that claimed to have defeated fascism and capitalism. *Der Verhör des Lukullus* was condemned by critics (as opposed to politicians) not for formalism as such, but for *anachronistic* formalism, for setting up in text and music a homology between aesthetic and social fragmentation and for favoring an open-ended dramaturgy that left the final word on the hero's war crimes to the audience. The estrangement of the war hero, which might have effectively exposed fascist abuse of power, was deemed by an orthodox critic in the SED journal *Neues Deutschland* as inappropriate in a society that had allegedly resolved fundamental social antagonism, and detrimental to the audience's loyalty to the GDR as anti-fascist state.[47]

Brecht's negotiation of the SED line in this period was critical, but his deployment of the SED vocabulary of raising the consciousness of the people suggests consent to the legitimacy of the state, if

---

[47] Anon., "Das Verhör des Lukullus," *Neues Deutschland*, 22 March 1951; reprinted in *Dokumente*, 186; Ulbricht, "Kampf gegen den Formalismus," 181. Brecht changed the title to *Die Verurteilung des Lukullus* and revised the text to emphasize the ideological *condemnation* of a war criminal rather than the open-ended *trial* of the protagonist in the first version. The revision was closed after four performances.

not its methods. In a note "on socialist realism," Brecht responded to Ulbricht's attack on *Lukullus* with a plea for critical representation of ongoing social problems, including the apathy of much of the population (*Werke* 23: 287). Even though Brecht regretted the absence of "the cleansing [*reinigende*] process of revolution" (23: 327–8) in the establishment of socialism in the GDR, his emphasis on "raising the consciousness [*Bewußtseinsbildung*] of the nation" as the duty or "privilege of the arts" (23: 306) echoes SED directives. Grappling with the project of a realistic theatre under social transformation, Brecht's notes in his last years suggest a shift away from specifically modernist techniques of theatre developed in the 1920s – montage, interruption, dissociation of actor and character – towards what he called "dialectical theatre" (23: 295–303). Acknowledging the hegemony of socialist *realism*, he argued nonetheless for ongoing *realistic* critique of failures under socialism. In an unpublished note at the time of the battle around *Lukullus* in 1951, Brecht invoked his 1938 argument against Lukács to turn the SED campaign against formalism against itself, attacking its program as the tyranny (*Vorherrschaft*) of anachronistic forms over a realistic reassessment of new forms appropriate to current political content ("aktuelle politische Inhalte," 23: 148). In his public statement "Cultural Policy and the Academy of the Arts", published shortly after the 1953 uprising, Brecht argued that the culture commissars' version of socialist heroism entailed a kitsch reduction of the Soviet tradition of "revolutionary romanticism" to a prescriptive affirmation or administration of state ideology at the expense of the facts of ongoing social transformation (23: 257–8). The superficial optimism celebrating the conversion of anti-social individuals into good socialist workers could not grapple honestly with the persistent contradiction between old and new between and within people; on the contrary, "it endangers the development of the new society" (258). In an unpublished response to the pointedly Leninist question "What is to be done?" (*Was haben wir zu tun?*), Brecht challenged Culture Minister Johannes Becher who had insisted that "socialist realism is the *only* creative method [*einzige schöpferische Methode*]" to further "great socialist art," arguing instead for a strategic exploration of means that might be "critical, realist and socialist *in different ways* [*verschiedener Art*]" (23: 266).[48] His argument for formal experiment was not based on mere novelty but on an urgent assessment of the danger of undoing the social revolution by distorting reality through officially sanctioned forms and their bureaucratic enforcement. To cut fiction against a pre-fabricated yardstick would be not merely an aesthetic error but a social and political failure, because it would resolve conflicts in fiction rather than in reality and thus provide illusory solutions ("soziale Scheinlösungen") as opposed to authentic social solutions ("echte soziale Lösungen") to real social problems (23: 258).[49]

Against this prescription, Brecht called for a diverse, flexible, and pragmatic conception of realism, derived from the changing shape of social reality and the challenge of representing these changes. As we shall see in the next chapter, however, his attempt to realize this conception in practice by producing representations of GDR reality on stage proved to be difficult.

[48] Becher, Discussion Paper at the Second SED Party Conference, 9–12 July, *Dokumente*, 241. Brecht's emphasis on *verschieden* (diverse) as against Becher's *einzige* (only one) highlights his critique of the SED's promotion of a single artistic method to the level of doctrine.

[49] In his critique of "'illusory'" or fictional "solutions to real problems," Brecht drew closer to Lukács's post-war critique of the tendency of revolutionary romanticism to degenerate into unrealistic portrayals of sudden conversion. Lukács expressed these doubts most forcefully after the Soviet repression of the Hungarian uprising in 1956, but suggested, in an earlier essay published in the GDR in 1949, that the presence of socialist themes or working-class characters did not in itself amount to "realism from a socialist point of view"; see Lukács, "Der höchste Grad des Realismus," in *Zur Tradition der deutschen sozialistischen Literatur* 3: 719. Brecht did not confine his criticism of the illusory representation of socialism to the GDR; he also criticized its application by American Communists. As early as 1936, in a letter to the American Communist V. J. Jerome, he used as analogy the notion that "syphilis might vanish after a couple of injections" to criticize Clifford Odets's appeal to socialism as a magic solution of the suffering portrayed in his play *Paradise Lost*; letter no. 712, *Werke* 27: 545.

2 Realism, socialism, and modernism in the production play

As the German Democratic Republic began to implode after the fall of the Berlin Wall in November 1989, many influential members of the West German press and academy dismissed GDR cultural production as a mere reflection of the official communist line. In a manner reminiscent of classic Cold War polemics in the 1950s, these critics attempted to discredit the very idea of the political engagement of art by attempting to reduce the complexities of commitment to a simplistic political message.[1] Against art allegedly corrupted by socialism, West German scholars as well as journalists after the fall of the Wall defended a notion of aesthetic modernism supposedly free from politics. The "new" Germany's not so new "ideology of modernism," to borrow a term from Fredric Jameson, represented East Germany as a pre-modern society unable to meet the standards of its fully modernized Western counterpart and doomed to a state of enforced primitivism.[2] Karl-Heinz Bohrer, aesthete and Nietzsche scholar, introduced the model when he dismissed the GDR as a *Kulturschutzgebiet* (culture reserve – an allusion to *Naturschutzgebiet*, the German term for "nature reserve," which dates from the Nazi

[1] For comparison between Cold War rhetoric and that of Western critics on the late GDR, see Loren Kruger, "'Wir treten aus unseren Rollen heraus': Theatre Intellectuals and Public Spheres," in *The Power of Intellectuals in Contemporary Germany*, ed. Michael Geyer (Chicago: University of Chicago Press, 2002), 183–211.

[2] Fredric Jameson, "Beyond the Cave. Demystifying the Ideology of Modernism," in his *The Ideologies of Theory. Essays 1971–86* (Minneapolis: University of Minnesota Press, 1988), 115–32.

period), whose terminally "obsolete civilization" should be an object of ridicule.[3] In general, the claim, shared by the SED and dissident GDR intellectuals, to have inherited and furthered the ideals of progress defined by international socialism and anti-fascism, which had been acknowledged if not always supported by the West European and West German left, appeared in the accounts of many former leftists in a grotesque inversion as the "preserve" of a parochial and outdated ideology.

Even before the breach in the Wall, Wolfgang Emmerich – once an informed explorer of the GDR literary landscape – argued in 1988 that GDR literature could only be described as pre-modern:

> At the outset, in the wake of devastation that is now difficult to comprehend, economic and technical modernization in the GDR was extremely slow. Already in 1948, under the aegis of "socialist [re]construction" [*Aufbau des Sozialismus*], the GDR wanted to be a "modern state" in which enlightenment and progress, the rational principle, were supposed to prevail. But, owing to the withholding of material assistance (in contrast to the Western sectors) and also to a dogmatic, authoritarian application of "socialist principles," the GDR continued to be a pre-modern state well into the 1970s [. . .] the all too well known doctrine of "socialist realism," which had emerged in the Soviet Union in the thirties and become "fixed" in debates among [German] exiles there and later became incontestable dogma in the form of a *continuity imposed from above*. At its heart was a narrowly conceived reflection theory and the non-negotiable command for *positive heroes* . . . Culture and literature were treated as cogs and screws factored into the planning of socialist production; in other words, they were instrumentalized. Thus, the modernization principle of total rationalization [*Durchrationalisierung*] was carried to extremes to include

---

[3] Karl-Heinz Bohrer, "Die Ästhetik im Ausgang ihrer Unmündigkeit," *Merkur* 500 (1990): 851–65.

even poetry. The result of this peculiar unification of art and life, agitational rhyme schemes and tractor poetry, affirmative plays [*Bejahungsstücke*] and workplace novels calling on people to exceed production norms, is well known.[4]

Despite an initial gesture towards "contradictory and colliding movements" (194), Emmerich relies on the very interpretation he claims to reject. His account of GDR literature is predicated on "a narrowly conceived reflection theory" and a teleological literary-historical model that resembles the object of his attack. His neat parallel between the GDR's economic and literary "underdevelopment" rests on a contradiction. If he regrets the GDR's "backwardness" in the modernization process, he nonetheless grants that its compensation was the survival of a pre-modern lifeworld, in which daily life was not yet completely rationalized by the demands of efficient production in a fully developed capitalist society. Divorced from modernist innovation, socialist realism appears here in crude caricature, as paternalist kitsch of the most dangerous kind, allegedly reinforcing the affirmative character of modernization while abandoning the epistemological freedom of the modernist aesthetic.

This view of East German culture as an instrument of the paternalist state corresponds more to the triumphal tenor of Cold War melodrama than to the actual complexity of GDR life. West German promotion of art above politics represses the very political history of the West's denial of politics, in particular the legacy of fascism, while attempting to discredit the founding claim of East German claims to represent the anti-fascist legacy of Weimar socialism rather than Nazism. While Emmerich is right to claim that the socialist and anti-fascist legacy represented a "continuity imposed from above" and that the orthodox prescription of socialist realist doctrine treated culture as an instrument of this imposed continuity, his presupposition that social and political conditions in the GDR could *only* lead to the instrumentalization of art ignores the aspirations of its practitioners

---

[4] Wolfgang Emmerich, "Gleichzeitigkeit. Vormoderne, Moderne und Postmoderne in der Literatur der DDR," in *Gegenwartsliteratur* (Munich: edition text + kritik, 1988), 199–200.

as well as the actual contradictions in artistic practice and in the state's legitimation discourse. Although the SED followed Zhdanov's call to promote the "achievements of socialism and the socialist individual in the present and future," GDR playwrights, directors, and audiences reformulated the parameters of socialism and realism in ways that allowed in part for a critical examination of formal and social norms, the local labor and life conditions that departed from the norms, and the tangled relationship between actual conditions and the conflicted legacies of fascism, imperialism and their opposites in the officially anti-fascist and anti-imperialist state.[5] Although dissidence in the theatre was circumscribed, its operation contradicts the Cold War cliché of primitive politics and formal crudity, and highlights instead the challenge of articulating a new artistic politics that might counter the subordination of culture to the commodity form, including the commodity of autonomous art.

Against the artistic politics that Emmerich dismisses as the "peculiar [and premature] unification of art and life, agitational rhythms and tractor poetry" in the affirmation of the state but also against the commodification of art under capitalism, GDR theatre intellectuals attempted, as Brecht put it, to argue that formal diversity was a political as well as aesthetic good (*Werke* 23: 266), to show "in victory" also "the threat of defeat," so as to avoid the "error" that "victories were easy" (25: 422–3). This argument for experiment was anchored in a belief in the historical legitimacy of socialism and anti-fascism, not merely as ideological program but as an emotionally appealing "new, infectious feeling for life" (423). The appeal to the *affect* of socialism certainly participates in what Julia Hell has called the "ideological fantasies" of "post-fascism," narratives of transformation in the political discourse and especially in the prose fiction in the GDR, which worked on GDR readers on the level of the psyche as well as social life.[6] But whereas the autonomous production and

---

[5] Zhdanov, "Soviet Literature. The Richest in Ideas, the Most Advanced Literature," 17.

[6] Julia Hell, *Post-Fascist Fantasies: Psychoanalysis, History, and the Literature of East Germany* (Durham, NC: Duke University Press, 1997), 19.

private reception of prose fiction may encourage play in the scene of the unconscious, the public character of the theatrical scene demands attention to the social, political, and artistic scripts shaping the roles of stage performers and their audiences. The stage here is not Freud's unconscious, nor yet Marx's farce of historical repetition, but rather the GDR as construction site, on which action emerges from the friction between institutional structures and social agency. The most realistic depiction of this construction site, particularly as the founding discourse of the GDR unraveled, may well have appeared *surreal* but the problem of creating society through staging it remained real. The production play, from Brecht's *Katzgraben* in the early years (1953) to the surreal revival of Heiner Müller's *Lohndrücker* (1956) in 1988, on the eve of the state's collapse, represented the national drama and its failure like no other genre.

Highlighting the social and historical ground of Brecht's and Müller's work is important because it reminds readers of these playwrights' engagement with the project of the GDR. This focus points not only to the historic attempt to establish a socialist society in a Germany dominated by Nazi habits at the sharp edge of Cold War Europe, but also to the internal complexities and contradictions of a state and society that appeared to the West to be a model heir of Stalinist dictatorship. The canonization of Brecht and, more recently, of Müller as international modernist – or post-modernist – heroes of formal experimentation has proceeded, especially in English, by uncoupling their work from its social and historical grounding.[7] This chapter argues that the international stature of these writers is enhanced,

[7] This canonization of Brecht often takes the form of decoupling epic theatre form from marxist politics and recoupling it with deconstruction, as in Elizabeth Wright, *Postmodern Brecht* (London: Routledge, 1989). Critics who came to Müller via his later collaborations with international figures like Robert Wilson highlight formal experiment at the expense of political engagements and the historical complexity of these engagements. Jonathan Kalb's *The Theatre of Heiner Müller* (Cambridge University Press, 1998) includes illuminating analyses, especially of Müller's later texts, but loses sight of politically charged history. Comparing Müller to modernists like Genet, Artaud, and Beckett, Kalb reduces Müller's production plays to

not diminished, by a clearer understanding of their engagement with the local conditions of the GDR, in particular with the anti-fascist and anti-imperial discourse that animated politics and culture in that country, since this understanding critically revises and expands the prevailing Western notion of international modernism.

Society as a construction site

Against the Stalinist prescription for ideological affirmation and for-mal closure, Brecht and his successors attempted to represent socialist society as a work in progress, a site not only of socialist construction, but also of social contradiction. The representation of the achieve-ments of labor and the citizen as producer played a fundamental role in the GDR's legitimation as the "worker's and peasant's state." While the manifest bankruptcy of that state in its final years certainly dis-credits the official honorific, the drama of work in the GDR, especially in its first two decades, attempted to address the lives of working peo-ple with a seriousness rarely found in capitalist cultures. Although not unique in this period, the work of Brecht and his most critical successor, Heiner Müller, is exemplary. In particular, Brecht's unfin-ished project on Hans Garbe (1951–6), master bricklayer and "hero of labor," engaged with the problem of the model worker, idealized citizen-producer in a not yet model society. Further, his controversial production of Erwin Strittmatter's *Katzgraben*, about local farmers' response to land redistribution and modernization (1953), highlighted not only new social content – the democratic potential of land redis-tribution to small farmers and the state's contradictory response to wealthier farmers' resistance to this transformation – but also the challenge to find appropriate dramatic form to represent not only con-flict but also pleasurable preparation for the future. After Brecht's death in August 1956, Müller addressed the problematic articulation of a new socialist society in a series of plays from *Der Lohndrücker*

variations on Mayakovsky without investigating the international socialism that both linked and separated these two authors, or the different historical forces that shaped Müller's work two decades after Mayakovsky's death, as well as the ambiguity of Müller's subsequent disavowal of this work.

(The Wage-Buster) (1956) to *Der Bau* (The Construction Site) (1965), in particular problems posed by actually existing inequality and repression in labor and social relations in the officially socialist state.

The workplace in the self-described socialist state is a telling site for investigating the contradictions within socialism, since it is here that the tensions between state socialism and the socialization of working subjects – between the immediate pressure for national unity and modernized production on the one hand and the socialist utopia of emancipation from exploitation on the other – are most vividly dramatized. As GDR critics Eva and Hans Kaufmann pointed out, the figuration of the new state as a construction site provided both trope and topos, in which the portrayal of social conflict strove to focus not on a simplistic dichotomy between individual and society but on conflicting patterns of socialization within and among individuals *in* society.[8] Brecht's GDR projects make more explicit the dramatic conflict between the worker-and-peasant state and actual working lives that his classical adaptations – such as *Der Hofmeister* (The Tutor) by J. M. R. Lenz – or his own historical drama – such as *Life of Galileo* – only hint at. They also reflect Brecht's difficulty in moving from anti-capitalist dissidence to writing within a society officially described as both anti-fascist and beyond capitalism. The fragmentary character of the Garbe project in particular suggests the difficulty of representing socialism-in-process. As Müller trenchantly observed, the transformation of Brecht from anti-capitalist dissident into a mascot of "actually existing socialism" embodies the central contradiction in the GDR's claim to exhaustively represent anti-fascist and post-capitalist Germany.[9] Loyal to the idea(l) of socialism, Brecht and Müller nonetheless shared a wariness of the SED's ambitions to create

---

[8] Eva and Hans Kaufmann, *Erwartung und Angebot: Studien zum gegenwärtigen Verhältnis von Literatur und Gesellschaft in der DDR* (Berlin/GDR: Akademie, 1976), 39–40, and, in English, Marc Silberman, *Literature of the Working World. A Study of the Industrial Novel in East Germany* (Bern: Peter Lang, 1976).

[9] Heiner Müller, "Fatzer±Keuner," in *Brecht-Jahrbuch 1980*, ed. Reinhardt Grimm and Jost Hermand (Frankfurt a.M.: Suhrkamp, 1981), 14–21.

by fiat a new socialist human being along with a new mode of production. Their writing in the crucial early years of the GDR treats the model worker as a subject of and in production, not as the rounded protagonist of a *Bildungsdrama* but a contradictory agent in a *Lehrstück*, comparing this worker explicitly with the anti-capitalist agitator and implicitly with the Nazi figure of the worker as massive but mute machine. This comparison challenges the normative Soviet paradigm of the Stakhanovite worker breaking production quotas and busting wages.[10] At the same time, the ongoing attack on this paradigm indicates the political stakes involved in the definition of socialist realism: the legitimacy and survival of the worker-and-peasant state itself.

The SED acknowledged these stakes by attempting to appropriate the *Lehrstück*, as part of the SED's exclusive inheritance of the Weimar left.[11] Acknowledging the "didactic *Lehrstück*" as a genre developed by and for workers by the KPD in the later Weimar period (1929–32) allowed the SED to claim Brecht's anti-capitalist agit-prop work as part of the historic anti-fascist struggle and thus also of the post-capitalist present of the "worker-and-peasant state," while continuing to dismiss more anarchic modernism (including Brecht's early plays) and to attack its latter-day advocates, including the worldly critic Hans Mayer, an admirer of Brecht, for "nostalgia for Weimar modernism."[12] It also created ideological space for the SED briefly to support sharply critical portrayals of SED policy it later repressed, such as Müller's production plays, *Der Lohndrücker*, *Die Korrektur*

---

[10] Alexei Stakhanov, a miner, exceeded the norm by 1400% in 1935 and became the model for Stalin's plan to accelerate production while reducing labor costs, i.e. wages. For Stakhanov's role in the GDR, see Annelli Hartmann and Wolfgang Eggeling, "Von Gremjatschi Log nach Katzgraben. Zum Transfer sowjetischer Arbeitskultur und ihrer Literatur," in *Literatur in der DDR: Rückblicke*, ed. Heinz Ludwig Arnold and Frauke Meyer-Gorsau (Munich: edition text + kritik, 1991), 12–13.

[11] See David Bathrick, "Agitproptheater in der DDR. Auseinandersetzung mit der Tradition," in *DDR-Dramatik*, ed. Ulrich Profitlich (Frankfurt: Suhrkamp, 1987), 128–49.

[12] Kurt Hager, Speech at the 3rd Plenum of the SED Central Committee (July 1957), *Dokumente*, 540.

(The Correction, 1959), *Die Umsiedlerin* (The Female Resettler, 1961), and *Der Bau* as contemporary representatives of socialist tradition.[13]

Production was not only a theme in the drama of work but also the mode of its aesthetic engagement. The production play treated dramatic structure as a form in process rather than a set of rules derived either from the received formulae of the Stalinist/Zhdanovite orthodoxy or from Brechtian epic theatre. Brecht's dialectical renegotiation of the theoretical gap between epic and dramatic theatre, between estrangement and empathy, between his name and Stanislavsky's, had practical consequences, most immediately for his work on *Katzgraben*, a "historical comedy," at once epic and empathetic, critical and appealing. Both *Katzgraben* and the unfinished Garbe project struggle with the tensions between affirmation and critique and between prescription and experiment. Both tried to avoid what Brecht called the "error" of "easy victories" by showing "the threat of defeat" (*Werke* 25: 422–3). In *Katzgraben*, the occasion for his reflections on the false impressions of "easy victories," Brecht produced a "historical comedy" about "manageable difficulties and corrigible incompetence" (424). Set in 1947–9, the play affirms the initial achievements of the socialist state established in that year, especially the redistribution to landless tenant farmers of property abandoned by Junker landowners fleeing west. It offers an optimistic view (hence "comedy") of the achievements of the "progressive, productive, revolutionary forces" represented by this "new class" and their "new, infectious feeling for life" (423) in the immediate past before the present new state (hence "historical"), but tempers that optimism somewhat by the "threat of defeat" not only at the hands of wealthy farmers but by their own resistance to change, especially to the status of women. However, the generic frame – the inherited *Volksstück* and the invented historical comedy – shapes the picture in unexpected ways, making the drama something more than merely didactic "agroprop".

[13] Ulbricht, "Der Weg zur Sicherung des Friedens," *Dokumente*, 543 and "Einige Probleme der Kulturrevolution" (10 July 1958), *Dokumente*, 534.

Given the disdain of many critics for any socialist culture and the tendency among marxists to focus on industrial rather than rural themes, we should not be surprised that this historical comedy has received scant attention in the West.[14] In the East, the play, or more often Brecht's notes, *Katzgraben-Notate*, appears as brief prologue to the work of Heiner Müller, Peter Hacks, and other playwrights who were associated, however briefly, with the *Bitterfelder Weg*. This program for promoting fiction and drama about socialist production was inaugurated at the SED Central Committee's Fourth Plenum in 1959 in Bitterfeld, a center of socialist industrial activity since the 1920s and centerpiece of GDR reindustrialization in the 1950s, and abruptly ended at the Eleventh Plenum in 1965. But *Katzgraben* appeared at the Berliner Ensemble (BE) in 1953, well before Bitterfeld. The production encouraged other playwrights to tackle production plays with rural as well as urban settings, whether they ultimately affirmed the leading role of the party, such as Helmut Baierl's *Die Feststellung* (The Determination, 1958) and *Frau Flinz* (1961; at the BE with Weigel in the title role) or offered more critical perspectives, such as Peter Hacks's *Moritz Tasso* (1961; produced and abandoned, Volksbühne, 1965) or Heiner Müller's *Die Umsiedlerin* (1961; staged as *Die Bauern*, Volksbühne, 1975).[15] Brecht's departure from his own modernist epic form to create

---

14 Liane Pfelling praised the play as part of the socialist legacy on the occasion of the GDR's twentieth anniversary: "Von der wirklichkeitsverändernden Kraft der Menschen," *Theater der Zeit* 24: 4 (1969), 4–10. Since unification, it has received a brief but thoughtful comparison with Mikhail Sholokhov's *kolkhoz* (collective farm) novel *Virgin Soil Upturned*, in Hartmann and Eggeling, "Von Gremjatschi Log nach Katzgraben," 19–21, and a tendentious dismissal by Carl Wege, "Spielplan(politik) und Inszenierungskalkül des Berliner Ensembles zwischen 1952 und 1956," in *Zweifel, Fragen, Vorschläge: Bertolt Brecht anläßlich des Einhundertsten*, Osloer Beiträge zur Germanistik, 23, ed. Thomas Jung (Frankfurt a.M.: Peter Lang, 1999), 93–8. David Bathrick discusses GDR "agroprop" (his term) in *The Powers of Speech: The Politics of Culture in the GDR* (Lincoln: University of Nebraska Press, 1995), 110–28, but not its source in *Katzgraben*.

15 The Bitterfeld program called for closer ties between "comrade writers" and labor organizations on the one hand, and more cultural

---

a new "people's play" in the historical comedy has received very little critical attention, even though this apparently anti-modernist experiment, as a genre of dramatic writing and a mode of social as well as theatrical production in and of the GDR, was received by Müller, as foremost writer of the modernist production play, and his director B. K. Tragelehn as "the beginning of GDR drama."[16]

Easy victories and the threat of defeat: history and comedy in *Katzgraben*

Katzgraben, the BE's adaptation of Erwin Strittmatter's *Szenen aus dem Bauernleben* (Scenes from Farming Life), proved to be the company's only representation of the contemporary GDR in Brecht's lifetime. Adapted by Brecht and dramaturgs Käthe Rülicke and Peter Palitzsch, the play depicted the reactions of small, middling, and wealthy farming families to the land reform in the difficult early years of reconstruction (1947–9) and land reform, especially the redistribution of abandoned Junker estates under Soviet occupation, before the introduction of rural collectivization in 1952.[17] Although Strittmatter's *Scenes* were rejected by the FDJ, who had commissioned the play for

production by industrial workers on the other; see Ulbricht, "Fragen der Entwicklung der sozialistischen Literatur und Kultur" (Speech to writers, socialist crews [*Brigaden*] of industrial and cultural workers, Bitterfeld, 24 April 1959), *Dokumente* 552–64. For an affirmative account of Bitterfeld dramatists, see Hermann Kähler, *Gegenwart auf der Bühne* (Berlin/GDR: Henschel, 1964); for a critical GDR perspective favoring Müller and Hacks, see Wolfgang Schivelbusch, *Sozialistisches Drama nach Brecht* (Darmstadt: Luchterhand, 1974), and, in English, Bathrick, *Powers of Speech*, 109–24.

[16] Heiner Müller, *Krieg ohne Schlacht: Leben in zwei Diktaturen* (Cologne: Kiepenheuer and Witsch, 1992), 240; Jan-Christof Hauschild, *Heiner Müller, oder Das Prinzip Zweifel: Eine Biographie* (Berlin: Aufbau, 2001), 189.

[17] Nationalization of industrial conglomerates already centralized by the Nazis was relatively easy; by 1952, 81 percent of industrial manufacture had been nationalized, but agricultural collectivization met with resistance from middling as well as wealthy farmers. Strittmatter wrote a *Nachspiel* to *Katzgraben* in 1958, which dramatizes collectivization and the alliance between small and

the *Weltjugendfestspiele* (International Youth Festival) in 1951, the BE's *Katzgraben* opened at the Deutsches Theater in May 1953, after the fortification of the East/West German border had slightly reduced the exodus to the West, but before the uprising in June punctured the SED's heroic depiction of the planned economy and its model workers and provoked a crackdown in the name of anti-imperialist defense.[18]

The play, especially its comic portrayal of conflict around the building of a new road to an imagined village in the Lausitz region of Brandenberg southeast of Berlin, may appear at first glance to correspond to SED propaganda of the sort represented by songs like *Fritz der Traktorist* (1952) or paintings like *Blick auf Stalinstadt* (View of Stalin City, 1955), Bernhardt Kretschmar's impossibly sunny depiction of the industrial infrastructure and green surroundings of the GDR's "first purely socialist city," and so to confirm Emmerich's cliché of "affirmative plays and tractor poetry."[19] *Katzgraben* offers a pointed satire of the rich farmer Grossmann's exploitation of his

middling farmers against their former patron; see *Katzgraben*, 122–31. Intended as a text for worker-players (*Laienspieler*), it was not added to the BE production.

[18] The discussion of *Katzgraben* draws on Strittmatter, *Katzgraben: Szenen aus dem Bauerleben* (1954; Berlin/ GDR: Aufbau, 1978), which was published after the revised production in May 1954 and differs from the production script at several points; published notes by Brecht and collaborators, *Katgraben-Notate* (1953; rpt in *Werke* 24); unpublished notes in the Bertolt Brecht Archive (BBA), and the BBA video of the stage production (1959) (Berlin: DEFA, 1992; dir. Manfred Wekwerth; script Käthe Rülicke). After ten thousand per month in 1952, emigration reached forty thousand in March 1953, and then dropped off after the border fortification, before rising again after the uprising in June; see doc. 5 in Friedrich, *Es hat alles keinen Zweck*, 20.

[19] *Fritz der Traktorist* (music Eberhard Schmidt; text Walter Stranka) was written after the SED Party conference of June 1952, where the collectivization program was announced. The lyrics reflect not only collectivization policy but also the incipient remilitarization of the GDR; the tractor driver is called to "protect his homeland" against "danger to happiness and peace." See Marcus Heumann, Liner Notes to *Fritz der Traktorist, Die Partei hat immer Recht* (Berlin: Hansa Musik, 1996), n.p.

Fig. 1. "The Factory in the Garden": Regine Lutz and Ekkehart Schall in *Katzgraben* (Berlin, 1953) by Erwin Strittmatter, adapted and directed by Brecht.

dependants and selfish resistance to the road, and the middling farmer Mittelländer's wavering dependence on his patron, as against an optimistic view of future social transformation led by the "new farmers," especially Kleinschmidt and his wife, and young workers, especially Kleinschmidt's daughter Elli, farm girl turned agricultural scientist. The staging certainly invokes the factory-in-a-garden motif in the backdrop to the scene of Elli's return to enlighten the village (fig. 1). Strittmatter's draft also indulges in what might be called socialist kitsch in the penultimate scene: the representatives of the MAAS (*Maschinen-Ausleihstation*, Machinery Rental Agency) drive the tractors into the village to the cheers of the young people, while Grossmann is jeered off the stage and mocked by children riding a straw facsimile of his horse. Nonetheless, Brecht's revisions to this and the final scene suggest a desire to make the cheers more muted. The play in performance ended as Kleinschmidt, his daughter and her beau Hermann, now released from serfdom as Grossmann's "adopted son," look forward to the coming year and offer a more sober assessment of ongoing problems; but the shadow of the tractor behind them promises future solutions.

Despite Strittmatter's apparently model plot, the BE's work on the play suggests the company's awareness of potential controversy. Notes from 1952, in which half a million people left the GDR, included the investigation of life on the East/West German border, where many villagers chose to work for western Deutschmarks, as well as the presence of refugees fleeing former outposts of the Reich such as East Prussia, part of which was annexed by the Soviet Union, or Silesia, absorbed into Poland.[20] Although these explosive topics, including

---

[20] The German–German border appears nowhere in the play, but the archive records the company's interest in it. Unsigned notes, probably by dramaturgs Palitzsch and Rülicke, include investigations of the border village Sommersdorf, where many worked in the FRG to earn western Deutschmarks, and where SED mayors and Soviet officers had to contend with villagers, ranging from Nazis to those nostalgic for the Junker baron who used to own the village to dissident socialists, and with the appeal of Western or Nazi films as against those produced in the GDR (BBA 962). Poland also provides an interesting counterpoint

the impact of a refugee tally close to a quarter of the general population, left only the faintest traces in the text (in which, for example, beggars appeared "from the city" rather than from the east), the play provoked sharply critical response from different sources, from a lay economist (*Volkswirtschaftler*) commenting on the adaptation to the leading actors in the production to farmers and Party members at the performances. The economist, Heinz Schmidt, is noteworthy, but not because he challenged Brecht's promotion of "theory" over "facts," as a post-unification critic has it.[21] Rather, Schmidt highlighted the difficulty of Brecht's attempt to honor his own rigorous model of realism, showing the "threat of defeat" rather than "illusory solutions to real problems" (*Werke* 23: 258), and, perhaps surprisingly, his recourse to conventional aesthetic criteria he had previously criticized. In an unpublished letter to Helene Weigel as director of the BE, Schmidt applauded the company's attempt to represent contemporary rural life on the urban stage, but suggested that the central agon Grossmann's opposition to the road was "hard to believe" (BBA 1331/150). Instead, he argued, one ought to distinguish between Junker landowners, such as the Junker baron who had abandoned his estate after living off his tenants' rents in the feudal manner, and capitalist farmers like Grossmann, who would be interested in maximizing profits through modernization:

> For decades, it has been the active landowning farmers [*Großbauern*], rather than the Junker aristocrats or middling or small farmers, who ran their land according to capitalist principles. They had the most tractors, machines, and other agricultural tools . . . applied intensive breeding techniques, and had for these reasons an interest in good transport. . . . [T]he capitalist in the country [*auf dem Dorf*] would profit the

to agricultural collectivization in the GDR: while the GDR programme was realized by force, the uprising against Stalinism in Poland in 1956 led the government to curtail collectivization at a mere 13 percent of agricultural land by 1960. See Hermann Weber, *Geschichte der DDR*, 2nd edn (Munich: Deutscher Taschenbuchverlag, 1999), 215.

[21] Wege, "Spielplan(politik) und Inszenierungskalkül", 95–6.

most from a new road. Why then is he against it? Only
because the reactionary must, for symbolic reasons, be against
new ways of doing things?

(BBA 1331/155)[22]

Schmidt's distinction between feudal Junker and capitalist farmer and
his concluding, thoroughly Brechtian appeal to the truth that is "concrete" (1331/169) has both ideological and dramatic salience. It highlights the progressive aspect of Grossmann's position and thus lends
conceptual and gestural depth to the character of the kind that Brecht
and the actor Erwin Geschonnek were seeking (Werke 25: 403), especially to avoid the crass comedy that rural spectators at rehearsals
found a grotesque rather than an effective portrayal of class struggle
(432). Despite this critical opportunity, Strittmatter's reply to Schmidt
conflates the Junker and the capitalist farmer as he asks rhetorically
"Where then are the model show-roads [Prachtstraßen], which should
lead from every Junker village to the towns . . . if, as you claim, Junker
and landowning farmers had such a great interest in the construction
of new roads?" (BBA 1331/170).

Brecht's response, "A Letter" (Werke 25: 459–60; 573), unpublished until 1967, is striking not so much because he reduces his interlocutor to an unnamed "expert" (459), but rather because he accuses
the latter of being alienated from theatre (theaterfremd, 460), and
insists, in uncharacteristically Aristotelian fashion, on the difference
between theatre and scientific inquiry, images and theses, poetry and
prose: "In art, unlike science, representation of reality must have the
quality of images [Bildcharakter]" (459). In response to the argument
that farmers like Grossmann would favor the road, Brecht invokes the
aesthetic authority of the typical over the probable:

> Even if the building of the road were utterly exceptional, it
> could be used in the play as the point of departure for the
> unfolding of a typical situation. It is false to choose a frequent
> everyday occurrence [alltägliches Vorfall], a common

---

[22] Wege carries both the literal meaning "roads" and the figurative
"ways."

undertaking [*übliches Unternehmen*], to depict the launching
of a great poetic conflict [*großen dichterischen
Auseinandersetzung*] between decisive historical forces. In a
poetic text [*einer Dichtung*] these forces could be unleashed
by a Martian.

(460)

In defending the philosophical and universal character of poetry, especially dramatic poetry, over the more prosaic, contingent writing of
history, Brecht appears to join his usual antagonists Aristotle and
Hegel and to depart from his characteristic argument in, for example,
"A Short Description of a New Technique of Acting" in favor of historicizing (*Historisierung*) the plot and grounding the theatrical gest
in realistic observation of social relations (22.2: 641–59). His appeal
to poetic license over daily life seems, like his defense of using verse
form as a "sieve" filtering out the "casual" and "unimportant" so as
to dignify formerly "primitive" farmers with the "essential lines" and
"loftiness" of the "classical drama" (25: 426), to constitute a regression
into the affirmative realm of pathos and beautiful resolutions (associated with Hegel and Schiller; *Werke* 23: 169). One could even detect a
relapse into bourgeois theatre's tendency to paint over (*verschmieren*)
contradictions and to simulate (*vortaüschen*) harmony (23: 294),
rather than the deployment of *Verfremdung* as a dis-illusion of such
simulation of harmony or, in the language of the *Katzgraben-Notate*,
"easy victories."[23] But, for all the citation of Schillerian idealism
mediated by socialist claims on the classical inheritance, Brecht also
suggests, in the abrupt decline from the lofty realm of "poetic conflict"
to the "Martian," an *alien ex machina*, a critique of heroic pathos and
an ironic reminder that his historical comedy does indeed deal with
the "difficulties and awkwardness" of everyday life.

[23] Brecht's affinities with Hegel and Schiller have received less attention
than his disputes with the German classics, but his interest in
combining instruction and pleasure in the theatre owes a debt to this
tradition; see Loren Kruger, "Making Sense of Sensation:
Enlightenment, Embodiment, and the End(s) of Modern Drama,"
Modern Drama 43:4 (2000): 543–63.

A closer look at the textual variants – the premiere in May 1953, the revival in May 1954 and the film made in 1959, three years after Brecht's death – reveals less an orthodox agon between "progressive" and "reactionary" class elements (*Werke* 25: 424) than a complex comedy probing "the crisis-, problem-, and conflict-filled character of the new life" (25: 423).[24] The production certainly registered SED hostility to the alleged formalism of dis-illusion and related techniques; Brecht's acknowledgment that "we are not yet far enough along" ("Wir sind nicht so weit") to "work with actual dis-illusion techniques" (25: 430) and his incorporation of techniques attributed to Stanislavsky, such as creating character-biographies for actors' study (25: 546–8), and public endorsement of this method at the Stanislavsky conference in April 1953, might suggest a capitulation to SED pressure. Nonetheless, the unidentified subject of Brecht's "we" (the BE, GDR theatre, society as a whole?) leaves open the question of agency. The shifts in allegiance followed by Kleinschmidt and his fellow poor farmers, Weidling and Mammler, from dependence on Grossmann to active support for collectivization may follow the Party line, but the line moves in fits and starts, leaving some like Mammler still poor and resentful and others, especially the miner and SED representative Steinert, continually exasperated by what he sees as the farmers' backward attachment to oxen rather than tractors, and other manifestation of their "cramped existence"

---

[24] For the 1953 production, Brecht cut most exterior scenes to concentrate on the action in the farmers' contrasting interiors and the pub attached to the community hall where the votes on the road take place. He also trimmed long speeches relying on abstract propaganda rather than concrete argument for particular proposals. In 1954, Brecht reduced the acts to three and cut the more grotesque comic business; see the four-act published version and the summary comparison between 1953 and 1954 production scripts (BBA 961/03). In the 1959 film, Wekwerth restored some of the apostrophes to the state and had Strittmatter write more optimistic songs for each act; compare the later stress on the "establishment" of the plan in the opening *Kalenderlied* (Strittmatter, *Katzgraben*, 7) with the earlier version on the "threatened" plan reproduced in the appendix (133).

(*Krötendasein*).[25] Brecht retained arguments for state intervention in general and the first Five Year Plan in particular in Strittmatter's text, but he moderated Strittmatter's tendency to pathos by cutting long apostrophes or arias to the tractor-borne blessings of the future and by subjecting remaining didactic speeches to partial *Verfremdung* by making their speakers tired and exasperated (Steinert) or as yet immaturely zealous (Elli).[26] Despite the authority of the tractor as icon of socialist progress, reiterated in the *Katzgraben* program's citation of martyred KPD leader Ernst Thälmann's polemical separation of those fighting for tractors and those ploughed under by them, Brecht continued even after the premiere in May 1953 to pare down the kitschier elements of the "tractor show," cutting the folk-dances and reducing the parade of machines and flags to a single tractor and one flag (*Werke* 25: 479).[27]

If Brecht appeared to retreat from a global application of *Verfremdungseffekte*, he found an alternative form of dis-illusioned theatre in the recontextualized *Volksstück*, which he had developed in the rehearsals and production of *Herr Puntila und sein Knecht Matti* (Mr Puntila and His Man Matti). In his notes on this production, Brecht

---

[25] Strittmatter, *Katzgraben*, 30; Act 1; third picture. *Krötendasein* translates literally as "toad existence;" the expression carries the connotation of "small-minded and primitive" as well as "materially deprived."

[26] For example, Elli's opening aria to "our first plan," which criticized previous planting habits as "anarchic" (*Katzgraben*, 14; Act 1; first picture), was reduced in both Brecht's manuscript (compare BBA 1894/04 with 1864/19)) and in the film to a short line to introduce her discussion with her father. Likewise, her father's final paean to progress in the shadow of the tractor (1899/86) was reduced in revisions (1864/90ff.) and in the published text (*Katzgraben*, 119–20; epilogue) to a series of alternating affirmations by Elli, Erna, Hermann, and other young people as well as Kleinschmidt. While these speeches are not cued for singing, the fervor of the presentation suggests the intensity and sometimes the sentimentality associated with the operatic aria.

[27] The citation comes from a speech to the embattled KPD in 1932 and reads "either you fight for victory on the tractor or you get ploughed under by it" (BBA 59, n.p.).

argued for a new *Volksstück*, which would combine physical comedy and satire to highlight the grotesqueries of class society and to transform crude caricature into the gest of critique (*Werke*: 23: 293–9). Three elements in the BE production of *Puntila* (1951), as documented by Hans-Jürgen Syberberg's rehearsal film, are relevant here.[28] The comic undoing of landowner Puntila's authority over his hired man Matti when the former is drunk anticipates the humiliation of Grossmann tossed into a wheelbarrow at the end of *Katzgraben*. Second, the comic potential of actors' bodies is both exploited and recontextualized by the social dimension of the action. The deployment of corporeal irony used the concrete plasticity of performance to dis-illusion the pathos of "tractor poetry" and show the "threat of defeat" in the contingencies of the body. Erwin Geschonnek's massive frame, which had emphasized Matti's power over the smaller Curt Bois as Puntila, served instead to highlight Grossmann's excesses in *Katzgraben*. Thirdly, women play pivotal roles as both objects and agents of comedy and social critique: Puntila's daughter, Eva (played as an old maid by Angelika Hurwitz) shifts from being a victim of Puntila's and Matti's antagonism to an agent of social transformation through cross-class marriage. In *Katzgraben*, Hurwitz played a crucial role as Frau Kleinschmidt, who promoted changes that benefitted her directly (buying a new ox), while resisting those that appeared to make life more difficult (letting her daughter off farm work to go to agricultural school). Helene Weigel, in a radical departure from her recent revival of the eponymous revolutionary in *The Mother* (1951), drew on the image of a *Volksstück* hag to portray Frau Grossmann as a barren and bitter miser hoarding her wealth and her extra food from others, from hungry casual laborers to her "adopted son" Hermann, played by Ekkehart Schall, Weigel's and Brecht's son-in-law. Regine

[28] Hans-Jürgen Syberberg, *Syberberg filmt bei Brecht* (1953; 1973; Munich: Progress, 1993). Recently arrived in East Berlin from Rostock in 1951, Syberberg filmed Brecht rehearsing *Die Mutter* and the *Urfaust* as well as *Puntila* in 8mm. In 1970/71, living in the FRG, he transferred the film to 35mm and added comments by fellow emigré Hans Mayer; see *Berliner Ensemble 1953 – Syberberg filmt bei Brecht* (Berlin: Berliner Ensemble, 1993).

Lutz as Elli and Sabine Thalbach as the Mittelländers' servant turned FDJ partisan, Erna, offer differently conflicted responses to new opportunities for young women to become producers of the new society. Especially in the first two acts, the plot develops through the juxtaposition of incompatible or incongruous words and bodies in contrasting "stage pictures" (*Bilder*). These "pictures" are the primary units of the drama, marked by changes of locale, from small to rich farmer and back, whereas the larger acts cover the years 1947, 1948, 1949, and the smaller scenes mark the arrival or departure of one or more characters. These parts, and the whole, Brecht argued, were to follow the classical form, rather than his former penchant for montage (*Werke* 25: 428). The comedy is most obvious, even crass, in the Grossmanns, who appear in the fourth "picture", after the audience has seen the Kleinschmidts grapple with both scarcity and new opportunities and the Mittelländers equivocate between their material interest in the road and their habit of following the rich. Weigel's Frau Grossmann, lamenting the departure of the Baron while attempting to imitate the Baroness, was thoroughly, even excessively grotesque (*Werke* 25: 427, 438). In contrast, Geschonnek's Grossmann was both comic and menacing, imposing his considerable weight at the dinner table or throwing it around the stage and up against his antagonists, while maintaining what Brecht called the humanization (*Vermenschlichung*) of the character (438). The pretension of the couple to replace the absconded feudal lords emerges especially in their treatment of those dependent on their favors; when the "beggar from the city" comes to the door for a hand-out, for instance, they ostentatiously refuse him the plenty on the table, while a religious plaque about charity at home highlights their hypocrisy. By contrast, Grossmann's loss of power at the end was expressed in his dependence on others, in his reckless drinking and ultimately in the humiliating experience of being tipped from a wheelbarrow. Members of the Farmers' Mutual Aid Union (VdgB: *Vereinigung der gegenseitigen Bauernhilfe*) present at the last preview performance (18 May 1953) argued for the socially critical value of this humanization, noting that the appealing side of Grossmann's role as paternalist patron of the small farmers should be acknowledged so as to show how difficult was the task of the latter's separation from him (BBA 1331/92–4). In addition, while city audiences found the punishment of Grossmann too crude, rural spectators thought it appropriately funny, but some observed that, like carnival, it might well be forgotten on the morrow (1331/96).

If Brecht drew on the *Volksstück* to satirize wealthy farmers, he was harder pressed to make "positive heroes" such as Elli or Steinert both comic and exemplary, without reducing them to "faceless, bloodless formulae for social types" (*Werke* 25: 441). This task proved easier for characters closer to the *Volksstück*. Angelika Hurwicz's Frau Kleinschmidt drew directly on the *Volksstück* in her comic mime of her battle with the hungry ox in the second act, but even the sheer delight of the mime did not abandon the critical edge of the action highlighting the family's gradual independence from Grossmann and his farm animals.[29] Her conflicted response to her daughter's impending departure to school in the first scene, which will make her own work harder in the short run, resolves itself in her comic but pointedly emphatic encouragement "Study him to death [Studiere ihn tot]!" or, by implication, "beat the bastard [Grossmann] by studying to take over", and foreshadows her own transformation into a formidable social actor at the end (figs. 2 and 3).[30] Regine Lutz's portrayal of Elli proved more complicated, in part because the pretty Lutz, who had previously played vamps like Yvette in *Mother Courage*, chose here to highlight Elli's awkwardness. Brecht, who had argued in another context against casting "pretty girls," contrasted her "charm" in making the new plan appealing to her father in the first act with her awkwardness masquerading as superiority in her treatment of Hermann on her return from agricultural school in the third (fig. 1; *Werke* 25: 428).[31] He

---

[29] Strittmatter, *Katzgraben*, 49–51; Act 2, picture 1.

[30] Ibid., 23; Act 1, picture 1.

[31] Discussing a proposed film of *Mother Courage* (which Wolfgang Staudte was to direct), Brecht stated "I am a [strong] opponent of pretty women in film. The pretty ones are almost always without talent" (BBA E44/42; 14 June 1950). Thanks to Katie Trumpener for this reference.

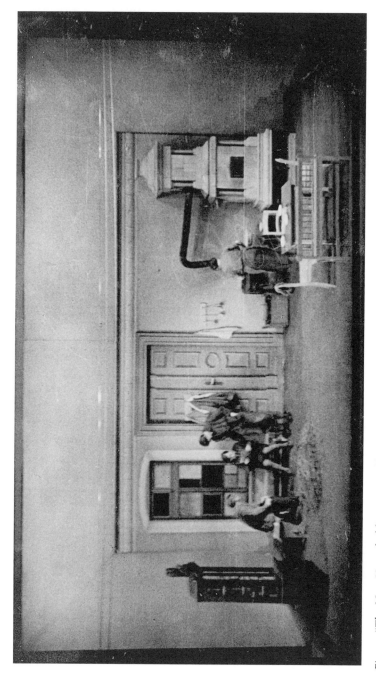

Fig. 2. "The New Household": Lutz as Elli, Günter Gnass as her father Kleinschmidt, and Angelika Hurwicz as her mother in *Katzgraben*.

Fig. 3. "Studiere ihn tot!": Lutz and Hurwicz in *Katzgraben*.

noted later that "cultural functionaries" could not follow her deliberate estrangement between the girl-in-love and the newly qualified
expert, or her attempt to use this estrangement to show that public and
private lives might not be so easily brought together (478–80). Against
the demand that "positive heroes be exemplary [vorbildhaft]," Brecht
followed Lutz in suggesting that an audience might learn from the
comic portrayal of a naive character and that comedy might be more
effective than the romance plot for "infecting" young audiences with
a "new feeling for life" (423). Even though critics in 1953 disagreed,
assistant director Wekwerth's comments in 1965 on this use of naivety
in the service of dis-illusion set the tone for GDR canonizations of this
play.[32]

If Lutz's comic but critical performance complicated responses
from audiences expecting "model youth," the Party secretary's role, in
orthodox terms *the* model character, proved to be especially difficult.
In rehearsal, Brecht returned repeatedly to the tension between the
exemplary character and the urban worker exasperated by the farmers' alleged attachment to what he calls their "cramped existence"
("Aufbau eines Helden" [Building a Hero], 25: 418–20; "Belehrung"
[Instruction, 456–7]; "Der positive Held" [The Positive Hero, 456];
"Die Rede Steinerts" [Steinert's Speech, 463]). Bothered by the role
even after the play opened, Brecht changed the actor from Willi
Kleinoschegg to Raimund Schelcher. Cast by Wekwerth in the 1959
film, Norbert Christian lacked the physical stature of Kleinoschegg
and Schelcher and perhaps also a compelling portrayal of the tireless-
ness (Unermüdlichkeit) of the committed socialist shining through
the physical fatigue (Müdigkeit) of the man doing double duty as
worker and Party secretary, as demonstrated by Schelcher's portrayal
of the Party secretary in Schlösser und Katen, a more orthodox feature

[32] For a critical response, see Lily Leder, "'Katzgraben' am Deutschen
Theater," *Theater der Zeit* 8:7 (1953), 57–60; for Wekwerth's
comments, his *Notate* (Frankfurt a.M.: Suhrkamp, 1967), 23, and for
the reappropriation, Pfelling, "Von der wirklichkeitsverändernden
Kraft der Menschen," 4–10.

film thematizing agricultural collectivization.[33] In Christian's performance in the BE video, Steinert's weariness is as palpable as his persistent effort. What the stage performance and the film recording bring out is a key element of this effort, lost in the imagined figure of the socialist novel or tireless propagandist of *Lehrstücke* like *Die Massnahme*: the acknowledgment of difficulty. His apostrophe to Soviet agricultural achievements in the final confrontation with Grossmann in the third act is followed in the film, but not in Strittmatter's text or Brecht's original production, by his attack on Grossmann as a Nazi. Accompanied by this assertion alongside his evident fatigue, Steinert's action represents not facile affirmation or a simple showdown with the class enemy but the prelude to the breakthrough in the more important and more difficult argument with his allies, Kleinschmidt and friends, about the value of learning how to use farm machinery and technology more generally.[34] Christian's Steinert ("stony") is not the tireless cliché of the Stalinist ("steely") leader, which Slavoj Žižek identifies as *the* "sublime object of [Communist] ideology," but rather the dogged prodder. It is this exhausted but persistent pioneer, rather than the impossibly steely leader, who will become the prototype for the world-weary but tenacious party men in critical GDR theatre and cinema in years to come.

Although Wekwerth's film restored some of the socialist kitsch cut by Brecht, notably the folk-dances and tractor parade at the end (perhaps to offset the manifest opposition to rural collectivization in 1959, after uprisings in Hungary and Poland in 1956 had led governments there to curtail the process), the figures of Elli and Steinert

[33] *Schlösser und Katen* (Locksmiths and Catalysts), directed by Nationalpreis winner Kurt Maetzig, was based on a more orthodox script by (anti-Brecht) journalist Kuba (Kurt Barthel). It came out in 1957, two years before the revival (and filming) of *Katzgraben*.

[34] Strittmatter, *Katzgraben*, 82–4; Act 3, picture 2. "Stalin", the Party name for Soviet leader Josef Vissarionovich Dzhugashvili, was intended to represent the steely quality of the ideal party man; see Slavoj Žižek, *The Sublime Object of Ideology* (London: Verso, 1989), 107–8. Steinert's name clearly alludes to this tradition.

break through the kitsch barrier. In Christian's impersonation, the
Party secretary is not the "historical metaphor for the necessity of
superhuman achievement . . . in a society of scarcity" which Bathrick
finds in Brecht's successors like Baierl, nor the "sublime body of the
Communist hero" which Julia Hell, following Žižek, finds at the core
of GDR fiction.[35] Instead, his unsettled combination of doggedness
and exasperation highlights the "threat of defeat" in the "Happy End
routine" (Happy-End-Schablone; Werke 25: 433), and provides a distinctively GDR model of the flawed Party secretary, who reappears
in Erik Neutsch's Bitterfeld novel Spur der Steine (Traces of Stones,
1964), as well as in Frank Beyer's suppressed film of the same name
(1965), and Müller's published but initially unproduced production
play Der Bau (1965), to personify "the crisis-, problem-, and conflict-
filled character of the new life" (Werke 25: 423). Likewise, Lutz's Elli
jettisons the cliché of the pretty ingenue in the romance plot for the
conflicted role of a woman who may be "clumsy in love" but strives
nonetheless to change her role in society; Müller's female protagonists, especially Niet the Umsiedlerin and Schlee, the engineer in
Der Bau, abandon roles in a romance plot along with their first names
(but not their sexuality) in dramas that push Brecht's social gest further than Brecht himself did. But Müller's experiment in the socialization of subjectivity takes its formal cues from Brecht's attempt, in

[35] Bathrick, Powers of Speech, 122; Žižek, Sublime Object of Ideology,
145; Hell, Post-Fascist Fantasies, 19. Given the high stakes in the
representation of the Party secretary, it is not surprising that reviews
diverged sharply: for the GDR National-Zeitung (30 May 1953),
"conflicts were stirred up, but not resolved," but for the
anti-communist Der Spiegel (3 June 1953), this was an out and out
"propaganda play" full of "lies" about "socialist achievements" (cited
in Brecht, Werke 25: 559–60). In a more sober assessment, Leder
("Katzgraben," 60) noted that Kleinoschegg's response to the "difficult
role" of Steinert overemphasized the "wise" but "distanced" leader,
while his replacements, Raimund Schelcher and Norbert Christian,
treated this cliché more critically. Arnold Zweig, who had returned to
East Germany from a kibbutz in Palestine, also regretted that Brecht
missed the opportunity to explore Steinert's "overconfidence" in
industrial agriculture: Sonntag, 14 June 1953.

the Garbe project, to highlight the model worker's conflicting social gests rather than his heroic attitude.

Producing Hans Garbe: from the *Lehrstück* of the model worker to the *Trauerspiel* of the fallen proletarian

If *Katzgraben* is a comedy of the "new, infectious feeling for life" as well as the "crisis-, problem-, and conflict-filled character" of the new society, Brecht's unfinished project on Hans Garbe looks like a proletarian tragedy. The project began with the bricklayer who was dubbed Hero of Labor in 1950 when he rebuilt one of a series of brick furnaces at the Siemens-Plania plant without interrupting firing in the others and thus accelerated production in the key construction industry, but ended not with Garbe's decoration, but with his death and the threatened overthrow of the SED after workers in the key construction sector struck to resist the impracticable acceleration of production by 150%.[36] Including a scene on the June uprising as well as the contradiction between calls for "building socialism" and the fact that the Red Army removed whole factories to the Soviet Union, Brecht engaged directly with the legitimacy claims of the GDR as a society produced and transformed by workers, and, indirectly, with his own doubts about the roles and responsibilities of intellectual workers in this society.[37] Brecht's sceptical attitude collided with the hagiographic *Mann im feurigen Ofen* (Man in the Fiery Furnace) by Karl Grünberg (1950) and with fictionalized versions of Garbe's story, Edward Claudius's novels *Vom schweren Anfang* (From Difficult Beginnings, 1950) and *Menschen an unserer Seite* (People at our Side, 1951). While Grünberg's text replicated the orthodox homology between the "inner struggle" of the recalcitrant proletarian and his social integration as model worker and model father, and thus represented a retreat from its much-cited Soviet model,

---

[36] The SED called for an increase in production by 150 to 200%; see "Production Quotas," 15.

[37] My comments on the Garbe project draw on volume ten of Brecht's *Werke* and archival material (BBA), as well secondary literature. Citations of the published fragments include text number (e.g. A10) as well as page number.

Fyodor Gladkov's *Cement* (1925/41), which highlighted the unresolved tensions between family and state, Claudius's narrative pushes his worker-protagonists, especially the crew leader Aehre in *Menschen an unserer Seite*, further than Gladkov's, sharpening the contradiction between the worker's social achievements and his increasingly fragmented self.[38] Brecht also struggled with the text based on interviews by Käthe Rülicke, *Hans Garbe erzählt*, which, while it did not reproduce Rülicke's shaping of Garbe's disjointed narrative into a harmonizing socialist *Bildungsroman*, nonetheless "improved" on Garbe by smoothing out his grammar and inconsistencies in his narrative.[39]

As the interviews reveal, Garbe's story was full of contradictions. Born illegitimate on an agricultural estate in Imperial Germany in 1902, he had little formal education but considerable talent as a bricklayer. Working after 1945 for a private factory, he tried several times to join the SED, and succeeded after being initially rebuffed because he had been a member of the Nazi Party during the war. At Siemens-Plania from 1949, he was known as a hard worker whose zeal

[38] Karl Grünberg, *Der Mann im feurigen Ofen* (Berlin/GDR: Neue Welt, 1950); Eduard Claudius, *Menschen an unseren Seite* (Berlin/GDR: Volk und Welt, 1951). *Cement* was lauded by Zhdanov and Gorky at the First Soviet Writers' Congress in 1934. Nonetheless, the first edition (1925) eschewed a premature resolution of this conflict, suggesting, in the broken marriage of the protagonists and in the death of their child, the cost of socialist reconstruction in the face of civil war and foreign intervention, even though it offers a critical endorsement of this sacrifice. The revision (1941) smooths out these contradictions and softens the radical treatment of women's rights, critical arguments against collectivization, and the undecided conclusion of the original version. Compare *Cement* (1925), trans. A. Arthur and A. Ashleigh (New York: Continuun, 1985) and *Cement* (Moscow: Raduga Press, 1941). For the critical reading of *Menschen an unsrer Seite* paraphrased here, see Hunter Bivens, "Concrete Utopias: Labor and History in East German Literature" (PhD dissertation, University of Chicago, 2004), chapter 2.
[39] Käthe Rülicke, *Hans Garbe erzählt* (Berlin/GDR: Aufbau, 1951).

and impatience with shirkers did not always endear him to fellow workers. Even the management was initially sceptical of his plan to rebuild the brick furnaces, although he was praised once the repairs were successfully completed.[40] Garbe's own account, as transcribed by Rülicke and published under her name as *Hans Garbe erzählt* (Hans Garbe Tells [his story], 1951), offers plenty of opportunity for heroic treatment as a progress from alienated laborer to worker hero.[41] Although Garbe's transcript lacks the narrative coherence of a *Bildungsroman*, his recollections nonetheless gloss earlier experience as stages of a socialist education. His memory of childhood on a Junker estate, for instance, is marked by a retrospective emphasis on the lack of educational opportunities, while his account of conflicts with private management emphasizes his differences with the owners more than his trouble with the SED, which would cast doubt on his role as model worker. Rülicke's revisions encouraged this retrospective reading. A comparison of the transcript of Garbe's responses (BBA 550) with Rülicke's revision (BBA 557/13–79) suggests not only a concern to correct his grammar (to lend his story a "classical" universality) but also a desire to read Garbe's personal recollection of his experience as a collectively valid prediction of the process of socialist education and the triumph of the model worker.

Insofar as he regarded Garbe's achievement as a result of socialist formation, Brecht followed the SED line mapped out by Rülicke for the "identity between what the Party plans and the proletarian does," as a journal note in July 1951 on a possible adaptation of Anna Seghers's story "Die Linie" suggests (*Werke* 27: 324). However, another note, written at the same time, on transcription of the interviews problematizes the identification of Garbe as the proletarian "subject of history" (324); and the plot outline produced after the 17 June uprising, but published as part of Brecht's works only in 1997, only deepens the contradictions:

[40] See Stephan Bock, "Hans Garbe. Ein Chronik, 1902–57"; appendix to his essay "Die Tage des Büschings. Brechts *Garbe* – ein deutsches Lehrstück," in *DDR-Dramatik*, 41–77.
[41] For the transcript, see BBA 500 and 557.

1. Garbe visits a lawyer, because he got a camp follower pregnant [during the war]. . . .
2. Released, Garbe works once more in the private sector . . . tries to get the property expropriated and has to flee the Party.
3. The ownerless company is dismantled [and removed to the Soviet Union].
4. . . . Garbe as ratebuster [*Tarifdrücker*].
5. Battle for the furnace.
6. Garbe battles in vain against further reductions in the [work] norms.
7. Can the government maintain the new [higher] norms? No! Can it give them up? No! The government gives them up!
8. 17 June.
9. The story of his apprentice. Flees to the West.
10. The Russians rescue the factory. Garbe dies.
11. The apprentice comes back. Too late. For now, but not forever.

(*Werke* 10: 971–2)

Rather than assuming a causal link between proletarian alienation and the overthrow of capitalism, Brecht plays special attention to the conflict between working-class solidarity, developed in opposition to the capitalist exploitation of labor, and the loyalty demanded by the SED state on the grounds that it represents the workers' long-term interests despite current hardship. In addition, by entitling the fragments *Büsching* Brecht draws a provisional but pointed connection between the model worker Garbe and the war deserter Büsching in *Der Untergang des Egoisten Johann Fatzer*. This unfinished play, which preoccupied Brecht intermittently from the late 1920s to the end of his life, dealt directly with deserters at the end of the First World War, but later drafts written in the 1950s also animated a dialectical tension between the model worker as socialist subject and the deserter as object lesson of asocial behavior. In order to push through his project, Garbe had to take on his comrades and their perception of their class loyalty, campaigning against their desire to lower the production quotas (10: 971). Brecht allows for the possibility of workers calling Garbe a traitor to his class for working harder than his peers and so lowering

86

wages (10: 974: A10; 10: 976: A17). He suggests in unpublished notes that Garbe's activism emerges in the first instance in opposition to his co-workers' perception of their interests as workers and only gradually develops into a defense of the GDR as the workers' state (BBA 200/14–16).

The fragmentary, intertextual character of Brecht's notes, as well as his splitting of the protagonist into socialist and asocialist agents connoted by the names Garbe and Büsching, makes it hard to see Garbe's story as a socialist *Bildungsroman,* in which the socialization of the hero as model worker fills the mold traditionally occupied by the bourgeois hero's deepening self-knowledge.[42] Garbe's transformation is to be understood not as psychological formation but rather as social production. In conceiving of the play as a *Lehrstück* on the model of *The Measures Taken,* Brecht resists an unconditional representation of Garbe/Büsching as a positive hero. Instead, he stresses the obstacles in the way of this socialist's progress. The double name of the protagonist, Garbe/Büsching, encapsulates the actual historical problem: the construction of a socialist society in the GDR would require not only the mobilization of socialist and anti-fascist resisters to Nazi rule but also the incorporation of former Nazis themselves in the ranks of the workers building socialism. Moreover, Garbe had also to deal with those socialist workers whose very commitment to workplace democracy in a hostile capitalist economy led them to wonder whether the SED's accelerated production goals amounted to exploitation by the employer-state. In both cases, he had to rely not on their unlikely psychological transformation as allegedly new "socialist human beings," but rather on their work as producers of socialist society. Brecht hoped to show this double crisis – contradiction and opportunity – by deploying a chorus of workers who were to articulate a critical counterpoint to the confident assertions of the protagonist. Brecht's notes offer neither a satisfying story nor a fully realized hero but rather an attempt to "represent socialism critically" (to recall his Academy speech in 1953). More than the resolution in *Katzgraben,* it

---

[42] Stephan Bock, in "Chronik zu Brechts Garbe/Büsching Projekt," 85, attributes the heroic emphasis to Rülicke.

is the fault-line in *Garbe/Büsching* that corresponds to Brecht's comments on the threat of defeat, even though he made those comments while rehearsing *Katzgraben*. Despite the models pressed upon him and his own search for the "subject of history," he remained sceptical of "socialist mythmaking"[43] and especially of uncritical attachment to the worker as heroic type.[44]

What appears to have stymied the project was the shock of the uprising on 17 June. In May 1953, the SED Central Committee decided to raise production quotas immediately by ten to thirty percent, on the way to the goal of 150% or more, but, faced with the impracticability of this acceleration, retracted the plan in early June – too late.[45] The vehemence of the strike by the construction workers building new model housing on the east-central Stalinallee (Stalin Boulevard; formerly and now once again Frankfurter Allee) took GDR intellectuals and the as-yet-inexperienced Ministry of State Security (Stasi) by surprise. This action by relatively well-paid and highly visible workers, including Garbe who joined the demonstration wearing his Hero of Labor badge (*Werke* 10: 1283), challenged the legitimacy of the "worker-and-peasant state" like no other. Brecht's subsequent notes

[43] Bathrick, "Affirmative and Negative Culture: Technology and the Left Avant-Garde," in *The Technological Imagination*, ed. Teresa de Lauretis, Andreas Huyssen, and Kathleen Woodward (Madison: Coda Press, 1980), 116.

[44] Jan Knopf, *Brecht-Handbuch* (Stuttgart: Metzler, 1980), 1: 374. Despite their clear-sighted analysis of prose fiction versions of the model worker, Hartmann and Eggeling repeat Knopf's opinion that Brecht saw Garbe in a heroic mode ("Von Gremjatschi Log nach Katzgraben," 16).

[45] For the SED line on the uprising as "armed violence against the people," see Torsten Diedrich, *Der 17. Juni 1953 in der DDR: bewaffnete Gewalt gegen das Volk* (Berlin: Dietz, 1991). For an eyewitness account from an SED dissident, see "Heinz Brandt: ein SED-Funktionär in der Opposition," in *Es hat alles keinen Zweck*, 21–41. In their preface to *Es hat alles keinen Zweck*, Armin and Thomas Friedrich praise Stefan Heym's documentary novel, *5 Tage in Juni* (1977: Frankfurt a.M.: Fischer, 1990), as the "first comprehensive representation" of the uprising (5); the novel effectively combines SED communiqués with fictional narrative from different perspectives, including those of strikers, SED loyalists and bystanders.

in October 1953 and plot outline produced in November 1954 allude to this crisis in the proposal of a chorus of workers in the "style of *Measures Taken*" (*Werke* 27: 348) to provide the problem of representing those who were at once adversaries and comrades with a framework broader than the scope of individual antagonists. Yet Brecht's notes on this chorus give no clue as to whether it should represent the authority of the party, as in *The Measures Taken*, or the conflicting voices of social and asocial subjects, in the manner of *Fatzer*. Brecht gives voice not only to Garbe's reluctant co-workers but also to the strikers who were the most visible participants in the 1953 rebellion. His shock at their justifiable reaction to the labor conditions resulting from accelerated production, as well as what he sees as their anarchic expression of these grievances, is above all shock at the discrepancy between the Party's program of "ideological re-education" and the "depravity" of the masses, mixed with the hope that the gravity of the crisis will provoke the hitherto lacking conscientization:

> But this untimely occasion [*Ungelegenheit*] provided a great opportunity to win over the workers. For this reason, I did not think that the effect of 17 June, however horrible, was simply negative. In the moment when I saw the proletariat . . . once more handed over to the class enemy . . . I saw also the only possibility of combating that enemy.
>
> (20 August 1953; *Werke* 27: 346–7)

It would be easy to read this journal entry as an expression of a desire to redeem the working class at the moment of its dissolution, or as the reification of members of the working class with conflicting desires as a monolith like its mythical antagonist, the capitalist class enemy. Yet it is noteworthy that, in this moment of crisis when Allied forces in West Berlin were literally a stone's throw away from the strike in the Stalinallee, Brecht still insists on the authentic agency of the strikers. His plea that the "only way to combat the class enemy" is to proceed from the workers' own response to what they perceive as deprivation, rather than from central Party directives, challenges the SED, but his concession to the SED, line on the "depravity" of the strikers reinvents the workers as objects of party education and enlightenment and treats Garbe as its exemplary product.

The strain on the Büsching/Garbe scenario is especially clear in Brecht's scene outline, which begins provocatively and ends in ideological and dramaturgical compromise. After scene headings that point directly to controversial issues – Soviet appropriation of factories and the rebellion of 17 June as well as the difficult work relations of the alleged model worker – the concluding headings suspend the drama of fundamental social contradictions, to juxtapose the death of Garbe with Russians "sav[ing] the factory," and thus to paper over these contradictions with the pathos of reconciliation.[46] This veneer of pathos is pretty thin, however. Garbe may strive for the noble but flawed hero of classical tragedy, but his antagonists are shadowy and his social environment too hastily constructed to constitute what Hegel identifies as the "organized national life" shaping the collision of subject and society in high tragedy.[47] Instead, it offers an outline for an undeveloped genre, a socialist *Trauerspiel* (mourning play) for a utopian society in still-birth. The blocked dialectic between subject and society, after the trauma of the June uprising, haunts the socialist *Lehrstück* or *Chronik* Brecht professed to write, and bears comparison with the disjunction between subject and society that Peter Szondi associates with the bourgeois *Trauerspiel*. If the Baroque *Trauerspiel* or "martyr play" appears to be, as Walter Benjamin argues, a distorted

[46] Stephan Bock, in "Chronik zu Brechts Garbe/Büsching Projekt und Käthe Rülickes Bio-interview *Hans Garbe erzählt,*" *Brecht-Jahrbuch* 1977 (Frankfurt: Suhrkamp, 1978), and "Die Tage des Büschings. Brechts *Garbe* – ein deutsches Lehrstück," in Profitlich, ed., *DDR-Dramatik*, 41–77. Echoing Brecht's play on the Paris Commune, *Die Tage der Commune*, the title of Bock's essay invokes the pathos of the failed revolution that pervades that play. Bathrick, "Affirmative and Negative Culture: Technology and the Left," counters this pathos by emphasizing the Garbe fragment's links to the *Lehrstück*, but it returns in his regret that the play's legitimating audience, the SED, was not ready to receive it.
[47] G. W. F. Hegel, *Vorlesungen über die Ästhetik* (Frankfurt a.M.: Suhrkamp, 1970), 3: 476; trans. T. M. Knoz, *Aesthetics* (Oxford: Clarendon Press, 1998), 2: 1159.

image (*Zerrbild*) of tragedy but turns out instead a more intensely apt representation of the violence of the age (the Thirty Years War in seventeenth-century Europe) than the orderly proportions of the classical form could offer, the bourgeois *Trauerspiel* from George Lillo's *The London Merchant* (1731) to Arthur Miller's *Death of a Salesman* (1947) portrays what Lillo called "private woe" rather than "royal woe" in response to the failure of a bourgeois subject to ride the tide of capitalism, mourned and redeemed by the "attention paid," in the words of Linda, the eponymous salesman's wife, by women in the domestic sphere.[48] Instead of "private woe" or individual formation, the socialist *Lehrstück* attempts to break with domestic sentiment to build the socialist public sphere. Nonetheless, although Brecht jettisoned the depiction of Garbe's private life attempted by Claudius, his protagonist's ascetic ethic of sacrifice pitted against a hint of former libertinage (suggested by the camp follower) suggests restraint rather than social agency, the Protestant ethic if not the spirit of capitalism.[49]

[48] Walter Benjamin, "Der Ursprung des deutschen Trauerspiels," *Gesammelte Schriften* (Frankfurt a.M.: Suhrkamp, 1980), 1.1: 230–3; trans. John Osborne, *The Origin of German Tragic Drama* (London: New Left Books, 1977), 50–3; Peter Szondi, *Die Theorie des bürgerlichen Trauerspiels* (Frankfurt a.M.: Suhrkamp, 1979); Lillo, *The London Merchant* (1731), ed. William McBurney (Lincoln: University of Nebraska Press, 1965); Arthur Miller, *Death of a Salesman* (New York: Viking, 1949). Drawing on Lillo's prologue to *The London Merchant*, and his emphasis on "private woe," Szondi argues that the Protestant ethic of the merchant and the sentiment of the family women, rather than the class origin of the protagonist, define the genre; see *London Merchant*, 5, and Szondi, *Theorie*, 15–90.

[49] Max Weber's *The Protestant Ethic and the Spirit of Capitalism*, trans. Talcott Parsons (1930; New York: Routledge, 1993) is the classic study of the ascetic subject as model entrepreneur, delaying the gratification of consumption or expenditure in order to accumulate wealth. E. P. Thompson notes in "Time, Work-Discipline, and Industrial Capitalism," in *Customs in Common* (New York: New Press, 1991) that this ideology of delayed gratification was reinforced by nineteenth-century socialist movements preparing members for a long wait for the revolution.

Crushed by the contradictions in this not-yet-socialist public sphere, however, *Lehrstück* relapses into *Trauerspiel*. This note of mourning under the utopian anticipation of the *Lehrstück* deeply affected Müller's "stories from the production line" as well as his better-known plays from *Hamletmaschine* (1977) on. The production plays are often forgotten in studies that focus on the later plays to represent Müller as an international (post)modernist and cosmopolitan sceptic.[50] Nonetheless, it is in his early plays, particularly *Der Lohndrücker* and *Der Bau* – in which he attempts to portray conscientization not as the realization, enlightenment, or mourning of the self, but as the *disassembly* of subjectivity through socialization – that the foundations of his scepticism (both the ground and the source) in the production of the GDR as utopia, dystopia and everyday life emerge. Even more than Brecht, Müller tackled the GDR's appropriation of the political and social as well as artistic legacy of the Weimar Republic, as these plays return to key sites in the history and iconography of socialist militancy from the 1920s.

The wage-buster, or the socialization of subjectivity

Written in collaboration with Inge Müller, Müller's wife at the time, in the same year (1956) as Khrushchev condemned Stalin's crimes only to suppress the Hungarian uprising shortly thereafter, *Der Lohndrücker* (The Wage-Buster) meets the contradictions of official socialism head on.[51] The playwrights refused the SED call to portray the triumph of the new society in the allegory of model worker, choosing instead

---

[50] Such studies proliferated after Müller's death in December 1995; Horst Domdey's *Produktivkraft Tod: Das Drama Heiner Müllers* (Cologne: Böhlau, 1998) places Müller in a Nietzschean tradition of radical nihilism, reducing the GDR to passing comment on the "illusory" character of its literature (67–76) or, more bluntly, to a "drug" (195–209). Exceptions tend to be GDR work, such as Joachim Fiebach's *Inseln der Unordnung* (Berlin/GDR: Henschel, 1990), and Frank Hörnigk, editor-in-chief of the definitive edition of Müller's work (2000–).

[51] The play first appeared in issue 5 of the Writers' Union journal, *Neue Deutsche Literatur* (1957), and was later revised for publication in West Berlin; see "Der Lohndrücker," *Geschichte aus der Produktion 1*

to highlight the deep divide between SED propaganda of future prosperity and the immediate scarcity of basic goods in 1949, as the new
state struggled against Soviet appropriations on the eastern front and
the lure of the Marshall Plan and the new Deutschmark to the west.
Despite its departure from the affirmative paradigm represented by
Der Mann in feurigen Ofen, *Der Lohndrücker* was performed first by
students at the prestigious Hochschule für Ökonomie und Planung
(HfÖ; College of Economics and Planning) in Berlin in early 1958,
followed by professional productions in Leipzig and Berlin.[52] In the
program at the Maxim-Gorki-Theater in Berlin (directed by Hans-
Dieter Mäde), *Der Lohndrücker* was accompanied by a companion
piece, *Die Korrektur*, based on conditions at the industrial conglomerate Schwarze Pumpe (near Hoyerswerda in the east) and revised in
the light of workers' responses.[53] Although initially hailed in SED circles as an exemplary portrayal of a "transformation in working-class
consciousness," *Der Lohndrücker* and *Die Korrektur* were denied the

(Berlin/ West: Rotbuch, 1974); this version was translated as "The
Scab," in *The Battle: Plays, Prose, Poems by Heiner Müller*, trans. Carl
Weber (Baltimore: Johns Hopkins University Press, 1989). In the
context of complex relations of worker solidarity and betrayal, and the
demands of the "worker-and-peasant" state, the more precise term
"wage-buster" makes more sense.

[52] Despite the claim, reiterated in Müller's *Stücke* (Frankfurt a.M.:
Suhrkamp, 2000), 1: 536, that the first production was in Leipzig in
March 1958, the editors of *Theater der Zeit* argue that the HfÖ
production was in fact first; see the editorial introduction to
"Faszinierendes Diskussionsangebot: Zuschauer diskutieren Heiner
Müllers 'Lohndrücker,'" *Theater der Zeit* 43: 5 (1988), 52. For
information about the HfÖ production, see Steffi Spira, "Damals und
Heute," *Theater der Zeit* 43: 5 (1988), 53–4, and the interview with
B. K. Tragelehn, who directed the HfÖ production of *Die Umsiedlerin*
in 1961: "Regisseur-Gespräch," *Theater der Zeit* 45: 1 (1990): 21–6.

[53] For analysis of worker disaffection in the 1950s, based on reports to
the official union, the FDGB, by concerned SED shop representatives,
see Mary Fulbrook, *Anatomy of a Dictatorship: Inside the GDR,
1949–89* (Oxford University Press, 1995), esp. 61–77, 154. For a
discussion of the revisions of *Die Korrektur*, see Müller, *Krieg ohne
Schlacht*, 144–53, and Bathrick, *Powers of Speech*, 112–15.

prize awarded by the Freies Deutsches Gewerkschaftsbund (FDGB; Free German Trade Union Congress), and had too short a run to reach the broader worker audience for which they were conceived.[54]

Given *Der Lohndrücker*'s harsh treatment of Party dogma about the superiority of socialism to the lures of the imperialist West, the ambivalence of the SED's response is not surprising. Following Brecht's rejection of illusory solutions to real problems, the text opens with the playwright's disclaimer of such solutions along with an appeal for active audience engagement with the problems:

> The play doesn't try to present the struggle between old and new – which can't be decided by a playwright – as if it were solved [*abgeschlossen*] with the victory of the new before the final curtain. It tries to convey the struggle to the new audience who will decide it. The play takes place in the GDR, in 1948/49. The history of the circular furnace is well known. The characters and their stories are invented.[55]

The action proceeds by way of a series of confrontations between the activist Balke (who shares Garbe's zeal on the job but not his sense of socialist formation from humble beginnings) and his co-workers,

---

[54] For SED praise for the play, see Willi Lewin, "Probleme unserer literarischen Entwicklung" (1960), *Dokumente*, 608, and Ulbricht's speech at the Fifth SED Congress (1958), "Einige Probleme der Kulturrevolution," *Dokumente*, 534. The pair of plays were initially nominated for the FDGB Prize by union members at Schwarze Pumpe but were withdrawn under SED pressure; *Der Lohndrücker* eventually received the Heinrich Mann Prize in 1959, awarded by the Academy of the Arts. See Müller, *Krieg ohne Schlacht*, 151.

[55] Heiner Müller, "Der Lohndrücker," *Geschichte aus der Produktion 1*, 15; "The Scab," 28 (trans. mod.). The 2000 edition cuts the appeal to an active public, leaving only the acknowledgment of the action's historical veracity: *Stücke*, 1: 28. Subsequent citations in the text follow *Geschichte aus der Produktion* followed by the translation in "The Scab," modified where necessary. Apart from familiarity with the BE repertoire, Müller's debt to Brecht lay in the latter's comments on Garbe and 17 June in his *Arbeitsjournal* and in Rülicke's account of Garbe's story, rather than in any archival material.

supervisors, and representatives of the SED. The dramaturgical structure follows the epic juxtaposition of scenes linked conceptually
rather than organically, which Brecht favored before he returned to
the "organic" architecture of *Katzgraben*. Rather than the didactic
prologues favored by the Party and applied to the "corrected" versions of *Katzgraben* (in the 1959 film) and *Die Korrektur*, this elliptical structure highlights the social gests of each character by inserting
pauses or silences at moments of sharp contradiction and thus leaving space for audience reflection. Presented in this epic manner, the
confrontations between characters reveal less about the make-up of
individuals than about the contradictions arising from the conflict
between their erstwhile and actual social positions, contradictions
that cannot be resolved in the fiction of the play but only in the public
sphere.

Müller's focus on the social parameters of action rather than
depth of character, and his commitment to epic form and the work of
the critical spectator, distinguish him from the Brecht whose production of *Katzgraben* retreated from montage and epic theatre. Müller
keeps a critical distance from Brecht's interest in Garbe's personal
history and his transformation from alienated prole to hero of labor.
Instead, he withholds information about his characters' domestic
lives; scenes portraying the private reflections of Barka, the model
worker/wage-buster, or Schorn, the SED secretary, which appeared in
the original publication, disappeared from the rehearsal script and subsequent published versions.[56] Cutting interiority and first names for

---

[56] In response to criticism from Peter Hacks that the action was too
"positivist," Müller added three scenes dealing with the characters'
private lives: Balke's conversation with an unnamed "woman,"
presumably his wife, about the shortage of coal (7b); a conversation in
which the Director discusses his wife, who has left him because he
was working too hard, and Schorn makes elliptical mention of his wife
who died apparently because he was condemned by a Nazi court (7c);
and Krüger's conversation with his son, in which he appears to support
his son's medical training which he criticizes at the site meeting (12b).
See Müller, "Der Lohndrücker," *Neue Deutsche Literatur* 5 (1957),
128–9, 137–8. Müller later rejected these scenes with a laconic "bad"

his characters, Müller treats their behavior as a product of contradictory social roles rather than the expression of inner conflict. Balke, a factory inspector during the war who reported anti-fascist sabotage to the Nazis, shows the same zeal for efficiency in this post-war situation when he offers to rebuild the furnaces single-handed. The Party secretary Schorn values this efficiency but still remembers Balke as the inspector who denounced him. Balke's activism on behalf of accelerated production provokes the hostility of the workers on his crew (*Brigade*), some of whom sabotage what they see as scab labor and collusion with the employer.

Far from underplaying the actual alienation of workers caught between rising production norms and stagnant living standards, between an as-yet-intangible socialist democracy and the lure of Western consumer society, Müller's deconstruction of the antinomy between saboteur and model worker emphasizes it. In the first scene, three exhausted workers unwittingly trample an SED poster; shortly thereafter, several others, angered by the scarce commodities and high prices of the VEBs (*volkseigene Betriebe*, people's own enterprises), raid the factory HO (*Handelsorganisation*, trading station). The play acknowledges the gap between the promises of the worker-and-peasant state and the indifference, frustrated idealism, or outright hostility of its citizens in the face of material scarcity. In the series of scenes at the core of the play, several interest groups debate Balke's plan to rebuild the furnaces while they are lit. In scene 8a, Schorn responds to the practical objections of the engineer (whose name, Kant, recalls the philosopher of practical reason) with an appeal to consciousness, ironically deflected by the other engineer, Trakehner:

KANT: It may be possible to work at a hundred
                 degrees. Question is: can we do quality work?
SCHORN: This isn't only a question of technology or
                 materials.

(*Krieg ohne Schlacht*, 142), but made no comment on the erasure of women, who otherwise appear nowhere in the play.

TRAKEHNER: "But a question of [class] consciousness". . . . You're the paid expert [on that question]. But we're dealing here with hard facts.
SCHORN: The working class is creating new facts.
TRAKEHNER: I take my hat off to the working class. But exploitation is not a new fact.

(29/43; trans. mod.)

The irony of a marxist appealing to consciousness in the face of material scarcity is brought home by the facts as well as the elliptical presentation:

TRAKEHNER: If a bricklayer rebuilds the furnace, he'll be a hero. If the furnace cracks, we'll be the saboteurs (SCHORN *smiles*)
BITTNER: The furnace is going to crack.
BALKE: It has cracked. . . . I request [*verlange*] permission to rebuild the furnace.

(29/44; trans. mod.)

For many of the workers schooled in the anti-capitalism of the Weimar era, socialism means solidarity against exploitation; for the union official, Schurek, the manipulation of other workers using party slogans like "The working masses [*Werktätigen*] demand the raising of the norm" (42/54, trans. mod.); for Party secretary Schorn, the as-yet-unconsolidated basis of the mass action that might give this slogan real force. Müller's presentation of this debate in scene 8b highlights the gaps between them:

DIRECTOR: We're going to show . . . what the working class can achieve. It should [*muß*] be an honor for you to participate. (*pause*)
KRÜGER: That's exploitation [. . .].
BALKE: The plan depends on it, colleagues.
VOICE (*in the background*) Shit on the plan.
BALKE: Question is: will you have something to shit without the plan? (*Man with Glasses bleats a laugh, then stifles it when no one else laughs*).

97

I can't rebuild the furnace on my own but we
need it (*Silence*).

DIRECTOR: Krüger, you said exploitation. All your life
you've been exploited. Today your boy is at the
university.

KRÜGER: Did I send him to the university? I was against
it (*Silence*).

BALKE: It will be hard, very hot. Twice the pay, three
times the work.

A WORKER: And eight years inside if something goes wrong.
[. . .]

BALKE: I know what I'm doing (*Pause*)

KOLBE: I sat in a tank until '45. That was no icebox
either. I'll join you.

KRÜGER (*steps forward*) If it has to be.

(30–1/45; trans. mod.)

The contradictory demands and expectations of the bricklayers, engineers, and the director, as well as the Party secretary, explode any single definition of socialist identity, consciousness, or interests, leaving shards of incompatible positions inherited from acquiescence to Nazism, organized or disorganized opposition to capitalism, marxist critiques of these, or new and unsettled legitimations of the state. The pauses and silences, especially after Balke's emphatic claims, leave room for a sceptical if not outright ironic response to his self-assurance. The threat of defeat – and the risk that the workers will have to take the blame – is palpable.

The play does not attempt to bridge the gap between the Party and the workers with the reaffirmation of the Party's authority or with the redemption of workers' alienation as the path to proletarian sovereignty. Where the moralizing strain of socialist realism would require that the wage-buster and the reluctant workers be redeemed as model workers in the making, or that the dubious habits and allegiances of these characters, including former and current Nazis as well as shirkers of all stripes, be reformed through socialist education, Müller's play confronts its audience with the possibility that the

work of building socialism may not transform these people into a new
"socialist" breed but rather, as the SED secretary noted in the first,
controversial version of *Die Korrektur*, "socialism won't be built only
by socialists, not here or elsewhere – here, least of all."[57] The audience is not invited to identify with Balke or his opponents but to
understand the historical and social relations which have led to the
conflict between them, and to see the connections between those circumstances and their own, even though living standards in 1958 were
substantially better than in 1948: the kilo of butter trampled by an
angry worker in the play cost 65 marks in 1948 but only 10 marks
after price stabilization in the 1950s.[58] The collaboration among people whose politics, social status and interest in the work at hand are
quite mixed does not resolve the contradictions of their several positions but proceeds from a recognition that their future depends on
negotiating them.[59] As the play's last words imply:

BALKE: I need you Karras. I don't ask as a friend.
             You've got to help me.
KARRAS (*stops*)   I thought you wanted to build socialism all
             by yourself. When do we start?

(44/ 56)

This ending is neither the transcendence of alienated labor by utopian
communism nor an admission of defeat. Rather, it suggests that exemplary work is not the property of any single model worker or the
creation of the party, but rather the product of collaborative labor

[57] Müller, "Die Korrektur," *Geschichten aus der Produktion*, 47; "The
Correction," in *Hamletmachine and Other Texts for the Stage*, trans.
Carl Weber (Baltimore: Johns Hopkins University Press, 1984), 33;
trans. mod.
[58] See the chart reproduced in *Geschichte aus der Produktion*, 34; also the
tariffs reproduced in the resource book edited by dramaturg Alexander
Weigel for the 1988 revival, *Spuren: Texte, Bilder, Dokumente zu
"Lohndrücker" von Heiner Müller* (Berlin/GDR: Henschel, 1988), 14.
[59] Schivelbusch, *Sozialistisches Drama nach Brecht*, 104, argues that this
cooperation does not stem from the workers' conversion to socialism
but rather from their recognition that their future depends on their
labor power.

in which the Party representative is not a leader or a judge but a facilitator.

Müller critiques the Stalinist orthodoxy of the SED, especially the absolute authority of the Party and the demand for loyalty to the command economy, by portraying the Party's potential for organizing labor and rationalizing production at a moment of severe social crisis, while at the same time criticizing its actual abuse of power and pretensions to infallibility.[60] He grounds this critique not in an attack on the Party as such but by invoking its most respected authority, Lenin, so as to challenge, if only implicitly, the official view of Lenin's emphasis on the modernization of the economy and on labor discipline as a necessary means to that end.[61] Lenin's authority for the SED as well as for the socialist opposition in the GDR was reinforced by marxist-leninist instruction in schools and unions.[62] While the SED's claim to political legitimacy rested on Lenin's famous endorsement of the authority of the vanguard party against the "formal democracy" of "bourgeois parliaments," the tension between the Party secretary and even the socialist workers in the play amplifies the critique, advanced inconsistently by Lenin, of the vanguard party's presumption of superiority over local workers' organizations.[63] The Director cites Lenin directly

[60] See Kurt Hager (Minister for Agitation and Propaganda): "All levels of the intelligentsia and labor force must attach themselves to the worker-and-peasant state," Sonntag (11 August 1952), in Dokumente, 478, and the unsigned affirmation of the second Five Year Plan in "Für eine sozialistische Kultur" (24 October 1957), Dokumente, 496–507.

[61] Lenin (Vladimir Ilyich Ulyanov), "The Immediate Tasks of the Soviet Government" (April 1918) and "Leftwing Childishness and Petit-bourgeois Mentality" (1922), in Works (London: Lawrence and Wishart, 1966), 27: 235–77 and 323–54.

[62] The official emphasis on Lenin over Marx is clear in Neues Deutschland and in educational textbooks such as Grundlagen des Marxismus-Leninismus (Berlin/ GDR: Dietzverlag, 1963). See also Kaufmann, Erwartung und Angebot, 33–40. Spira's account of the student production includes their responses to workers' comments, which suggest willingness to test socialist ideas against frustration with actual practice (Spira, "Damals und Heute," 53).

[63] Lenin, "State and Revolution," in The Lenin Anthology, ed. Richard Tucker (New York: Norton, 1975), 341–6.

when he suggests that "fewer [Party recruits]" would be "perhaps better" than premature or mandatory Party membership.[64] What is at issue in the Party's relationship to the workers is not moral persuasion or even solidarity, but the troubled dialectic between productivity and emancipation, between the Party's claims of direct democracy in the workplace and the actual discipline exercised by Party representatives. This was a dialectic that a Party governed by an infallible *Führungsanspruch* (as in the Stalinist anthem, "The Party is Always Right") could not acknowledge.[65]

This "story from the production line" ("Geschichte aus der Produktion") resists the socialist realist temptation to dissolve workers' alienation from their labor in an uncritical assent to the leninist assertion that *they* are the state. Instead, it dramatizes the contradictory and uneven development of their sense of entitlement, ownership and responsibility alongside the uneven attempts of engineers and Party officials to set aside their own privileges. The critique of Party infallibility as well as the ironic treatment of "people's own enterprises" challenges the claim that "ideological re-education" in the interests of modernization and productivity necessarily leads to socialism. While the managers reiterate the need for discipline and

---

[64] Lenin notes: "We must understand that trade unions are not government departments like the People's Commissars, but comprise the whole organized proletariat" (the "Second All-Russia Congress of Miners") and "trade unions are the principal means of combating the bureaucratization of the economy . . . and making possible the truly popular control of production" ("Once Again on the Trade Unions": *Works* 32: 56, 100). The Director's comment that "fewer are perhaps more" in *Der Lohndrücker* (38/ 50; trans. mod.) alludes to Lenin's last essay, "Better Fewer but Better," *Works* 33: 487–502, known for its prompt suppression by Stalin rather than for its critique of bureaucratic patronage in the Bolshevik Party.

[65] "Die Partei had immer Recht" (The Party is Always Right) (1950: text and music by Louis Fürnberg), a.k.a. "Song of the Party," salutes the Communist Party as "mother of the masses" born of "Lenin's mind" and "Stalin's might"; it remained in the SED repertoire after Stalin's death – but without his name. Heumann, Liner Notes to "Lied der Partei," *Die Partei hat immer Recht*, n.p.

indispensable "bourgeois experts," the range of sceptical responses recalls Lenin's critique of the overzealous application of communist dogma such as nationalization and central state control, on the grounds that premature centralization may diminish productivity and so exacerbate the scarcity of commodities.[66] Although the critical treatment of the tensions between industrial modernization and modern consumer culture, as the legacy of the command economy, would not appear in Müller's work until the 1980s, this early play highlights the discrepancy between central economic command and actual experience of deprivation at a moment, in 1956, when the SED's stubborn adherence to Stalinist orthodoxy (even after Stalin's death and disgrace) contrasted with destalinization efforts in the Soviet Union and Poland, to say nothing of the Hungarian uprising.[67]

Der Bau: construction sites on cracked foundations

Der Lohndrücker opens and closes with a sceptical analysis of the present and a determined prognosis for the future of socialism, a future "to be decided by the new public" rather than party officials, as dramatized by Karras's decision to work with his former foe, Barka. If this play expresses what Antonio Gramsci called "optimism of the will," the determination to make socialism succeed against the odds, the opening of *Der Bau* (The Construction Site), Müller's next play to investigate the GDR as construction site and, in Joachim Fiebach's view, his most important, seems to speak more to a "pessimism of

[66] On distinguishing between mere confiscation of assets and the collective redistribution of capital, see Lenin, "Leftwing Childishness," 334; on the implications of the New Economic Policy for industrial labor, see "The Role and Function of Trade Unions under the New Economic Policy," *Works* 33: 184–96.

[67] While the Hungarian uprising in June 1956 was crushed by Soviet tanks, public dissent in Poland led to the release of 100,000 political prisoners and the relaxation of programs such as rural collectivization. For pointed comparison between the GDR and other Soviet allies in 1956, see Armin Mitter and Stefan Wolle, *Untergang auf Raten: Unbekannte Kapitel der DDR-Geschichte* (Munich: Bertelsmann, 1993), 163–295.

the intellect" with a sceptical view of construction on cracked foundations.[68] The play was commissioned by the Deutsches Theater as an adaptation of Neutsch's *Spur der Steine* (Trace of Stones), which sets the plot at the same time as *Der Lohndrücker* – the retrospectively heroic early years of the republic – and locates the story in Leuna, near Bitterfeld, the site in the 1920s of repeated strikes, industrial resistance and violent response by the Weimar state and the conglomerate I. G. Farben, which later supplied the chemicals for Nazi death gas.[69] Unlike the novel, which brings the asocial rebel worker into the Party in the final pages, *Der Bau* refuses the consolations of nostalgia for the pioneer past or fictional solutions to intractable social problems in the present. Müller jettisoned Neutsch's title, plot, and timeframe, but retained references to the location in Leuna, the better to address current taboos, including the Party's bureaucratic mismanagement of production and the environment in supposedly model cities like Leuna. It also alludes critically to the Berlin Wall, built to seal the last porous border between East and West Germany on 13 August 1961 and touted in government communiqués and propaganda songs as an "anti-fascist protection barrier." The play was published in April 1965 in the Academy of Arts journal *Sinn und Form*, but subjected to SED attacks and dropped from rehearsal in early 1966.[70] Written

---

[68] Fiebach, *Inseln der Unordnung*, 132.

[69] As Eric Weitz argues, in *Creating German Communism: 1890–1990* (Princeton University Press, 1997),188–205, armed uprisings against exploitation and unemployment in 1921 and 1923 were led by radicalized industrial workers and the unemployed in the KPD, predominantly in the Leuna area. These uprisings and their graphic representation provided the basis for GDR appropriation of the legacy of anti-fascist resistance.

[70] Müller's first two drafts for the Deutsches Theater still bore the title "Spur der Steine." After objections by Neutsch, he changed the title and the names of the characters. The revision appeared in *Sinn und Form* 17 (1965), 169–227. The text published in 1974 is the seventh draft, which restores elements cut after criticism of the *Sinn und Form* version at the Eleventh Plenum. For an account of the drafts, see Hörnigk, "'Bau'-Stellen: Aspekte der Produktions- und Rezeptionsgeschichte eines dramatischen Entwurfs," *Zeitschrift für*

in face of the uneven development and partial thaw that followed the building of the Wall, *Der Bau* seems in retrospect to be written as if for the last decade of the GDR, by which time stagnation had choked cultural as well as economic production in the whole country. Performed for the first time in 1980 (directed by Fritz Marquardt at the Berlin Volksbühne) and again in 1986 (in Chemnitz, formerly known as Karl-Marx-Stadt, directed by Frank Castorf, later director of the Volksbühne), *Der Bau* dug up communism's cracked foundations. Along with Müller's own ironic deconstruction of his foundational play, *Der Lohndrücker*, in 1988, it seems to anticipate the final demolition of the worker-and-peasant state in 1990.

When Müller received the commission for *Der Bau* in 1963, he had already been expelled from the Writers' Union as a result of the SED's rejection of his previous play, *Die Umsiedlerin oder das Leben auf dem Lande* (The Female Resettler or Life on the Land, 1961). Written initially in response to *Katzgraben* in the 1950s and revised in the light of the collectivization consolidated by 1960, *Die Umsiedlerin* was performed for one night in September 1961 by the same HfÖ group as had performed *Der Lohndrücker*, and then shelved. Although the completion of rural collectivization in 1960, by which time over eighty percent of farmers had joined agricultural production collectives (LPGs, *Landwirtschaftliche Produktionsgenossenschaften*), and the erection of the Wall gave intellectuals the fleeting reassurance that the SED would now relax its vigilance against alleged counter-revolution, *Die Umsiedlerin* was treated as an attack on collectivization, and thus on the fundamental principles of the worker-and-peasant state. While propaganda jingles like "Now you're in the LPG / Now the work will be easier" provided upbeat cover for the SED's coercive pressure at a time when other socialist states were easing up on rural collectivization, *Die Umsiedlerin* dramatized the

Germanistik 6: 1 (1985), 35–52, and his editorial comment in Müller, *Stücke*, 1: 549–51. Propaganda songs promoting the Berlin Wall included "Wir sind wachsam" (We are on Guard) (text Heinz Kahlau (former Brecht student); music Joachim Werzlau) and "Die 13" (text and music Kallies), reputedly aired on radio on the very day the Wall was built. See Heumann, Liner Notes, *Die Partei hat immer Recht*, n.p.

disorderly reality and probed taboo topics such as local resistance to refugees from the East and, despite official support for female emancipation, the tension between independent women and a prudish party hierarchy.[71] Despite an attempt by Helene Weigel to get Müller to write a self-criticism that would satisfy the Party of his contrition, he was expelled from the Writers' Union and subjected to informal but effective marginalization from GDR theatre for a decade.[72] As

[71] Although LPGs managed 93% of agricultural land by 1960 (up from less than 50% in 1959), this happened only after farmers were threatened with confiscation. The hasty collectivization in the last year led to a distribution crisis reminiscent of the early years of scarcity. The artistic limitations of "Jetzt bist du in der LPG / Jetzt wird die Arbeit leichter sein" (text by Werner Lindermann, repeated to a slow polka by Hans-Georg Mühe) offered sad testimony to the limits of its message: see Heumann, Liner Notes to "Jetzt bist du in der LPG," *Die Partei hat immer Recht*, n.p. Gender equality was enshrined in the GDR constitution but, while women did heavy work on industrial crews, most were active in conventionally feminine service jobs and were largely absent from the SED hierarchy. See Hildegard Maria Nickel, "Women in the German Democratic Republic and the New German States: Looking Backward and Forward," in *Gender Politics and Post-Communism: Reflections from Eastern Europe and the Former Soviet Union*, ed. Nanette Funk and Magda Mueller (New York: Routledge, 1993), 138–50.

[72] For the attack on the text of *Die Umsiedlerin* as well as the production directed by B. K. Tragelehn (who later left the GDR), see the reports and "operational plans" circulated among officers in the Writers' Union, SED, FDJ and the Stasi, reproduced as appendices to Matthias Braun, *Drama um eine Komödie: Das Ensemble von SED, Staatssicherheit, FDJ, und Ministerium für Kultur gegen Heiner Müllers "Die Umsiedlerin oder das Leben auf dem Lande" im Oktober 1961*, Scholarly series published by the Federal Authority Responsible for the Former GDR's Security Service Records, vol. 4 (Berlin: Links Verlag, 1996), 89–165. Braun's long-winded commentary replicates Stasi obfuscation; for a clearer assessment, see Marianne Streisand, "Der Fall Heiner Müller: Dokumente zur 'Umsiedlerin,'" *Sinn und Form* 43 (1991): 429–86. The play received its first professional production in 1975 under the blander title *Die Bauern* (The Farmers), directed by Fritz Marquardt at the Volksbühne; but by that time, in Müller's view,

indicated in the extensive documentation on the case of *Die Umsied-lerin*, the SED suppressed opposition not only by applying the coercive methods of the Stasi, but also by appealing to the loyalty of intellectuals, like Weigel and union president Anna Seghers, to the idea of a socialist society beleaguered by a triumphal capitalism at the height of the Cold War.[73]

Remarkable for its provocative lines on immediate Cold War politics and its allusive titles (such as "Carpenters' Dance" and "Dance of Stones"), and arias on the ironies of history and production, *Der Bau* marks both the apotheosis of the production play and its dissolution.[74] The title evokes a generation of verbal and visual representation of the GDR as construction site, but it also recalls Kafka's story with the same title about a man engaged in endlessly building a labyrinthian bunker supposed to provide refuge from enemies and "life in the open."[75] Although Kafka was officially taboo, *Der Bau* draws

the play had only limited relevance to GDR reality (*Krieg ohne Schlacht*, 186).

[73] The documents demonstrate not only collaboration between the Stasi and Party loyalists but also the effective deployment of conflicted participants, such as Seghers, as instruments of the SED attack on "enemy" ideology, which allowed the SED to avoid overt coercion. In this case, the Stasi noted Seghers's appeal to Weigel (Braun, *Drama um eine Kömodie*, 162) but also her silence during the discussion before the vote against Müller (159).

[74] The German title of this first scene, "Zimmermannstanz," translates literally as "Carpenters' Dance" and so foreshadows the argument about wood versus plastic later on. It also refers to the game known in English as arm-wrestling or "Indian boxing," in which seated contestants rest their elbows on a table, clasp hands and try to pull the opponent's hand down. In the immediate context, it dramatizes the contest between work-team leader Balla and Party secretary Schorn.

[75] Müller, *Krieg ohne Schlacht*, 196. Although Müller mentions only "Kafka's title," his play evokes "Der Bau"; see Kafka, *Sämtliche Erzählungen* (Frankfurt: Fischer, 1970), 359–88; here: 368. The standard English translation of the story, "The Burrow," overemphasizes the mole-like behavior of the protagonist and thus encourages a reading that privileges animal instinct at the expense of the social construction and control denoted by the German original.

on his impossible construction in a drama that pits builders against planners, and both against intellectuals – the SED secretary and the two engineers, the energetic Schlee and the hesistant Hasselbein, "Hamlet in Leuna." The allusion is most obvious in the denunciation of the Berlin Wall as a "prison" by the rebellious Barka, leader of the crew notorious for stealing concrete for their work-site when the Party does not deliver; but Kafka's portrayal of workers and intellectuals alienated from bureaucracy is also apt here.[76] The action of disaffected workers in *Der Bau* draws on *Der Lohndrücker* and on the gestic language of Brecht, but their speech as well as that of alienated intellectuals like Hasselbein recalls Kafka's ironic phantasmagoria of bureaucracy as well as the alienated figures in the dramas of Georg Büchner, one of Müller's favorite authors. The opening question by the new SED secretary, Donat, "Warum zertrümmert ihr das Fundament?" ("Why are you demolishing the foundation?") receives an immediate if metaphorically mediated response from a construction worker, Dreier, who indicts the wielders of paper in Party offices for keeping workers to irrational plans while delaying delivery of essential materials. As he puts it, "paper explodes concrete and buckles the floor" but does not solve the problem: the foundation is still cracked (*gerissen*) at the end of the play.[77] Despite the Kafkaesque arrest of time, the historic crisis of the Cold War looms already in the first question: "zertrümmert" connotes not just "demolished" but also

---

[76] The vehemence with which the SED dismissed Kafka's depiction of alienation as irrelevant to a society that had allegedly overcome it only confirms Kafka's power. Defending the "national role of our republic" at the Presidium for Writers and Artists in March 1963, Alexander Abusch denounced the poet Günter Kunert as an apologist for Kafkaesque subjectivism and a "traitor" to the "world-liberating ideology" of socialism: "Zur nationalen Rolle unserer Republik und ihrer Kunst," *Dokumente*, 897–98. In "Fünf Jahre nach Bitterfeld," *Dokumente*, 941–50, Hans Koch sharply criticized those, including the eminent philosopher Ernst Fischer, who implied that Kafka's depiction of "alienation from bureaucracy" might be "topical" in the GDR.

[77] "Der Bau," *Geschichte aus der Produktion 1*, 85, 136. The text published here formed the basis of the performance in 1980 and restored the lines cut from the 1965 publication.

"smashed" like atoms in a bomb – and takes explicit if ambiguous shape in Donat's response to Dreier's indictment of paper and construction supervisor Belfert's defense of it. Addressing Belfert, Donat says:

> They are ripping up the very foundation that they've built. Khrushchev can talk to Kennedy about coexistence, which will bring down [umbringt] capitalism sooner or later, [but] you can't talk to your VVB [Vereinigung Volkseigener Betriebe, Union of People's Own Enterprises] about correcting the plans, which will save us I-don't-know-how much money in propaganda costs. When a painter turns a tree upside-down, we make him eat his canvas and in our offices, Abstraction is Fact.
>
> (87)

The present tenses in the German imply a certain rather than conditional future for both the end of capitalism and the savings to be had from correcting the plan, even though Kennedy was dead and Khrushchev ousted by the time the play was in rehearsal, the Nuclear Test Ban Treaty of 1963 had established mutual deterrence, and capitalism remained intact.[78] The contrastive "but" which is implied by the syntax of the quotation but does not appear in Müller's text, might have made explicit an implicit contrast between the punishment of the abstract painter and the impunity of the abstracted Party officers.

[78] Wilhelm Girnus, editor of Sinn and Form, required that this section be edited as follows: "We can talk with capitalism about coexistence, which will bring it down, but not with our VVB about correcting the plan. . . ." (Müller, "Der Bau," Sinn und Form 17 (1965), 172). Writing in 1992, Müller read this as caution in the face of the "military balance of power" (Krieg ohne Schlacht, 197), but the phrase "bring it [capitalism] down" is more emphatic in the published version without the qualifying "sooner or later," while the elimination of Khrushchev lessened the likelihood of complaints from the new Brezhnev administration. Writing after the 1980 premiere, Hörnigk ("'Bau'-Stellen," 48), noted more cautiously that the "global political context" of NATO versus the "socialist camp" affected contemporary literary depictions of the GDR.

The suppression of this word, however, both pinpoints the discrepancy between the grand anti-imperial gesture abroad and the stagnation of production at home, and mutes the obvious didactic emphasis that the SED might prefer. The juxtaposition of the punishment of the abstract painter with the impunity of bureaucratic abstraction also operates on multiple levels. Alluding to Brecht's indictment of formalism in the ranks of those SED functionaries who condemned formal and social innovation, Müller has his Party secretary suggest that the Party should pay more attention to real rather than formal problems. As author of these words, however, he also implies that formal experiment and economy might make the essence of the problem emerge more clearly than it would in a text cluttered with naturalistic details and emotional characters.

The economy of the play stands out against its source, the 800-plus-page novel *Spur der Steine*, but this economy is not merely formal. Whereas Neutsch provides his central character, the rebellious crew-leader Balla, with a classic narrative of personal formation, in which his initially asocial attitude is transformed not only by his unrequited love for the engineer (who is caught up in a problematic romance with the married SED secretary) but also by an epiphanic return to his father and home village, Müller's characters have only surnames and appear mostly on the construction site, where all actions are social. The presentation of social gests in epic or narrative fashion rather than the expression of private feeling highlights the public impact of the romance between the secretary and the engineer in three brief scenes: on the construction site, where Donat's "I love you" is followed by "forget it. Party orders" (110); in a landscape, where any allusion to the pretty country resort in the novel is dissipated by Schlee's ironic opener "they're building a chemical factory there. Don't ask me why" (117); and in the snow at the end, when Schlee agrees to deny to the Party that she knows the father of her unborn child, sends Donat packing, but reflects nonetheless on the communist future their child may inherit (136).

While potentially romantic encounters are subject to disillusion, spoken always in prose and often in the third person (reminiscent of the third-person courtship in Brecht's *Caucasian Chalk*

Circle), moments of productive breakthrough or, more often, tentative movement on the work-site appear in blank verse. The verse does not turn the speeches into subjective monologues, however. Dreier's response answers Donat's opening question to the extent that it pinpoints blame – not by naming names but by creating a phantasmagoric scene in which paper, rather than the bureaucrats wielding it, seems able to blow up or bury the "embryo of a factory" in his mind's eye. These speeches function as arias not in terms of the sentiment usually associated with the operatic form but rather to the degree that they offer a heightened expression of the social gest of the scene and the character's investment in it. If Dreier's indictment of paper highlights the structural, even political, character of the obstacles to social production rather than the personal failings of individuals like Belfert in the earlier drafts, Barka's aria at the end conjures up a communist future that seems as yet without a solid foundation but depends on assent from the others in this play and the social space around it.[79] This aria does not come when he decides to join the Party; that possibility occurs only as an ironic aside after a drinking bout with an ex-Nazi crew-mate (119). Rather, in the long final scene in the snow, as he carries the pregnant Schlee after she faints on the construction site, Barka apostrophizes the "cities that we will build tomorrow":

[79] Ziemer/Dreier's criticism of personal failings in the first draft – "We are all saboteurs on the side" – may seem at first more critical, but it suggests resignation to corruption; the revision, which indicts bureaucratic overplanning as a matter not of corrigible corruption but of unproductive *policy*, is both more critical and more accurate, hence the hostile response. See Hörnigk, " 'Bau'-Stellen," 39–40. Fiebach, *Inseln der Unordnung*, 54, calls these speeches monologues because he sees them as "foreign bodies" in Müller's otherwise "Brechtian dramaturgy." He suggests that the give and take of dialogue is only apparent, but nonetheless acknowledges the *episch* (narrative and analytical) character of the speeches by Dreier, Barka, Donat and Schlee. Despite the implication of Fiebach's title, I would argue that these speeches are bridges rather than islands; they pick up questions raised by others in the scene and, even if they do not address other characters directly, still open up a dialogue with the audience.

And in factories that are as yet in your head / that have not
yet grown out of my handwork / Runs their as-yet-unknown
production.
   And from the stars as yet under Plough / Grows bread from
their thirty-two teeth. . . . My life is building bridges. I am
the / Ferry between ice age and commune [*Kommune*].

(134)

Although Barka ends the aria by referring wistfully to the child in
Schlee's womb that could have been his, Müller pared away his
original characterization of Schlee's professional persona, "colleague
beardless with a woman's breasts," which highlighted Barka's personal attachment to Schlee and suggested that her status as engineer
was anomalous, even unnatural, to emphasize instead the concord
between her fertility and the factories generated in her head.[80] Juxtaposing the evocation of factories as yet unbuilt from Mayakovsky's
revolutionary fable *Mystery Bouffe* with the teeth under plough from
the Greek legend of Cadmus, Barka's vision is utopian but not predictable according to any purportedly scientific socialism. The teeth,
as in the legend, may yet produce soldiers of war rather than workers for peace.[81] More provocatively, his role as "ferry" between the
"frozen relations" of capitalism and a future egalitarian communism
he won't live to see pointedly implies that the GDR's "actually existing socialism" is still a long way from a communist utopia.[82] Although
this personification could also be read as an allusion to the Hades
ferryman Charon, which would place utopian communism in the

[80] See Müller, "Der Bau," *Sinn und Form*, 223. This 1965 version has
   "Fähre [ferry] zwischen Eiszeit und Kommune," which was changed
   later to "pontoon" (*Geschichte aus der Produktion 1*, 134), despite
   Müller's later assertion (*Krieg ohne Schlacht*, 158) that "ferry" was
   preferable. "Kommune" connotes both communism and the Paris
   Commune, the short-lived egalitarian workers' government crushed
   by Prussian and French ex-imperial forces in 1871.
[81] In the legend, Cadmus obeys the Delphic oracle's injunction to sow
   the teeth of a slain dragon to produce warriors to build Thebes; he is
   also supposed to have brought writing from Phoenicia to Greece.
[82] Müller, *Krieg ohne Schlacht*, 201.

afterlife, the play's conclusion returns to pragmatic prose, to Schlee's resolve to lie for Donat, but also to the implication that this lie will not upend the world: "the snow won't last until next winter" (136), and the work will go on.[83] In this open ending and in Balke's aria to the future, Müller reworks the production play from *Katzgraben* to his own *Lohndrücker*; stripped of the rosy haze of the tractor parade, his arias concentrate the white heat of utopia to pierce the affirmative fog gripping the Party.

While Müller's transgression of Party norms in *Die Umsiedlerin* was punished in the secretive manner of the "family business," from which he was expelled after quasi-kin such as 'party mothers' Weigel and Seghers failed to get him to submit to the paternalistic authority of the SED, *Der Bau* received public discussion in *Sinn und Form* in early 1966, even after the restricted discussion at the Eleventh Plenum of the SED Central Committee (hereafter "the Eleventh Plenum") in December 1965 and denunciations by SED loyalists.[84] The full force of SED censorship fell on films on contemporary GDR life, especially Kurt Maetzig's film of Manfred Bieler's novel, *Das Kaninchen bin ich* (I'm the Rabbit) and Frank Vogel's *Denk bloß*

[83] The ending of the *Sinn and Form* version maintains this pragmatic register, moving from Schlee's laughter in response to Donat's cowardice ("Der Bau," *Sinn und Form*, 226–7) to her offer to lie on his behalf, but the final version inserts a meditative exchange between laughter and concluding determination. In response to Donat's apocalyptic question "What do you want, a foundation cracked, a cooling tower burned, a star unhinged?", Schlee returns with the pragmatically rhetorical: "Who needs the stars?" before going on to offer both her lie and her assertion that the snow will melt and work will go on (136).

[84] "Gespräch mit Heiner Müller," *Sinn und Form* 18 (1966), 30–47. Wilfried Adling and Renate Geldner, "Zur Bedeutung des Konflikts für unsere sozialistische Gegenwartsdramatik," in the SED journal *Einheit* (July 1965), 95–103, dismissed the play with familiar charges of "bourgeois decadence" (103), while Hermann Kähler (author of *Gegenwart auf der Bühne*) argued in "Der Alltag und die Ideale – Bau oder Chaos," in the FDJ paper *Junge Welt*, 18/19 September 1965, 1–3, that the play was out of line because it juxtaposed a "bleak present" with a "distant future" communism (3).

nicht, ich heule (Just Don't Think I'll Bawl), which were screened at the Eleventh Plenum, and secondarily on historical revisions, such as Frank Beyer's film of Neutsch's *Spur der Steine*, which treated asocial workers as appealing cowboys and eschewed the uplifting resolution of the novel. Despite the stress on film, SED officers like future general secretary Erich Honecker criticized *Der Bau* for tarnishing the "clean state" ("sauberer Staat") GDR with its "vulgar bourgeois scepticism" ("spießbürgerlicher Skepticismus"), and singled out the phrase "ferry between ice age and communism [sic]" as evidence for Müller's disrespect for the "comprehensive development of socialism in the GDR."[85] While the SED indicted *Der Bau* and the films in Cold War terms for focusing on internal contradictions rather than affirming the SED's claim to defend "freedom, humanism, and democracy" against the alleged "militarism, imperialism, and neo-Nazism of West Germany," the discussants in *Sinn und Form*, including theatre scholars Werner Mittenzwei and Rudolf Münz, attempted to save the play for performance by placing it in a lineage of formal experiment from Mayakovsky to Brecht, as well as by praising the play's representation of "contradictions and their overcoming," while Müller tactically deployed the language of the SED on the "'GDR' achievement" (*Errungenschaft*) in the mouth of the regional SED secretary to authorize his critique of bureaucracy.[86]

Although Müller retrospectively dismissed this strategy as "good lying" and the discussion as a whole as an "interrogation" rather than a debate, the published text suggests a more complex negotiation

[85] Erich Honecker, Politburo Report to the Eleventh Plenum of the SED Central Committee, in Günter Agde, ed. *Kahlschlag: Das 11. Plenum des ZK der SED1965: Studien und Dokumente*, 2nd edn (Berlin: Aufbau, 2000), 238–51; here: 241–3. Honecker's misquotation – "communism" – misses the allusion to the Commune, but nonetheless registers Müller's critique of the pretensions of "actually existing socialism."

[86] Werner Mittenzwei, in "Gespräch mit Heiner Müller," 40; Müller, ibid., 31. For the multiple meanings of "Errungenschaft GDR," see Martin Ahrends, *Allseitig gefestigt: Stichwörter zum Sprachgebrauch der DDR* (Munich: dtv, 1989), 50.

of a restricted public sphere.[87] The editor, Wilhelm Girnus, may have been, as Müller asserts, "chief warrior against modern art," but Mittenzwei and Münz championed the play's critique of "conventional, traditional dramaturgy" and the way in which the "flexible epic linking of scenes" allowed for "different readings of the plot" and for making connections between social transformation and the "stations on Barka's path to the knowledge that the concept of happiness would need to be redefined through building socialism."[88] Despite a lively exchange, the conspiratorial tone of SED surveillance seeped into the debate, not only in charges of "decadence" made by party men but also in the discussants themselves resorting to similar tactics of exclusion by praising *Der Bau's* "productive" spirit at the expense of unnamed "DEFA films," condemned for "resignation," and by declining to name the relevant film, *Spur der Steine*.[89] This conspiratorial habitus also shaped Müller's recollection of the subsequent private discussion with the SED's "regional representative for ideology," who condemned the play, and the response of the Deutsches Theater, which dropped the play without its being formally banned.[90] For the rest of the decade, Müller made a living as a translator, adapting, among other

[87] Müller, *Krieg ohne Schlacht*, 198–9.

[88] Ibid., 197; "Gespräch mit Heiner Müller," 33 (Münz), 31–2 (Mittenzwei), 41–2 (Müller).

[89] Mittenzwei, "Gespräch mit Heiner Müller," 40. Unlike the other films withdrawn directly after the Eleventh Plenum, *Spur der Steine* had an authorized public screening – at the Workers' Festival in Potsdam in mid-1966 – and a few appearances at cinemas before being shelved until 1989; see Agde, ed., *Kahlschlag*, 380.

[90] Müller, *Krieg ohne Schlacht*, 201–2. The Party representative, Roland Bauer, criticized a passage in which the supervisor, Belfert, blames the engineer, Hasselbein, for not opposing him and claims that "I have learnt to obey, as if my head were bowed from a stammer attack, I almost have a right to my cowardice, where is your Hitler?" (122). His complaint was ostensibly not that Hitler's name appeared (and with it a reminder of the unfinished fascist debris under GDR foundations), but rather that Müller did not make clear who "Hitler" was and, presumably (but not explicitly), did not identify the current "class enemy."

texts, American folk songs criticizing the Cold War and the CIA, confining his theatrical activity to classical adaptations like *Philoktet* and *Oedipus Tyrannos*. Only with the publication of the first collection of Müller's plays in West Berlin in 1974 and in East Berlin in 1975 did *Der Bau* and other plays on GDR subjects re-emerge from the realm of secrecy into the public sphere.

By 1980, however, Müller had become a public intellectual. The thaw that opened the 1970s had allowed for productions in the GDR of Müller's provocative historical plays such as his series of sketches on the Nazi legacy, *Die Schlacht* (The Battle) and the now-historical *Die Bauern* (i.e. *Die Umsiedlerin*; Volksbühne, 1975). It also allowed Müller to travel to the United States and elsewhere, which in turn increased his prestige, foreign earnings, and ability to maneuver within SED constraints. At the same time, international legitimation of both Germanies by the Unitied Nations in 1973 helped to open the GDR to the world; the SED ceased official jamming of Western media and relaxed cross-border visits – albeit mostly in one direction only. Despite the freeze caused by the Biermann affair in 1976, and despite SED pressure, Müller was able to ensure that the Volksbühne showcased his preferred version of the play, without concessions to "illusory solutions to real problems."[91] The production, which opened in September 1980, was well received – even by the reviewer for *Neues Deutschland*, who argued that Müller's alleged "pessimism" was here replaced by an admirable "cutting severity" in exposing social as well as individual conflicts.[92] Although a more sceptical Hörnigk later implied that the production of this "unique play of the 1960s" was "historical" if not dated, the audience's intensely silent response

[91] Versions five and six, written in response to the Eleventh Plenum in an attempt to save the Deutsches Theater production, add the Regional Secretary's defense of the "Errungenschaft 'DDR,'" and allow for a happy ending by making Donat single and thus able to marry Schlee (Hörnigk, "'Bau'-Stellen," 50–1), the final published version (no. 7) cut these concessive modifications, to acknowledge but not to justify Belfert's and Donat's equivocations.
[92] Rainer Kerndl, "Bildkräftige Szenen von Prozeß revolutionärer Veränderungen," *Neues Deutschland* (11 September 1980), 7.

to Barka's equation of the Wall with a prison suggests, in Müller's account in an interview with Sylvère Lotringer a year after the premiere, that the production had current as well as historical significance, even though he argued later that the response was "boring . . . affirmative."[93]

The currency of this production and its successor in 1986 depended not only on actualizing GDR history on the level of everyday life as well as the epochal hinge "between ice age and commune," but also on establishing a critical distance between 1965 and 1980. Marquardt created this double perspective in part by deploying costume and music in the "cabarettish" style he had developed for Müller's *Schlacht*, a style which at times recalled the grotesquely dismembered clown in Brecht's *Badener Lehrstück vom Einverständnis* (Lehrstück on Consensus, 1928) rather than the analytical gests of the later parables or *Katzgraben*, while keeping the set to a minimalist black and white box framed with a grille that descended across the back of the stage over the course of the action, eventually sealing off the space.[94] Although Müller's biographer, Jan-Christof Hauschild, claims that the production focused on Schlee and was therefore "almost an emancipation play," the appearance of Schlee (Hildegard Alex), in a slick black trouser suit reminiscent of Diana Rigg in the 1960s British television series *The Avengers*, but with kewpie-doll eyelashes and make-up, at least complicated this scenario.[95] The make-up seems to correspond

<hr/>

93 The sceptic here is Hörnigk, "'Bau'-Stellen," 52; for Müller's comment on the audience, see "Walls" (1981), in *Germania* (New York: Semiotexte, 1990), 61, and his subsequent claim that the critical response was only affirmative (*Krieg ohne Schlacht*, 202).

94 English-language readers should note that the "kabarettistisch" style that Müller attributes to Marquardt (*Krieg ohne Schlacht*, 256) is a politically sharper cousin of the French cabaret; the former is grotesque where the latter may be merely sexy. Comments on the production are drawn from the 1980 program; the compilation edited by dramaturgs Otto Fritz Hayner and Lily Leder, *Heiner Müller: Bilder und Texte: Der Bau* (Berlin/GDR: Henschel, 1980) in the Akademie der Künste: Theaterdokumentation 527 (hereafter: AdK/TD 527), and the video of this production.

95 For the "emancipation play" see Hauschild, *Heiner Müller*, 235.

initially to Belfert's jaundiced view of her as a "ballerina" not an engineer (88). This expression and Donat's command to "dress appropriately" or else face the "Party leadership" (99) suggest the opposite
of emancipation.[96] Adding a hard hat and subtracting the jacket did
not make Alex's Schlee look like a worker; she retained the clownish
make-up and donned an overall only in the next-to-last scene. Cross-
casting Dreier as a woman (Ursula Karusseit) in a more heavily padded
pastiche of the worker's overall-cum-football uniform worn by the
other workers may have given her more muscle than her initial antagonist, the slighter Party secretary Donat, played by Michael Gwisdek
as a disheveled intellectual in workerist leather jacket. Despite this
possibility, she could not deliver her indictment directly to Donat on
stage, or to Belfert in the wings from her initial position hidden behind
the audience. Belfert's shifty position off stage anticipated his reprise
of the *Avengers* look in bowler-hat and dark glasses, suggesting clandestine spookiness rather than transparent management.[97] As Barka,

[96] Page references to "Der Bau," *Geschichten aus der Produktion*.
Photographs of rehearsals in 1979 show Alex in a skirt and high heels;
her costume was later changed to the pantsuit (TD 527). Despite
Hauschild's retrospective judgment, even enlightened critics such as
Martin Linzer of *Theater der Zeit* saw the pantsuit as excessive
"masculation" (*Vermännlichung*) rather than emancipation; see Linzer,
"Spur zwischen gestern und morgen," *Theater der Zeit* 6: 11 (1980), 12.

[97] Belfert's costume may well cite Magritte's bowler-hatted bureaucrat,
as dramaturgical notes imply (TD 527), but the dance by Belfert and
Hasselbein recalls the opening credit of *The Avengers*. The "secret
agent" motif may seem out of place on a construction site – until one
remembers the Cold War paranoia quoted in the play and in its
reception. Karl Grünberg's 1953 play *Golden fliesst der Stahl*, which
had a controversial revival under Castorf's direction in 1979, featured
CIA men disguised as steelworkers. The leather jacket has a long
association with socialist leaders, often modeled on Ernst Thälmann, a
KPD leader killed by the Nazis, whose likeness graced not only GDR
stages but also West German treatment of classical roles such as the
lead in Hans-Günther Heyme's 1986 revival of Schiller's *Wilhelm Tell*
in Stuttgart. In *Der Bau*, the epithet "Thälmann" is used by Bolbig, the
unreformed anarchist, to refer to Barka, but Dieter Montag wears the
same uniform as the rest of the crew, not the trademark leather jacket.

Dieter Montag defined the role of the stubborn but not always savvy worker he would carry over into his performance of the wage-buster Balke in the revival of *Der Lohndrücker* in 1988, albeit dis-illusioned, like the rest of the crew, with half-mask and white face as well as the padded uniform which he peels off during the course of the play. Hermann Beyer as Hasselbein "Hamlet" in tuxedo and white gloves would later bring his world-weary irony to the role of the director in *Der Lohndrücker* revival. In *Der Bau*, however, his patent for rationalizing construction, represented theatrically by his arrival in the supervisor's office on stilts, is cut down from under him by the supervisor who steals his patent, and he is left walking on his knees.[98]

This production followed a fine line between critique and parody, highlighting, as one critic put it, the "impure truth of history," and, in the words of the director, Marquardt, the as-yet-unbridged gap between "subjects" and the "system" that cannot function without subjective as well as social engagement.[99] It marked the distance between 1965 and 1980 in allusions to commodity culture, from the spy movie images to the ironic love scene between Donat and Schlee, which took place not in a picturesque resort but on a beach signified by deck-chairs but dis-illusioned by the truck from the construction site that still marked the upstage borderline. In the final scene, framed by the black grille against the white cyclorama, which indexed but did not attempt to imitate snow, Marquardt attempted to show not only the end of this play's relationships, especially among Donat, Schlee, and Barka, but also the start of new relationships. The white backdrop allowed in his view both for the catharsis of Barka's vision and for the temporary freeze in Schlee's; further growth, personal or social, can

[98] Hayner and Leder, eds., *Heiner Müller: Bilder und Texte: Der Bau*, 36 (image 24).

[99] Michael Hubert, with Fritz Marquardt and Rainer Vangermain, "Gespräch über die Bau-Inszenierung an der Volksbühne" (final previews on 28 and 29 June 1980), in Hayner and Leder, eds., *Heiner Müller: Bilder und Texte: Der Bau*, 31–5, here: 34; Marquardt's comment is on p. 31. Subsequent citations in the text to "Gespräch." An abbreviated version of this debate was published in *Theater der Zeit* 6: 11 (1980), 9–13.

come only from the recognition of the real limits on the present state of society; "screaming pain" alongside visions of utopia ("Gespräch," 35). But, whereas Müller's later plays, including *Die Schlacht* and *Hamletmaschine*, present a more subjective view of history, Marquardt argued that *Der Bau* retains a greater measure of objectivity and thus allowed, despite its parodic moments, for the historicization of the present as well as the past.

If Marquardt's *Bau* attempted to balance parody with social critique in the name of the socialization of subjectivity that had characterized the production play since *Katzgraben*, Frank Castorf's four-hour montage of scenes and sounds from *Der Bau* and other sources jettisoned any pretense of faithfully representing Müller or GDR society, while nonetheless satirizing the SED's cherished assumptions about the modernity of "actually existing socialism" on the eve of perestroika, the restructuring of the command economy that would ultimately undo state socialism.[100] Castorf had already earned a reputation for controversial productions of orthodox plays like Grünberg's *Golden fliesst der Stahl* (Golden Flows the Steel, 1979) as well as revivals of other plays by Müller like *Die Schlacht* and *Der Auftrag* (The Mission; Theatre Anklam, 1982, 1983).[101] Opening in November 1986 in Chemnitz/Karl-Marx-Stadt, the center of the GDR's brown coal industry in Müller's home region of Saxony, Castorf's *Bau* reeked of the notion already in the air if not in official documents: the failure of the command economy.[102] Using repetition of recurring leitmotifs

[100] Comments on the production, which opened at the Schauspielhaus, Karl-Marx-Stadt, in November 1986, are based on the program and dramaturgical notes (Adk/TD 535a), and the video of the production (TD 535b); on the discussion "Nachdenken über Kunst und Leben," *Theater der Zeit*, 42: 3 (1987), 26–30; and on conversations (in September 2000) with Dr Peter Ullrich, who participated in the 1980 discussion as secretary of the Theatre Union.

[101] See Jürgen Balitzki, "Von Donald D. zu Rosa L: Eine montierte Biographie," and "Regieverzeichnis," in *Castorf, der Eisenhändler: Theater zwischen Kartoffelsalat und Stahlgewitter* (Berlin: Links, 1995), 11–104, 234–7.

[102] On the environmental impact of brown coal, see Rudolf Bahro, *Elemente einer neuen Politik: zum Verhaltnis von Ökologie und*

from *Der Bau*, the recently revived *Umsiedlerin* (directed by B. K.
Tragelehn in Dresden in 1985), and other texts, Castorf highlighted
two themes. The first, the demolished or smashed foundation, had also
structured Marquardt's production; but the second, the substitution
of plastic (Bakelite in Müller's text) for the traditional construction
material wood, and its implications for GDR modernity, dominated
the production, in which the set was reduced to green and yellow plastic sheeting on the floor, cabaret curtains on the walls and a few props,
including newspapers, brooms and an accordion. The newspapers periodically spread over the floor and swept away amplified Barka's scorn-
ful comment, "Communism is for the newspapers" (92), as well as
Dreier's attack on paper; the sheeting transformed (Western) Bakelite,
the model material in the text, into GDR plastic (*Plast*) as *the* modern material, the foundation and the emblem, in new brightly colored
objects from furniture to radio and television sets, of the consolidation of consumer society in the 1960s after the drab years of scarcity
in the 1950s.[103]

Despite the historical material in the program, the performance
stripped away the social action of the collective, the work-crew, in
favor of encounters between two or three people that highlighted physical, subjective, affective associations rather than analytical interaction. As the aural signature of the production, the accordion brought
out the arias in Müller's text, while also infusing the most lyrical
moments with the kitschy associations of this *völkisch* instrument.
From the initial tangle between Donat (Kurt Naumann) and Belfert

Sozialismus (Berlin: Alemania, 1980) and Monika Maron's
documentary novel *Flugasche* (Frankfurt a.M.: Fischer, 1981).

[103] The program had a naked woman on the cover, superimposed on a
construction site in the same bright yellow as the set, and included
paeans to GDR plastic from Ulbricht downwards, as well as icons of
Western pop culture, such as the Beatles (also in yellow). Thomas
Beutelschmidt, *Sozialistische Audiovision: zur Geschichte der
Medienkultur in der DDR* (Potsdam: Verlag für Berlin-Brandenburg,
1995), 124–5, highlights the iconic value of bright plastic design in the
crafting of consumer modernism in the GDR.

(Wolfgang Sörgel) to Schlee's (Katherina Lange) opening dance with Hasselbein (Peter Lüdicke), after which her 1930s cabaret dress and fur coat are stripped by crew members Bolbig and Klamann (in a series of repetitive gestures recalling Pina Bausch), to Donat's retreat to a clapping game with a female regional secretary (Annie Stöger; the party representative as "mother of the masses" from the "Song of the Party"), the accordion provides a leitmotif of parodic pathos punctured by period sound-bites, from the GDR National Anthem at the opening – "*Auferstanden aus Ruinen*" (Arisen from the Ruins) – to Ulbricht's speech about the Wall before Barka calls the Wall a prison, as against the voice of Yuri Gagarin, the first man in space and the primary exemplar of the communist advance in the Cold War.[104] Schlee's changes of clothing, from the cabaret outfit to a 1960s red shift dress (accompanied by the blues number "I'm a little red rooster," and later by the love lament from *Carmen*), and finally to a schoolmarm outfit in which she lectures Donat about lying, mark a trajectory that passes through emancipation on the way, not to communism, but to the schoolmarm state. The performance ends with Barka's utopian aria, but accompanied here not by music but by a wind-up toy; the actors paper over the entire stage, the paper blows away as the toy whirrs, and Hasselbein give the victory sign in the void.

Castorf's deployment of the aural subconscious of the Western 1960s (especially the Beatles and Rolling Stones) to challenge the nostalgic sound of socialism (from *La Paloma* from the Spanish Civil War to the GDR's own *Auferstanden aus Ruinen*) is not new. Of two works published in 1978, Erich Loest's novel *Es geht seinen Gang* features a protagonist who finds in the Beatles an alternative to GDR drab, and Ulrich Plenzdorf's story "Kein Runter, Kein Fern" hinged on the desire of a disabled teenager, abused by his militarist father,

[104] Castorf mentions the influence of Bausch in "Nachdenken über Kunst und Leben," 28. Gagarin's pioneering orbit around the earth functioned in 1961 not only as a point scored against the West in the Cold War but also as a counter-image to the enclosure of the Wall. He appears in texts ranging from propaganda songs to Konrad Wolf's 1965 film of Christa Wolf's novel *Der geteilte Himmel* (Divided Heaven).

to join crowds gathered on the eastern side of the Brandenburg Gate to hear the Rolling Stones rumored to be playing on the Western side of the Wall. But Castorf's play with transnational consumer culture on the subsidized GDR stage represented not only a challenge to SED dogma but also a confrontation with the pressing gap between consumer desire and state ideology.[105] Consumption in this sense is not merely a site for individual gratification, but an alternative public sphere, in the sense that Oskar Negt and Alexander Kluge give that term, a realm in which the experience of alienation can act as "a kind of unconscious critique of . . . alienating social conditions."[106] Although the production's associative logic may have risked reducing the story of the construction site and history itself to recyclable material for ironic replay, the production's acknowledgment of the power of consumer longing spotlighted the command economy's crucial failure to recognize that producers are also consumers and that longing, like work, is a productive – and destructive – social force. Castorf's exploration of the social force of longing would find its echo in the revival of *Der Lohndrücker*, especially in Erich Wonder's prescient screen image of bananas and other tropical fruit projected over the nearly empty counter of the stage HO, and in the later documented banana craving of many GDR consumers pouring into West Berlin in November 1989.[107]

[105] See comments by the director Wolfgang Hauswald, the academic Erika Stephan, and the critic Peter Ullrich in "Nachdenken über Kunst und Leben."

[106] Oskar Negt and Alexander Kluge, "Public Sphere and Experience," in *Selections*, trans. Peter Labanyi, *October* 46 (1988): 67. For analysis of the failures of the command economy from critical GDR perspectives, see Wilfried Ettl, Jürgen Jünger, and Dieter Walter, "Von der Zentralverwaltungswirtschaft zur sozialen Marktwirtschaft," and Thomas Blanke, "Versuch, das Scheitern des Sozialismus zu erklären," in *DDR: Ein Staat vergeht*, ed. Thomas Blanke and Rainer Erd (Frankfurt a.M.: Fischer, 1990), 171–82 and 183–204.

[107] On the (Austrian) designer Wonder's prescient representation in 1988 of the GDR as a "banana republic" (Müller's phrase), see "Bananenlicht" (conversation between Müller and Wonder, 20 June

Archeology and the farce of history: the swan song of the GDR

Opening on 29 January 1988, a few weeks after the controversial Luxemburg Day demonstration for free speech that led dissidents like Freya Klier and Stefan Krawcyk to prison and exile, Müller's revival of *Der Lohndrücker* juxtaposed the historical alienation of workers in the early years of absolute scarcity with the present disaffection of intellectuals and others with the relative poverty of the SED in retreat. While Czechoslovakia and Hungary responded to the new Soviet line on glasnost (openness) and perestroika (restructuring) by promoting economic reforms and greater freedom of expression, the SED hierarchy increased repression and publicly disdained its alliance with the Soviet Union by banning the magazine *Sputnik* and claiming that the GDR had no need of glasnost or perestroika, despite evident stagnation.[108] At the International Writers' Congress in Berlin in mid-1987, Müller had praised Mikhail Gorbachev's program as an "incredible renaissance of hope" for "a real alternative to capitalism," as against the "bureaucratic treatment of art, literature, theatre" and other "relics of Stalinism."[109] Despite this and other expressions of hope, Müller directed the revival of *Der Lohndrücker* in an archeological rather than utopian mode. Citing a remark attributed to Brecht in 1948 about the risky business of building new houses before clearing out old cellars, Müller's production unearthed the prehistory of the GDR, to make manifest the unprocessed debris of history, the mix of Nazi inheritance with anti-fascist aspirations that had been denied

---

1993), in *Regie: Heiner Müller,* ed. Martin Linzer and Peter Ullrich (Berlin: Zentrum für Theaterdokumentation, 1993), 52.

[108] Mikhail Gorbachev became Soviet Communist Party general secretary in 1985 and instituted perestroika the same year, hoping to diversify the command economy to allow for production of scarce consumer goods. *Sputnik,* published by the Soviet Foreign Affairs Ministry, was banned in the GDR in November 1988, but the SED had already impounded issues with articles critical of Soviet policy. On stagnation in the GDR in the 1980s, see Weber, *Geschichte der DDR,* 313–33.

[109] Müller, "Berlin – ein Ort für den Frieden" (6 May 1987), in *Heiner Müller Material* (Leipzig: Reclam, 1990), 112.

by the official line.[110] This unprocessed historical residue, pressing, in Marx's apt phrase, "like a nightmare on the brains of the living," was realized on stage not only in the workers' costumes – overalls patched with items from both Wehrmacht and Red Army uniforms – but also in Dieter Montag's embodiment in his hunched shoulders of the burden carried by the model worker on a socialist construction site (fig. 4), which replayed a more somber version of the more rebellious Barka he had played in Marquardt's *Bau*.[111] The program supplemented this critique with material judged too provocative for performance: the juxtaposition of "hero of labor" Hans Garbe with his contemporary, gangster and dandy Werner Gladow – who was tried for robbery, smuggling, and murder the same year Garbe was honored, and executed a year later – and with the uprising of 17 June 1953, suggested the power of uncontrolled social energy whose force could not be diverted with mere charges of asocial hooliganism.[112]

Müller's archeological dramaturgy entailed more than digging up inert historical remains, however. Treating archeology in Michel Foucault's genealogical sense, the production probed the "conditions

---

[110] For Müller's comments on the archeological principle, see his conversation with dramaturg Alexander Weigel, "Etwas für das Programmheft," reproduced in *Regie: Heiner Müller*, 26–8.

[111] Karl Marx, "The Eighteenth Brumaire of Louis Napoleon," in *Marx–Engels Reader*, ed. Richard Tucker (New York: Norton, 1971), 595. The costumes and Montag's performance are clear in the video of the performance (AdK/TD:144b) but also noted by critics: see Carena Schlewitt, "Dieter Montag", and Marianne Streisand and Bernd Kott "Wieder eine Botschaft," in *Regie: Heiner Müller*, 38, 48–50.

[112] A newspaper report on Gladow was to be read against another extolling the achievements of the heroes of labor over the bodies of exhausted workers collapsed on the floor (scene 8d). Although recorded by the video of the preview, the second report was cut before the premiere. Nonetheless, the program included photographs of Gladow and his gang with their trademark silk ties, together with Gladow's statement to the court and comments from his mother: Weigel, ed., Program Notes to *Der Lohndrücker* (Berlin/GDR: Henschel, 1988), n.p. Charges against the gang included smuggling during the Soviet blockade of Berlin as well as robbing wealthy jewelers in West Berlin.

Fig. 4. "The Model Worker's Burden": Dieter Montag in *Der Lohndrücker* (1956) by Heiner Müller. Adapted and directed by the author (Berlin 1988). Set design by Erich Wonder. Photograph by Sybille Bergemann.

of emergence" of GDR institutions and ideologies as well as the "monument" of the state, in particular the SED appropriation of a workforce disciplined by the Nazis as well as the Soviet glorification of the model worker.[113] It also exposed the narrative and dramatic discourses supporting and undermining this monument, highlighting the mythological as well as ideological dimensions of these discourses and their embodiment in political as well as theatrical performances. The deconstruction of mythology drove the anti-heroic portrayal of the weary workers, whose sloping shoulders contradicted the heroic upward gaze of the anti-fascist and stakhanovite poster. The stage picture also acknowledged the power of myth: the blazing red opening of the furnace at the center of the stage floor recalled the tanks in which workers had served Hitler's army and also suggested the legend of Prometheus, who stole fire from the gods to unleash creative productivity in humanity.[114] The red hands of the workers glowed against their blackened faces, suggesting mythic power against the naturalistic reproduction of soot and sweat.[115] Juxtaposed with the image-repertoire of classical mythology in three dimensions was the two-dimensional representation of socialist myths. The upstage door to the bureaucrats' offices, likewise red, suggested a zone of danger, like the red telephones on the desks of Cold War presidents. Periodically on screens, images of 1980s Berlin, especially the television tower behind the exhausted Barka (see fig. 4, p. 125), showed the result of the construction of socialism, while the portrait of Stalin as supervising gaze and ghost in the machine appearing occasionally stage left

[113] Michel Foucault, "The Discourse on Language", trans. Rupert Swyer; appendix to The Archeology of Knowledge, trans. Alan Sheridan (New York: Pantheon, 1972), 230; Müller, "Etwas für das Programmheft," 26.

[114] On the resonance of the myths of Prometheus in this play, see Stefan Schnabel, "Szenische Mythographie," Theater Zeitschrift 30 (1991): 109–32.

[115] Make-up man Wolfgang Utzt used the graphite grime observed on power-plant construction workers as a basis for the make-up, noting that the black stuff appeared to penetrate the skin and turn men into machines; against the black faces, the blood-red hands absorbed the gaze that would have gone to the natural red of the workers' mouths. See Utzt, "Masken," in Regie: Heiner Müller, 60.

Fig. 5. Visions of abundance and the HO queen in *Der Lohndrücker* (1988).
Photograph by Sybille Bergemann.

was challenged by the fantastic picture of abundant fruit above the
HO stand stage right, the HO "queen" in unlikely party clothes stage
left, and workers lined up for rations in the middle (fig. 5). The phantasmagoric image of overabundance made manifest a hidden history
in the GDR of ideological window-dressing manifest in the actual HO
window displays – displays of an abundance at odds with actually
scarce consumer goods.[116]

The performance framed by these images was stylized, even
ritualistic at times, but sharpened rather than defused the audience's
focus on the substance of the action. The Director's call for "sacrifice

[116] In "Schaufenster des sozialistischen Konsums," in *Akten. Eingaben.
Schaufenster: Die DDR und ihre Texte*, ed. Alf Lüdke and Peter Becker
(Berlin: Akademieverlag, 1997), 91–118, Katherine Pence documents
both HO fakery and popular resentment at the discrepancy between
propaganda and actual goods for sale, especially after the currency
reform of 1948, the period dramatized by *Der Lohndrücker*.

for socialism" was ambiguously anticipated in the first scene, "Arbeiterbier", not only by the workers' enforced abstinence from beer they cannot afford, but by the portrayal of a visiting secret service man as an insatiable idol breathing smoke and consuming beer. The call was also interrupted by the interpellation of two actors reciting "Der Horatier," Müller's 1965 dramatic poem on state violence by way of the story of the Horatian who saves ancient Rome by killing his adversary, only to start an internal battle by killing his sister (who was betrothed to the adversary), after which the workers drink their beer with Nazi salutes to the Communist holiday 1 May.[117] Drinking schnapps rather than "worker beer," the Director and Schorn later toast Balke as "our best horse" (scene 6b), but their drinking indicates weakness rather than power. The depiction of a party and a state both autocratic and ineffectual spoke directly to the moment of 1988, albeit with materials from 1948 and 1953. In the penultimate scene (14), "Arbeitermacht" (Worker Power), Schorn, played by Michael Gwisdek (recapitulating his Donat from Der Bau to play Schorn as a hesitant figure rather than the authoritative Schorn from Der Lohndrücker of 1956), urges Balke to denounce the furnace saboteurs and thus to repeat in the name of socialism the very act of denunciation that he committed against Schorn under the Nazi regime. Schorn's previously encouraging words "the factories are ours and the state and its power. We'll lose it if we don't use it" (40/52) were accompanied in this performance by the sudden sound of tanks (and thus echoing the repression of 17 June) through the red door, so that Balke's decision came as if coerced. The violence of this coercion resurfaced in the final image where, instead of the provisional reconciliation between Balke and Karras, Balke repeated his earlier rejection, "I can't work with Karras",

---

[117] Müller, "Der Lohndrücker," 15; "The Scab," 28. Weber's translation of *Geheimrat* as "privy councillor" is at best anachronistic; "secret service man" better captures the status of pre-Stasi surveillance c. 1948. "The Horatier" recalls Müller's 1976 sketch of Nazi and Communist brothers in "Die Schlacht" but also alludes to Stalin's slaughter of alleged internal enemies as soon as the heroic defense of the Soviet Union in the Second World War was over: Martin Linzer, "Trilogie des Umbruchs," in *Regie: Heiner Müller*, 15.

and Schorn repeated his question "Who asked me if I could work with you?", while Montag and Gwisdek appeared locked in a an attitude half-strangulation, half-embrace.

In a controversial insertion between these scenes, Gwisdek sat at his desk in a gloomy posture that directly quoted his Donat in *Der Bau* as he recited the dramatic poem, "Centaurs: a Horror Story [*Greuelmärchen*] about a Saxon, Gregor Samsa," the fourth section of Müller's *Wolokolamsker Chaussee* (Volokolamsk Highway: the road followed east to Moscow by Hitler's army and later west to the Soviet satellite states by the Red Army). The speaker in the poem is, like Schorn, a Party secretary, but, unlike Schorn, he is confronted with his own superfluity in a utopian or dystopian dream in which there is "No incident, no threat to order / No crime. Our people are / As they appear in books and papers / That I'd like to see. Or rather not see / This is the end", to which an unnamed "comrade superior" responds with a call to create enemies because "the state needs enemies like the mill the corn / the state with no enemies is no longer a state." These lines recall Brecht's poem on 17 June, in which he noted ironically that "the people / Had squandered [*verscherzt*] the trust of the state / And could only through redoubled effort / Win it back" and that "Perhaps it would be easier if the state / Dissolved the people and elected another."[118] When the secretary tries to follow his superior in flight out of the window, he cannot move:

> I had grown into my desk / And my desk into me. . . .
> Thus does consciousness make *sitzfleisch* [bureaucratic bums]
>   of us all
> My desk is my Caucasus, my cross
> The Communards' dream from I to We. . . .
> The marriage of function and functionary
> 'Til death do us part And perhaps

[118] Müller, *Die Schlacht. Wolokolamsker Chaussee* (Frankfurt a.M: Verlag der Autoren, 1988), 59, 60. Brecht, "Die Lösung," *Werke* 10: 1009–10; my translation. For a freer but misleading version, see "The Solution," trans. John Willett, *Bertolt Brecht: Poems* (London: Methuen, 1976), 440.

Death will simply not take place
But humanity's dream of eternal life. . . .
Everyone so to speak his own monument
The class standpoint is the monument's base
Good wood and dialectic at a standstill.[119]

The lapidary assemblage of allusions in this passage begins with the
translation of Hamlet's meditation on paralysis into a bureaucrat's
Kafkaesque lament, juxtaposed with the visual citation of Gwisdek's
more optimistic portrayal of Donat in 1980, and ends with Benjamin's
image of the dialectic at a standstill freezing the contradictions of history, rendered visible on stage by the paralyzed functionary watched
by the worker (Montag) on the one hand and the director, Hermann
Beyer, with a secret service look reminiscent of *Der Bau* (1980) on
the other (fig. 6). Along the way it evokes and disavows the utopia
of the Commune and the dystopia of human flesh become machine,
as well as the counter-image of the wild and mobile centaur in the
immobilized functionary, speaking to the future as well as the past
and present of the socialist state and its audience, and, in Müller's
later judgment, of the failure of that future.[120]

In ironic reversal of Marx, Müller dubbed this moment in the
performance the farce *before* the tragedy that would be the collapse
of the GDR.[121] In retrospect, however, farce and tragedy seem closely
entwined, not only in these stage images but in the later actions in
the world and the media that they eerily anticipate: from the scene of

---

[119] Müller, *Die Schlacht. Wolokolamsker Chaussee*, 63–5. The bureaucrat
fused with his desk draws on the myth of the centaur, half-man,
half-horse, as well as on Kafka's story about the bureaucrat Gregor
Samsa's metamorphosis into a cockroach; but Müller's claim (65) that
"centaur" is Greek for red tape (Ger. *Amtsschimmel*, office mold) is
unlikely. Κένταυρος (centaur) has no etymological link to κεντηνάριος
(*centenarios*, officer drawing a salary of 100,000 *sesterces*); see Henry
George Liddle *et al.*, *Greek–English Lexicon* (Oxford: Clarendon Press,
1968), 938–9.
[120] Streisand and Kott, "Wieder eine Botschaft," 48; Müller, *Krieg ohne
Schlacht*, 344.
[121] Ibid.

Fig. 6. The paralyzed functionary and the secret service man. Michael Gwisdek and Hermann Beyer (right) in *Der Lohndrücker*. Photograph by Sybille Bergemann.

consumers in search of bananas in the immediate wake of the fall of the Wall in November 1989 to the thousands of private *Trauerspiele* playing out the loss of jobs, autonomy, and a sense of identity in greater Germany. The characters in this play are less subjects of socialist modernization than objects of a *post-modernization* in which most workers lack agency, heroic or otherwise. This post-socialist post-modernization differs from post-modern capitalism in that it is characterized not by the surfeit of commodities and the apparent evaporation of the current of history but rather the reverse: the ongoing and anachronistic scarcity of commodities in a region still burdened by its unfinished history. For the citizens of the former GDR, this burden of anachronism has been felt above all as a need for historical overtaking, a demand for the pleasures of consumption rather than, as Müller put it, "pleasure in productivity."[122] The promise of a synchronization and a share in the abundance of the West has not been

---

[122] Heiner Müller, *Gesammelte Irrtümer* (Frankfurt: Verlag der Autoren, 1988), 189.

fulfilled, however, but remains as it were in a different – and inaccessible – time-zone. The present moment is marked by the persistent underdevelopment of Eastern Europe as well as of the new *Länder* of a Germany that has been officially united for more than a decade, but remains economically, socially, and psychically divided. In this context, post-modernization cannot replace temporal discontinuities with spatial coexistence, but rather leaves the ruins of history and their inhabitants alienated from and resentful of Western affluence.[123] The alienation of masses of people from the culture of abundance might caution us against a premature celebration of the triumph of capitalist culture. Our late modern era of declining production, closing borders, and the violent scapegoating of ethnic minorities appears to be the mirror image of international socialism or, indeed, of global capitalism, but it also exposes the illusions of the so-called free world and of the Cold War teleologies that can no longer be sustained in a world that is post-imperial in the sense that even the self-described single super-power is far from super-powerful. In this world of scarcity and uneven development, Brecht's and Müller's "stories from the production line" represent the *disassembly* not only of socialist utopias in Central and Eastern Europe but also of anti-utopian assertions of the "end of history" closer to home.

[123] The idea that post-modernism privileges spatial rather than temporal relations is now a critical commonplace. For the locus classicus of this argument, see Fredric Jameson, *Postmodernism, or the Cultural Logic of Late Capitalism* (Durham, NC: Duke University Press, 1990), 3–54. For the ramifications of post-modernization in the late GDR, see Marc Silberman, "Postmodernized Brecht?", *Theatre Journal* 45 (1993): 1–19.

3 Broadcasting (a)socialism: Brecht, Müller, and *Radio Fatzer*

In "Fatzer ± Keuner," a lecture to the International Brecht Society in 1979, Heiner Müller pointed to a link made by Brecht between the Fatzer project from the 1920s and the unfinished Büsching/Garbe project on the model worker in the 1950s.[1] Although Müller alluded also to Brecht's *Keuner Stories*, about a cunning survivor of the "dark days" of the 1930s and 1940s, as well as the stage production of his own edition of Brecht's fragment *Der Untergang des egoisten Fatzer* (The Downfall of the Egoist Fatzer) by former GDR directors Manfred Karge and Matthias Langhoff in Hamburg in 1978, he had a broader context in view.[2] His emphasis on Brecht's attempts to link egoist and

[1] Heiner Müller, "Fatzer ± Keuner," *Brecht-Jahrbuch 1980*, ed. Reinhardt Grimm and Jost Hermand (Frankfurt a.m.: Suhrkamp, 1981), 14–21; published in English as "To Use Brecht Without Criticizing Him Is to Betray Him," trans. Marc Silberman, *Theater* 17: 2 (1986), 31–3. Brecht makes the connection between the form of *Fatzer* and the proposed chronicle form for the Garbe material in a journal entry from 10 July 1951, but his use of the name of Büsching, one of the anarchic deserters in *Fatzer*, as an alternative name for the model worker suggests a more substantial link: *Werke* 27: 327.

[2] Brecht links *Fatzer* and *Keuner* first by using the latter's name to replace the character Koch in later drafts of the *Fatzer* fragments, as indicated in the notes in *Werke* (10: 1115–20) and second, by emphasizing the "high technical standard" of *Fatzer*'s deployment of the chronicle form in a journal note of 25 February 1939 (26: 330) when he was working on the *Keuner* stories. Frank-Patrick Steckel's staging of the *Fatzer* fragments at the Schaubühne am Halleschen Ufer in West Berlin in March 1976 used a montage of texts prepared by dramaturg Wolfgang Storch, based on selections from the Brecht

model worker pointed the predominantly Western audience to the signal contradiction in GDR cultural politics, between the anti-fascist revolutionary and the loyal socialist functionary, which Brecht himself embodied. The revolutionary, Müller argued, had become frozen in the "father figure" cast in cement by "socialist cultural politics" (31). Brecht had private doubts about the SED, but nonetheless made public his commitment to the "great production [plan]" ("große Produktion") of socialism. This submission to Party discipline threatened to turn the egoist researcher (*Forscher*) into a functionary. The Fatzer fragments and their revision over the years from the 1920s to Brecht's death in 1956 trace their author's preoccupation with a key historical and dramatic problem: the contradiction between the individual experimenter whose individualism may be asocial and the socialist organic intellectual demanded by the embryonic socialist state.³

Müller's speech relocates this contradiction to the context not of dissident GDR theatres such as the Volksbühne, but rather of

archive edited by Reiner Steinweg, *Brechts Modell der Lehrstücke: Zeugnisse, Diskussionen, Erfahrungen* (Frankfurt a.M.: Suhrkamp, 1976). Müller's edition was subsequently produced in Jean Jourdheuil's French translation by Bernard Sobel at the Théâtre de Gennevilliers in 1981. The US premiere took place in Chicago in 1996, translated and directed by Stefan Brün, grandson of Fritz Kortner, actor and Brecht associate in the 1920s. Judith Wilke provides a thorough analysis of text and sources in her doctoral dissertation, *Brechts "Fatzer" Fragment: Lektüren zum Verhältnis vom Dokument und Kommentar* (Bielefeld: Aisthesis, 1998), but only supplementary chapters on productions in *West* Germany, and on Müller's staging at the Berliner Ensemble (BE) in unified Berlin in 1993.

³ For the concept of the organic intellectual as the indigenous representative of the emerging class, see Antonio Gramsci, "On Intellectuals," in *Selections from the Prison Notebooks*, ed. and trans. Quentin Hoare and Geoffrey Nowell Smith (London: Lawrence and Wishart, 1971), 12ff. Gramsci's reflections on the ambiguous nature of hegemony, at once the exercise of power by means of an enforced consensus and the goal of general social and political legitimacy striven for by counter-hegemonic groups, are peculiarly appropriate for characterizing the enforced consensus of a post-war Communist bloc that typified the founding moment of the GDR.

the mass-media institutions more directly under state control, especially radio.[4] Although the SED had by the 1970s subordinated radio
to television as the primary instrument of propaganda, radio played
an important role from the outset in the Leninist model of media
directed to "shape our mental and cultural life" and the "future of
socialism."[5] Days after the end of the Second World War in May
1945, even before the restructuring of the media, the authorities in
the Soviet Occupation Zone revived cultural as well as news programming on Berliner Rundfunk. This station would later broadcast Müller's critical revision of Brecht's *Fatzer.* By the 1950s radio
had become a key instrument for GDR nation-building, as the slogan "Jawohl, der deutsche demokratische Rundfunk kann sich hören
lassen" (Yes! German Democratic Radio can be heard) makes clear.[6]
In the 1960s, after the building of the Berlin Wall, the GDR broadcast cultural and political programming in the name of international

---

4 The State Committees for Radio and for Television reported to the
 Press Office of the Cabinet as well the Ministry of Agitation and
 Propaganda, rather than to the Ministry of Culture (founded in 1954);
 see Reiner Stein, *Vom Fernsehen und Radio der DDR zur ARD*
 (Marburg: Tectum, 2000), 38–40.
5 For the subordination of radio and television to the overall SED goal of
 shaping our "mental and cultural life" and the "future of socialism,"
 see the Politburo's statement of 7 November 1972 in *Die Aufgaben der
 Agitation und Propaganda bei der weiteren Verwirklichung der
 Beschlüsse der VIII. Parteitage der SED* (Berlin: Dietz, 1973), 84–6.
 For the argument that mass media should develop socialist society and
 the socialist human being, see the GDR edition of Lenin, *Agitation
 und Propaganda* (Berlin: Dietz, 1973), 212; for Lenin's influence on
 SED management of GDR radio, see Adelheid von Saldern and Inge
 Marssolek's introduction to *Radio in der DDR der fünfziger Jahre,*
 which they edited (Tübingen: diskord, 1998), 11–16.
6 On the restitution of music programming on radio in May 1945, see
 Manfred Jäger, *Kultur und Politik in der DDR: 1945–1990* (Cologne:
 Edition Deutschland Archiv, 1995), 5. "Jawohl, der deutsche,
 demokratische Rundfunk kann sich hören lassen," quoted as the
 epigraph to *Radio in der DDR der fünfziger Jahre,* 11, was the slogan of
 DDR[adio] from the 1950s; the initials "DDR" stand for the republic as
 well as the radio association.

anti-imperialism against the Voice of America and other Cold War institutions, while jamming access to these Western sources at home. Although Erich Honecker's "thaw" of 1971 ended the jamming, his government reiterated the instrumental role of the media by, among other measures, renaming the over-the-border broadcaster the Voice of the GDR ("Stimme der DDR") to highlight its opposition to the Voice of America and other instances of "imperialist hegemony."[7] The SED's expatriation of Wolf Biermann in 1976 while he was on tour in the FRG demonstrated the limits of tolerance: those who supported Biermann found their work, including television films, shelved without appeal.[8]

In this context the emancipatory potential of technology, especially media technology, had, in Müller's view, been stymied by the "imbecility [Verblödung] of the media." A paternalistic top-down apparatus of functionaries obeying the directions of the state leaves no room for any critical refunctioning (Umfunktionierung) of the media or the message. Against these "petrified conditions [versteinerten Verhältnissen]," Müller invokes Brecht's Fatzermaterial as a gesture of research and self-understanding, but also as an unpredictable and dangerous moment of anarchy imported from the turbulent years of the late Weimar Republic, which might puncture the effigy of the Staat der Sekretäre (State for [Party] Secretaries), in the stagnation known as "actually existing socialism." The experimental character of Fatzer – Great War deserter, anarchist rebel, and finally, perverse antagonist of his erstwhile comrades in arms – shatters in Müller's view the petrified self-image of the "actually existing socialist" state. As an asocial

---

[7] The claims for the Voice of the GDR against "imperialist hegemony" were reiterated in 1987 in a GDR textbook by Erwin Pracht et al., Ästhetik der Kunst (Berlin/GDR: Dietz, 1987), 79.

[8] On the impact of the Biermann affair on the media, see Gunter Holzweissig, Massenmedien in der DDR (Berlin: Holzapfel, 1984), 102–30, esp. comments on the commissioning and subsequent suppression of Geschloßene Gesellschaft (Private Party, 1978), a television fiction film about the alienation and banalization of intellectual and personal life in the GDR as seen through "scenes of a marriage" between two GDR professionals, directed by Frank Beyer (127–8).

protagonist, Fatzer flirts with solidarity rather than committing to it: he turns to his comrades, to other foot-soldiers on both sides of the Great War and, more vaguely, to the protagonists of the abortive German socialist revolution of November 1919, but ultimately refuses to align himself with any collective, even if that refusal kills him. Moreover, his downfall resists inscription as a deterrent in which authoritative commentary (including Brecht's) could explain away the asocial rebel as a socialist lesson. As Müller sees it, the anarchist moments in the *Fatzer* project critique the authoritarian moment in Brecht's theoretical practice as well as the domestication of Brecht as a socialist classic.

The transformation of this oblique textual critique of the SED line into a publicly broadcast challenge was delayed, however. Karge and Langhoff staged Müller's edition of *Fatzer* in Hamburg with Müller's participation and with the approval of the Brecht heirs. The GDR theatrical premiere took place at the BE only in 1987 without direct input from Müller. As a member of the SED Central Committee as well as a "special collaborator" for the Stasi, BE director Manfred Wekwerth was able to pre-empt the broadcast of the radio version on Berliner Rundfunk, with which Müller was working closely.[9] The

---

9 Müller worked as dramaturg at the BE under the direction of Ruth Berghaus, who ran the theatre from Helene Weigel's death in 1971 until Brecht's daughter Barbara Brecht-Schall restored Wekwerth in 1975; he then ran the theatre until the end of the GDR in 1990. In Müller's view, Berghaus's tenure was the "only period after Brecht's death when the BE was alive. Under Wekwerth, it became a closed space, in which doctrinal history [*Kirchengeschichte*] was restored"; see Müller, *Krieg ohne Schlacht*, 249. This view is corroborated by Joachim Walther, *Sicherungsbereich Literatur: Schriftsteller und Staatssicherheit in der Deutschen Demokratischen Republik*, Analysen und Dokumente: Wissenschaftliche Reihe der Bundesbeauftragten für die Unterlagen des Staatssicherheitsdienst der ehemaligen DDR (scholarly series published by the Federal Authority responsible for the former GDR's State Security Records), vol. 6 (Berlin: Ch. Links Verlag, 1996), 622–5. Wekwerth claims that he dismissed the Stasi on the sole occasion that he was approached during Brecht's lifetime (in interview with Thomas Grimm, *Was von den Träumen blieb: Eine Bilanz der sozialistischen*

BE production, directed by Wekwerth in collaboration with Joachim Tenschert, starred Brecht's son-in-law Ekkehart Schall as a middle-aged version of the young anarchist. This line-up appeared to legit-imate the eponymous anti-hero as a national hero comparable with Faust and thus reinforced the status of the Brecht repertoire at a time when the BE had long lost any pretensions to critique. By contrast, the radio version, in which Brecht's granddaughter Johanna Schall shared the role of speaker with Müller, reflected Brecht's interest in the revo-lutionary potential of radio in the 1920s and his engagement, from the 1920s until the 1950s, with the contradiction between asocial rebel and socialist state, as well as Müller's interpretation of the thematic and institutional resonances of Brecht in the GDR in the late 1980s. The radio production of *Fatzer* exploited radio's marginality (and thus its relative neglect by the SED) as well as Müller's prominence to generate critical interference in the SED's propaganda echo chamber at a time, in the late 1980s, when cultural policy had lapsed from systematic censorship to inconsistent suppression of or concessions to dissent. This pattern was more disorganized than the rigid adher-ence to the party line of the 1950s and 1960s, but was not so much "chaotic" (as Manfred Jäger maintains) as a variation on the paternal-ist alternation of despotism and benevolence that characterized the "family business" of the Party from the outset.[10]

Utopie (Berlin: Siedler, 1993), 135). Walther argues that he was promoted to "secret collaborator for special missions" (624–5) shortly before the death of Brecht's widow, Helene Weigel, in 1970, and went on to hold key positions including the chair of the Academy of Arts.

[10] On the "chaotic" character of SED cultural policy in the 1980s, see Jäger, *Kultur und Politik in der DDR: 1945–1990*, 187–263, and on the logic of paternalism in GDR culture as "family business," Kruger, "'Wir treten aus unseren Rollen heraus'," 189–97. Despite getting permission for a trip to the USA in the 1970s after a decade of enforced marginalization, Müller publicly criticized SED repression by signing the petition against Biermann's expatriation. The denunciation of Müller in 1993 by an erstwhile acolyte, Dieter Schultze, relied ironically on Müller's acknowledgment that he had used Stasi contacts to get Schultze an exit visa in 1983, and was rebutted by two colleagues, B. K. Tragelehn and Lothar Trolle, who argued that Müller

Whereas the theatrical *Fatzer* invoked the faded glories of the BE, *Radio Fatzer*, punctuated by the industrial music of Einstürzende Neubauten, the West German band whose name roughly ("Imploding Prefabs") recalls the post-war housing blocks that were to have marked the arrival of a distinctively *GDR* Modern style, heralds the future, not only through East/West collaboration but also in the deployment of a relatively low-tech and low-profile medium, rather than the dominant institution of television, to realize the drama of the collapsing state. In broadcasting *asocialism* rather than either "actually existing socialism" or any easily anarchic rejection of it, *Radio Fatzer* counters the emphatic ideological affirmation of the SED contained in the slogan "Yes! German Democratic Radio can be heard," not by shouting a simple "no" but rather by claiming the right to change the terms under which "yes" would indeed be democratic, rather than merely centralist, and in which the people, not the Party, would decide. Müller reiterates this utopian view as he reads from Brecht's text at the end of the broadcast: "the state is not finished / allow us to change it / according to the conditions of our lives" and, finally, "may the order of things please you, regulator / the state no longer needs you / hand it over" (*Werke* 10: 513).[11] Müller and his collaborators not only challenge the

protected dissidents. In "Literatur und Staatssicherheit," *Frankfurter Allgemeine Zeitung* (28 January 1993), Frank Schirrmacher argued that Western critics denouncing Müller's dealings with the Stasi had invested these dealings with the "seductiveness of the forbidden" and thus were deceived by their own creation. For an example, see Michael Merschmeier who, in "Heiner und 'Heiner'. Im Dickicht der Stasi. Ein deutsches Leben?", *Theater Heute* (February 1993), 2–3, regretted that Müller did not live up to the cynical persona fostered by influential Western sources like *Theater Heute*. Prodded by this debate, Müller added documents on his Stasi contacts to the second edition of his memoir *Krieg ohne Schlacht* (1994). For a review of this controversy, see Jan-Christian Hauschild, *Heiner Müller oder das Prinzip Zweifel: eine Biographie* (Berlin: Aufbau, 2001), 473–83.

[11] In the current edition of Brecht's *Werke*, this meditation on the state forms part of the last fragment of the play from the fifth round of revisions before the selection of texts called *Fatzerkommentar*. As the editors indicate, this round of revisions took place at roughly the same

undemocratic centralism of the SED state but also criticize authoritarian elements in Brecht's version of Leninist notions of media as well as in his aggressive, even brutal, depiction of the deserters. This discussion of *Radio Fatzer* in the context of GDR media institutions thus complements the analysis of Brecht's and Müller's contributions to GDR theatre in the preceding chapters and extends the overall investigation of the critical and post-imperial dimension of this practice.

Completing the state's "unfinished music": revolution, radio theory and the teacherly attitude

Before locating *Radio Fatzer* in and against the repression of the "actually existing socialist" state, we should begin by re-examining the tension between the Leninist and the asocial protagonist of and in Brecht. The tensions between socialized production and individual whim, discipline and desire, which reached a crisis for Brecht after the workers' uprising dealt a blow to GDR socialism in 1953, emerge already in his essay on radio written after the crisis of capitalism in 1929. Conceived at about the same time as the first Fatzer fragments and the *Lehrstücke* and published in 1932, Brecht's essay on "The Radio as Institution [*Apparat*] of Communication" (1932) turns on the crucial distinction between radio as a functional means of *broadcasting* or propaganda and radio as a means of *communication* and interaction:

> Radio should be transformed from a distribution apparatus into an institution of communication. It would conceivably be the most extraordinary communication institution of public life . . . , i.e. if its task were understood as not only broadcasting but also reception.
>
> (*Werke* 21: 553)

In this scenario, the act of listening constitutes not merely consumption of information but the active production of a public sphere and a shared sense of "publicness" or publicity (both implied by the

time (1929–1930) as Brecht was immersing himself in communist theory and preparing his *Lehrstück* on Party discipline, *The Measures Taken* (1930) (*Werke* 10: 1118–20).

German *Öffentlichkeit*) in which that information can become a means of self-representation, as the articulation of the mass public in the public sphere.[12] Indeed, Brecht maintains that, in a capitalist society, which does not foster the development of an active mass public sphere, the technological developments of the electronic media are meaningless: *"Suddenly, it seems possible to say everything, but, thinking it over, one may find that there is nothing to say"* (553; italics in original). Only with the revolutionary transformation of society can listeners become distributors and producers as well as consumers, who could in turn transform radio from a stand-in (*Stellvertreter*) for the public to a publicly accessible institution of communication.

Although Brecht notes the authoritarian implications of one-way state-run radio, the terms he uses to describe mass publicity tend to reinforce those implications. Alongside the participatory gloss of proletarian publicity, his notes on radio suggest modes of broadcasting and a reception of a rather different kind. Determined to wrest radio from its habitual association with the "home delivery" (*Hausablieferung*) of commodities passively consumed in the family circle, Brecht favoured the reception of radio in public places. Yet his list of suitable public sites for radio receivers includes not only rallies and union halls but also "public" institutions like prisons or shelters for the homeless, which are sites not of enfranchisement but of social discipline. In

---

[12] Habermas's analysis of the bourgeois public sphere in *The Structural Transformation of the Public Sphere*, trans. Thomas Berger (1962; Cambridge, MA: MIT Press, 1989) is foundational, but the work of Habermas's critics, Oskar Negt and Alexander Kluge, on proletarian public spheres is more pertinent here. See Negt and Kluge, *Öffentlichkeit und Erfahrung* (Frankfurt a.M.: Suhrkamp, 1972); trans. as *Public Sphere and Experience* by Peter Labanyi, Jamie Owen Daniel, and Assenka Oksiloff (Minneapolis: University of Minnesota Press, 1993), especially appendix 2 on the proletarian public sphere of the Weimar Republic. Hans Magnus Enzensberger's meditations on communicative radio in "Constituents of a Theory of the Media" are less analytical than those of Negt and Kluge, but are perhaps closer in spirit to the utopian moment in Brecht's essay. See Enzensberger, *Einzelheiten* (Frankfurt a.M.: Suhrkamp, 1964), vol. 1; *The Consciousness Industry*, ed. Michael Roloff (New York: Seabury, 1974).

these regulated spaces, the public looks more like a captive audience than the agent of its own emancipation. Despite his arguments for a decentralized democratized institution of communication that might wrest control from the hands of the state, his radio theory and, to a large extent, his radio practice appear to be driven by a "teacherly" (*belehrende*) rather than a learning attitude (*lernende Haltung*), despite the dialectic relation between them set up in his notes on a "theory of pedagogics" (*Werke* 21: 298).[13] The *Ozeanflug* (Flight across the Ocean) is perhaps the best-known experiment in this area; it was presented at Baden-Baden Festival in 1929 as the *Lindbergh-flug*, but Brecht changed the title after the aviation pioneer Charles Lindbergh declared his sympathies for Nazi Germany in the 1930s. In the 1929 presentation, the radio orchestra faced an actor who played the "listener" and also sang the part of the trans-Atlantic pilot. Both parties thus performed a written text and score on a platform stage for the essentially captive audience below. Brecht's note on the pre-view performance describes the introduction of the "listener" in terms that make quite clear the *staged* character of the actor's performance and the illusionist character of that staging: "on the one side of the stage . . . the radio apparatus, singers, musicians, speakers, etc. and on the other . . . , behind a screen, a room is suggested. . . . a man in shirt-sleeves sits with the score and hums, speaks and sings the Lindbergh part."[14] This performance puts on display an *imitation* of communicative interaction between listener and radio, rather than challenging the effectively uni-directional functioning of the apparatus, and thus unwittingly affirms its central control. Despite Brecht's

[13] In this period, the RRG (*Reichsrundfunkgesellschaft*, State/Imperial Radio Association) was 51% state-owned. Broadcasting and distribution (including the licencing of radio sets) was centrally controlled by the post office: see Jürgen Seifert, "Probleme der Parteien-und Verbandkontrolle von Rundfunk-und Fernsehanstalten," in *Massenkommunikationsforschung: I: Produktion*, ed. Dieter Prokop (Frankfurt a.M.: Fischer, 1972), 304.

[14] See "[Zur öffentlicher Generalprobe]," *Brechts Modell der Lehrstück*, 37. For a more affirmative view of this production, see Roswitha Mueller, *Bertolt Brecht and the Theory of the Media* (Lincoln: University of Nebraska Press, 1989), 26–36.

critical comments in a 1928 note on radio (*Werke* 21: 263) about the manipulation of "illusory collectives" by state-run media, this display affirms just such an illusion rather than criticizing the power of radio as an institution of broadcasting.

Brecht's endorsement of the emancipatory promise of radio technology as a means of individual communication is not easy to square with a radio practice that obeys the Leninist injunction that "discipline is the foundation of freedom" (*Werke* 24: 88) and shares with that injunction and its author the paradoxical notion of demo-cratic centralism. The association of Brecht's radio theory with Lenin's theory of the revolutionary state is not anomalous, since Brecht him-self draws the analogy between active radio listeners and the revo-lutionary state and calls explicitly for a "listener uprising" against the status quo.[15] The analogy which he draws between the educa-tional function of the radio apparatus and the revolutionary state also includes an allusion to the role of the citizen-listener: "as the state gives forth unfinished music, so will the listener make it complete" – but it rests firmly on the foundation of the better wisdom of the rev-olutionary state which, in the form of the vanguard party, in Lenin's terms, provides indispensable guidance for the spontaneous agency of the working masses.[16] Brecht's conception of the citizen-listener in the radio theory and of the participant in the *Lehrstück* chorus recalls Lenin's notion of a state made up of armed workers whose authority is ultimately ideally disseminated throughout the population rather than concentrated in the hands of a few.[17] Brecht's well-known, if enig-matic, argument in "Pedagogics Great and Small" ("Die große und die kleine Pädagogik") for a theatre which would abolish the "system of player and spectator" and make a "statesman" out of every specta-tor (*Werke* 21: 396) echoes the utopian notion, offered by Marx and reiterated by Lenin, of the "withering away" of the state with the

[15] Brecht and Elisabeth Hauptmann, "[Entwurf für 'Anmerkungen zum Lindberghflug']," in *Brechts Modell der Lehrstücke*, 64–65.

[16] "Entwurf," 65; Lenin, "What Is to Be Done?"(1902), in Tucker, ed., *The Lenin Anthology*, 24, 43.

[17] Lenin, "State and Revolution" (1917), ibid., 380 and "Can the Bolsheviks Retain Power?" (1917), ibid., 405.

transformation of passive subjects into active citizens. Yet, just as Lenin's praise for direct democracy in principle is complicated by his claim for the pressing need for central control in practice, so Brecht's ideal view of the participant audience rests on central authority.[18]

The phrase "discipline, the foundation of freedom" appears in this light to mean freedom to act *as if* active Party leaders indeed included the entire population, and *as if* the radio listeners were indeed citizen-rulers. Brecht's idea of appropriating the radio without the top-down organization of the actual institution of the State [or Imperial-*Reich*] Radio Association, as it was at the time, shares in Lenin's desire to appropriate the "splendidly equipped mechanism" of the bourgeois state without taking on the oppressive structures of that former state.[19] Both ideas have considerable resonance as utopian ideals but tend in practice to favor centralism at the expense of democracy. Under the aegis of an apparatus that compels attention by excluding the diversion of "free-floating feelings" ("freischwerfende gefühle"), radio listeners resemble not so much active citizens, empowered to appropriate the public sphere, as *Volksempfänger*, "splendidly equipped mechanisms" of reception.[20] Brecht's assertion that "doing is better than feeling" appears in the same unpublished note on the *Lindbergh-flug* as his call for a "listeners' uprising," but this appeal to militant, disciplined action relegates "free-floating feelings" to the realm of the unproductive and asocial. Although a journal note of 7 March 1941 (*Werke* 26: 468) argues that socialism should be understood as the "great production [plan]" ("große Produktion") rather than the "great order or system" ("große Ordnung"). This utopian plan promises to

---

[18] Lenin, "State and Revolution," 369.

[19] Lenin, "What Is to Be Done?", 50.

[20] The critique of "free-floating feelings" is Brecht's and Hauptmann's in "Entwurf," 64; the phrase recalls Karl Mannheim's notion of the "free-floating intellectual" disconnected from social action. Mannheim's reflections first appeared in *Ideologie und Utopie* in 1929; see "The Sociology of the 'Intelligentsia,'" in *Ideology and Utopia*, trans. Louis Wirth and Edward Shils (New York: Harcourt and Brace, 1963).

emancipate individuals through production and thus to socialize not only productive individuals but also stubbornly egotistical or asocial individuals, but it is stymied by the "system" of the actual – that is, allegedly fully realized – socialist state.

In this closed system, desire is short-circuited by discipline masquerading as fulfilment. Treating "distraction" as an unwanted diversion (*Ablenkung*) from the main business of great pedagogics rather than as the modern mode of perception through which the "[mass] audience encounters itself; its own reality [. . .] revealed in the fragmented sequences of [. . .] sense impressions" which Siegfried Kracauer attributes to distraction (*Zerstreuung*) in his 1926 essay on the "Cult of Distraction," Brecht seems to leave little room here for the free, "egoist" exploration of the unexpected.[21] In Leninist fashion, he stresses the value of the asocial protagonist as deterrent or negative model for socialist conduct and argues in a note on the "Theory of Pedagogics" that a lesson is to be learnt from the fall of the egoist: "it is precisely the representation of the asocial [*Darstellung des Asozialen*] by future citizens of the State that can be very useful to the state, especially when this representation follows precise and broadly conceived models" (*Werke* 10: 525; 21: 398). In this scenario, the asocial figure is made useful by being harnessed to the great(er) production of the social(ist) State, but Fatzer's resistance to usefulness continues to trouble the Leninist project of freedom through discipline. The tension in the *Lehrstücke*, especially in the controversial *Measures Taken*, between collective discipline and the emancipation of audience members as participants in the drama of social transformation returns in the early GDR years of the BE in Brecht's imposition of the disciplinary cohesion of the teacherly attitude deemed necessary for the consciousness-raising of audiences whose collective experience as Nazi subjects had left them, as he put it in a discussion with dramaturgs Palitsch and Wekwerth in 1955, not so much critically

---

[21] Brecht and Hauptmann, "[Entwurf für 'Anmerkungen zum Lindberghflug']," 64; Siegfried Kracauer, "Kult der Zerstreuung" (1926), in *Das Ornament der Masse* (Frankfurt a.M.: Suhrkamp, 1977), 315; trans. by Thomas Y. Levin as "Cult of Distraction", in *The Mass Ornament* (Cambridge, MA: Harvard University Press, 1995), 326.

"asocial" or even "egoist" as "depraved" or merely "resigned" (*Werke* 23: 328).

Despite Brecht's attempt to re-present the egoist as the asocial subject of a socialist lesson, the egoist remains an irrepressible foil to the good socialist subject, lurking in his notes on the Garbe project and in the name of his alter ego, Büsching, as one of Fatzer's fellow deserters as well as the alternative name for the Garbe figure. In the revisions of *Fatzer* up to 1930, in the unprocessed remainder of the *Fatzerkommentar*, and in journal notes from the GDR period, Brecht tries to mediate between the unmediated experience of flesh and the rational claims of the great pedagogic project. Making the argument for materialist judgment – Fatzer's attitude (*Haltung*) should be derived from his action (*Handlung*) – he suggests that both constitute a desperate response to a desperate state of emergency (*Not*) occasioned by the war and the stalled revolution in Germany, and thus, like the social conditions that provoke Fatzer's actions, subject to change (*Werke* 10: 520). Like "Bad Asocial Baal [*der böse Baal der Asoziale*]" in Brecht's 1938 revision of the youthful rebel hero of his first play, Fatzer "honors things as they are," not as ideologues might wish them to be (26: 323). Even more than Baal, who "does as he pleases," Fatzer is a provocation to those who claim to be able to transform the subjects of the old regime into new socialist people.[22] Brecht's single mention of Fatzer in connection with the Garbe project (in a note dated 10 July 1951) is elliptical; he mentions only that he "brought the Fatzer experiment along" with him while working on the Garbe project, but even this laconic mention implies that the two need to be read together, so that the limits of the model worker can be brought into focus. Where Garbe, or at least Garbe's labor, becomes a machine in the service of the "great production plan" Fatzer resists instrumentalization

---

[22] In this journal entry of 11 September 1938, Brecht calls Baal a "provocateur" who "does what he wants" (*Werke* 26: 323); his praise of the *Fatzer* fragment as "technically of the highest standard" (25 February 1939; 330) seems understated by comparison, but nonetheless classes *Fatzer* with the politically and formally avant-garde *Lehrstück* as a drama potentially capable of abolishing the gap between actor and spectator and so challenging the latter to act as asocial actor as well.

in the service of war or any other social transformation. Proclaiming "a person is no lever" (10: 495; B77) and insisting that "Fatzer" is the remainder left over when others have taken "what is useful," Brecht challenges not only instrumentalization by the state, but also exploitation at the hands of comrades. If, despite his refusal to be fully useful, Fatzer remains a foil to Garbe, it is perhaps because he shows the limits of state socialist claims that the new mode of production would be a sufficient condition for transforming human consciousness, as well as the limits of Brecht's willingness, in the first decade of the new state, to show the egoist remainder that escaped the orderly equation of socialism.

Remaindered voices and asocial noise

If Brecht's Fatzer functions, in his 1951 note, like a remainder that will not be resolved in the socialist equation of discipline and freedom, Müller's *Radio Fatzer* broadcast in the last full year of an intact GDR seems retrospectively like a problem set to cancel that equation. Even if Müller could not anticipate in early 1988 the demise of the state he addresses directly at the end of the broadcast, his appropriation of radio exploited its marginal status in the Ministry of Agitation and Propaganda and the apparent willingness of a more benevolent – but no less arbitrary – management, an era of inconsistent but no less paternalist cultural policy, to countenance experimental work, at least on a showcase station such as Berliner Rundfunk, officially the "mouthpiece of the capital."[23] While recognizing the limits of the Honecker regime's tolerance for even this contained dissent, we can argue that Müller uses radio, one branch of the centralized media apparatus which he had dismissed as "imbecilic," to test those limits by using a medium on the margins of the apparatus and by juxtaposing an anarchist figure with the persistently paternalist cultural politics of the GDR state, even in a period when this paternalism was expressed

---

[23] By 1988, the Committee on Radio under Achim Becker was willing to countenance critical and avant-garde work within limits, for example at a late hour on Berliner Rundfunk, which was dedicated to cultural programming reflecting its status as "mouthpiece of the capital"; see Stein, *Vom Fernsehen und Radio*, 33.

in artistic rather than explicitly political constraints. Müller and his ally at the Berliner Rundfunk, Matthias Thalheim, an assistant director there from 1984, took advantage of the administration's tendency to mask political objections with artistic ones; to the chief dramaturg's objections that this fragment was simply too fragmented and therefore "unsuitable" for radio, Thalheim was able to respond by demonstrating the text's aesthetic power as a play for listening without exposing the subtext of unspoken censorship and thus calling his superiors' bluff.[24]

Der Untergang des Egoisten Fatzer was adapted and directed by Heiner Müller, and performed by friends who had produced new stagings of Müller's theatre work, such as Frank Castorf and Jörg-Michael Koerbl from the Volksbühne, Johanna Schall, granddaughter of Brecht and daughter of Ekkehart Schall, principal of the Berlier Ensemble but engaged at the rival Deutsches Theater, and non-subsidized independents such as Iduna Hegen, Werner Hennrich, and Ulrich Zieger from Zinnober, whose unofficial space in Kollwitz Street (now the center of the thoroughly gentrified Prenzlauerberg scene) served as an improvised recording studio (fig. 7). Einstürzende Neubauten provided ambient sound in the form of heavy metal industrial music. The play was recorded in June 1987, mixed the following month, and broadcast at 10 pm on Berliner Rundfunk on 10 February 1988, on the occasion of Brecht's ninetieth birthday. The broadcast was not the first airing of Müller's edition of the play; the stage production by Karge and Langhoff at the Deutsches Schauspielhaus in Hamburg in 1978 used Müller's edition of Brecht's fragments, but failed to gain critical acclaim. Karge and Langhoff intended to highlight the contemporary resonances of anarchic and violent rebellion against an oppressive regime by including statements from the Red Army Fraction in the program and suggesting links in the production between the murder of the Weimar Republic-era Communists Karl Liebknecht and Rosa Luxemburg by fascist Freikorps soldiers and present-day repression

[24] Matthias Thalheim, "'Fatzer im Radio,': Heiner Müller inszeniert Brechts Dramenfragment als Hörspiel," *Theater der Zeit* 52: 1 (1997), xix. The dramaturg was Wolfgang Beck.

Fig. 7. Right to left: Heiner Müller and Jörg-Michael Koerbl rehearsing *Radio Fatzer* (Berlin 1987). Photograph by Grischa Meyer.

of the "Stammheim dead" by the West German government and media, through projections like "Liebknecht, Luxemburg, Meinhof." Ostensibly provoked by the production's apparent endorsement of the Red Army Fraction's tactics, the director of the Deutsches Schauspiel-haus removed statements by the Fraction's lawyer Marieluise Becker and the contemporary anarchist Peter Paul Zahl, but left citations from Ernst Jünger's memoir of trench warfare in the First World War, *In Stahlgewittern* (Storm of Steel).[25] Purged of the provocative

[25] The Red Army Fraction was a group of urban guerrillas, led in the 1960s and 1970s by Andreas Baader and Ulrike Meinhof, who moved from the legal exposure of residual fascism (and former Nazis) and persistent social inequities in West Germany to the use of sabotage, kidnaping, and assassination in the name of a challenge to the excesses of capitalism and state violence in the affluent North and its domination of the rest of the world, tactics shared in part with other contemporary groups from the Italian Red Brigades to the Movement for the Liberation of Quebec. The programme notes included comments from Becker, a lawyer, on the FRG's abuse of prisoners' rights through isolation cells and Zahl's condemnation of the

149

juxtaposition of contemporary commentary on asocial violence and historical views of the man who went on to write the Nazi war manifesto, *Die totale Mobilmachung* (Total Mobilization, 1934), the production failed, in part because, in Müller's view, the directors tried to engage too many points of reference, from the Nazi era to the sexual anarchy of the 1960s to the US Army in Vietnam, and in part, in the view of Henning Rischbieter (editor of the influential West German *Theater Heute*), because Müller's penchant for the more discursive passages of Brecht's political revisions weighed down the dramatic potential of the naked physical violence of the bodies on stage.[26] Against Rischbieter's aestheticism, I would argue that it is precisely this discursive turn that constituted the originality of *Radio Fatzer*. While the display of naked bodies was by 1978 routine rather than sensational on Western stages, the punctuation (and puncturing) of the conflict among the four deserters by the present-day commentary in the voices of Brecht's granddaughter and Müller himself highlighted the historical force and present-day resonance of the contrasting voices speaking from and against these bodies.

Before analyzing *Radio Fatzer* in detail, we should look briefly at the production that preceded, and possibly pre-empted, the planned recording and broadcast of Müller's edition.[27] The BE production of

unexplained deaths of Meinhof (1976) and later Baader (1977) in the maximum-security Stammheim Prison, after Red Army Fraction members involved in the hijacking of a Lufthansa airplane in Mogadishu, Somalia, were killed by German commandos. Red Army Fraction activities ended in 1992 after German unification cut short former lines of support from the Stasi, but trials of former members continued through the 1990s. For a documentary account of the group misrepresented as the "Baader-Meinhof Gang," see *Rote Armee Fraktion: Texte und Materialien zur Geschichte der RAF*, ed. Martin Hoffmann (Berlin: ID Verlag, 1997). For a brief note on the controversy, see Wilke, *Brechts "Fatzer"-fragment*, 222–4.

[26] For Müller's comments on the production, see *Krieg ohne Schlacht*, 311–12; for Rischbieter's review, see "Fatzer fatal," *Theater Heute* 19: 4 (1978), 9–10.

[27] Thalheim claims that Barbara Brecht-Schall granted recording rights in April 1987 to Berliner Rundfunk on condition that it did not broadcast

1987 is significant for its resistance to the contemporary implications of the material. With the middle-aged Ekkehart Schall in the role of the young rebel Johann Fatzer, and a mise en scène by Wekwerth and Tenschert that rationalized his behavior partly as a world-historical symptom of bad times and partly as that of a tragic hero on the model of Johann Faust, the production shirked a serious confrontation with Brecht's notes. In particular, it avoided Fatzer's challenge to the teleological closure of actually existing socialism exemplified by the model worker Garbe as well as with the SED state's routine relegation of dissent to the taboo realm of the asocial.[28] Claiming to produce Müller's edition of Brecht's play, the directors nonetheless cut Müller's preferred ending, in which the speaker calls on the "regulator" to "hand over" the state that "no longer needs [him]." Instead, this production followed the fatal explosion with an epilogue in which Schall reappears as Fatzer to reassert: "I will not die like a dog. [*Ich will nicht verrecken.*] . . . I am Fatzer" (*Werke* 10: 449). It thus reinforces the self-regard of the company's lead actor (and Brecht's heir-by-marriage) as if the character alone could not sustain Brecht's portrayal of the self-destructive egoist. The discrepancy between the deliberate emphasis of the producers and the persistently uncertain character of the product was noted even by a reviewer bent on seeing in the downfall of the

until after the BE production with Ekkehart Schall in the title role, which was to have its premiere in June 1987 ("'Fatzer im Radio'," xx).
[28] The contradictory assertions by principal collaborators on the BE production of June 1987, as documented in *Berliner Ensemble 1987: Untergang des Egoisten Fatzer von Bertolt Brecht*, Theaterarbeit in der DDR, 15, ed. Eva Förster (Berlin/GDR: Brecht-Zentrum der DDR, 1987), provide ample evidence of the tension between the impulses to treat the central figure alternatively as the protagonist of classical tragedy or as the object of marxist recuperation. For the former (including the comparison with Faust), see Schall, "Zur Fatzer-Figur," *Berliner Ensemble 1987*, 68, and "Kräftige Figuren, Spannende Vorgänge," conversation between co-director Joachim Tenschert and critic Dieter Kranz, *Berliner Ensemble 1987*, 110. For the latter, see academic Werner Mittenzwei, "'Fatzer' oder Die Möglichkeit des Theaters im Umgang mit einem Fragment," 114–28, and dramaturg Holger Teschke, "Fünf Punkte zu Brechts 'Fatzer'," 62–7.

egoist the allusion to Faustian tragedy as well as a defense of "politically engaged action."[29] Against this affirmation, Müller and his associates criticized the BE for producing a "huge hammy chunk of history [*riesiges Geschichtsschinken*]" or an array of "stuffed animals" displayed in a "diorama," and, by implication, for treating Brecht himself as an effigy in a museum.[30]

The radio format, on the other hand, provided a place and an occasion, at several removes from the legitimate theatre and from the strict control of the Brecht heirs, where that legitimacy could be subverted, precisely because of the relative poverty of radio as against the more expensive and more prestigious theatre and television. Intimate rather than ostentatiously public, cheap and mobile rather than too expensive to move, it offered a site for a critical experiment as well as a certain skeptical regard for the "socialist" re-presentation of the "asocial" deserter. Although the project, especially the provocative critique of the state that ends Müller's version, met with an initial veto from the department head, Christa Vetter, the full text was recorded in the same month as the BE premiere. Müller had to wait several more months to get authorization to use the music of Einstürzende Neubauten and to allow the Brecht heirs to reap the prestige due to the GDR premiere of the play.[31]

Despite these obstacles, Müller's *Fatzer*, especially its final injunction against the "men of state," pushed further the critique of the "petrified condition" of socialism already undertaken in his archeological production of *Der Lohndrücker*, which had had its premiere a few weeks earlier in January. Like that revival, Müller's *Fatzer* challenges Brecht's attachment to the collective force of the "greater production" and the good socialist subject pledged to advance it. Like Balke, the activist protagonist of Müller's play *Der Lohndrücker* – especially in Dieter Montag's performance within the hellish work environment created by Erich Wonder's set in the 1988

[29] Dieter Krebs, "Noch und Schon-Stirb und werde," *Theater der Zeit* 9 (1987), 73. His title quotes Goethe's Faust.
[30] Thalheim, "'Fatzer im Radio'," xxii.
[31] Jan-Christof Hauschild, *Heiner Müller oder Das Prinzip Zweifel*, 436.

production – Johann Fatzer is a saboteur of received collectivity. Unlike Balke, however, he owes no allegiance to an explicit alternative collectivity. Balke's activism and egoist zeal can be said instead to sabotage the immediate well-being and labor relations of his fellow workers and thus also the anti-capitalist proletarian collectivity which they represent. Nonetheless, his action can be recovered within the drive to maintain the "great production" of the socialist state as an act of solidarity, the necessary sacrifice of the smaller collectivity – the brigade of workers – in the interests of the greater society. Fatzer, however, deserts in the first instance to save his skin and only intermittently acknowledges the revolutionary potential of his behavior or even its status as a reaction to the events of the Great War and the November Revolution. His resistance to the instrumentalization of his body and his ego is aimed not only at the war, but also at his companions.

Radio Fatzer, by which I mean not only the broadcast "listening play" (*Hörspiel*) but also the fluid and anarchic *gest* articulated by the central character and, by indirection, those collaborating on the project, juxtaposes the immediate behavior of Fatzer and friends with narrative and interpretive commentary, spoken by Johanna Schall and by Müller himself. This commentary appears to illuminate Fatzer's cunning and all-consuming attention to his immediate physical needs by setting his avowedly egoistical behavior against the Bolshevists' world-historical rejection of the war in the interests of social revolution. Significant as these references to the larger historical context may be, they do not constitute an intervention in the action or dialogue of the characters. Like Mother Courage, Fatzer and his companions, Büsching, Kaumann, and Koch, do not learn to interpret their individual experiences in the light of epochal social movements. The tension between what Louis Althusser calls in his homage to Brecht the "dialectical temporality" of comprehensible historical processes and the "non-dialectical temporality" of a disengaged subjectivity remains irreducible here.[32] Whereas Althusser glosses this

---

[32] Louis Althusser, "Le 'Piccolo': Bertolazzi et Brecht. Notes sur un théâtre matérialiste," in *Pour Marx* (Paris: Maspéro, 1965), 137, 143;

disengagement as an ideological dead-end as opposed to a historicizing critique of it, which would be properly Brechtian, Müller undoes
any simple dichotomy between world-historical authority and the asocial individual. Even when the speaker-narrators provide elucidating
commentary, the structure and tone of the play, as well as the punctuation by Einstürzende Neubauten, deny these speakers the authoritative pathos of socialist realist history-makers.

The residue is Fatzer: conflict, heterophony and the limits of society

Brecht's last sustained work on the project divided the *Fatzer* material into the "*Fatzer*-document," or fragments of monologue, dialogue
and choral speeches documenting an unwritten and perhaps unper-
formable play, and "*Fatzer*-commentary," which covered notes offering "directions for players" (*Werke* 10: 515), parables from other fictions (especially the *Keuner* stories), and theoretical comments on
learning through performing that link the *Fatzer* project to the publicly produced work on the explicitly socialist *Lehrstück* as well as
to unpublished meditations on "unfettered sexual intercourse" (517,
527), violence and other asocial tendencies (525). In keeping with the
fragmented state of Brecht's work on the material, as well as with
his argument that the "*Fatzer*-commentary belongs to the *Fatzer*-
document" and provides "guidelines for its representation" (515),
Müller's dramaturgy for *Radio Fatzer* stresses the alienation of the
characters who often speak past rather than to each other, but also
punctuates this alienation with analytic and historicizing commentary. Situated in a sparsely defined space and time, with a minimum
of ambient sound or naturalistic indices of a publicly inhabited space,
the voices of Fatzer and his companions are alternately isolated and
intimately bonded in an environment that remains only abstractly and
intangibly social.

> trans. Ben Brewster as "The 'Piccolo Teatro': Bertolazzi and Brecht:
> Notes on a Materialist Theatre," in *For Marx* (London: Verso, 1990),
> 137–8, 142–3.

Consider the opening sequence:

(*Hammering . . . electronic percussion over wind machine*)
SPEAKER [Johanna Schall]
Fatzer's resting place.
Fix in the mind
this dark square between cranes and ironwork
through which Johann Fatzer passed his last days
stopping, the wheel
Bertolt Brecht, *Downfall of the Egoist Fatzer*. A Fragment.
  Edition: Heiner Müller[33]

(*Rapid heavy metal percussive representation of battle – or
  moving train; continues over voices*)[34]
KOCH [Frank Castorf]: Which of you is my friend and will bury
me? [. . .]
BÜSCHING [Werner Hennrich]: Everything that is must *go*
[*sound fades*]
KOCH: Let no-one ask after us. We are
Lost. We must go.
They ask us why

[33] I am following the text of the broadcast radio play adapted by Müller
from the *Fatzermaterial* contained in the Brecht Archive. Volume 10 of
Brecht's *Werke* contains previously unpublished material arranged in
five "work phases" from 1926, as well as critical notes under the
rubric of the *Fatzerkommentar*. References in the text include page
and fragment numbers in the published text (here *Werke* 10: 463; B45),
the archive (BBA 109/45), Müller's manuscript (M, 23), the tape of the
broadcast (T000–035), and finally the *Hörspiel* script used by Berliner
Rundfunk (HS 1). Note however that some fragments remain
unpublished and do not therefore include a reference to Brecht's
Werke. Translations are mine, and italics indicate sound effects or
emphasis in delivery.
[34] Thalheim, "'Fatzer im Radio'," notes that the sound of a freight train
recorded outside was more effective than the recorded sounds of tanks
reproduced in the studio, and compliments sound editor Günter Wärks
on his "sharp cuts" (xxix).

We were born today. Then
The air was full of iron and bane [. . .]
Humanity is the enemy and must come to an end.
(*Short percussive blast as punctuation*)
    ("Fatzer's Voice from the Tank," *Werke* 10: 452; B30;
        BBA 109/45; T035–54; M, 2; HS 2)

This opening offers us a concatenation of an immediately dramatized *fall* in the tumult and incoherence of the dialogue with the measured, even plodding, announcement of the title.

At the outset, Fatzer and his comrades allude, albeit obliquely, to the perishable and used-up nature of human beings in war, but not as yet to the ideology of soldiers' sacrifice for the interests of leaders fomenting war. By overlaying the delivery of the opening lines with Einstürzende Neubauten's simulation of war noise that drowns human speech, Müller brings out what is lurking in, but not articulated in, Brecht's text: the memory of dismembered flesh, fragmented metal, *and* wilful engagement in the trenches of the First World War, as captured in Jünger's *Storm of Steel*.[35] Even though the sound of this opening scene can plausibly be heard as a literal echo of the "storm of steel," the effect is not simply mimetic. The force of the punctuating of the dialogue by patterned industrial noise and the concatenation of sound is dis-illusioning; it holds the hearer at bay and defers the apparently natural "feeling of being encompassed that envelopes the individual listener" which one might be tempted to associate with the experience of music or mimetic sound.[36] Although the percussion can be naturalized as the noise of battle, its abstract minimalism

[35] Ernst Jünger, *In Stahlgewittern* (Berlin: Mittler and Son, 1929); trans. Basil Creighton as *The Storm of Steel* (London: Chatto and Windus, 1929) had gone through ten German editions by the time Brecht had finished work on *Fatzer*, and was undoubtedly known to him. *Die totale Mobilmachung* (Berlin: Junker and Dunnhaupt, 1934), Jünger's paean to all-out war under Nazi leadership, appeared a year after Brecht had left Germany and five years before Germany invaded Poland and provoked the Second World War.

[36] T. W. Adorno and Hanns Eisler, *Komposition für den Film* (Frankfurt a.M.: Suhrkamp, 1976), 30; *Composing for the Films* (New York:

keeps it at one remove from the mimetic. Rather than enveloping the listener with the illusion of three-dimensional space, the ostentatiously fabricated sound, along with the stylized, indeed *flattened,* delivery, emphasizes the perspectival character of recorded sound and the chamber containment of its reception while highlighting the disconnection of the characters from the larger context of the war.[37]

Brecht never alludes to *Storm of Steel* in the context of *Fatzer,* nor does he mention Jünger's promotion of "total mobilization" in 1934, a year after the Nazis seized power. Later that year, however, he produced notes for a critical explication of published speeches by Hermann Goering and Rudolf Hess, adding phrases that analyze the implications for ordinary people of the Nazi call for *Opfermut* (sacrificial courage; *Werke* 22: 93), thus highlighting the chilling logic of fascist subjection by repeating and rehearsing rather than merely demolishing its lexicon, as Roland Barthes notes in commenting on Brecht's explication of Hess's "Christmas Message from the Führer's Representative."[38] Half a century later Müller accredited Jünger for

Oxford, 1947), 21. The German edition represents Adorno's revision of the original text.

[37] On the perspectival character of recorded sound, see Tom Levin, "The Acoustic Dimension," *Screen Education* 25 (1984): 66; on the chamber character of recorded music, however symphonic in intention, see T. W. Adorno, "The Radio Symphony," in *Radio Research 1941,* ed. Paul Lazarsfeld and Frank Stanton (New York: Duell, Sloane and Pearce, 1941), 119.

[38] Roland Barthes, "Brecht et le discours: contribution à l'étude de la discursivité" (1975), in *Essais critiques IV: Le Bruissement de la langue* (Paris: Seuil, 1984), 245–6; trans. Richard Howard as "Brecht and Discourse: A Contribution to the Study of Discursivity," in *Critical Essays IV: The Rustle of Language* (New York: Hill and Wang, 1986), 214–16. The "Christmas Message" was published on 26 December under Hess's name in the *Nationalzeitung* of Basel, in neutral Switzerland, alongside messages from King George of England and the Pope (*Werke* 22: 911). Barthes does not mention the most likely source for Brecht's "exercise": Austrian satirist Karl Kraus's pointed quotation of Nazi bombast in *Die Fackel* (The Torch), the satirical magazine that he produced until Austria capitulated to Nazi annexation in 1938.

the first "materialist" representation of modern warfare without the moralizing or rationalization of Nazi discourse.[39]

The historical allusions that follow the opening of Radio Fatzer come from the fourth period of work (c. 1929), at a time when Brecht's intensive reading of marxist texts led him to a historical materialist analysis of the war as an outgrowth of a capitalist munitions industry rather than a battle for national honor, and of desertion as potentially an act of solidarity between foot-soldiers on both sides against the profiteers. The lines point to a historical context, but stop short of an overriding historical explanation, despite the speaker's opening invitation to consensus:

SPEAKER:
As you know,
in the second decade of this century (*short blast*)
All nations were at war (*short blast*) [. . .]
This war lasted four years (*short blast*)
And now in our time is considered a crime.
And it spat out a race (*short blast*)
Covered with scabs,
which did not last long
In its downfall,
Ripped up the old world (*short blast*).

('Fatzer-document 1', *Werke* 10: 481; B63; BBA 109/40;
M, 4; T055–077; HS 2)

Commenting on the rehearsal, Thalheim noted that Schall's voice carried something of the authority of her grandmother, BE director Helene Weigel, into the commentary, but that this "reasoned" and "pure" delivery "cries out to be punctured" ("danach schreit, perforiert zu

[39] Jünger's work continued to be published in post-war West Germany and enjoyed a revival after he received the Goethe Prize in 1982 (despite protests from the West German left). Like many Germans of his generation, Müller read Jünger in school in the Nazi era, but his later public interest raised hackles among dissidents in both East and West; for comments on his reading and on his meeting with Jünger in 1988, see Müller, *Krieg ohne Schlacht*, 275–82.

werden").[40] And so it is, as the listener confronts in succession the loud confusing roar of Büsching and Koch and the lofty explanation of the narrator, and is left at this point – despite the confidential solidarity implied by the collective "you" at the start – in limbo between the evocation of experience and the teleological ordering of that experience under the aegis of history.

As *Radio Fatzer* unfolds, the tension between inchoate experience and immediate response on the one hand and historical explanation on the other only deepens. To be sure, the text includes the account of Fatzer's probing of the social exploitation underlying warfare, as he comes to realize that he and his foot-soldier foe have more in common with each other than with their respective commanders:

> FATZER [Jörg-Michael Koerbl]:
> This is me and here against me
> Unavoidable a line, those are
> Soldiers like me, but my foe
> But here suddenly I see
> Another
> Line behind me; it is
> Also against me what is this. They are
> Those that send us here; that is the
> Bougie-oisie [*Burschoisie*]
> > (*Werke* 10. 476–77; B57; BBA 520/05; M 13–14;
> > T164–68; HS 7)

At this point the half-jesting attack suggests plebeian disdain for the airs of the "bougie-oisie" rather than a Marxist analysis of the capitalist war-machine. The German neologism *Burschoisie* combines the slangy *Bursche* (guy) with the standard French *bourgeoisie* to highlight the vulgar familiarity of low-class scorn for bourgeois pretensions, as does the (African) American "bougie." As the speech continues, however, using a variation not included in the published text, Fatzer turns suddenly serious:

---

[40] Thalheim, "'Fatzer im Radio'," xxiv.

And so I saw
After four years of furious war
Suddenly behind me
Everything all at once, namely
in front my brother against whom I fought
behind him and behind me, our foe [. . .]
I
will make war no more
(BBA 520/06; M, 14–15; T169–76; HS 8)

Here the banter freezes suddenly in a flash of recognition and an equally sudden revelation of what appears to be anti-war analysis and decision to "make war no more," as though anticipating the critique of the war-mongering talk of "sacrificial courage" that Brecht will launch against the Nazis in 1934.

The flash of enlightenment is brief, however. The speaker's commentary that follows in the broadcast (but not in the published version of this fragment) treats this intimation of anti-war analysis as a manifestation of a revolutionary truth sealed by the link between Fatzer's outburst and the intervention of Lenin:

Furthermore, a man named Ulyanov called *Lenin*
Living in exile in Zürich
Socialist and rabble-rouser
A destructive element (*percussive punctuation*)
(At his request passing through our territory
in a sealed car)
Like a fungus (*percussion volume rises to the end of the speech*)
Seeks the shapeless body of our eastern enemy
To hollow it out from within and so
Unknowingly furthers our cause (*loud blast*)
(BBA 820 Fatzerdokument 5; M, 25; T201–20; HS 15)

Weighty as this world-historical moment appears to be, its authority is called into question by the reference to "us" and "ours" in an echo of the abstract manner of *The Measures Taken*, and by the percussion that first punctuates and then blocks the account of Lenin's movements. The reference to "our cause" in the final line may allude to the German socialists who, inspired by the Bolshevist revolution of November 1917, fomented revolution in Germany two years later, but the loud blast that drowns this allusion reminds listeners that this revolution failed.

Any attempt to read Fatzer's anarchic behavior as proto-socialist solidarity cannot rest with explicitly communist supplements to the egoist protagonist; it must contend with his resistance to his companions' desire to make his desire for meat into a planned act of socially justified subversion:

> I'm against your mechanical ways,
> Since a person is no lever
> And I strongly dislike doing
> Among many deeds only those that are useful
> But want rather to bury good meat
> And to spit in potable water [. . .]
> From everything of mine, keep only
> What serves your needs.
> The residue is Fatzer
> > (*Werke* 10: 495; B77; BBA 110/47; M, 55–6;
> > T487–500; HS 33)

Reacting to his comrades' attempts to employ him as a food thief, Fatzer refuses to be a useful instrument. As Barthes says of Brecht himself, Fatzer's language or acts are not "currency."[41] He insists instead on his desire "to bury good meat / and to spit in drinking water" and thus on his egoist drive to what Georges Bataille calls "unproductive expenditure" ("dépense non-productive"): libidinal investment in apparently inexplicable behavior which, rather than being reduced to rationally calculated social or even asocial use value, expresses the drives of the flesh.[42]

---

[41] Barthes, "Brecht et le discours," 244; "Brecht and Discourse," 213.
[42] Georges Bataille, "La notion de dépense," in *Oeuvres complètes* (Paris: Gallimard, 1970), 1: 302–22; trans. Allen Stoeckl as "The Notion of Expenditure," in *The Bataille Reader*, ed. Fred Botting and Scott Wilson (Oxford: Blackwell, 1996), 165–81.

Fleisch in Fatzer denotes both meat and flesh: the most immediate object of need and desire for the starving deserters, and the mediated but equally compelling compulsion to sex, both of which leave
subjects at the mercy of desire. The two meanings of *Fleisch* come
together in the encounter between Fatzer and Therese Kaumann – but
only fleetingly. Earlier, Therese is introduced as a subject of desire,
lamenting the absence of someone who might "lie on top of her" and
give her "gratification" (*Werke* 10: 485; M 27–8; T 201–10; HS 16).
Once the deserters return, however, she is reduced to an object, forced
to share her bed with four men, and practically disappears from the
scene while the action focuses on the men's attempt to find meat, and
later on their punishment of Fatzer when he fails to deliver. When
Therese reappears, in a section called the "Sex Chapter," it is in a sexual encounter with Fatzer that seems at first to suggest equal interaction between two subjects of desire:

> (*Therese releases Fatzer [from the bonds in which his
> comrades placed him when he refused to get meat for them].
> He seduces her*)

> FATZER [and THERESE; Iduna Hegen]:
> And he grasped her breast under the shirt, the lovely one
> His crude hand persuaded her breast, made her/it
> Stand up and harden. And he gently grasped
> Her backside and weighed it
> With joy and watched the
> Closely pressed thighs open and
> Her hand pulled him to her and the game, so old,
> renewed itself and also
> the beloved movement
>
> (*Werke* 10: 456; BBA 10/434; M 64–5; HS42)

The language of romantic union at this moment, and the radio play's
incorporation of the voices of Koerbl and Hegen, rather than just
Koerbl as Fatzer alone as Brecht's fragment has it, might suggest liberation from what Brecht, in a note "On Fatzer as 'sex play,'" calls
the "possessiveness" of man over woman in the bourgeois family in

the name of a mythic "unregulated sexual intercourse" (*Werke* 10: 517).

But patriarchal sexual norms prove stronger than this whiff of liberation that Brecht picks up from Friedrich Engels, glossing Engels's speculative remarks in *The Origin of the Family* on an alleged "freedom from jealousy" characterizing pre-historic "group marriage."[43] Instead of a revolutionary sexual epiphany, the talk turns to hunger and, in the scene that Brecht identifies as the "Fear Center of the Play" ("Furchtzentrum des Stücks"), the action reinforces the reduction of human beings to instruments. The scene is interrupted by Kaumann, who attempts in a "fit of possessiveness" to throw Fatzer out, and this is followed by the speaker (Müller) reading: "The four consult around a table. One presents revolutionary theses on the freedom of sexuality and: what one needs, one should get. But then they had to go outside and outside it was – raining. The theses were retracted; now hunger was their advisor" (*Werke* 10: 428; A9; M 66; T599–601; HS 51). Therese becomes no more than a silent witness to her reduction to an instrument of what Fatzer euphemistically calls "housework"; the men try to extract surplus value (cash for food) from her labor as a sex worker and to rationalize this exploitation on the grounds that they can question her factory laborer clients for information about the coming revolution. What is noteworthy here is not only that the utopian moment of unproductive expenditure, of escape from the economy of exploitation and profit into a realm governed by the gratuitousness of the gift, is crushed by the act of reducing a human being to an instrument. It is also striking that, at a moment when he might have indicted the persistence of sexual exploitation as exploitation, Brecht retreats into a decidedly bourgeois form of expression; in his euphemistic renaming of pimping as "housework," he deflects the act of exploitation engaged in by desperate men at a woman's expense

[43] Friedrich Engels, *The Origin of the Family, Private Property, and the State in the Light of the Researches of Lewis H. Morgan* (New York: International Publishers, 1972), 100. As the title indicates, Engels used Morgan's anthropological research as the source for an alternative to bourgeois marriage, which he argued was based on the economic dependence of women on men.

and thus the implications of their incoherent talk of freedom and the unraveling of their claims to reason.

It is to this unraveling of reason and of the coherent egoist self that the final scene returns. As Koch dies and the others threaten to kill Fatzer, he responds by proclaiming "shit on your reason" and reiterating that he is merely a "point," a site for the intersection of competing vectors of desire, rather than an agent of politics, reason, or honor. This point is no geometric abstraction but takes on the fleshy weight of Fatzer's body, whether at the moment that Kaumann complains about the blood dripping from the meat under Fatzer's arm – the last piece of meat they see – or when Büsching threatens to kill Fatzer for not living up to his promises, or, after this threat leads Fatzer to betray all of them to the army, in the final moment of the action when Kaumann shoots down Fatzer and the army outside blows up the room and all those remaining in it. In inviting his comrades to take the "useful part of him" and leave him the rest – the provocation that leads them to take all of him – Fatzer offers them what Georges Bataille would call a *potlach*: that is, a gift that takes the form of the "spectacular destruction of wealth" and is thus both a challenge to rivals and a form of self-destruction – because it reinforces the power of giver over receivers, while turning the force of that power on the giver as well.[44] Fatzer's potlatch consists not only in giving away meat and making it inedible but in giving away his own flesh and in provoking the sacrifice of all the men as the explosion consumes both the egoist and his would-be rivals.

To be sure, the BE production of *Fatzer* under Wekwerth focuses on Koch's argument for the "necessity" and "utility" of Fatzer's death and thus attempts to restore the downfall of Fatzer and his foe/friends as a legible political act, but this invocation of the classical Communist reasoning of *The Measures Taken*, despite his emphatic rejection of the *"Lehrstück* line," only shows the strain of this reading.[45] Unlike the notorious execution in *The Measures Taken*, performed

---

[44] Bataille, "La notion de dépense," 308–10; "The Notion of Expenditure," 172–4.

[45] For Wekwerth's rejection of the *Lehrstücklinie*, see his "Notizen und Gesprächen," *Berliner Ensemble 1987*, 12; for the affirmative reading

by the members of the clandestine party cell after the young comrade agrees that his enthusiasm has endangered the mission and merits his death, this explosion shatters attempts to render Fatzer a coherent political subject. The potlatch, the gift as (self)destruction, becomes, in the context of modern war and post-war, beyond measure; it can no longer be a "measure" to be taken and rationalized according to the demands of politics in the manner characteristic of Brecht the "poet of reason." Rather, as Hans-Thies Lehmann argues, moments of sacrifice in the *Lehrstücke* are an exception to the rule of rule, the "revocation of measure" ("die Rücknahme der Maßgabe").[46]

Hearing this final explosion in Einstürzende Neubauten's semiotic rather than mimetic sound and in Müller's matter-of-fact repetition of the passage "Destruction of the Room," one can argue that *Radio Fatzer*'s arbitrary or egoist use of signs deconstructs the traditionally *private* character of radio perception and reception. In this understanding of radio, whose best-known proponent is Martin Esslin, radio makes possible the direct and immediate communion of the inner selves of character and listener, representing the solitary experience on the "stage of the listener's mind, turned inward to a field of internal vision."[47] But, where Esslin argues that this experience is at once the *essence* of radio drama and the proof of the medium's authentic transparency to social as well as private experience ("the mere sound of a vast crowd easily suggests these multitudes"), *Radio Fatzer* problematizes any simple equation of intimacy of reception with an immediately collective affect. Rather it explores to the full the tension between the affective quality of radio sound at the

---

of Koch's argument as his "recognition" of the necessity of Fatzer's death, see rehearsal notes for 17 March 1987 by Eva Förster, Holger Teschke, and Margit Vestner, ibid., 102.

[46] Hans-Thies Lehmann, "Die Rücknahme der Maßgabe: Schuld, Maß und Überschreitung bei Bertolt Brecht," in *Drama und Theater der europäischen Avantgarde*, ed. Frank Norbert Memmemeier and Erika Fischer-Lichte (Tübingen: Francke, 1994), 104. The characterization of Brecht as a "poet of reason" ("Dichter der Ratio") is Lehmann's.

[47] Martin Esslin, "The Mind's a Stage," in *Mediations: Brecht, Beckett and the Media* (New York: Grove Press, 1982), 171–87, here 172.

intimate scene of reception and the voice of authority of the commentator along the road of history. While interior scenes, especially the opening scene in and around the tank as well as those in Kaumann's house, were recorded in the Berliner Rundfunk studios, Müller broke with the convention that imposes "dead silence" on the studio space before creating sound for recording. Not only the designated outside scenes in which Fatzer prowls through Mülheim in search of meat, but also the final "destruction of the room" were recorded outside at night, near an electrical plant, capturing the disorientation of the characters in the echoing sound "found" outdoors in open (literally "free") space (*im Freien*) and in turn disorienting the listener when broadcast in a stereo format that reproduced this fragmentation rather than the illusion of a place made coherent by clearly coordinated boundaries.[48]

Against the force of a centralized and centralizing broadcasting system designed to reinforce the illusion of perspectival and ideological coherence, Müller's *Radio Fatzer* highlights the tension between public and private, enclosed and "free" space. It does so by deploying the subversive potential of that very private character of radio *reception* that Brecht deplored and that GDR media organization could not fully control. As Frances Gray and Janet Bray suggest in their critique of Esslin, "the inevitable intimacy of radio [reception?] means that codes employed by political theatre are not helpful . . . A radio crowd is simply another sound effect, and while the function of that effect may be clear, it has no inherent power to move us."[49] In other words, radio offers no immediate access to compelling political representation. Rather, as they suggest, radio's critical potential lies in the very gaps in the medium, between naturalistic sound and the deliberately artificial sound-sign, between dialogue and commentary, for example, and the consequent ambiguities of interpretation it presents. Instead of Esslin's notion of radio as a compelling *visual* medium, whose elusive clarity might encourage a didactic intention to contain that image, the concatenation of competing sounds unravels attempts at an

---

[48] Thalheim, "'Fatzer im Radio'," xxii–xxiii.
[49] Frances Gray and Janet Bray, "The Mind is a Theatre: Radio Drama since 1971," *New Theatre Quarterly* 3 (1986): 292–300, here 294.

authoritative hierarchy of voices. Unlike the theatre spectator, whose view is generally organized by the proscenium arch and the very act of going to the theatre, the listener receives and entertains anonymous cries of pain, industrial noise, the expressions of the characters, and the analysis of the commentators in the same perceptual space: all sounds come from the same speakers. Despite the deliberate evocation of authority in Johanna Schall's delivery, for instance, the broadcasting of authority is muffled by other voices as well as by the echoing found sound recorded outside the confines of the studio.

"Let us become statesmen, man of state": sounding out political agency

The authority of the sovereign point of view, which Brecht found so seductive, dissolves in the play of voices whose heterophony complicates the opposition of performers and captive spectator that defined the realm of the *Lindberghflug*. While we can certainly hear in this heterophony the harbingers of citizen voices beyond the state, it is important to remember that as a radio play, *Radio Fatzer* is more than a *Hörspiel*, or a work of art composed of sound and voices. Contrary to much mainstream (West German) *Hörspiel* theory, which has only reluctantly engaged with the institutional context of broadcasting and reception and tries rather to shield the autonomous work from the apparently inevitable stultification of what Klaus Schöning calls, following T. W. Adorno, "administered art" ("verwaltete Kunst"), *Radio Fatzer* reminds its listeners of the institutional context of cultural production and concludes with a critique of central control and a call for the appropriation of this and other institutions:[50]

> Draw breath, speaker
> Your name is erased from the board. your commands
> Are not carried out. let
> New names appear on the board and let

---

[50] Klaus Schöning, "Verwaltene Kunst," in *Neues Hörspiel: Essays, Analysen, Gespräche*, ed. K. Schöning (Frankfurt a.M.: Suhrkamp, 1970), 248–65.

New orders be followed. [. . .]
Abandon old position. [. . .]

You are finished, man of state [*Staatsmann*].
The state, however, is not.
Permit us to change it
According to the conditions of our lives.
Permit us to become statesmen, man of state [. . .]
Forget the name
Obey your laws, lawgiver

May the order of things please you, regulator
The state no longer needs you
Hand it over
"Come, Fatzer/Fatzer Comm." (*Werke* 10: 512–13; BBA
1014/ 48–50; M 97–9; T 1000–16; 1033–41; HS 61–3)

Coming, as it does in Müller's edition, after the death of Fatzer and
his companions turned antagonists, this call sounds like a sober critique of the excesses of the state rather than a confident announcement of a future utopia. Müller's sense of the tentative, risky nature
of this speech came to the fore in the recording; apparently, his voice
shook so much during the final lines – "The state no longer needs
you / Hand it over" – that these lines had to be recorded several times
before he regained his customary "sober," "unpretentious" delivery.[51]
If Müller's doubt about the future has a provisional cast, his critique
of the past is sharply focused in the prominent placement of the line
"Abandon old positions." This injunction quotes the young, doomed
comrade in *The Measures Taken* only to unravel the earlier play's reiteration of party authority in the twilight of state socialism.

In his decision to end *Radio Fatzer* by making public this speech
from the archive, Müller presents not only a provocative apostrophe to
the SED state but also a solution in performance to a problem in Brecht
philology. Brecht's editors currently argue that the section is titled
"Come" (*Komm*) to herald the final critical apostrophe to the state

---

[51] Thalheim, "'Fatzer im Radio'," xxiv.

168

rather than "comm[entary]" (*Komm[entar]*) and thus that the speech is part of the "Fatzer-document" or drama rather than the "Fatzer commentary"; but Müller's presentation emphasizes Brecht's characteristic combination of performance and critique and the performance of critique that complicates this distinction.[52] It also highlights the fundamental role of performance in the determination of meaning. The Brecht philologist Judith Wilke may argue that the text confirms Brecht's commitment to the Leninist view of the Party's seizure of power in the name of the masses; but the performance on GDR radio by Müller and his collaborating dissidents, framed by Einstürzende Neubauten, suggests rather a decentralized movement away from the Party.[53] This ending to *Radio Fatzer* revises Brecht's appropriation in "Pedagogics Great and Small" of Lenin's notion of a militant citizenry in which spectators become social actors and "statesmen" (*Werke* 21: 396) to grant greater authority to democratic citizen-statesmen (sic) as against the functionary "man of state" who, like Andrzej Wajda's "man of marble," reflects the petrification of the state that he serves.[54] It may herald a challenge to the centralist power of the "regulators" by participatory democracy, but may also indicate a future of deregulated discontinuous social collisions that do not add up to a coherent alternative.

Müller's direction of the radio play, like his deliberately dry presentation of the open conclusion, eschews the "actually existing

---

[52] See notes to *Fatzer* (*Werke* 10: 1134) and comments by Wilke, *Brechts "Fatzer" Fragment*, 23–35, 48–64.

[53] Ibid., 59.

[54] The distinction between the "man of state" and the "[citizen-]statesman" emerges from my differentiated translation of *Staatsmann*. This interpretation rests on the negotiation by Brecht and Müller in the GDR, and their counterparts elsewhere in Eastern Europe, of the tension between working citizens and the functionaries of the "worker-and-peasant states" that claim to represent them. Andrzej Wajda's film *Man of Marble* (*Czlowiek Z Marmur*, 1977) is literally about a statue of a model worker but alludes figuratively to the growing Solidarity Movement in 1970s Poland and its members' critical reformulation of the model workers, in this case against the state.

socialist" temptation of identification with the sublime ideological object of the "man of state" or any clear-cut rival, such as an impecca-ble dissident. It consists rather in the orchestration of voices, in part outside, in part inside the system, rather than their subordination to the master's voice of the SED – or the FRG. Produced in the first instance for a GDR audience for whom the social was only indirectly "manageable," in the Brechtian sense, this radio play and its "asocial" heterophony offer a critical negative dialectic to the voice of the state and its effigy of sovereign socialist subjectivity frozen in "actually existing" subjectedness. It is the aural fluidity of the *Hörspiel*, but also the institutional marginality of radio that enabled Müller and his collaborators to set in motion the "cement" of the authoritarian state in the name of potential future "statesmen." Müller went on to produce another stage version of *Fatzer* (in combination with his meditations in *Wolokolamsker Chaussee* on the beginning and end of the GDR) in *Duell Traktor Fatzer* in 1993, in his final role as head of the BE, the theatre that had inspired but not fully admitted him in the SED era.[55] While formally impressive, this production could no longer – in 1993 – carry the political force that had resonated in Müller's risky but compelling call at the end of *Radio Fatzer* in 1988. Today, more than a decade after unification, the "egoist" resistance of the still-second-class citizens in the Eastern states may be muffled somewhat by mass media representations of a new "asocial" genera-tion, but Brecht's troubled experiment with the downfall of Fatzer and other "egoists" still offers a timely reminder, in the hardening pub-lic sphere of a globally competitive *Großdeutschland* (greater [West] Germany), of those left behind in the rush to reunification, rational-ization, and redundancies in the new Germany.

[55] For a discussion of *Duell Traktor Fatzer*, see Wilke, *Brechts "Fatzer" Fragment*, 240–53.

4   Specters and speculation: Brechtian futures on the glocal market

"Wars bring the world to ruin, and through the rubble goes /
... a specter ... / come to change everything and to stay
forever; its name is / *Communism.*"

(Brecht, Werke 15: 148)[1]

Celebrated on 10 February 1998, the centenary of Bertolt Brecht's birth anticipated by a week or so the hundred-and-fiftieth anniversary of the Communist Manifesto published in late February 1848. Whereas the first event was commemorated with great enthusiasm – and not a little irony – in Germany, and acknowledged, albeit grudgingly, in the United States (almost always by Marc Blitzstein's sweetened adaptation *Mack the Knife*), the second event received relatively little attention.[2] As the communist Brecht has been buried – along with Communism – under the weight of classical prestige, a monumentalization even more impenetrable than the steel coffin in which he chose to be interred, it is all the more important to remember Brecht's debt to Marx. So long as functionaries like the Minister for Culture in Brandenburg (the state that surrounds but does not incorporate

---

[1] This citation is from the opening lines (1–2, 15–16) of Brecht's versification of the *Communist Manifesto* (third draft, July 1945). The emphasis on Communism is Brecht's.

[2] Only the formerly GDR daily, the *Berliner Zeitung* carried a detailed commentary on the 150th anniversary of the Communist Manifesto. The article "So viel Hoffnung war nie. Gleiches Stück, wechselnde Personal," *Berliner Zeitung* (21–2 February 1998): II–III, by Wolfgang Engler (author of the influential book *Die Ostdeutschen*, 1998) discussed Brecht's interest in the text as well as the manifesto's relevance in a Europe shaped by transnational capital.

the state of Berlin) represent this anti-bourgeois activist as a poet of "tender verses" ("zärtliche Verse") on the local landscape, Brecht's decidedly untender versification of the knotty argument of the *Communist Manifesto*, whose opening lines form the epigraph to this chapter, call for renewed attention.[3] The coincidence of Brecht's centenary and the hundred-and-fiftieth anniversary of the *Communist Manifesto* in 1998, and the travails of a not-so-triumphant capitalism in the opening years of the twenty-first century, provide a timely opportunity to re-evaluate Brecht's contribution to anti-capitalist culture locally, globally, and in the *glocal* situation of Berlin, pre-eminent city of central Europe.[4]

The demise of the GDR ended the official sponsorship of both Brecht and Marx as icons of Communism, and thus also removed the rationale for anti-Communist counter-images of Marx as the avatar of Stalinist dictatorship and of Brecht as Stalin's dupe. In a post-Cold-War era in which the specter of Communism no longer haunts the counting houses of the world, Germany has become the dominant capitalist power in an unevenly capitalized Central Europe. The earlier political division between East and West has not disappeared but has rather changed into a shifting boundary between haves and have-nots, a boundary monitored less by nations than by the interests of transnational capital. In this environment of newly unfettered capitalism, Marx's view of a juggernaut that "has left remaining no other nexus between people [*Menschen*] than naked self-interest, than unfeeling [*gefühllose*] 'cash payment'" remains more pertinent than ever, and

---

[3] For the minister's comment, see Jörg Wagenau, "Zum Abschied Amselgesang", *die tageszeitung* , 27 January, 1988; at
<http://www.taz.de/~taz/spezial/brecht/pb-T980127.188.html>

[4] For "glocal," see Eric Swyngedouw, "The Mammon Quest: 'Glocalisation,' Inter-Spatial Competition and the Monetary Order," in *Cities and Regions in the New Europe*, ed. Mick Dunford and Grigoris Kafkalis (London: Belhaven, 1992). The term, in common use by urbanists, refers to the intersection of global and local concerns in cities that function both as national or regional capitals and as destinations for transnational migration of peoples, markets, and culture. It thus focuses more precisely than glib "globalization" on the sites and intersections of exchange.

Brecht's attempts to make drama and social poetry out of Marx's analysis of the contradictions of capitalism is likewise of renewed interest.[5] Yet, while Brecht's centenary was commemorated by staged readings of early and previously unproduced fragments, from *Jae Fleischhacker von Chikago* (1926) to *Judith von Shimoda* (1940; about Japanese resistance to penetration by the US Navy, c. 1850), which highlighted his anti-capitalist and anti-imperialist engagement, it was also marked by revivals of well-known plays, such as *Der aufhaltsame Aufstieg des Arturo Ui* (The Resistable Rise of Arturo Ui), or much-discussed if rarely produced critical milestones such as *Die Massnahme*, which were characterized by marketing cloaked in respect, in short, by commodification rather than critique. While the glamorous "gangster show" (Brecht's term) version of *Ui* promoted by Martin Wuttke, its star attraction (1995), was nothing new, the respectful red drapes around the revival of *Die Massnahme* (1997) evoked, as did the red flag on the cover of Verso's hundred-and-fiftieth-anniversary reprint of *The Communist Manifesto* (1998), the museum cabinets of yesteryear, while at the same time marketing the product as a valuable collector's item. This combination of reverence and commodification was highlighted (especially in the former case) by the marketing of the revival as an object of original rediscovery, as the first professional production to break Brecht's 1956 ban on performances of the play, even though professional productions had recently taken place in London and student productions in several places, including Berlin.

This evocation brings the revivals and their agents into the realm of socialist kitsch or, in East German parlance, of *Ostalgie* (nostalgia for things east) and thus into the market niche carved out already in the late Soviet period by Vitaly Komar and Alexander Melamid, who painted ironically faithful replications of socialist

<hr />

[5] Karl Marx and Friedrich Engels, *Manifest der kommunistischen Partei* (1848; Stuttgart: Reclam, 1999), 22; trans. Samuel Moore, *Manifesto of the Communist Party* [1888], ed. Engels., with a new introduction by Eric Hobsbawm (rpt London: Verso, 1998), 37; trans. mod.; hereafter cited as Marx/Engels, *Manifest/Manifesto*. I follow Hobsbawm in attributing primary authorship to Marx; see Hobsbawm, Introduction, *Manifesto*, 4.

realist images as an ironic comment on the decline of the Soviet empire. Now based in the United States, they have turned their ironic gaze on "actual existing capitalism" to produce standardized "popular" images based on mass market surveys and, occasionally, invented examples of heroic capitalist images, usually featuring the American flag.[6] This *ostalgisch* niche, occupied by found objects from Soviet army paraphernalia, GDR domestic objects, and idiosyncratic red and green men still gracing East Berlin traffic lights, as well as ironic quotations of such objects on postcards, t-shirts, compact disks and board games, may also accommodate the apparently high-art revival of Communist iconography at the Berliner Ensemble (BE), even if the latter were not intended as kitsch. This phenomenon raises the question of the future of Brecht and of Brechtian futures, or, rather, the question whether Brechtian futures allow a future for Brecht other than the commodification of his communism as a novelty item in an increasingly competitive theatrical marketplace. Characterized since unification by the closure of many theatres, mostly in Eastern states, and the rationalization and curtailment of regional and national subsidy to others, even in the capital Berlin, the German theatre institution has had to borrow the marketing tactics of more aggressively privatized institutions, such as those in post-Thatcherite Britain: in particular, the tactic of a distinctive brand or proper name.[7]

In the 1990s, the iconography of *Ostalgie* took precedence over a critical working through of the recent past. At the end of the decade, GDR board games and reissues of satirical and even official songs of the old regime, such as *Die Partei hat immer Recht* (The Party is Always Right), garnered more publicity than the invaluable but weighty tomes of the Christof Links Press series of studies based on Stasi and other GDR archives opened in the 1990s. Stage productions tended to be likewise nostalgic. For instance, *Helden wie wir* (Heroes like Us),

---

[6] See *Komar and Melamid*, ed. Carter Ratcliffe (New York: Abbeville, 1989).

[7] For the rationalization of German theatre after unification, see Adolf Dresen, "Statt Theater Stadt-theater," in *Hinterm Vorhang das Meer*, ed. Hans-Dieter Schütt (Berlin: Das neue Berlin, 2001), 13–47, and Kruger, "'Wir treten aus unseren Rollen heraus.'"

Thomas Brussig's best-selling comic novel about the good-for-nothing son of a Stasi underling whose outsize member allegedly broke the first hole in the Wall, became after the release of the film version (directed by Sebastian Peterson, who got his start at the Prenzlauerberg community Theater unterm Dach), and the stage adaptation (by Peter Dehler) opening at the Deutsches Theater on 9 November 1999 (exactly fifty years after the grounding of the GDR state and a decade after the fall of the Wall) a prime exhibit of *Ostalgie*.[8] Returning to the Deutsches Theater stage to commemorate the tenth anniversary of unification on 3 October 2000, and still in the repertoire in 2003, the play encouraged a sentimental response to *Ostalgie*, which Brecht would have called culinary. More ambiguously, perhaps, Volksbühne director Frank Castorf, who had made a reputation of wrapping post-Brechtian critical theatre texts such as Heiner Müller's *Bau* in post-modern pastiche in 1986, continued in the 1990s to use the iconography of GDR modernity – from the old SED Party songs to the local unfashion worn by those rendered redundant by the demise of the GDR – to draw former GDR audiences to the Volksbühne's deconstructions of modern classics and of late modern consumerist society, in productions of *Hauptmanns Weber* (1998) and *Endstation Amerika* (2000; a version of *A Streetcar Named Desire* disavowed by the Tennessee Williams

---

[8] Although enlivened by the comic talents of Götz Schubert as the hapless Klaus Ultzsch, and enriched by the program (a parodic recreation of *Trommel*, the newsletter of the Young Pioneers), the GDR organization for children, the one-man stage adaptation offered a rosy view of a GDR childhood. *Sonnenallee* (1999: directed by Leander Haussmann, who had also previously worked in theatre) and also written by Brussig, also softened the rough edges of GDR adolescence with the hues of 1970s sex, drugs, and rock and roll to the horror of older, more politically focused dissidents – but nonetheless captured the contradictory anarchism of the younger generation and the specifics of location more effectively than *Helden*. *Sonnenallee* links the working-class districts of Neukölln and Treptow, previously divided by the Wall. For comment on the films, see Christiane Peitz, "Alles so schön grau hier: Leander Haußmanns *Sonnenallee*, Sebastian Petersons *Helden wie wir*: Der Osten ist jetzt Kult–auch im Kino," *Die Zeit* (28 October 1999).

estate). Although dismissed by some younger East German commentators as marketing for West Germans nostalgic for a socialist utopia that never existed in the GDR, these East German restagings of GDR life have drawn a sizable GDR audience.

Where Castorf and Brussig clearly addressed East Germans discomfited by the end of the GDR, the Berliner Ensemble seemed at a loss in the mid-1990s after the death of its celebrity playwright-director Heiner Müller, and its interim management seemed unclear about its audience and mission. Nonetheless its contribution to the Brecht centenary included staging and staged readings of fragments from the archive such as *Jae Fleischhacker von Chikago* and *Judith von Shimoda* as well as a scrupulously faithful revival of *Die Massnahme*, whose very fidelity to the initial production of 1930 raised charges of *Ostalgie*. From the late 1990s, Brecht's BE was under new management by the former Vienna Burgtheater director, Claus Peymann, who initially shunned Brecht in favor of his man from Vienna, Thomas Bernhardt. Despite this initial retreat, Peymann returned to his earlier career as a leftist director and came round to (the brand of) Brecht with committed and notably unironic productions in 2003 of Brecht's most militant plays after *Die Massnahme*, namely *Die Mutter* (1931) and *Die Heilige Johanna der Schlachthöfe* (St Joan of the Stockyards, initially written in 1932, but not performed until after the war).

Precisely because they cannot be simply reduced to a univocal expression of *Ostalgie*, the events staged in commemoration of Brecht's centenary provide a point of departure for exploring the marketing of *Ostalgie* and the decline of Brechtian futures, as well as opportunities for critique. In particular, the rediscovery and re-evaluation of items in Brecht's archive that were neglected by Cold War regimes on both sides offer new ways of describing and perhaps also prescribing Brecht. From the exhibition of the hitherto archived contents of Brecht's library to the marketing of the revival of *Measures Taken* as if it were the recovery of a hitherto forbidden object, this revival calls in general for new ways of configuring the relationship between the preservation and commodification of cultural heritage,

and in particular for an examination of the irony of the current and
future commodification of this anti-capitalist author.

"I'm at home in Asphalt City" ("On poor B. B.": *Werke* 11: 119)

A key contributor to Brecht production and to the production of Brecht
is the city of Berlin. Although Brecht was born in Augsburg, the city
fathers there put up a plaque at his birthplace (and, more recently,
opened a museum and a Brecht shop) only in 1991, after shunning
him for nearly half a century. Berlin, by contrast, was the only place,
from 1924 to 1933 and later, from 1949 to 1956, the year of his death,
where Brecht had extensive and intensive access to the collaborators
and audiences who shaped his theatre practice. While he may have
written plays, poetry, fiction, and theory more extensively in exile in
Scandinavia and the United States, exile deprived him of the language,
the institutions, and the social support – and antagonism – vital for
the production and reception of a "theatre for instruction" that could
be pedagogical, playful, and politically provocative all at once. Berlin
in 1998, eleven years after the rival celebrations of the 750th anniversary of the city and eight after the reunification of Germany, was a city
in the process of reinventing itself after being divided for over forty
years, an exemplary place and occasion for investigating the historical foundations and present contestation of cultural politics. In the
early years of the twenty-first century, Berlin was still literally and
figuratively a building site, on which the activity of construction (and
deconstruction) called attention to the still-potent tensions between
past and present, East and West, communism and capitalism, as well
as to the literary history of the material and ideological construction of
different Germanies discussed in this and the two previous chapters.

Walking tours organized for the centenary under the rubric of
"I'm at home in Asphalt City" ("In der Asphaltstadt bin ich daheim")
addressed these tensions indirectly. "Brecht's unknown stages"
included lesser-known places of Brecht performances, particularly
in the period, the mid-1920s, contemporaneous with his celebration of "Asphalt City," but left unexplored sites in working-class

districts, such as Neukölln, where Brecht worked with communist choir and acting groups to perform the *Lehrstücke* (learning plays), his most politically and theatrically advanced theatre for actors without spectators.[9] Even if the halls and the party that maintained them are no longer there, this tour might have provided a useful counterweight to Brecht's big hit in this period, *The Threepenny Opera* at the Theater am Schiffbauerdamm, and to the presentation of Brecht as a cultural monument among other city monuments, which was notably more prominent. "Brecht and the Powerful" toured Unter den Linden, once the main thoroughfare of inter-war bourgeois culture, and the quarters of the Weimar and Nazi governments, and now in the twenty-first century once again the center of consumer capitalism. "Brecht in Stalinallee" used the site of the SED's most ambitious urban planning venture and the construction workers' uprising against it in June 1953 to explore the tensions in Brecht's uneasy loyalty to the GDR. Linking Alexanderplatz in the center with the working-class neighborhood of Friedrichshain (renamed Horst-Wessel-Stadt by the Nazis), Frankfurter Allee had been the highway of the Red East. As the proletarian counterpart to haut-bourgeois Unter den Linden in the 1920s, it was the primary site of urban renewal and national self-representation for the SED government in the 1950s. The boulevard was renamed Stalinallee within weeks of the GDR's inauguration in 1949, and retained the name well after Stalin's death (in 1953) and disgrace (in 1956) until 1961, when it was renamed Karl-Marx-Allee.[10] The

---

[9] Michael Bienert, *Mit Brecht durch Berlin: ein literarischer Reiseführer* (Frankfurt a.M.: Insel, 1998), 71–128, contrasts Brecht's haunts in the "New West" of 1920s Berlin, including commercial houses like the Theater des Westens, with his later work with the Marxist Workers' School, and school *Lehrstück* productions in working-class Neukölln, as well as more visible leftist productions such as his adaptation of *Die Mutter* at the Volksbühne on Rosa-Luxemburg-Platz. For an alternative guide to sites associated with Brecht, see Michael Rutschky and Jürgen Teller, *Der verborgene Brecht: Ein Berliner Stadtrundgang* (Berlin: Scalo, 1997).

[10] For a critical account of the Stalinallee project, see Simone Hain, *Warum zum Beispiel die Stalinallee? Beiträge zu einer Transformationsgeschichte des modernen Planens und Bauens* (Erkner:

western portion of the boulevard still bears Marx's name and, despite criticism of its monumentalism, is now an official landmark hailed as in 1996 as "the only boulevard to be built in post-war Europe."[11]

The centenary exhibition of Brecht's work at the Akademie der Künste (AdK) pointed towards some of these and other unexplored sites. The very procedure of preparation and exhibition reinforced the impact of the Cold War on city geography even after unification. Materials housed in the Brecht museum and the academy's archive in central (formerly East) Berlin were exhibited in the western academy of arts. The AdK West's first director, Hans Scharoun, was to lead the Stalinallee project in the *east* until the SED rejected his modernist, Bauhaus-influenced designs for an open and interactive *Stadt-landschaft* (city landscape: low-rise modernist buildings in green settings), which led to his departure for West Berlin and his realization of these designs in the anti-monumental modernist buildings in the Hansa district, which in 1998 still housed the AdK's primary exhibition space.[12] One cabinet in the open airy exhibition space of the AdK West highlighted Brecht's ties to the architect Hermann Henselmann, who won the commission to direct the renovation of the bombed-out Frankfurter Allee as Stalinallee (Stalin Boulevard), but

Institut für Regionalentwicklung und Strukturplanung [IRS], 1999), and for its contribution to controversies about the failure of GDR modernity, see Wolfgang Engler, *Die Ostdeutschen: Kunde von einem verlorenen Land*, 2nd edn (Berlin: Aufbautaschenbuchverlag, 2002), 34–51.

[11] Helmut Engel and Wolfgang Ribbe, Editors' Preface to *Karl-Marx-Allee: Magistrale in Berlin. Die Wandlung der sozialistischen Prachtstraße zur Hauptstraße des Berliner Ostens* (Berlin: Akademieverlag, 1996), 9.

[12] The AdK West was designed by Werner Düttmann and Sabine Schumann in 1957 as part of Scharoun's overall plan for the Hansa district. The Arnim Palace in Pariser Platz (1737; renovated by Heinrich Knoblauch in 1857) housed the AdK from 1907 until 1937, when it was taken over by the Nazi architect Albert Speer as his planning headquarters. Bombed near the end of the Second World War, it was left in ruins in the space between Soviet and Western zones, which become the no man's land around the Berlin Wall. After renovation (led by Günter Behnisch), it is now once again the headquarters of the AdK for the whole of Berlin.

who claimed that without Brecht he would not have remained in the GDR.[13] Henselmann's association with Brecht included the collaboration between architect and poet on the Stalinallee; texts by Brecht were set in stone on the portals of Henselmann's signature buildings, beginning with the "Hochhaus [high-rise apartment building] an der Weberwiese [weavers' meadow]". Located in the central section, named for the meadow where weavers in pre-industrial Berlin washed their textiles, the building, a block-wide eight-storey apartment building flanked by towers and covered with tiles in the Moscow style, provided more interior space and better plumbing than the proletarian backyard apartments of the nineteenth century, but sacrificed the closed but neighborly space of the central yard of nineteenth-century Berlin apartments to the monumental boulevard leading ever onward.

The project represented the triumph of Soviet notions of modernity, not only over pre-modern residues like inadequate plumbing but, more pointedly, over competing traditions of modernity, especially the pre-war Bauhaus tradition represented by Scharoun. Despite its antifascist reputation, subsequent destruction by the Nazis, and rehabilitation by authorities like Henselmann (who cited Brecht covertly to praise modernists Ludwig Mies van der Rohe and other Bauhaus associates as exemplary architects engaged with a realistic transformation of form in the interests of modernity rather than a formalist attachment to outdated ornament), the Bauhaus did not suit the Moscow orientation of the SED.[14] Ulbricht dismissed Scharoun's *Stadtlandschaft*

---

[13] Herman Henselmann, quoted in *Und mein Werk ist der Abgesang des Jahrtausends: 22 Versuche, eine Arbeit zu beschreiben*, catalogue for the Bertolt Brecht centenary exhibition, ed. Erdmut Wizisla (Berlin: Akademie der Künste, 1998), 114.

[14] In "Formalismus und Realismus," *Bauplanung und Bautechnik* 4 (1950): 244–8 and 282–7, Henselmann attacks as formalist architects' attachment to archaic ornament and an illusion of craft in the era of industrialism, while praising architects who tackle new ways of unleashing and representing new forces and means of production. Despite an obligatory nod to Lukács, Henselmann uses terms that reiterate Brecht's critique of Lukács's formalism. In his essay "Die Gestalt der neuen Stadt," *Bildende Kunst* 1: 6 (1947), 10–15, Scharoun

as more appropriate for the "South African landscape" and therefore by implication primitive and pre-modern, and insisted that the
monumental high-rise apartments reflected post-capitalist modernity
in "the power of our will to rebuild" and the "grandiose ideas" of
socialism.[15] Ulbricht's debt to Moscow may have reinforced his government's "colonial" relationship to the "Stalinist empire," but one
should not forget that, while GDR architects made their journey to
Moscow, their Western counterparts were sent to North Carolina for
"reorientation," and that both camps in the Cold War campaigned vigorously for their version of a new international style.[16] The tension
between this "colonial" monumentalism and an interactive international modernism was made concrete – but also rendered ironic – by
the academy building's prominent place in the Hansa district, designed

> does not mention the term "Bauhaus" but nonetheless invokes the
> contribution of Walter Gropius and associates in the "reshaping of
> Berlin" and argues that form should follow function in the creation of
> an architecture on a human scale to bring together city and green
> space.
>
> [15] Ulbricht, "Die Großbauten im Fünfjahrplan," *Neues Deutschland* 23
> (July 1950), quoted in Hain, "Strategien des Monumentalen am
> Beispiel der Gestaltung der Hauptstadt der DDR Berlin," *Warum zum
> Beispiel die Stalinallee?*, 100, 102.
>
> [16] For the Stalinallee project's debt to Moscow, see Hain, "Reise nach
> Moskau: Wie Deutsche 'sozialistisch bauen lernten,'" *Bauwelt* 83
> (1992): 2546–58, and Hain and Herbert Nicolaus, eds., *Reise nach
> Moskau: Dokumente zur Erklärung von Motiven,
> Entscheidungsstrukturen und Umsetzungskonflikten für den ersten
> städtebaulichen Paradigmawechsel in der DDR* (Erkner: IRS, 1995). In
> "Cities of the Stalinist Empire," in *Forms of Dominance: On the
> Architecture and Urbanism of the Colonial Enterprise*, ed. Nezard
> Al-Sayyad (Brookfield: Avebury, 1992), Greg Castillo argues (270ff.)
> that this relationship was colonial to the extent that Moscow
> enforced ideological conformity through massive urban projects, but
> bases his claims exclusively on English-language sources and tends
> (despite a concluding acknowledgment (284) that the United States
> conducted its own ideological re-education) to reiterate the Cold War
> line that the program to house workers was merely Stalinist
> propaganda.

as the organic antithesis to the monumental Stalinallee. The display inside also reiterated the contradictions of the Stalinallee project. While providing undoubtedly modern quarters for the construction men and *Trummerfrauen* (rubble women) who worked on the site, the accelerated construction schedule also provoked the rebellion of construction workers whose resistance to speeded-up work schedules organized around Stalin's birthday led, several months after Stalin's death in March 1953, to the uprising that undermined the 'worker-and-peasant state', and to the doubts of critical intellectuals about its continued legitimacy.

"The cunning needed to disseminate the truth" ("Five Difficulties in Writing the Truth," *Werke* 22: 81)

While this particular cabinet offered a synecdochic display of Brecht's locations in the city outside, the exhibition as a whole followed his placement and displacement in different locations in the world and in multiple sites and genres of production. Under the motto of the telling but ephemeral nature of the essay, which Brecht himself noted in the quip "my work is the swan song of the millennium" ("der Abgesang des Jahrtausends"), the exhibition displayed in twenty-two cabinets "22 essays in describing [a way of] work[ing]" ("22 Versuche, eine Arbeit zu beschreiben"). The title alluded to Brecht's serial publication of *Versuche* (essays, experiments), which included plays, poetry, fiction, and non-fiction prose and so escaped the conventional distinction between "creative" and "critical" work, and thus the pressure to commodify the former as an object of culinary or leisure consumption and the latter as hard-to-swallow theory. Arranged in an area called the rehearsal space (*Probebühne*), the cabinets were offset by photographs of Brecht's family and friends on the walls and by selected stage objects made for pioneering BE productions in Brecht's last few years, from masks for *The Trial of Lucullus* (1951) and *The Caucasian Chalk Circle* (1953), to the globe of the world for *The Life of Galileo* (1956). The largest and perhaps most-symbol laden object was the fully fitted wagon for *Mother Courage and Her Children* (1949), which inaugurated Brecht's return to Berlin and his battles with Fritz Erpenbeck, who denounced the production for "decadence alien to the people."[17] In contrast to the flimsy cardboard flats complete with painted books, representing a composite of Brecht's workrooms in various sites around the world, the solidity of these objects, too solid to be called props, amply realized Brecht's call, in a note on stage construction written at the time of the *Mother Courage* production, for usable stage objects whose use might demonstrate the labor and social value imprinted on them (*Werke* 23: 116).

Whatever the sensuous pleasures to be had from (almost) touching these objects, which were still protected by the usual museum prohibitions against actual handling, the greatest use value of the exhibition lay in the documentation of the textual and visual matter that stimulated Brecht's production, as well as in the display of a plethora of works-in-progress previously known only to the archivists and their professional clients. This material cast light (and shadow) on better-known plays on similar themes. "The Life of Einstein" highlighted Brecht's concern in 1945 about annihilation by the atom bomb, which *The Life of Galileo* addressed only indirectly; the photograph of Einstein putting out his tongue at a photo-journalist registered Brecht's perception of the connection between experimental thinking and a cheeky sense of fun (*Spaß*). On the other hand, "Die Horst-Wessel-Legende," notes for a play on the Nazi theme-song, suggested a more pointed attack on Nazi propaganda than the glamorous "gangster-show" on Hitler's rise to power in *The Resistable Rise of Arturo Ui. Jae Fleischhacker* [meat-chopper] *von Chikago* (one of the fragments receiving a world premiere at the BE in 1998) and the accompanying materials assembled by Elisabeth Hauptmann – from the floorplan of the Chicago Board of Trade and Frank Norris's novel *The Pit* to German economic textbooks – highlighted the "random and reckless character of world markets" in the 1920s that surfaced

---

[17] Fritz Erpenbeck, "Formalismus und Dekadenz," in *Dokumente zur Kunst-, Literatur- und Kulturpolitik der SED*, ed. Elimar Schubbe (Stuttgart: Seewald, 1972), 109–13.

later and more enigmatically in the play *St. Joan of the Stockyards* (1932). A note titled "Confucius or Ford?" suggested not only the difference between bureaucratic traditionalism and imperial capitalism but also the possibility of affinities between two variations on the concentration of power.

As this note suggests, Brecht's exploration of capitalist and anti-capitalist themes and topics followed some unexpected paths. His versification of *The Communist Manifesto* (1945; unpublished until 1993) drew not only on his study of Marx with Karl Korsch and Fritz Sternberg at the Marxist Workers' School (MASCH) in the Berlin of the Weimar Republic and on his observation of American capitalism during the Second World War, but also on earlier experiments with *Lehrgedichte* (pedagogical poems) on the model of Lucretius' ruminations on natural science. Brecht's reading of Marx was supplemented not only by Lenin but also by one of Lenin's fiercest critics, Rosa Luxemburg, who was to have been the subject of a play but whose critique of Party infallibility encapsulated in the famous defense of freedom as necessarily "the freedom of those who think differently" may have proven too touchy for the GDR state. More surprising than the material on Luxemburg was Brecht's extensive collection of writing by and about Trotsky (Lev Bronstein). Trotsky was erased from communist history during Stalin's rule and even after Stalin's death, yet Brecht's library contained Trotsky's *Geschichte der russischen Revolution* and *Flucht von Siberien*, published in Germany shortly before Hitler came to power, and Trotsky's controversial edition of *The Suppressed Testament of Lenin* (in US translation). Displayed alongside Brecht's notes and typescript of *Me-Ti: Book of Changes*, they highlighted the topicality of his allegorical narrative analysis of state socialist sclerosis in Confucian costume.

Although he was a lifelong critic of capitalist society and bourgeois culture, Brecht's own connection to official communism was ambiguous. As he told HUAC in 1947 (the year after he completed a draft of the versified Communist Manifesto, and the year before he left the United States for good), he was never a member of any

Communist Party.[18] Nonetheless, even his crafty response to HUAC reiterated the anti-fascist commitments of his Weimar and exile years in his defense of a democratic anti-militarism under threat by preparations in both camps for a not-so-cold war. Brecht's anti-militarist and anti-imperialist sentiment, along with his interest in the artistic as well as pragmatic challenge of making poetry out of political prose, inform his endeavor to versify the *Communist Manifesto*. Composed in the last months of the Second World War, as the end of the war in Europe shaded, via the atom bombs on Japan, into the foreshadowing of another, nuclear world war, this project also looked forward to the centenary of the manifesto and to what Brecht saw as an opportunity, outlined in a journal entry on 11 February 1945, to renew the "propaganda impact [*Wirkung*]" of the manifesto as "political pamphlet" and as "work of art" (*Werke* 27: 219). The actual labor on this project suggests, however, that the barrier between Marx's pointed account of contemporary political conflict and his specific "technical" terms for its protagonists, such as the bourgeoisie and the proletariat, on the one hand, and the constraints of what Brecht's collaborator Leon Feuchtwanger called the "smooth flow of the hexameter" on the other, remained difficult if not, as Feuchtwanger had it, "hopeless" (*Werke* 15: 393–4, 400).[19]

In keeping with his defense, in a rare article in *Das Wort* (1939; *Werke* 22: 357–65; *BoT* 115–20), for rough, irregular translations of dramatic verse, Brecht used rougher, less predictable hexameters to evoke the violence of class struggle rather than the smooth transmission in the classical epic of Homer or Virgil. He was nonetheless not

---

[18] See the exchange in US Congress House of Representatives, *Communist Infiltration in the Motion Picture Industry*, 495–6. For an edited version, see *Thirty Years of Treason: Excerpts from Hearings before the House Committee on UnAmerican Activities*, ed. Eric Bentley (New York: Viking, 1971), 201–25; here: 209.

[19] After the third draft of 1945, Brecht dropped the project, despite encouragement from Karl Korsch, who hoped that Brecht would finish in time for the hundredth anniversary of the manifesto in 1948 (*Werke* 15: 390).

immune to the temptation of substituting elevated epithets for Marx's terms of analysis. Marx's first paragraph opens succinctly:

> Ein Gespenst geht um in Europa–das Gespenst des Kommunismus. Alle Mächte des alten Europa haben sich zu einer heiligen Hexenjagt gegen dies Gespenst verbündet, der Papst und der Zar, Metternich und Guizot, französische Radikale und deutsche Polizisten.
>
> (Marx/Engels *Manifest*, 19)

This introduction is rendered in Samuel Moore's evocative if not always precise translation as:

> A spectre is haunting Europe – the spectre of Communism. All the powers of the old Europe have entered into a holy alliance [or *witch-hunt*] to exorcize this spectre: pope and Czar, French radicals and German police [spies].
>
> (*Manifesto*, 33)

The introductory section goes on to argue that Communists should show themselves as the force that their enemies acknowledge them to be:

> Es ist hohe Zeit daß die Kommunisten ihre Anschauungsweise, ihre Zwecke, ihre Tendenzen vor den ganzen Welt offen darlegen und dem Märchen vom Gespenst des Kommunismus ein Manifest der Partei selbst entgegenstellen.
>
> (*Manifest*, 19)

> [It is high time that Communists openly before the whole world publish their views, their aims, their tendencies and confront this nursery tale of the Spectre of Communism with a manifesto of the Party itself.]
>
> (*Manifesto*, 34; trans. mod.)

In contrast, Brecht's third and final full draft opens with a long verse paragraph about the specter of Communism and the legacy of war:

Kriege zertrümmern die Welt, und umgeht zwischen den
  Trümmern
Sichtbar und groß ein Gespenst, und nicht erst der Krieg hat's
  geboren.
Auch im Frieden schon ward es gesichert, den Herrschenden
  schrecklich
Aber freundlich den Kindern der Vorstadt. Im ärmlicher Küche
Liegte es oft, kopfschüttelnd, voll Zorn, in halbleere Töpfe.
Oft die Erschöpften paßte es ab vor Gruben und Werften.
Freunde besuchte es im Haft, passierend ohne Passierschein
Oftmals. Selbst in Kontoren wird es gesen, und im Hörsaal
Wird es gehört. Zu Zeiten dann stülpt es von Stahl einen
  Hut auf
Steigt in riesige Tanks und fliegt mit tödlichen Bombern.
Vielerlei Sprachen spricht es, alle. Und schweigt in vielen.
Ehrengast in den Hütten sitzt es, Sorge der Villen
Alles zu ändern und ewig zu bleiben gekommen; sein
  Name ist
Kommunismus.

                    (*Werke* 15: 148; ll. 1–14)

[Wars bring the world to ruin, and through the rubble goes /
Conspicuously large a specter. The war did not create it /
Already in peace was it sighted, fearsome to the rulers / But a
friend to [slum] children. In poor kitchens / It lay shaking its
head in anger, in half-empty pots / Often it passed by weary
[workers] in quarries and docks / Attending friends in
dungeons, passing without a passbook / Often. Even seen in
counting houses, in assemblies / Heard. At times then forges
from steel a hat /And rises up in giant tanks and flies with
deadly bombers / Many tongues it speaks and in many holds
its tongue / Honored guest in hovels, the mansions' grief /
Come to change everything and to stay forever; its name is /
Communism]

Brecht attempts to expand Marx's cardinal agon between reactionary
European powers and the insurgent Communist International to

include a role for Communism as the agent of change in the ruins of post-war Europe. His paratactic track of the specter's path through particular sites in these ruins evokes its many ministrations to the victims of war and those compelled to wage it in battle or industry, as well as, briefly, its presumed torment of the rulers.

But this evocation of ruin, however compelling, favors a series of vivid tableaux of suffering and struggle rather than Marx's original analysis of class struggle and of the bourgeoisie's revolutionary capacity to completely transform productive relations by reducing all to the cash nexus. Marx's key paragraph reads:

> [d]ie Bourgeoisie hat in der Geschichte eine höchst revolutionäre Rolle gespielt. Die Bourgeoisie, wo sie zu Herrschaft gekommen, hat alle feudalen, patriarchalischen, idyllischen Verhältnisse zerstört. Sie hat die buntscheckigen Feudalbande, die den Menschen an seinen natürlichen Vorgesetzten knüpften, zerrissen und kein anderes Band zwischen Mensch und Mensch übriggelassen als das nackte Interesse, als die gefühllose "bare Zahlung." Sie hat die heiligen Schauer der frommen Schwärmerei, der ritterlichen Begeisterung, der spießbürgerlichen Wehmut in dem eiskalten Wasser egoistischer Berechnung ertränkt. Sie hat die persönliche Würde in den Tauschwert aufgelöst und an die Stelle der zahllosen verbrieften und wohlerworbenen Freiheiten die *eine* gewissenlose Handelsfreiheit gesetzt. Sie hat, mit einem Wort, an die Stelle der mit religiösen und politischen Illusionen verhüllten Ausbeutung die offene, unverschämte, direkte, dürre Ausbeutung gesetzt.
>
> (Marx/Engels, *Manifest*, 21–2)

> [The bourgeoisie historically has played a most revolutionary part. The bourgeoisie, wherever it has got the upper hand, has put an end to all feudal, patriarchal, idyllic relations. It has [pitilessly] torn asunder the motley feudal ties that bound people [*Menschen*] to their 'natural superiors' and has left remaining no other nexus between people [*Menschen*] than naked [self-]interest, than unfeeling [*gefühllose*] 'cash

payment'. It has drowned the [most] heavenly ecstasies of religious fervour, of chivalric enthusiasm, of philistine sentimentalism in the icy water of egoistical calculation. It has resolved personal worth into exchange value and in place of the numberless indefeasible chartered freedoms it has set up that *single* unconscionable [freedom –] free trade. In a word, for exploitation veiled by political and religious illusion, it has substituted naked, shameless, direct, brutal exploitation.]

(Marx/Engels, *Manifesto*, 37–8; trans. mod.)

Apart from adding some superfluous adjectives to Marx's well-chosen ones, Moore's translation follows Marx's surgical exposure of bourgeois and feudal illusions to the light of capitalist facts. Although Marx reinforces this thrust through the flesh of ideology to the bones of actual social relations with a series of qualifiers calculated to make those wounds bleed and bleed again, the paragraph ends in a sharp but simple point: the indictment of the end of freedoms, values, and ideals in the fact of unlimited exploitation.

Brecht's corresponding verse paragraph begins by omitting Marx's revolutionary point about the revolutionary role of the bourgeoisie and replacing it with the following:

> Und sie [die Bourgeoisie] erwies sich als harte und
> ungeduldige Herrin.
> Eisener Stirn und eisenr Ferse zertrat die das faule
> Patriarchalisch stille Idyll, zerriß die feudalen
> Alt buntscheckigen Bande, geknüpft zwischen Schützling und
>   Schutzherr
> Duldend kein anderes Band zwichen Menschen als nackte
>   Intresse
> Barer Entlohnung. "Adlige Haltung", "Ritterlichkeit", und
> "Treues Gesinde", "Liebe zum Boden", "ehrliches Handwerk"
> "Dienst an der Sache" und "innre Berufung", alles begoß ihr
> Eisiger Strahl der Berechnung. Menschliche Würde
>   verramscht sie
> Grob in den Tauschwert, setzend brutal an der Stelle der vielen
> Heilige verbrieften Freiheiten nur die Freiheit des Handels.

Stille Ausbeutung war es gewesen, natürliche, immer;
Offene wurde es nun und schamlos wurd es betrieben.
(*Werke* 15: 151; ll. 83–95)

[And the bourgeoisie appeared a hard, impatient mistress /
With iron mien and iron heel she crushed the idle / Patriarchal
idyll, ripped up the / Old and motley feudal ties that bound
vassal to protector lord / Allows no other tie than naked
interest / Of cash amends. "Noble bearing," "chivalry" and /
"true retainer," "love of land," and "honest craft" / "Service
to the cause" and "inner calling," all basted by the / Iron ray
of calculation. Human worth sold short / For crass exchange
value, brutally replacing many / Holy chartered freedoms with
mere free trade / Hidden exploitation it had been, natural,
enduring / Open now and shamelessly conducted.]

Brecht's personification of Marx's abstract enumeration of "motley
feudal ties" in the figure of the neutered "vassal" (*Schützling*) or
"true retainer" (*treues Gesinde*) to the masculine "lord protector"
(*Schutzherr*) aptly dramatizes feudal relations and Marx's ironic dis-
section of the "natural superiority" of feudal rulers, but his treatment
of the bourgeoisie as Iron Lady blunts Marx's key point that capital's
power to *dissolve* (*auflösen*) human relations and values into calcu-
lable exchange value is at once brutal and revolutionary. The heavy
emphasis on iron leads not only to a muddled metaphor, in which
the iron ray of calculation "basted" (*begoß*) feudal values rather than
simply dissolved them, but also to an implicit equation of capitalism
and fascism as the apotheosis of the reign of iron. While this characterization reiterates the line of the Moscow group poised in 1945 to
take over the Soviet Zone of Germany, it leads Brecht to miss not only
Marx's understanding of the revolutionary and repressive dimensions
of capitalism, but also a crucial opportunity to apply this understanding, in the brief moment before the hardening of the Cold War camps,
to the development of a critical socialist analysis of the allure as well
as the shortcomings of capitalism, the better to contest it. This clumsy
rather than critical *Episierung* suggests not simply, as the editors of
his *Werke* suggest, that Brecht treated the *Communist Manifesto* as

part of the Communist "classics" despite his desire to reactivate its political force in the present (*Werke* 15: 393), but rather that he struggles between these two impulses, between the orthodox imperative to make of Marx's text a classical epic, elevating the struggle of the proletariat to the triumph of the Communist International, and the critical imperative to use *Episierung* as a tool of dis-illusion and revision of Marx in the light of contemporary conflict and contradiction.[20]

"The contradiction between learning and enjoyment must be clearly grasped and its significance understood – in a period when knowledge is acquired in order to be sold for the highest possible price" ("Appendices to the Short Organum," *Werke* 23: 288)

Completed in 1948 after Brecht had left the United States and effectively abandoned the *Communist Manifesto* project, the *Short Organum for the Theater* is Brecht's most systematic presentation of his method. Whereas the former attempt to create an epic poem out of Marx's manifesto seems overloaded with the pressure of the orthodox teleology that brings the epic to conclude in Soviet hegemony over the Communist International, the latter, with its series of notes in dialogue with one another, succeeds in applying a marxist critique of capitalist social relations and bourgeois culture in a manner both experimental and systematic. The appendix to the *Organum*, from which the epigraph of this section is taken, was compiled as Brecht revised his method while working for the first time with a stable long-term ensemble (1949–56), and, finally at the end of this period in Berlin, his return, under socialist conditions, to the theatre on Schiffbauerdamm where he had his greatest hit under capitalism, *The Threepenny Opera* (1929). The quotation above represents a delicate balance between an orthodox dismissal of entertainment

---

[20] Korsch found the text "wonderfully useful," whether or not the "hexameters scanned," while Eisler, composer himself of dissonant music, regretted that Brecht's rough verses had failed to cohere in a "good, strict form" and thus left "us" without the promised "epic of *The Communist Manifesto*, which would have been a quite remarkable work of art" (*Werke* 15: 400).

under capitalism and a characteristically Brechtian recognition of the productive tension between enjoyment and learning, pleasure and instruction. Brecht's emphasis on this tension is perhaps his most famous and most misunderstood tenet. Yet his remark, which highlights the tension as well as the mutual influence of learning and consuming, offers a timely reminder, in an early twenty-first-century culture much more saturated with commodification than anything Brecht experienced, that the capitalist culture industry thrives by marketing anti-capitalist messages as commodities, from the revival of *Die Massnahme* to revolution jeans.

Once again, the material and theatrical production around Brecht's centenary in February 1998 provide food for thought. If the Academy of Arts exhibition offered a rehearsal space in which visitors might learn from staging experimental variations on Brecht in their mind's eye, the theatres in Berlin used the centenary in part to re-evaluate the canon not only of Brecht plays and productions but also of Brechtian performance conventions more generally – and also in part to make of this canon an object of consumption. The centenary celebrations took place slightly more than two years after the death of Heiner Müller, Brecht's successor, critic and, briefly, director of Brecht's erstwhile theatre, the Berliner Ensemble. The BE was still dealing with the monumentalization of Brecht perpetuated by his heirs, especially his daughter Barbara Brecht-Schall and his son-in-law, the leading actor Ekkehart Schall, as well as managing director Manfred Wekwerth, who ran the theatre from 1975 to the demise of the GDR in 1990. By the 1980s, the theatre that astonished the world in the 1950s and 1960s had become little more than a museum for archival productions of the master. It was taken over in 1990 by five prominent German directors but run essentially by Müller until his death in 1995. During this period the theatre was enlivened with a mixture of maverick productions of unfamiliar Brecht texts – including Müller's version of the *Fatzer* fragments – revivals of Müller's critical dramas on the contradictions between socialist theory and GDR reality – *Der Lohndrücker*, *Der Bau*, and *Mauser*, and new versions of classic Brecht, such as *Arturo Ui* (1995), directed by Müller, with Martin Wuttke as Ui. Although featured in the centenary season, this production was edited after Müller's death by Wuttke, who served as interim director until the appointment of Claus Peymann in 1999. Where Müller's staging maintained and sharpened the topical edge of Brecht's critique of fascism, especially in the scenes depicting Ui's perversion of justice and the thuggery of his followers which alluded to the rise of right-wing violence in the 1990s, Wuttke's version dispensed with these contextualizing scenes to focus on his own bravura performance as a demon dog in an entertaining but essentially toothless gangster-show.

While Wuttke's truncated version of *Arturo Ui* represented a defeat of sorts, a capitulation of critical dis-illusion to the illusory charm of the charismatic star, Robert Wilson's version of *Der Ozeanflug* (Flight over the Ocean, 1929) and Klaus Emmerich's revival of *Die Massnahme* (1930) both attempted critical re-presentations of charisma, albeit in rather different ways. Wilson is not in any obvious sense a Brechtian director, since he is less interested in the theatrical analysis of social contradiction that might instruct the audience than in the creation of a modernist *Gesamtkunstwerk* of minimalist but captivating image, sound, and movement. Like his early and exemplary work, *Einstein on the Beach* (1976), Wilson's *Der Ozeanflug* was a visual essay on the contiguity and incongruity of science and art. Initially produced as *Der Lindberghflug* for radio broadcast and performance at the Baden-Baden Festival in 1929, with music by Kurt Weill and textual work by Elisabeth Hauptmann, the published title, *Flug der Lindberghs* (1930), referred to the "flight of the Lindberghs" (plural) and so celebrated less the charismatic figure of Charles Lindbergh himself than the technological achievement of his flight across the Atlantic in 1927, and the possibility of educating the "boys and girls" to whom the play was dedicated to emulate the chorus of "Lindberghs" rather than any single individual (*Werke* 3: 7; 403–7). Wilson's mise en scène included an ingenious imitation of a minimalist flying machine – a table suspended in mid-air, at which the pilot (Stefan Kurt) sat, balancing on a unicycle – which aptly indicated not only Lindbergh's stripped-down aircraft but also his understanding that plane and pilot together constituted the flying machine. The stage image omitted any visual reference to Lindbergh's own fascination with the social as well as technological engineering of the Nazis that compelled Brecht to cut the man's name from his play for its post-war revival on Süddeutscher Rundfunk in 1950 (*Werke* 3: 403). While an incisive biographical essay in the program documented Lindbergh's trips to Nazi Germany and explored his more lasting promotion of American prowess and the "imperial" if not directly imperialist idea of America, the majority of spectators, who would not read this before the show, would more likely have been captivated by the image of flight and the small-boy-with-radio in period dress partially representing the "boys and girls" to whom Brecht dedicated his radio play.[21] The anti-fascist critique in the program vanished behind the haunting images of flight on the stage and the international reputation and brand name of the American creator of these images.

"Dialecticians bring out the contradictory elements in all phenomena and processes; they think critically; that is, they bring phenomena to crisis, so as to grasp them"
("Katzgraben-Notate," *Werke* 25: 416)
Although the BE, the theatre of Brecht and his heirs, had the lion's share of Brecht productions and reproductions in the centenary year, other Berlin theatres offered new perspectives on old plays which, in retrospect, appear to engage more productively and critically with Brecht's legacy. The Volksbühne, whose director, Frank Castorf, expressed contradictory opinions about Brecht, staged only the agit-prop fragment "The Bread Shop."[22] Brecht reappeared nonetheless

---

[21] Bernd Böhmel, "Charles August Lindbergh: Landesplatz für Dämonen," in *Bertolt Brecht: Der Ozeanflug* (Berlin: Berliner Ensemble, 1998), n.p.

[22] In *Die Erotik des Verrats: Gespräche mit Frank Castorf*, ed. Hans-Dieter Schütt (Berlin: Dietz, 1996), Castorf distances himself from the early anarchic Brecht allegedly favored by "Western directors in the 1970s" to defend on the one hand the parable plays as directed by Wekwerth in the 1950s and 1960s in the BE's heyday and, on the other, the "orthodox" *Massnahme* (93). Elsewhere in this series of interviews, however, he praises Brecht's early interest in *Spaß* (fun) and a theatre for sport spectators (109).

in the text and the technique of Castorf's adaptation of *the* pre-Brechtian socialist classic, Gerhart Hauptmann's *Weber* (*Weavers*, 1892) as *Hauptmanns Weber*. Post-modern in his ironic, even cynical deconstruction of Hauptmann's modern (progressivist, committed, even heroic) depiction of the plight of textile workers in 1840s Silesia on the eve of the revolutionary surge across Europe that inspired Marx's and Engels's *Manifesto* in 1848, Castorf used anachronism to deconstruct the calcified socialist rhetoric of solidarity in struggle, even more radically than he had done in the 1986 revival (or reburial) of Müller's production play, *Der Bau*. His adaptation juxtaposes the story of the Silesian weavers with that of present-day former GDR workers, Hauptmann's 1892 recovery of the weavers' failed revolution of 1848 with the iconographic allusion to the weavers set in stone in the Hochhaus an der Weberwiese and thus the failed revolution of *1948*, while refusing to weave these elements into a tidy heroic narrative. Castorf's scorn for master-narratives, especially for the GDR's foundational myth of the march onward to socialism, might seem to separate him definitively from Brecht, but his deconstruction of these narratives and the corresponding iconography proved a more compelling contribution to the centenary than the respectful homages at the erstwhile house of Brecht.

Hauptmann's play is noteworthy for its naturalistic recreation of the environment, dialect, and miserable condition of German workers in Silesia, a region which became part of Poland after the Second World War, the source of "re-settlers" in the GDR and refugees to the FRG, and thus the object of nationalist propaganda by "expellee" organizations in Germany. The actors used the Silesian accent not to replicate naturalistically a remote outpost of the Prussian Empire in the 1840s, or the dialect of documented refugees in the late 1940s, but rather to bring these scraps of history into a collage of allusions to the present-day layered inheritance of multiple histories. In tandem with the representation of the weavers as former GDR citizens dressed in the distinctive unfashion of the East German prole in a makeshift unemployment office, waiting for non-existent jobs, this collage suggested the current alienation of relatively affluent Berlin theatre-goers from the plight of East Germans and others east of Berlin (fig. 8).

Fig. 8. "The New Capitalists and the GDR Proles": Henry Hübchen, Silvia Riegel, and cast in *Hautpmanns Weber*, adapted and directed by Frank Castorf (Berlin 1998). Photograph by Ingolf Seidel.

These workers are caught between old socialist slogans and newly triumphant capitalism, neither of which offers them a way out. The rabble-rousing "red baker" who motivates the down-trodden weavers was played in Castorf's production by a woman, Silvia Rieger (third from left), who offered her listeners a pastiche of the heroic socialist rhetoric in the original text, and a range of historical and contemporary allusions. These allusions included not only the veteran actor Ernst Busch's vigorous rendition of "The Party is Always Right" (1950), in its time a thoroughly Stalinist anthem that has become an object of com-modification as well as derision in *Ostalgie* shops, but also citations about direct action from Brecht, Zapatista *subcommandante* Marcos, and Quentin Tarantino's film *Pulp Fiction*, juxtaposed in a manner that eluded a clear political line. At the same time, however, portraying the weavers as former GDR citizens waiting for non-existent jobs and the factory-owner, Dreissiger (played by Volksbühne leading man Henry Hübchen), as a new German capitalist in designer wear was not only pointedly topical but a constant reminder of the local conditions of arrested modernity in eastern Germany, sustained through the kaleidoscope of allusions to post-national post-modernism.

The local resonance of this international pastiche emerged in audience commentary, especially during the interval. The staging was met by a thoroughly Brechtian reaction from members of the audience whose interaction with the actors, especially with the favorite Hübchen, who remained on stage during the interval, apparently drew on sustained engagement with the ensemble, made possible (at least until budget cuts in the new century) by subsidy that had kept Volksbühne ticket prices well below those of other theatres such as the BE. Several spectators challenged the perceived motives of the character Hübchen, the factory-owner bent on rationalizing workers out of jobs, as well as those of his antagonists, providing a striking contrast to the usually polite German theatre audiences, who tend to confine themselves to final applause (or the occasional boo) at the end of the show. Others picked up on the irony of the program, a cast-list on a single sheet of GDR-era roughly recycled paper sold in a wrapper of multiple-page glossy advertising for the transnational firm Daimler-Chrysler's high-end Mercedes under the rubric "All people are not equal," with remarks that varied from quips about being conned by the packaging to broad attacks on globalization and its most immediate expression in West German colonization of the East. Hübchen's response, in character, was to suggest in effect that the only way to beat them was to join them: it would be better to be fired by a home-grown East German capitalist than a Westerner.

> **The bourgeoisie cannot exist without constantly revolutionizing the means of production, and thereby the relations of production, and with them the whole relations of society . . . All that is solid melts into air, all that is holy is profaned, and people [*die Menschen*] are at last compelled to see with sober eyes [*mit nüchterner Augen*] their real conditions of life, and their relations with humankind.**
>
> (Marx/Engels, "Manifest," 23; *Manifesto* 38–39 (trans. mod.))

Castorf's transformation of an East German version of Hauptmann's factory-owner into a late twentieth-century capitalist ironically enacts Marx's and Engel's dictum of the revolutionizing energy of transnational capital even though the new capitalist's antagonists – in his *Hauptmanns Weber*, in the Volksbühne house, and in eastern Berlin, eastern Germany and eastern Europe more generally – continue to escape the reach of this dictum, if only by remaining unemployed. While Wilson's *Ozeanflug* veiled this economic scene outside and instead blithely enacted the power of marketable image-making as it staged the eclipse of critique by spectacle, the revival of *Die Massnahme*, Brecht's most notorious play, offered a more ambiguous engagement with its own commodification, haunted by the tension between the heroic image of an international proletariat taking on capital with its own weapons and the sobering picture of the localization, even isolation, of labor struggles against the globalization of capital. Although Brecht argued in 1936, and again in 1956, when he withdrew the play from further production, that *Die Massnahme* was written for the education of the performers, not for spectators, the original performance in the Berliner Philharmonie in December 1930, accompanied by three worker-choirs representing the "control choir" or the voice of the Party, and animated by performance by the actors Weigel and Busch as well as the tenor Anton Topitz as the agitators reporting to the Party on their activities in China and their decision to take measures against their errant comrade, was received as a *Schaustück* in that it was explicitly presented as an "exhibition" of Communist theory and practice. Praised by some communists for its clear representation of the difficult necessity of revolutionary discipline – the young comrade agrees to his own death after jeopardizing the group's efforts at underground organization by emotionally exposing himself as sympathizer with the suffering of the locals – the performance was blamed by others for oversimplifying the complexity of Party work and thus for endangering the Communist cause on the eve of Nazi victory, the play was treated by the HUAC congressmen who interrogated Brecht and Eisler as a transparent apology for the brutality of the communist enemy.[23] Brecht's

---

[23] See critical responses in *Die Massnahme: Kritische Ausgabe mit einer Spielanleitung*, ed. Reiner Steinweg (Frankfurt a.M.: Suhrkamp, 1972),

ban on future production of the play was no doubt a response to its appropriation as a weapon in the Cold War. His concern about inappropriate "moral effects" (Steinweg 258) arose out of the Cold War interpretation of the text as a Stalinist apology and thus a serviceable weapon against any other attempts to represent communist revolution. But his attempt to protect the play from political manipulation by withdrawing it from public spheres of exchange (but not, it turns out, from informal circulation) did not anticipate the commodification of the text and, equally, of the event of its theatrical revival, as an object of the culture-and-heritage industries of a united capitalist Germany.

Despite Brecht's ban and its enforcement by his daughter Barbara Brecht-Schall, the BE production was not the first public revival of the play, although it could claim to be the first public and professional performance for a German-speaking audience. Apart from the production in Uppsala (Sweden) in 1956 that went ahead despite Brecht's attempt to stop its "moral effects," numerous student productions took place around the world, including in the United States after the New Left sparked renewed interest in marxism.[24] In West Germany, the New Left returned in the 1960s to the antifascist legacy in general and to Brecht in particular as a model for

319–471, hereafter cited as "Steinweg." For HUAC's interrogation of Eisler, see US Congress House of Representatives, *Hearings Regarding Hanns Eisler: Hearings Before the Committee on Un-American Activities, House of Representatives, Eightieth Congress, first session. Public law 601 (section 121, subsection Q (2))* (Washington, Govt. Printing Office, 1947), 10–62; edited version in *Thirty Years of Treason,* 73–91.

24 Steinweg lists several West German high school (*Gymnasium*) productions beginning as early as 1961 as well as productions at US universities from Pittsburgh (1966) and Berkeley (1967) to the first International Brecht Society meeting at the University of Wisconsin-Milwaukee (1970) (Steinweg 470). For further comment on *Lehrstück* productions with US students, see Andrzej Wirth, "Lehrstück als Performance," in *Massnehmen: Kontroverse, Perspektive, Praxis: Brecht/Eislers Lehrstück Die Massnahme* (Berlin: Theater der Zeit, 1999), ed. Inge Gellert *et al.,* 207–15.

a progressive critique of residual authoritarianism in a self-declared democratic state.[25] The Brecht heirs' insistence on enforcing Brecht's ban may have thwarted attempts by rising leftist directors in the West like Peymann and Peter Stein to direct *Die Massnahme;* they could not prevent unauthorized citation of the play by controversial political figures from the turmoil of the 1970s to the uncertain period after unification.[26] An experiment based on the play and Brecht's comments on it was conducted over seven days in December 1990 at the then separate Akademie der Künste (Academy of the Arts) in East Berlin by the Austrian director Josef Szeiler and twenty-four other formal participants, whose comments on and images of confrontations inspired

[25] Extracts from Brecht's work in this period, including his debates with Lukács and others, and his correspondence with his marxist mentor Karl Korsch that had not appeared in the authorized *Gesammelte Werke* (1967), were published in the West German *Alternative* in the 1970s.

[26] The question "Welche Niedrigkeit begingest du nicht um / Die Niedrigkeit auszutilgen?" appears in all four complete versions of *Die Massnahme,* which Steinweg labels as A1, A2, A3, and A5 (Steinweg 25, 54, 85, 123), as does the "Praise of the Party." An anonymous reviewer of the 1997 revival in *Der Spiegel* reprinted the BE program's citation of former GDR spy chief Markus Wolf's reference to this phrase in his memoir *Spionenchef im Geheimen Krieg* (Berlin: Econ, 1997), 346, and claimed that the Rote Armee Fraktion's spokesperson, Ulrike Meinhof, had cited both in a letter from Stammheim Prison and also penned a companion "Praise of the RAF." Although this citation does not appear in any of Meinhof's published writings, the Rote Armee Fraktion cited Brecht as an observer of the left's historical betrayal by its apparent allies in their analyses of Germany's fascist history and, in their view, authoritarian present. See "Über den bewaffneten Kampf in Westeuropa" (1971) and "Erklärung zur Sache" (1976), in *Rote Armee Fraktion: Texte und Materialien zur Geschichte der RAF,* ed. Martin Hoffmann (Berlin: ID Verlag, 1997), 104, 202. Subsequent fictional treatments of the Fraktion, especially films from *Deutschland im Herbst* (Germany in Autumn, directed by Fassbinder, Kluge, Schlöndorff, 1977) to Schlöndorff's *Die Stille nach dem Schuß* (1998) reflect on the German inability to come to terms with the history of conflict between fascism and anti-fascism, which resonates with the problem posed by Brecht's question even without citing him directly.

by Brecht's texts were subsequently published. Although it was not performed for an audience, the duration of the experiment and its location compelled those entering or working in the Academy building to engage with the events if only by "taking measures" to avoid them.[27] In 1995, directing and acting students at the (former GDR) Ernst Busch Theatre School produced two variations of the play in the BAT (Berliner Arbeitertheater, Berlin Workers' Theatre); the first replaced the visible figures (but not the voices) of the worker-choir with midget hand-puppets sitting as if in judgment on the four agitators and doubled the latter with puppets that looked like the four actors; this staging, and the long pause before judgment, seemed to encourage sympathy for the young comrade. The second, which took place after an interval, featured the actors speaking directly to the audience and so shifted the weight of the action towards collective decision-making rather than the sympathetic individual.[28]

Unlike the experiment at the Academy or the BAT student production, which were both framed as private performances and thus in theory opted out of the realm of commodification, even though both circulated in the marketplace of ideas through published critical comment, the BE production did not pretend to be anything other than a *Schaustück*, a display of the theatrical and musical heritage

[27] This experiment was conducted by and for participants in the Academy building without being displayed for an audience. Published documentation emphasized its open-ended character by juxtaposing reports by participants without drawing conclusions from them; see Angela Haas and Josef Szeiler, comp., *Menschenmaterial 1: Die Massnahme* (Berlin: Basis Druck, 1990).

[28] The play was directed by Tom Kühnel and Robert Schuster. Although a graduation project and thus an "internal presentation for school purposes," the production received numerous reviews and other public acknowledgments. See Dirk Nümann, "Bertolt Brecht ist für alle da," *die tageszeitung* (30 December 1994); Stefan Amzoll in discussion with academic Jürgen Schebera in *Neues Deutschland* (7 February 1995); veteran Brecht critic Ernst Schumacher, "'Weiss ich was ein Mensch ist?'," *Die deutsche Bühne* 66: 5 (1995), 44–8; and Amzoll's later revaluation, "Modelle der 'Massnahme,'" *Theater der Zeit* 50: 5 (1998), 55–7.

of Brecht and Eisler, and of virtuoso skill on the part of the present stage director Klaus Emmerich, the music director, Roland Klüttig, and the performers, for a paying audience. The value of this commodity could only be enhanced by the claim put forward by the producers, and largely repeated by the press, that this event was an original – of sorts – in that, despite the evidence to the contrary, it was allegedly the first to break Brecht's ban on public professional performances of the play. However problematic, this claim of originality carried the authenticating stamp of the Brecht heirs; its ambiguous status can be clarified in part by the heirs' curious procedures, which continue in the post-Cold War era to represent a Cold War division of rights and labor. Whereas Stefan Brecht, based in New York and responsible for Western rights, had given permission for several American student performances since the 1960s, as well as a professional London production under the aegis of the Almeida Music Festival's celebration of composers from Vienna including Eisler (who studied there with Arnold Schönberg but spent most of his working life in Berlin) in 1987, Barbara Brecht-Schall, based in (East) Berlin and responsible for German-language rights, had regularly refused requests through the 1970s and 1980s, even from Western directors with leftist credentials such as Stein and Peymann.[29] But, when critics and even the dramaturg of the 1997 revival at the BE continued to refer to the ban as though it had been absolute and as if it thus guaranteed the singularity of the revival, this reiteration took on the appearance of a marketing device designed to inflate the value of the production as

[29] The London production used a translation by John Willett rather than the earlier American translation by Eric Bentley; the director was Stephen Unwin and performers included Tilda Swinton. As dramaturgical collaborator on the BE production, Susanne Winnacker reinforced its claim to singularity, ignoring the professional London production as well as student and experimental productions in German. See Winnacker, "Der Tod des Genossen," *Freitag* 38 (12 September 1997), 14–15. Given that Winnacker and her colleagues also wrongly date the actual premiere to December 1931 (according to the program for the BE revival) rather than the actual date of 1930, their lack of comment on revivals preceding theirs is perhaps not surprising.

theatrical commodity, as an object of display and consumption rather than as a disposable learning tool.[30] The meaning of the play at the moment of its revival after the demise of the revolutionary communism that had inspired it remains ambiguous. Several critics, especially in papers associated with the West German New Left that had revived interest in the play in the 1970s without managing to stage it publicly, argued with regret that this production evacuated the play's historic dramatization of the key tension in Leninism between discipline and freedom and thus of any political resonance it might have had for present-day conflicts, leaving only "historical entertainment matter for the triumphant bourgeoisie [*Unterhaltungsstoff für die siegreiche Bourgeoisie*]."[31] Others probed the paradox proposed by Adorno, that the play's elimination of artistic ornament, and even its apparent rejection of artistic autonomy as a learning tool for the left, only highlighted its formal character as an

---

[30] Led by Winnacker's statement, most critics reiterated the assertion that this production broke a "fifty [or even 'sixty']-year-old ban"; from the right, e.g. Peter Göpfert, "Die Partei, die Partei, hat immer Recht," *Berliner Morgenpost* (15 September 1997), to the left – whether orthodox, e.g. Gerhard Ebert, "Was ist eigentlich ein Mensch?", *Neues Deutschland* (15 September 1997), or critical, e.g. Gustav Seibt, "Die Partei hat tausend Augen," *Berliner Zeitung* (15 September 1997). Only later commentary in specialist journals acknowledged the impact of the revivals, from the Almeida Festival in London in 1987 to the BAT production in Berlin in 1995; see Amzoll, "Modelle der 'Maßnahme.'"

[31] Seibt, "Die Partei hat tausend Augen," 11. Writing for the *Berliner Zeitung*, Seibt and his colleague Ingo Arend, writing for the former GDR *Freitag* ("Offenes Denkmal," *Freitag* 39 (19 September 1997)), read the production's parodic tone as a comment on the defunct GDR. Critics writing for Western leftist papers, especially those founded by the New Left, regretted that this production did not attempt to invoke more topical "measures" that might be taken by NGOs and other activists to "change the world"; Nikolaus Merck, in "Vorwärts und nicht verbessern!" (Forward and Don't Improve) ironically echoes the socialist solidarity song from *Kuhle Wampe*, "Vorwärts und nicht vergessen! [Forward and Don't Forget]," *die tageszeitung* (17 September 1997). See also Klaus Dermetz, "Abgeschobene Rückblicke," *Frankfurter Rundschau* (25 September 1997).

autonomous work of art rather than a reflection of or comment on political realities.[32] To be sure, the mise en scène staged the tension between learning and consuming by juxtaposing the matter-of-fact delivery and the simple white tops and black bottoms of the singers (recalling both GDR young pioneer uniforms and Christian confirmation garb) representing the agitators (including the Young Comrade when still part of the collective) with the tenor (Götz Schulte) quoting Anton Topitz (who originated the role in 1930) in full tuxedo, Richard Tauber-ish coiffure and red handkerchief, performing (while clearly not in any naturalistic way embodying) the Young Comrade in full empathetic flight (fig. 9).[33] While several critics noted the tendency to kitsch, especially Frank Bruch who hailed, in an ironic echo of Nietzsche, the "birth of the *Lehrstück* out of the spirit of the sentimental hit [*Schlager*]," none remarked that the decision to dress the young female soloist (Mira Partecke) in a short skirt contrasted not only with the trousers worn by the other three women in this production (fig. 10) but also with the uniformly long trench-coats of the soloists in the 1930 premiere and, in its indulgence of the male spectators in the house, suggested that the commodification of the play as a whole should perforce include that of the young woman.[34]

---

[32] Adorno, "Engagement," in *Noten zur Literatur*, 418–19; "Commitment," *Aesthetics and Politics*, 185; Frank Bruch, "Die Geburt des Lehrstück aus dem Geist des Schlagers," *Frankfurter Allgemeine Zeitung* (15 September 1997). Bruch's title alludes to Friedrich Nietzsche's *Birth of Tragedy out of the Spirit of Music*, but twists the allusion to stress not the aesthetic value of the *Lehrstück* as literary work but its commercial value as a commodity, like a sentimental hit-song.

[33] For the reading of the costumes as alluding to the uniforms of SED-affiliated youth organizations, despite the latter's trademark *blue* shirts, see Seibt, "Die Partei hat tausend Augen"; for confirmation garb, see Bruch, "Die Geburt des Lehrstücks aus dem Geist des Schlagers."

[34] Winnacker, in "*Die Massnahme* von Bertolt Brecht – ein unspielbares Stück," *Massnehmen*, 268–73, here: 272, recalls Brecht's textual reference to a single woman among the male activists and the 1997 stage representation of the woman in a skirt, but makes no further

Fig. 9. The Young Comrade as romantic tenor (Götz Schulte) in *Die Massnahme* (1930), directed by Klaus Emmerich (Berlin 1997). Photograph by Ute Eichel.

This tendency to commodification made the play's historical politics look like obsolescent merchandise. By doubling the four young agitators standing to attention stage center with older actors from the GDR era of the BE, who echoed the choir's Praise of the Party with citations from Marx and Lenin and whose evident stage weariness could be read as a pointed alienation from the official marxism of the former regime, the performance also encouraged an estrangement in the

comment. This eroticized representation of the activist as young woman in 1997 contrasts with the more neutral treatment of Weigel: in 1930, she was dressed like the other activists in a leather trench-coat, which minimized the fact that she wore a skirt rather than trousers. See photographs in *Brecht: Versuche 9: Die Massnahme, Lehrstück: Das Exemplar eines Kritikers von der Uraufführung am 13.12.1930*, ed. Reinhard Krüger (Berlin: Weidler, 2001), 80–1, 117.

Komm heraus, Genosse! / Riskier
den Pfennig, der kein Pfennig mehr
ist, / die Schlafstelle, auf die es
regnet, / und den Arbeitsplatz, den
du morgen

Fig. 10. Mira Partecke (in skirt) and comrades face the control chorus in *Die Massnahme* (1997). Photograph by Ute Eichel.

audience that could be understood as critique or merely loss of inter-est, but by draping the stage and backing the control choir with plush red curtain, it tipped the balance towards socialist kitsch.[35] The over-all effect was that of a polished museum piece glowing with *Ostalgie*, like Komar and Melamid's portraits of Stalin against the Red Flag. The Western counterpart of this expression of *Ostalgie* would be a little black book with red binding and a red flag on the cover also designed by Komar and Melamid: the anniversary reprint by Verso, offspring of New Left Books, of the first English edition of *The Communist Manifesto*.

If the performance of *Die Massnahme* in Brecht's former house confirmed the Brecht heirs' desire to maximize their cultural capital through the limited unveiling of a rarely viewed museum treasure, it

---

[35] Bruch, "Die Geburt des Lehrstücks", reads this weariness as deliberate disdain for the "dogmatic content" of the lines so recited.

also, to take the critical view, threatened to turn this objet d'art into its kitschy counterpart: the *Lehrstück* begat the *Schlager*. Prevented by the Brecht heirs, in collusion with Brecht publisher Suhrkamp, from following its usual practice of publishing the text of the play in the program, the BE published instead *Das Manifest der kommunistischen Partei*, a text in the public domain, presented in an "abridged version annotated with commentary for the revival of Brecht/Eisler's *Die Massnahme.*"[36] In this form, the program accompanying the performance engaged in a rearguard action against (if not a full-scale critique of) this strategy of profit-making through deliberate scarcity. Clad in a scarlet cover (as opposed to the BE's usual programmatic grey) adorned with portraits in profile of the "classics" (Marx, Engels, Lenin and Stalin), which would have graced the covers of excerpts of these writers in the era of Stalin but not at any time after his posthumous disgrace in 1956, with the title and subtitle of the play in front and the questionnaire from the 1930 premiere on the back, this volume sold for the same price (DM5.–) as the unabridged version of the *Manifesto* sold by the prince of public domain publishers, Reclam's Universal-Bibliothek. Reminding its readers of the rarity of the play, enforced by the Brecht heirs' ban on performance, the preface to this edition highlighted the proliferation of copies of the *Manifesto*, published in two hundred languages and five hundred million copies from 1848 to 1989, the year that state socialist subsidy for its dissemination dwindled almost to nothing (BE *Manifest* 1). An editorial footnote in a section of the *Manifesto* criticizing bourgeois ownership relations quotes the letter from the director of Suhrkamp, Siegfried Unseld. Even though the proliferation of performances in the 1990s was beyond the control of Suhrkamp and the Brecht heirs and the publication of the text in the program would not have competed with Suhrkamp's very expensive volume in Brecht's *Werke*, or with the cheaper but more exhaustive paperback edition of Brecht's multiple versions of the play edited by Steinweg, and published and reprinted by

---

[36] Marx/Engels, *Das Manifest der kommunistischen Partei*, ed. Claus Hegemann and Susanne Winnacker (Berlin: Berliner Ensemble, 1997), i. Subsequent references in the text to 'BE *Manifest*'.

Surhkamp since 1972, Unseld argued that "the text [*Die Massnahme*] has a very awkward history and must therefore be published only in book form" (BE *Manifest* 25, n. 84), without explaining why publication as a theatre program or theatre performance itself would aggravate this history.

This edition of the *Manifesto* modifies the text of Marx and Engels in two apparently contradictory ways. On the one hand, it adds to the text by including as footnotes comments that would have been appended to the edition of *Die Massnahme*, had it appeared in the program, as well as references to and brief quotations from *Die Massnahme* and other works by Brecht. On the other, it subtracts from the text not only by trimming sections of exposition or historical summary but also by excising key points or turns essential to the argument. The proliferation of footnotes annotating the edition of the Manifesto in the *Massnahme* program sometimes resembles academic parody, as in the note to the sentence which opens the section "Bourgeois and Proletarians," "Die Geschichte aller bisherigen Gesellschaft ist die Geschichte von Klassenkampfen" (The history of all hitherto existing society is the history of class struggle, Marx/Engels, *Manifest* 19; *Manifesto* 34) just after the call for a "manifesto" to counter the "nursery tale" [*Märchen*]. Following this allusion to the nursery tale is a footnote citing an interview by Frank Castorf that seems to run counter to Marx's project for radical transformation. In the interview cited in that footnote, Castorf proclaims that he can "do nothing with freedom" of the sort proffered by a no-holds-barred capitalist marketplace and that he would prefer a strong state against which he "can act in opposition" (BE *Manifest* 4, n. 10).[37] The sentence has two different notes attached to each instance of "history." The first is from Einer Schleef, another former GDR *enfant terrible* on the directing scene and a frequent guest director during Müller's regime at the BE: in an essay on Wagner, Schleef alludes to a(n anti) history that recalls Nietzsche's "eternal return of this same" in its "ceremony of repeatable representative events" rather than the progressivist history

[37] Castorf, cited in *Die Erotik des Verrats*, ed. Schütt, 156.

of Marx or Brecht for whom Wagner was anathema. The second cites musicologist Joachim Lucchesi's analysis of the pre-marxist Brecht's use of ballad music less to conduct class struggle than to play with the tension between plebeian and petit-bourgeois elements.[38] Finally, "class struggle" is glossed by a citation from the first scene of *Die Massnahme* in which the three activists admit that "we have nothing for you, but over the border in Mukden we bring the Chinese workers the writings of the classics and the propagandists, the ABC of Communism; for the ignorant instruction about their condition, for the oppressed class consciousness, for the class conscious experience of revolution" (BE *Manifest* 4, n. 13; Steinweg A2, 39; Bentley 79; trans. mod.). Marx's emphatic claim for the universal history of class struggle is thus amplified but not simply endorsed by these comments. Rather the notes bring to the surface eddies and counter-currents to the evidently blocked mainstream marxist line.

While some cuts to the text, such as the summary of historical modes of production leading up to the emergence of the stark opposition between bourgeoisie and proletariat, appear motivated by economy, others, such as the omission of the notorious reduction of value to "cash payment," seem more ambiguous. In the latter case, the program preserves the bourgeoisie's destruction of "all feudal, patriarchal, idyllic relations" and the consequent shift from "veiled" to "shameless" exploitation (BE *Manifest* 11) and retains Marx's subsequent indictment of professionals reduced to "paid wage labourers" and of family relationships to relations defined by money (Marx/Engels, *Manifest* 22; *Manifesto* 38; BE *Manifest* 12) but excises the argument that links these points, especially the dissolution of bourgeois as well as feudal values and relations in "the icy water of egotistical calculation," of "personal worth" in "exchange value" and "numberless chartered freedoms" into the freedom of trade alone (Marx/Engels, *Manifest* 22; *Manifesto* 37–8). This omission is slight

---

[38] Einar Schleef, *Droge, Faust, Parzifal* (Frankfurt a.M: Suhrkamp, 1997), 247 (BE *Manifest* 4, n. 11); Joachim Lucchesi, "Impuls zur literarischer Produktion," *Musik und Gesellschaft* 6 (1985): 309–10 (n. 12).

but symptomatic. Although the program's editors return in conclusion to Marx's general formulation of the "ownership question" and
to the particular issue of Suhrkamp's exclusive and excluding copy-
right to *Die Massnahme*, they appear reluctant to examine their own
promotion of the BE production as a unique, "priceless" and therefore
highly priced commodity.

> **Constant revolutionizing of production, uninterrupted**
> **convulsion [*Erschütterung*] of all social conditions,**
> **everlasting uncertainty and agitation distinguish the**
> **bourgeois epoch from all earlier ones. All fixed, utterly**
> **rusted [*eingerosteten*] relations, with their train of ancient**
> **and venerable prejudices, are swept away, all new ones**
> **become antiquated before they can ossify. (*Marx/Engels,***
> **"*Manifest*," 23; *Manifesto* 38 (trans. mod.))**

Filling out the ellipsis in the previous epigraph from *The Communist Manifesto*, the citation above offers a prophetic image that might
aptly represent not so much the industrial capitalism of Marx's time
but rather the post-industrial capitalism of our own. Indeed, Marx's
image of *rusted* (rather than the usual translation of "frozen") relations conjures up a picture of rust-belt cities and industrial parks
in the formerly affluent North, abandoned as capital has moved to
exploit cheaper labor and looser labor laws South and East. In the economic geography of Berlin and its environs, this movement has led
to the desertion of former industrial parks in Eastern Berlin. While
the former GDR center of Berlin, and inner-city, formerly working-
class, neighborhoods like Prenzlauer Berg, have been absorbed into the
domain of the post-industrial capitalism of real estate, insurance, and
tourism, neighborhoods further east remain stuck in no-man's land
between rusted-up socialist modernization and immaterial information age post-modernization. Attempts to integrate former industrial
parks in depressed areas like Schöneweide (literally "beautiful pas-
ture" – well southeast of Karl-Marx-Allee, and the location, during
the Second World War, of forced labor by eastern European prisoners,
before it became part of the GDR national-industrial complex) into
the space of immaterial capitalism through art (and, by extension,

tourism) have been problematic, in large part because they shy away from incorporating the depressed present and its unemployed inhabitants (who call the place "Schweinöde," pigshit desert) into schemes for artists' installations and performances in former industrial sites.

A series of displays and performances under the rubric of *Helden der Arbeit* (heroes of labor) in the margins of the annual Day of the Open Monument (*Tag des offenen Denkmals*) in September 2002 suggests that questions about the commodification of socialist history and capitalist present thrown up by events at the Brecht centenary are still pressing.[39] Whereas most of the other "open monuments" were churches, graveyards, and monumentalized secular landmarks in the center and the peripheries of Berlin, including the Mies van der Rohe house in northeast Hohenschönhausen and the former Stalinallee in the southeast as well as, in central Mitte, former synagogues and the Church of Zion, seat of anti-fascist pastor Dietrich Bonhoeffer in 1931 and of anti-SED groups in the 1980s, *Helden der Arbeit* was staged in a place without authorized claims to monumental status. The Reinbekhallen, a series of brick buildings along a post-industrial stretch of the Spree, were part of a former transformer factory, and are now an artists' exhibition and performance venue. Although the exhibition included documentation of forced labor, especially by Russian and Polish women pulled in from the Slavic periphery of the Nazi empire, in keeping with exhibitions in neighborhood museums such as the Heimatmuseum Friedrichshain, most objects, installations and performances offered variations on the familiar repertoire of *Ostalgie* rather than systematic analysis of the historical use and abuse of the designation "hero of labor" from the Stalinist era in the Soviet Union and the GDR through Hans Garbe and his successors to the end of the GDR in 1989. Most unabashedly sentimental was

[39] Comments about the *Helden der Arbeit* installations and events are based on personal observation of the "art festival" in and around the former TRO transformer factory in the Reinbekhalle on the opening day, 7 September 2002; the program published by the sponsors, Kulturwerk Oberschönweide; and the overall program for the Day of the Open Monument published by the Berlin Monument Office.

the "singing ship," a barge trip along the Spree in the rusty twilight, accompanied by recordings of socialist anthems. But the installations inside the Reinbekhallen also played with tension between critical and nostalgic evocations of GDR labor: Peter Bastian's *Lorbeerkranz*, a meter-high victor's wreath made from workers' gloves rather than laurel leaves, rested against one wall, while in the center, M. Lohe's *Erwachsenes Spielzeug* (Adult Toy) had cardboard figures on a platform shoveling thin air to the strains of a "young pioneer" refrain celebrating manual labor: "Wer will fleissiger Handwerker sein? tüchtig, tüchtig . . .") (Who wants to be a hard-working craftsman? sound and strong . . .).

Most interesting was an installation that attempted to conjure up the absence of actual workers in the space without resorting, as did the previous two works, to replicating them in effigy. Roland Führmann's *Produktivitätssimulator* (Productivity-simulator) revealed itself initially only as a caption on the wall, compelling the viewer to look for the object and to think about the absences suggested by its title. The object itself was an assemblage of machine wheels hanging, one welded to the next, from the ceiling, ending with a "black box" (albeit painted red) at the viewer's eye level, containing the computer program that turned the wheels at different speeds while alternately extending and contracting the whole hanging assemblage towards the floor and back towards the ceiling, and generating sudden bursts of factory noise not immediately connected to any visible movement. The gaps between sound and movement, and between the title of the work and the opacity of the object, compels observation of the absence of the producer and the product that might have turned the simulation into the production of productivity as a supplement to a real product. In the long view, the work invites reflection on the failed system of state socialism whose agents squandered energy (and scarce capital) on the production of the illusion of productivity in the image of the labor hero busting quotas, but at the cost of producing goods and services and of generating the social and cultural capital of legitimate consent to the system. The absence of any figurative representation of the hero of labor highlights the illusionary nature of the figure and the difficulty of representing its impotence (as experienced also by Brecht) as well as the work of dis-illusion performed by the installation. Even though the object did not speak to or of the absent and now idle workers who walked their angry dogs in the abandoned industrial site outside, it allowed space to think about those workers and the visibly out-of-work men in the neighborhood, who might have been employed assembling the artists' machines but instead were left to haunt the site, taunting tourists along this post-industrial river bank.

This low-level but potentially dangerous conflict between artists and (former) workers reveals the limits of *Ostalgie*. Whereas *Ostalgie*, as nostalgia for a no-longer-existing socialist society, rests on the presumption that remnants of the GDR, from small-scale objects to barely visible memorials of Luxemburg's failed Spartacist uprising of 1919 (removed to make way for condo development), are remnants of a dead past whose consumption can be detached from the agency of their production, the undeclared but palpable conflict over the use and abuse of history in these erstwhile workplaces reminds Western sceptics, as urbanist Simone Hain argues, that the experience of the GDR is living as well as lived experience, created by the actions of people in the region.[40] The ghost in the productivity-simulating machine may be conjured by the imagination of artist and connoisseur, but the people left outside resist appearing merely as spectral supernumeraries in this rarefied drama. Their belligerent presence serves as a reminder to those inside that the Berlin Wall has not disappeared but has only shifted eastward. As the center of capital has moved east from the former "New West" into Berlin-Mitte, former center of the "actually existing socialist" state, the line between affluent West and left-behind East has shifted and fractured against the industrial dilapidation within eastern Berlin and in the abandoned factories and towns in eastern Germany in an as yet "uninterrupted convulsion of all social conditions." To bear witness to this persistent inequality,

[40] Hain, "Zur Konstitution eines wissenschaftlichen Interesses," *Warum zum Beispiel die Stalinallee?*, 6.

however obliquely, artists have first to see clearly, as Marx has it, "with sober eyes," the "real conditions of their existence"; the temporal and historical links between past and present in this city and the spatial and structural connections marked by this and other wealthy capitals as a nodal point between North and South. We shall explore these connections in the following chapters.

5 The dis-illusion of apartheid: Brecht and South Africa

A literal-minded historian might begin a discussion of Brecht in South Africa with the first professional production of a play by Brecht in South Africa. This would be *The Caucasian Chalk Circle*, produced by the then newly established state-subsidized Performing Arts Council of the Transvaal (PACT) in 1963. A more critical historian might point out that the terms "professional" and "state-subsidized" hide the discriminatory character of the apartheid-era provincial arts councils and other state-subsidized institutions that denied blacks professional training in the name of preserving and developing "[European] civilization in a young country."[1] The PACT production of *The Caucasian*

---

[1] For the promotion of South Africa's contribution to "Western civilization," see *Performing Arts in South Africa: Cultural Aspirations of a Young Country* (Pretoria: Dept of Information, 1969), 1. This pamphlet takes pains to emphasize the progress of the "young country" towards the "best in drama, ballet, opera and music" and thus its identification with Europe and the West. Published after the crisis of the Soweto Uprising in 1976, the later *Report of the Commission of Inquiry into the Performing Arts* (Pretoria: Government Publications, 1977) mentions "early indigenous theatre in South Africa" (19) once and returns in a short chapter at the end to suggest that facilities could be provided for the "black, coloured and Indian population groups" (92–7) but devotes most of the document to increased subsidy for ballet, opera, music, and theatre, especially theatre in Afrikaans, the language of the party of apartheid. For a critical history of PACT, see Carol Steinberg, "Towards an Arts Council for South Africa", *South African Theatre Journal* 7: 2 (1993), 8–40. For the historical context of these institutions, see Martin Orkin, *Drama and the South African State* (Manchester University Press,

215

Chalk Circle took place half a decade after the first student and amateur productions of Brecht's classic plays, such as *The Good Woman* [sic] *of Setzuan*, which opened at the University of Cape Town's (UCT) Little Theatre in January 1958, or *The Threepenny Opera*, a hit on Broadway in 1953 (Library Theatre, Johannesburg, 1958). It followed the precedent set by those amateur productions in that it set greater store by Brecht's status as a canonized European playwright than by anything the political theatre practitioner might have had to say to an institution sponsored by a state that had recently and brutally suppressed almost all non-violent opposition. By 1963, the leading anti-apartheid groups, the African National Congress, the Pan-Africanist Congress and the South African Communist Party, were banned and new legislation made possible detention without trial and conviction thereafter on very broadly defined grounds of treason against and sabotage of state security.[2] Thus at the same time as the officially socialist GDR was elevating the troublesome Brecht posthumously to the pantheon of socialist classics, the officially anti-communist South Africa was looking to Brecht to guide its way into the exclusive club of Western European civilization.

Bearing in mind these ironies, the critical historian might wish to compare the subsidized *Circle* with the more modest, but ultimately more influential, production of the same play the following

1991) and Loren Kruger, *The Drama of South Africa: Plays, Pageants and Publics since 1910* (London: Routledge, 1999). Note that in South Africa, "coloured" has come to mean "mixed ethnicity" for the people concerned, as well as denoting the apartheid category for people supposedly between black and white. The American word "colored" is a synonym for "black" and is therefore not an appropriate substitute.

[2] See Arnold Blumer, "Brecht in South Africa," *Communications from the International Brecht Society* 13: 1 (1983), 30–8. "The Good Woman of Setzuan" mistranslates Brecht's title, *Der Gute Mensch* [Person] *von Setzuan*. For the history of the anti-apartheid struggle and its suppression, see *From Protest to Challenge: A Documentary History of African Politics in South Africa: 1882–1964*, ed. Thomas Karis and Gwendolyn Carter (Stanford: Hoover Institution, 1977), 4 vols., and Tom Lodge, *Black Politics in South Africa until 1985* (London: Longman, 1986).

year by the Serpent Players, a group of black worker-players who
earned their living as teachers, clerks, and industrial workers, and cannot thus be considered amateurs in the manner of leisured whites.[3] In
collaboration with Athol Fugard and under surveillance by the Security Police, the Serpent Players used Brecht's elucidation of gestic acting, dis-illusion, and social critique, as well as their own experience
of the satiric comic routines of urban African vaudeville, to explore
the theatrical force of Brecht's techniques, as well as the immediate
political relevance of a play about land distribution. Their work on
the *Caucasian Chalk Circle* and, a year later, on *Antigone* led directly
to the creation, in 1966, of what is still South Africa's most distinctive *Lehrstück*: *The Coat*. Based on an incident at one of the many
political trials involving the Serpent Players, *The Coat* dramatized the
choices facing a woman whose husband, convicted of anti-apartheid
political activity, left her only a coat and instructions to use it. In
Lehrstück manner, the performers focused not on the embodiment of
sympathetic character but rather on the representation of social relationships – between the waiting wife and her impatient son, between
the police and members of the political group to which the convicted
man belonged – as well as the conflicting demands made by these people on the coat and each other. The participants were engaged not only
in representing social relationships on stage but also in enacting and
revising their own dealings with each other and with institutions of
apartheid oppression from the law courts downward; this engagement
testified to the real power of Brecht's apparently utopian plan to abolish the separation of player and audience and to make of each player
a "statesman" or social actor (*Werke* 21: 396). Work on *The Coat* led
indirectly to the Serpent Players' most famous and most Brechtian productions, *Sizwe Bansi is Dead* (1972) and *The Island* (1973), devised in

---

[3] For discussion of the ideological overdetermination of "professional"
and "amateur" in the institutionalization of theatre, and the case for
"worker-player," see Loren Kruger, *The National Stage: Theatre and
Cultural Legitimation in England, France, and America* (Chicago:
University of Chicago Press, 1992), 3–29, 140–55; for the
contextualization of these concepts in South Africa, see Kruger,
Drama of South Africa, 50–9, 86–92.

collaboration by Fugard and the actors John Kani and Winston Ntshona. Both plays evinced a Brechtian attention to the demonstration of gest and social situation and encouraged audiences to analyze rather than merely applaud the action. *Sizwe Bansi*, which combined Brechtian critique and vaudevillian irony, especially in Kani's virtuoso improvisation, even provoked an African audience's critical interruption and interrogation of the action. Both plays are also credited with preparing the ground for the distinctively South African political theatre of the 1970s and 1980s. Characterized by the vigorous movement, rousing song, direct testimony of the oppressed and ironic impersonation of the oppressor, these fundamentally collaborative ventures included *Survival* (1976), *Woza Albert* (1981), *Born in the RSA* (1986), Junction Avenue Theatre Company's (JATC's) critical history plays such as *Sophiatown* (1986), and the workers' theatre of mobilization and education produced by former JATC members working with industrial union workers in the Durban Workers' Cultural Local in the 1980s.

However influential Fugard may be, an account of South African political theatre that leads from Fugard's experiments with the Serpent Players through his famous collaborations with Kani and Ntshona to the surge of political theatre, which followed in the wake of the student and worker unrest that galvanized anti-apartheid opposition first in Soweto and then in the whole country in June 1976, and which attributes the emergence of political theatre in large part to Brecht, is at best incomplete.[4] Oppositional theatre in South Africa

[4] Although the idea that Fugard initiated political theatre in South Africa has been disputed by scholars from Robert Kavanagh to Bhekizizwe Peterson, it remains the prevailing account abroad and persists among critics at home. Carol Steinberg and Malcolm Purkey begin their brief account of anti-apartheid theatre, in "South African Theater in Crisis", *Theater* 25: 3 (1995): 24–37, with Fugard. Zakes Mda argues, in "Theatre and Reconciliation in South Africa," *Theater* 25: 3 (1995), 38–45, that "Fugard introduced political theatre in the western mode in South Africa" (39); he allows that "indigenous performance modes often served a political function" (39), but not that other "western" political theatre forms arrived a generation before Fugard. The validation of very different forms and techniques of

existed well before Fugard's debut in the 1950s but did not make extensive use of Brecht until the 1970s. The black literate class that emerged
in the late nineteenth and early twentieth centuries made innovative
use of a range of African, European, and (African) American performance practices – from indigenous praises and storytelling to school-
taught literary drama, by way of a plethora of syncretic forms like
nationalist hymns, minstrelsy, and vaudeville sketches, as well as literary plays – to challenge exclusive Western claims to civilization and
modernity in the name of universal emancipation.[5]

By the 1930s, this activity included theatre workshops sponsored on the one hand by the neocolonial institutions such as the

theatre with even subdued political content as Brechtian is likewise
prevalent; Orkin credits the playwright H. I. E. Dhlomo, influenced in
the 1930s by English admirers of Hegel and Schiller from Thomas
Carlyle to John Drinkwater, with "Brechtian" treatment of his
colonialist villains (*Drama and the South African State*, 41). Temple
Hauptfleisch, in *Theatre and Society in South Africa: Reflections in a
Fractured Mirror* (Pretoria: Van Schaik, 1997), calls Brecht an
"important influence" on "community theatre," "workers' theatre,"
or "what you will" (42), but does not differentiate between the impact
of diverse modes of political theatre; Marcia Blumberg and Dennis
Walder, in their introduction to *South African Theatre as/and
Intervention* (Amsterdam: Rodopi, 1998), credit Brecht with setting the
terms within which "theatre as a weapon in the class struggle" was
conceived in South Africa (13). Steinberg and Purkey, who have
worked more closely with staging Brecht, are more circumspect in the
attribution of politics to theatre; they identify Fugard's politics more
precisely as "liberal humanist" and reserve the attribution "Brechtian
theatre" to the "self-conscious" appropriations by the Junction Avenue
Theatre Company (directed by Purkey) ("South African Theater in
Crisis," 27).
[5] For a ground-breaking account of the African intellectual class or
"New African," see Tim Couzens, *The New African: The Life and
Work of H. I. E. Dhlomo* (Johannesburg: Ravan, 1985); for the role of
New Africans in the development of urban music, see Veit Erlmann,
African Stars (Chicago: University of Chicago Press, 1990), and for
New Africans in theatre, see Kruger, *Drama of South Africa*, ch. 3, and
Bhekizizwe Peterson, *Monarchs, Missionaries, and African
Intellectuals: African Theatre and the Unmaking of Colonial
Marginality* (Trenton: Africa World Press, 2000).

British Drama League, and on the other by the integrated leadership of growing industrial unions and by the turbulent but influential Communist Party of South Africa (CPSA), the only integrated political party at the time. While the Drama League encouraged companies like the Bantu Dramatic Society to produce English comedies like Oliver Goldsmith's *She Stoops to Conquer* and Oscar Wilde's *Lady Windermere's Fan*, the unions provided space (such as union halls) and personnel for anti-colonial performance. Local union activists, whether white (Guy Routh) or black (Gaur Radebe) contributed plots (often in sketch format) on topics such as segregation and forced removals from the land, and leftist immigrants and visitors such as Kurt Joachim Baum from Weimar Germany, or André van Gyseghem from Belgium, passed on the techniques of European avant-gardists such as Vsevolod Meyerhold and Erwin Piscator, as well as the Living Newspapers and other American experiments. Groups like the Bantu Peoples' Theatre and the African National Theatre produced local versions of the metropolitan avant-garde, such as Eugene O'Neill's *Hairy Ape* (1936), and agit-prop on pressing social issues such as Routh's *Patriot's Pie* (1940), about African conscription, I. Pinchuk's *Tau* (1941), about African farmers' right to land, or Radebe's *Rude Criminal* (1941), about men caught by the pass laws forbidding unauthorized Africans to live or work in South African cities.[6]

Although their names may be unknown even to many South African readers, these people created an urban political theatre in South Africa a generation before Fugard and two generations before the angry young men who stormed the stages of the Space and the Market Theatre in the decade and a half between the Soweto Uprising in 1976 and the release of Mandela in 1990. Whereas Brecht's name does not appear alongside his colleague Piscator or his senior contemporary Meyerhold as a possible source for the theatrical activity of the South African left in its first generation, his work bears the imprint of the same internationalist socialist culture that informed proletarian

[6] See Guy Routh, "The Johannesburg Art Theatre," *Trek* (September 1950): 25–7, and "The Bantu People's Theatre," *Trek* (October 1950): 20–3.

theatre in the 1920s and 1930s, from Germany and the Soviet Union to the United States and Japan. This culture, which shaped Brecht's most politically and theatrically advanced work – the *Lehrstücke* – also influenced worker-players in South Africa, from the Afrikaner working-class women in the Garment Workers' Union to the mostly African male white-collar workers (teachers and clerks) of the Bantu Peoples' Theatre. Even though these groups knew little of Brecht, their use of theatrical form in the formation and transformation of passive spectators into social and political agents resonates with Brecht's call, in the essay on "Pedagogics Great and Small" (*Die grosse und die kleine Pädagogik*) for the transformation of spectators into "statesmen" [sic] through theatre (*Werke* 21: 396). While acknowledging the peculiar character of South African conditions, the Bantu Peoples' Theatre members invoked international socialism directly, when they argued, in an unpublished program note in 1940, that their subject was the "economic disintegration, the breakdown of tribal economy, and the impoverishment of Europeans, the massing of classes in their trade unions and employer organizations," as well as the "emotional complications of race and colour."[7] In so doing, they joined African intellectuals and leaders in the 1930s who challenged on the one hand the conservative, rural bias of the traditional leadership by arguing, as did Professor D. D. T. Jabavu, that "our situation is symptomatic of the world-wide travail of all repressed communities and dominated classes" and on the other the hegemony of "white savages" wearing the "mask" of "European civilization."[8]

These and other unacknowledged moments in the history of political performance and the performance of politics in South Africa must be acknowledged if we are to understand the ground on which an exploration of Brecht's traces can be conducted. In order to evaluate the literal history of "Brecht in South Africa," which appears to begin with white student and amateur groups in the late 1950s, we

---

[7] Bantu Peoples' Theatre, *Drama Festival Program* (25–7 July 1940), 10; Johannesburg Public Library, Strange Theatre Collection (hereafter: JPL/STC).

[8] Speech at the AAC, December 1935; quoted by M. L. Kabane, "The All-African Convention," *South African Outlook* (August 1936): 185–9.

need first to investigate its virtual history, the history of the intersection of international socialist politics and syncretic agit-prop performance forms from the 1920s – forms which have since been claimed as Brechtian, even though, as chapter 1 indicates, Brecht himself was at this time one of many in a milieu influenced by the agit-prop of worker-players from the Soviet Union alongside the satirical business of the Berlin cabaret and the Bavarian *Volksstück*. This chapter will show how theatre institutions with socialist aspirations in the 1930s and 1940s created a model for this productive fusion, and how the history of this early political theatre in South Africa can enrich our understanding both of the more explicitly Brechtian political theatre projects that followed, from the Serpent Players in the 1960s to JATC from the 1970s to the present, and of the effective suppression by neglect as well as outright censorship of this history in the minds of many South Africans.

Nationalism, Communism, and performance on the South African left

Before we can plot the intersection of international socialism and syncretic performance forms that together found what I have called the virtual history of "Brecht in South Africa," we should outline the political and social context that made this intersection possible. In this period, South Africa was not yet governed by the explicitly racialist ideology of apartheid but it was in practice already thoroughly segregated.[9] White people by law owned all but thirteen percent of the land and most of the capital, especially concentrated in mining and related industries. The few Africans who passed stringent property and education qualifications were after 1936 confined to voting for white "Native Representatives", while the vast majority had little formal education, no property, and no political representation. Those who

---

[9] For basic social, political, and economic history, see John Omer-Cooper, *History of Southern Africa*, 2nd edn (London: James Currey, 1994) and Nigel Worden, *The Making of Modern South Africa*, 3rd edn (Oxford: Blackwell, 2000); for the history of struggle see Karis and Carter, eds., *From Protest to Challenge*, and Lodge, *Black Politics in South Africa until 1985*.

migrated to the cities were constrained by a series of Urban Areas and Labour Acts in their search for work and lodging; in order to remain in the cities, African men had to carry passbooks with an endorsement from an employer. Although initially exempt from the pass laws, educated Africans were customarily segregated in or excluded from theatres and other entertainments, although some were able to gain access with the help of white patrons or to organize their own performances in institutions such as the Bantu Men's Social Centre in Johannesburg. A few musicians were able to support themselves as performers and arrangers, but most African writers and performers were compelled to earn their living as teachers or journalists.[10]

In this context, the CPSA and its publications *Umsebenzi* (The Worker) and *Inkululeko* (Freedom) provided a rare location for non-racial political and cultural organization.[11] The CPSA was founded in

[10] For the social and cultural contexts of urban Africans in the 1920s and 1930s, see Luli Callinicos, *Working Life 1886–1940* (Johannesburg: Ravan, 1985); for the ambiguous position of educated Africans, see Couzens, *The New African* and Shula Marks, *The Ambiguities of Dependence* (Johannesburg: Ravan, 1986).

[11] The role of the Communist Party in South Africa is subject to dispute. An "official" *History of the African National Congress: South Africa Belongs to Us* (Bloomington: Indiana University Press, 1989) by Francis Meli, educated in exile at the University of Leipzig in the GDR, argues for a close association between the ANC and SACP from the 1930s. Stephen Ellis and Tsepo Sechaba, *Comrades against Apartheid: The ANC and the South African Communist Party in Exile* (London: James Currey, 1992) present a more conflicted picture from the perspective of a former party member keen to expose abuses in the military camps run by the ANC in exile in 1970s. *Political Profiles*, vol. 4 of the *Documentary History of African Politics in South Africa*, compiled by the non-Communist Thomas Karis and Gail Gerhart, demonstrates that several leading figures in the ANC were also CPSA/SACP members, and that CPSA members played important roles in industrial unions in South Africa and in the political use of the strike. For a collection of documents that emphasizes Communist unity, see *South African Communists Speak* (London: Inkululeko, 1980); for a more nuanced collection that includes statements by Trotskyites and dissident CPSA members, see *South Africa's Radical Tradition*,

1921, nine years after the African National Congress (ANC, founded in 1912). While the ANC at the time had an exclusively African membership divided among conservative chiefs and more progressive "new Africans," the CPSA and its Trotskyite rival, the Workers' Party, were initially dominated by unionists from Britain, but by the end of the decade Eastern European Jewish immigrants from the socialist Bund movement and a growing black membership, supported by Soviet interest in anti-colonial rebellion in South Africa, India, and other outposts of the British Empire, pushed the party into a more militant position. Jewish socialists such as Ray Alexander (b. 1913), Eli Weinberg (1908–81), and E[mil] S[olomon] "Solly" Sachs (1900–76), organized workers in key industries, joined by black men who had gained experience as activists in the Industrial and Commercial Workers' Union (ICU), which, with 100,000 members, was in the 1920s the most significant challenge to white power. Key black leaders such as James La Guma (1894–1961), who came to the CPSA from the ICU; J[osiah] T. Gumede (ca. 1870–1947), who was also president-general of the ANC in the late 1920s, and J. B. Marks (1903–72) studied at the Lenin School in Moscow, and later organized the massive miners' strike in 1946. These men and others pushed the CPSA to greater representation of black unionists and other workers, and the ANC towards a greater engagement with a growing black working class.[12] When the ANC returned to its conservative roots in the 1930s (before rebounding under pressure from Nelson Mandela and other members of the Youth League in the 1940s), the CPSA joined forces with the short-lived All-African Congress, which challenged the ANC in 1935 with the internationalist analysis voiced by Professor Jabavu, cited

ed. Allison Drew (Cape Town: University of Cape Town Press, 1996), 2 vols. Note that the Afrikaner Nationalist government's ban on the CPSA's legal activities in 1950 led to its dissolution and reformation as the underground SACP, which was to contribute substantially to the organization of *UmKhonto we Sizwe* (MK), the ANC's guerrilla arm, after the banning of the ANC in 1960 and the imprisonment of its leaders, including Nelson Mandela, in 1964.

[12] For these biographies, see Karis and Gerhart, *Political Profiles*, 53–4, 34–6, 75–6.

earlier: "our situation is symptomatic of the world-wide travail of all repressed communities and dominated classes." Its most long-lasting impact on the anti-colonial movement, however, was organizing and educating industrial workers, including those such as miners who, as migrants, were not legally allowed to join unions, as well as union intellectuals. Examples include Moses Kotane (1905–78), who went from setting type for *Umsebenzi* via the Lenin School in the 1930s to working on major policy documents of the anti-apartheid movement such as the *Freedom Charter* (1955), which would be the cornerstone of the post-apartheid constitution of South Africa, and Gaur Radebe (1908–) who founded the African Mineworkers' Union, worked with the African National Theatre on his play *The Rude Criminal*, and, after leaving the CPSA, led boycotts in Alexandra Township against the high prices of the government bus monopoly (1943–4).

But, before the African intellectuals at the Bantu Peoples' Theatre and its successor, the African National Theatre, began to work on a repertoire that might bring together African Nationalist and international socialist themes and a variety of local and imported forms, socialist theatre had a place among radical immigrants, especially Jews who had been affiliated with socialist organizations in Tsarist Russia and the Soviet Union and who established institutions like the Jewish Workers' Club (JWC) in Johannesburg (1928–48). In contrast with the middle-class profile presented by Jews in South Africa in the later twentieth century, many members of this club were industrial workers, artisans and lower-level white-collar workers who favored Yiddish socialist culture, including choirs singing the *Internationale* on May Day and theatre producing Yiddish melodrama as well as socialist classics such as Maxim Gorky's *Lower Depths*.[13] While not so moved by socialist fervor, the middle-class, educated and, in key cases, Jewish South Africans who ran amateur and semi-professional art theatres also included plays on social themes in their repertoires. The long-standing Johannesburg Repertory Society (1928–69), led by

[13] Taffy Adler, "Lithuania's Diaspora: The Johannesburg Jewish Workers' Club: 1928–1948," *Journal of Southern African Studies* 6: 1 (1979): 70–92.

Muriel Alexander, began with Karel Čapek's *RUR* (1928; revived 1936) and included many plays by G. B. Shaw in its 1930s repertoire. The Repertory Reading Group staged Jewish South African playwright Lewis Sowdon's *Red Rand*, about the 1922 Miners' Strike, in 1937, and Kurt Joachim Baum ran a short-lived Johannesburg Art Theatre (1934–8) to introduce South African audiences to the formal and political innovations of Meyerhold and Piscator.[14]

While radical European immigrants interested in socialist and experimental theatre had counterparts among the politicized working classes of Germany (until 1933), France, and Britain, and among similar immigrant groups in North America, the development of political theatre among young, white Afrikaner women who came from isolated farms and puritan families to work in the garment industry in Johannesburg may seem surprising. Led by Solly Sachs, active member of the JWC and the CPSA (until he was purged in the 1930s) and father of Albie Sachs, political prisoner, writer, and now judge on South Africa's Constitutional Court, the Garment Workers' Union educated young rural women in urban life and culture as well as work discipline. Radicalized by the experience of working alongside Indian, coloured, and African men as well as Jewish immigrants who were veterans in the garment industry, activists such as the sisters Hester and Johanna Cornelius led other Afrikaner women away from a strictly ethnic affiliation with Afrikaner nationalism towards socialist solidarity with fellow workers, including blacks. As the historian Iris Berger notes, this solidarity had its limits; the first major strike of the growing industry, in May 1928, called for "no victimization of 'either Europeans or Natives,'" but white women and black men had to hold separate meetings.[15] Despite this customary segregation, the strike evinced not only documented inter-racial solidarity but the

[14] On the Johannesburg Art Theatre, see Routh, "Johannesburg Art Theatre"; on *Red Rand*, see Kruger, *Drama of South Africa*, 52–4, and Lewis Sowdon's *Red Rand* in Witwatersrand University's Cullen Library (WC/A406).

[15] Iris Berger, *Threads of Solidarity: Women in the South African Garment Industry, 1900–1980* (Bloomington: Indiana University Press, 1992), 95–8.

performance of that solidarity; it was, as the *Rand Daily Mail* reported, a "strike of bright colours, of gay processions, of laughter and joking, of music and dancing."[16] Later strikes in the 1930s, especially a divisive and unsuccessful strike in November 1932, revealed unresolved tensions between the GWU and the Communist-affiliated and largely black African Federation of Trade Unions, and received harsher treatment from both the media and the police. Some journalists called the strikers "wild women" and the police attacked them with batons and horses. The women responded by drawing on the legacy of Afrikaner rebellion in the Anglo-Boer War, as well as their more recent affiliation with socialism, by performing in prison and after songs ranging from the South African War favorite *Sarie Marais* and the Afrikaner anthem *Die Stem van Suid-Afrika* (The Voice of South Africa) to the *Internationale* and the *Red Flag* sung in Afrikaans.[17]

Intensifying educational efforts in the wake of the strike, the union leaders, Sachs and the Cornelius sisters, developed this turn to culture with a bilingual union paper, *Garment Worker/Klerewerker*, which published letters, reports of strikes and clashes between the workers and Afrikaner nationalists, and announcements of short plays, such as *Eendrag* (Unity) or *Die Sklavin van Suid-Afrika* (The Slave of South Africa), on the struggles of working women and the value of solidarity.[18] Although it lacked the history of socialist culture that characterized the activities of the Jewish Workers Group, the GWU broke new ground in training socialist worker-players from a puritan nationalist culture and transforming Afrikaans from the language of racial nationalism to a vehicle for an ecumenical socialism.[19] Before they wrote and produced their own plays, however,

---

[16] *Rand Daily Mail* 22 May 1928; quoted in Berger, *Threads of Solidarity*, 95.

[17] Ibid., 101.

[18] Manuscripts of these plays and copies of the *Garment Worker/ Klerewerker* are in the Garment Workers' Collection in Cullen Library (WC/GWU)

[19] Afrikaans touring companies, which took theatre to audiences in small towns in the rural areas where most Afrikaners still lived, were pioneered in the 1920s. They produced European classics and light

the women of the GWU attempted to use emerging institutions of Afrikaner nationalism, such as the Federasie vir Afrikaanse Kultuur (Federation for Afrikaans Culture) to represent a socialist subculture. In particular, by sending a Kappiekommando (a delegation of women dressed in pioneer dress complete with bonnets) to the Voortrekker Centenary Celebrations in December 1938, the culmination of the re-enactment of the Great Trek by tens of thousands of Afrikaners traveling in covered wagons following the original trek from the Cape to Pretoria, they hoped to show that it was possible to be both social-ist and Afrikaans.[20] After altercations with members of the Witwa-tersrand Centenary Committee who wanted to bar "followers of the Communist Sachs," Johanna Cornelius led a delegation to the gather-ing in Pretoria.[21] Writing in *The Garment Worker*, Hester Cornelius defended their socialist affiliation as the logical outcome of Afrikaner

comedy in translation, with the occasional drama of Afrikaner nationalism, such as J. W. Grosskopf's *As die Tuig Skawe* (When the Harness Chafes, 1926), about a hapless farmer allegedly exploited by Jewish money-lenders. In the Depression years of the 1930s, the commercial enterprises foundered, leaving the field to educated amateurs such as Anna Neethling-Pohl, director of Greek tragedy, modern European drama, and the theatrical program at the massive Voortrekker Centenary Celebrations in 1938. While this last event appealed to working-class Afrikaners, the others were directed at a small elite. For a rare English-language affirmative account, see S. C. Naudé, "The Rise of the Afrikaans Theatre," *Trek* (April 1950): 8–10; for critical remarks, see Kruger, *Drama of South Africa*, 35–40, 77–80, 100–28.

[20] For critical analysis of this event, see Albert Grundlingh and Hilary Sapire, "From Feverish Festival to Repetitive Ritual: The Changing Fortunes of Great Trek Mythology in an Industrializing South Africa," *South African Historical Journal* 21 (1989): 19–37 and Kruger, *Drama of South Africa*, 38–43.

[21] A Rev. De Klerk from Brixton, quoted in [Johanna Cornelius], "Die Kappiekommando ontmoet die Reëlingskomitee," *Klerewerker* (November 1938), 5; Cornelius' account of the trip in "Eeufees," *Klerewerker* (December 1938) optimistically claimed that the festivities "showed that our people [*volk*] can unite, even if we belong to separate political groups and churches" (1) (UW/WC/GWU). As

resistance to the "imperialist yoke" and as the best defense against the
"new danger threatening the world: namely Fascism."[22] As the photograph of the Kappiekommando member in Voortrekker dress holding
a copy of *Die Klerewerker* suggests (fig. 11), this performance was read
less as an inclusive "claim on this [Afrikaner] cultural heritage," as
Elsabé Brink maintains, than a pointed challenge to those Afrikaners
who openly supported Hitler and who called garment workers "com-
munistic accomplices" whose attempt to participate in the Centenary
was a "Jewish plot" and a "mockery of our national traditions."[23]
   Although neither the brief appearance of the socialist *Kappiekommando* at the Voortrekker Centenary in 1938 nor the plays and
"Pageants of South African Labour" performed at May Day celebrations and other occasions through the mid-1940s quote Brecht directly,
the GWU performances offer an exemplary instance of what Brecht
called, in an article written in the late 1930s with the anti-fascist
project in mind, the task of reclaiming "popular" or *volkstümlich* culture from the "history of its falsifications" and its contemporary abuse
by fascists (*Werke* 22: 407; *BoT* 108). By attempting to present themselves as critical socialists reforming an exclusivist narrative of *volk-
seie* (ethnic, rather than strictly "popular", identity) and *volkseenheid*
(ethnic unity), the Afrikaans members of the GWU hoped to challenge

Sachs later noted, the Afrikaner Nationalist government made union
and social association between Afrikaner women and men of color on
the shop floor increasingly difficult, while Afrikaner cultural
institutions fomented racist and anti-Semitic opposition to those who
held fast to the GWU's original non-racial policy; see E. S. Sachs, *Rebel
Daughters* (London: MacGibbon and Kee, 1957), 223–9.

[22] Hester Cornelius, "Ons en die Voortrekker-eeufees," *Garment Worker/
Klerewerker* (October 1938), 4.
[23] E. Brink, "Play, Poetry and Production. The Literature of the Garment
Workers," *South African Labour Bulletin* 9: 8 (1984): 32–51; for the
contemporary debate, D. B. H. Grobbelaar, "Do Not Forget to Be an
Afrikaner!", letter to E. S. Sachs, reprinted in *Garment Worker*
(November 1938), 9; "Sachs' Reply to a Hitlerite," *Garment Worker*
(November 1938), 9–10; and Petronella van Heerden, "Waarom ek 'n
sosialis is," *Klerewerker* (November 1938), 9, 12 (UW/WC/GWU).

Fig. 11. Garment worker in the Kappiekommando (Johannesburg, 1938).

the ideology of the racially exclusive *volk* and the Nazi discourse borrowed by key members of the Afrikaner elite. Instead they wanted to ground a broader-based "popular" movement in a non-racial working class, as reflected, for example, in the partnership of Weinberg and Kotane directing the May Day Pageants of Unity. The GWU's attempt to create a counter-public sphere at the intersection of socialism and Afrikanerdom offers a compelling concretization of Brecht's theory of the *Lehrstück*; their appearance at the Voortrekker Centenary Celebrations, like their strike actions and their formal plays, all had the goal of the "transformation of spectators" into social and political agents (or "statesmen" in Brecht's phrase, *Werke* 21: 396). Although they were not allowed to represent themselves as socialists *and* members of the *volk*, their rehearsal of this performance makes visible a key moment in the history of a progressive moment in an otherwise apparently monolithically right-wing Afrikaner revival movement in the era of fascist expansion in Europe and abroad and, in retrospect, suggests both the local and the international resonances of both the "small pedagogics" of the learning play and the "greater pedagogics" of social transformation, in the appeal for an anti-fascist and popular front.

The dis-illusion of race: estrangement effects in the Bantu Peoples' Theatre

Although the African intellectuals, white-collar workers and union activists who formed the Bantu Peoples' Theatre (1936–9) and later the African National Theatre (ANT, 1939–41) occupied quite different social, racial and geographical spaces in 1930s Johannesburg from those of the Afrikaner women of the GWU, they shared with the latter the desire to harness together the causes of national and anti-colonial struggle and the striving of socialism in "the massing of classes in their trade unions and employer organizations," as their program notes attest.[24] Whereas the first constitution of the Black Peoples' Theatre in 1937 claimed that the group was "non-political," the second in 1939

---

[24] Bantu Peoples' Theatre, *Drama Festival Program* (25–7 July 1940), 10; JPL/STC; hereafter BPT Festival.

reconstituted the BPT "on the model of the Unity Theatre, London"; like the Unity Theatres in London, Glasgow, Toronto and elsewhere in the Commonwealth and the Theatre Unions in the United States, it was dedicated to producing theatre on the themes of class struggle and social justice.[25] Although its membership overlapped with the more genteel Bantu Dramatic Society, which was founded in 1932 and sponsored by the British Drama League, it distinguished itself from its predecessor by staging Eugene O'Neill's social expressionist play *The Hairy Ape* in December 1936.[26] The producer was André van Gyseghem, a Belgian socialist who came to South Africa after an extended tour of the Soviet Union to direct the Pageant of South Africa (in English and Afrikaans) at the Johannesburg Jubilee in 1936. This *Hairy Ape* sharpened the portrayal of the conflict first between Yank, the physically powerful but confused worker deep in the engine room of an ocean liner, and the bright but brittle rich girl on the deck above, and secondly between Yank and the union men he briefly encounters, by making the workers, including the actor, sportsman, and later radio personality Dan Twala in the role of Yank, all black rather than the "white ethnics" (Irish, Polish, etc.) in O'Neill's play, and by having them speak what Mary Kelly, secretary of the Drama League, called "American slang [. . .] translated into the Bantu idiom of English."[27] Whether or not this "Bantu idiom" was Fanagalo, the pidgin spoken by white bosses to black workers in the gold mines, as a marxist critic later claimed, the production certainly highlighted the racial inflection of class conflict in the Johannesburg context and, in the traces of American slang transformed by this context, also produced the critical effect to which Brecht had that year given the name *Verfremdung*,

[25] For reference to the second constitution, see BPT Festival, 10; for the first, see the "Bantu Peoples Theatre Draft Constitution" in the South African Race Relations Collection (SAIRR: AD843 N6.14; UW/WC).

[26] For the Bantu Dramatic Society and its association with the British Drama League, see Peterson, *Monarchs, Missionaries, and African Intellectuals*, 156–93; for contrasting remarks on the BPT's *Hairy Ape*, see ibid., 167–8, and Kruger, *Drama of South Africa*, 58–9.

[27] Mary Kelly, *Conference on African Drama. 1938* (London: British Drama League, 1938), 3.

estrangement or *dis-illusion*, as the first English translation had it
(*Werke* 22: 960–8).[28]

While the Black Peoples' Theatre's production of *The Hairy Ape*
used O'Neill's stylized representation of class conflict as a basis for
highlighting the bleak divide between white and black in South Africa,
and the whites' inability to comprehend the blacks, the work of the
revived company appeared to return to the confines of domestic drama.
The Black Peoples' Theatre's Drama Festival in mid-1940 featured two
short plays by O'Neill, *The Dreamy Kid*, set in "the Negro quarter
of New York," and *Before Breakfast*, set in "an American tenement
house," as well as two new plays by a unionist and veteran of Baum's
Johannesburg Art Theatre, Guy Routh.[29] *The Word and the Act*, set in
"1937, at the height of the public controversy over the Native Bills,"
dealt with the hypocrisy of the Native Representation Act, which
removed the last "qualified" Africans from the common voters' roll,
and *Patriot's Pie*, set "in the early days of the Greater War 1939" (BPT
Festival, 3–4), broached the controversial subject of African conscription in the Second World War in the story of "a young African who
attempted to fight for his King and Country."[30] Setting both plays in
the home of one *Sonke* (Zulu, "all of us"), Routh emphasized the township context of urban African life, while using the domestic format
to bring public political issues closer to home. Despite this format,
the acting drew more on the presentational style of African variety
"concerts" (still today the local term for variety shows), whose satiric
and sentimental modes of direct audience address had been honed
by well-known performers like Twala and Griffiths Motsieloa rather
than on naturalist restraint, "achieving," as Routh had it, "a more
direct form of self-expression" (Routh, BPT, 21).[31] Buoyed by its

---

28 The marxist critic is Robert MacLaren, who writes under the
   pen-names of Mshengu or Robert Kavanagh; here: Kavanagh, *Theatre
   and Cultural Struggle in South Africa* (London: Zed, 1985), 46.
29 Routh, "The Johannesburg Art Theatre."
30 Routh, "The Bantu Peoples Theatre," 21; subsequent references in the
   text to Routh, BPT.
31 African concerts drew on models from the Ziegfeld Follies to Bert
   Williams and George Walker and other pioneers of the

modest success, including positive reviews in the CPSA organ *Inkululeko*, the company changed its name to the African National Theatre and was briefly able to pay actors for rehearsals (22).[32]

Despite this promising run, the tension between African preferences for a presentational mode of performance and the satiric stage treatment of serious matters, such as police brutality, and the white director's belief that serious drama called for "the audience to identify themselves with our stage characters" exploded in the company's "last major show" (Routh, BPT, 22–3) in a manner both unexpected and arguably Brechtian. *The Rude Criminal* (1941), the company's only play by an African, satirically depicted the all-too common scenario of an African arrested for not having his passbook in order, and may have been the first of many plays on this topic to be performed.[33] The author was Gaur Radebe, founder of the African Mineworkers' Union, then a CPSA member and later a major influence on Nelson Mandela; the play was performed at the Gandhi Hall in Fordsburg for an audience that included CPSA members of all races, unionists, and a few "wealthy patrons" (Routh, BPT, 23).[34] Nonetheless, despite the

African-American stage, but had by 1940 developed their own distinctive combination of vaudeville gags, jazz and marabi musical numbers, nationalist hymns, and occasional social drama, such as "The 'Cruiter'" by African-American folklorist John Matheus, performed by Motsieloa's Pitch Black Follies in 1938; see Kruger, *Drama of South Africa*, 25–9, 44–7.

[32] Anon., "The African National Theatre," *Inkululeko* (June 1941) 5, 7. *Inkululeko* means "freedom."

[33] *The Pass* (1943), by H. I. E. Dhlomo, now feted as the "father" of black South African theatre, was written shortly after, but never produced. Fugard's first play, *No-Good Friday* (1958), draws in part on his experience as a clerk in the Pass Office, but the play does not deal in detail with African experience of the humiliating and often arbitrary regulation of their daily lives.

[34] Radebe left the CPSA in 1942, but went on to lead the bus boycotts in Alexandra township to the north of Johannesburg in 1943 and 1944; see Karis and Gerhard, *Political Profiles*, 130. He proved a major influence on Nelson Mandela at the time, when Mandela was a law clerk and Radebe an "interpreter and messenger." Mandela called him

reputation of the playwright and of the potential audience, Routh did not trust Radebe's bent for satire. He argued instead that:

> Our African audiences had a horrible way of laughing in the wrong place. If anyone got a blow in the face, they would shriek with laughter; if someone died, they would go into hysterics. It was explained psychologically that they were expressing their pleasure that it wasn't them. But, if that were so, then we were failing in our artistic task of causing the audience to identify with our stage characters.
>
> (Routh, BPT, 22–3)

Like other white liberals working with black actors, Routh read this laughter as evidence of failure, of the cast's inability to compel audiences to empathy and of the audience's inability to take the play seriously. The problem, however, is that Routh failed to take seriously the political implications of the "psychological" explanation. African audiences then and now have agreed that they take pleasure in knowing that they aren't targets – for the moment – but have also used this pleasurable distance as an opportunity to evaluate the actors and comment on the action in relation to their own experience of similar abuse.[35]

Even though Routh did not see the critical potential of this *disillusioned* spectatorship, which we have come to admire in Brecht,

a "troublemaker in the best sense of that term, and an influential man in the African community": see Nelson Rohihlahla Mandela, *Long Walk to Freedom* (Boston: Little, Brown, and Co., 1995), 71–4, 85–9.

[35] Leontine Sagan, working with black actors at the Hofmeyr School for Social Work (1941–2), noted not only the tendency to laugh but also that Africans judged characters on grounds that were different from but no less reasonable than the judgments of schooled (mostly white) audiences. For example, her students found Polonius more interesting than Hamlet because he was trying, however clumsily, to focus on "social" rather than "emotional" problems, and they considered the former paramount: see *Lights and Shadows: The Autobiography of Leontine Sagan*, ed. Loren Kruger (Johannesburg: Witwatersrand University Press, 1996), 211. Over the last quarter century, I have heard similar arguments by African spectators and scholars.

the performance of the play invited critical dis-illusion all the same. *The Rude Criminal* opened with a "policeman" striding into the hall, demanding passes from members of the audience. Africans were so alarmed, according to Routh's account (23), that they "huddled into themselves," while "the wealthy patrons leapt to their feet with squeals of terror and disappeared through the backdoor." This strategy anticipated by more than twenty years the direct assault on audiences that was to become a familiar device in Soweto-era protest plays such as Workshop '71's *Survival* (1976), produced just before the uprising in June – by which time the director would be deliberately invoking Brecht. Although many white patrons left, the review in *Inkululeko* suggested that those who stayed saw in the play the argument that the "African nation" could "fight for its rights and win."[36]

The organizers of the ANT clearly saw no contradiction between African nationalism and international socialism. Like its counterparts in the leftist Unity Theatres in Europe and North America, the ANT targeted urbanized and urbanizing workers as well as intellectuals. Local actors may not have had direct knowledge of political theatre overseas, but the reception suggests that their theatre strove to meet the demands of a proletarian avant-garde and its institutions rather than those of any single individual pioneer, and to live up to the argument, in the words of former Berliner John Bonn, later director of the New York Proletbuehne and editor of *Workers Theatre*, that "simplicity does not mean crudity or the absence of art. On the contrary, the more artistic our productions are, the better our political education will be."[37] But whereas their counterparts in Europe and the United States could expect support from well-established unions, the South African theatre could not. While state harassment and lack of funds were probably the primary cause of the group's demise, in addition to the "pressures of war," the lack of universal primary education, and thus of a broadly literate membership able to contribute written plays and criticism for wider circulation, is also significant.

[36] Anon., "Three Good Plays," *Inkululeko* (September 1941).
[37] John Bonn, "Dramburo. Chairman's Report," *Workers Theatre* (May 1932): 9–11.

Like most politically inclined cultural groups in this period, the BPT relied on an educated core of English-speaking (black as well as white) organic intellectuals and were not able to mobilize much beyond the minority of black workers who understood English.[38] The BPT organizers' idea of drama largely relied, like that of the Unity Theatre and Theatre Union movement, on written drama rather than the short agit-prop sketches of the *Arbeitertheater* (Germany), Workers' Theatre Movement (Britain) the League of Workers' Theatres (USA), or locally, the "mass pageants" of the GWU, which deployed disciplined choreography and choral delivery that did not depend as much on naturalist acting techniques or on players learning lines from written texts.

Despite these shortcomings, the BPT's national aspirations, its intercultural membership, the topical themes of its plays, and its exploration of innovations in performance *and* in spectatorship are remarkable, as was its case for a people's theatre grounded on class as well as racial affiliation. With the banning of the CPSA in 1950, however, and the suppression of even distantly related organizations over the next forty years, the legacy of leftist theatre like the BPT and the GWU vanished. So effective was its erasure from South African history that Astrid von Kotze, founding member of Junction Avenue Theatre Company and the Durban Workers' Cultural Local (DWCL), chronicler and director of workers' theatre in the 1980s, could begin her account of the DWCL with the claim that "there is a long history of working class struggle in South Africa. But it is only in the last few years that workers have organised to fight their oppression on the cultural front."[39] Before examining the intersection of academic and unionist activities and individuals in Junction Avenue, South Africa's most self-consciously Brechtian theatre company, we should pay due attention to the Brechtian experiments which Athol Fugard conducted with the Serpent Players in the 1960s and early 1970s.

[38] Routh, BPT, 23.
[39] Astrid von Kotze, *Organise and Act: the Natal Workers Theatre Movement, 1983–87* (Durban: Culture and Working Life Publications, 1988), 8.

Enter Bertolt Brecht

Brecht's plays began appearing in university and art theatres in the late 1950s, but, as Arnold Blumer shows in his survey of Brecht in South Africa, these productions challenged neither the administrative and artistic hierarchy of the drama schools nor the ideological and material power of the apartheid state.[40] Noting that out of twenty-six Brecht productions in twenty-five years, from 1958 to 1983, fifteen took place at drama schools, seven at fringe or art theatres, and only four at the subsidized provincial arts councils, Blumer suggests that these productions primarily served the purpose of formal education for drama students by means of "Brecht the great dramatic artist in the bourgeois sense of the word" (38), and had little social impact outside the narrow confines of the white Europhile art theatre. The first production of *The Caucasian Chalk Circle*, for example, was directed by Fred Engelen, of the Royal Flemish Theatre, at UCT's Little Theatre in September 1959, and was praised by the Little Theatre's director, an English expatriate, for its "richly imaginative use of up-to-the-minute technique" and for launching the "show-business career" of Percy Sieff in the role of Azdak.[41] Not until the turmoil of the 1970s did these theatres engage with the political questions raised by Brecht in his critical writing and in his work as an educator and agitator about the critical role that theatre might play in and against an oppressive state.

---

[40] Blumer, "Brecht in South Africa," 30–8.

[41] Donald Inskip, *Forty Little Years: The Story of a Theatre* (Cape Town: Howard Timmins, 1972), 93. According to Blumer ("Brecht in South Africa," 37), UCT's first Brecht production, *The Good Woman of Setzuan* (1958), was dismissed in a routine Cold War manner as "proletarian propagandistic drama." It was not until the 1970s that Brecht was produced with any frequency. In addition to revivals of *The Caucasian Chalk Circle* and productions of acknowledged classics, *Mother Courage* and *The Threepenny Opera*, there were localized stagings of *Puntila and his Man Matti*, in Afrikaans by the Cape Performing Arts Board (CAPAB) in 1973, and in English at the UCT Drama Department (directed by the noted experimental director Mavis Taylor) in 1982.

The value of Brecht's theory and practice in and for South Africa emerges well before the student activism in the 1970s, however. In the critical period of the early 1960s, the government used its own assault on unarmed protesters at Sharpeville in March 1960 to ban legitimate opposition and to drastically increase police power to detain and torture suspects without trial, driving resistance underground.[42] It is in this repressive context that Athol Fugard's work with the Serpent Players, a group of black worker-players in the historically politicized area of the Eastern Cape, should be judged. Although different accounts of the founding of the Serpent Players in 1963 replay tensions that were characteristic of asymmetrical collaborations between liberal, educated whites and militant but often impoverished blacks in the apartheid years, all agree about the achievements of a company that created compelling theatre under very difficult circumstances, including the arrest and trial of members for political offenses, revocation of permits allowing blacks and whites to occupy the same room, and the pressures of arbitrary labour conditions and long commutes for factory and domestic workers from their homes in the black township of New Brighton to work in white Port Elizabeth.[43] Under

---

[42] The banning of the ANC and PAC in 1960 was followed by the Criminal Law Amendment Act to permit the police to detain suspects for up to ninety days without trial in cases of alleged "sabotage," "treason," and "terrorism." For a brief account of these acts, see Leonard Thompson, *A History of South Africa* (New Haven: Yale University Press, 1990), 198–200.

[43] According to Fugard, the Serpent Players emerged after Norman Ntshinga asked Fugard for help setting up a theatre group; see Fugard, *Notebooks, 1960–1977*, ed. and selected Mary Benson (New York: Theatre Communications Group, 1984), 81; hereafter cited as *Notebooks* in the text. Kani acknowledges that he and Ntshona joined a well-established group with the production of *Antigone* in 1965, but claims that the group was formed before Fugard: see J. Kani and W. Ntshona, "Art is Life and Life is Art: An Interview with John Kani and Winston Ntshona of the Serpent Players, South Africa," *UFAHAMU: Journal of the African Activist Association* 6: 2 (1976): 5–26; here: 15–17. For further comment see Russell Vandenbroucke, *Truth the Hands Can Touch: The Theatre of Athol Fugard* (Johannesburg: Ad

Fugard's direction, the group first performed *The Cure*, an adaptation of Niccolò Machiavelli's play *La Mandragola* which shifted the story of quackery from Renaissance Florence to contemporary townships, and the form from classic *commedia dell'arte* to the local fusion of music hall, (African) American vaudeville, and indigenous story-telling in the "concert." The next production, a local version of Georg Büchner's *Woyzeck* accompanied by an original jazz score by Mike Ngxolo, depicted the soldier Woyzeck (Welcome Duru) as a "black labourer," the Drum Major (Norman Ntshinga) as a "boss boy," and Marie as a black domestic servant (Mabel "May" Magada) and dropped much of the comic concert business in favor of focused representation of these social roles.[44] This focus led Fugard to praise the actors' sense of responsibility and to argue that he could "go further with this group than any group of white professionals or high class amateurs" (*Notebooks*, 134). He was particularly impressed with their work discipline as against the "dreaming and bitching" of the black intellectuals and "situations" he had encountered in Dorkay House, Johannesburg, working on *Nongogo* (1959) and *No-Good Friday* (1958) (*Notebooks*, 96).[45] For their part, company members emphasized in letters to Fugard not only that they appreciated his commitment to the Serpent Players and to their individual contributions but also,

Donker, 1986), 132–4, and Kruger, *Drama of South Africa*, 138–9, 233, n.18. Similar disputes have since surfaced in accounts of other collaborations such as the collectively authored workshopped plays directed by Barney Simon at the Market Theatre (1976–95).

[44] Vandenbroucke (*Truth*, 133) mentions the male members of the cast but not May Magada, despite the fact that she had previous experience as a blues singer and was an original member of the group; see Fugard, *Notebooks*, 81.

[45] "Situation" was the label used by gangsters and township toughs to belittle the aspirations of black white-collar workers (applying to "situations vacant" in the papers); it was adopted ironically by African intellectuals, including Fugard collaborators Bloke Modisane and Lewis Nkosi, who felt themselves caught in an untenable situation between black and white culture from which exile was the only escape, and who spent much time and ink lamenting their condition; see Kruger, *Drama of South Africa*, 86–91.

and crucially, that they saw theatre as a means of social and political education. As the actor and director Mulligan Mbikwane put it, theatre provided a way to "put across certain truths to my people."[46]

Rehearsed over the second half of 1964, *The Caucasian Chalk Circle* opened to a white audience at Rhodes University in the small settler and educational town of Grahamstown in November and in New Brighton on 10 December. Fugard was initially ambivalent, noting that reading Brecht provoked "doubt and suspicion" about his own work, and complaining in rehearsal that the actors "were as bourgeois in aspirations and morality as most white people [. . .] The fight is for the slice of the same cake. No one wants to bake a different one. This is the hardest – showing that *The Chalk Circle* is a different recipe" (*Notebooks*, 119), but later considered the production "one of the best he had ever mounted" (Vandenbroucke, *Truth*, 135). Unlike the all-white productions at UCT (1959) and PACT (1963), this performance highlighted South African conditions. Grusha (Magada) was dressed as a domestic servant, the Iron Guard wore local police helmets and the palace clique white masks, while Duru drew on the concert persona of the alternately cunning and servile black to play the maverick Azdak. Even though Duru was "taken for ninety days" detention without trial before the New Brighton performance, leaving Fugard to play Azdak to the township audience, Fugard remained impressed by the "usefulness" of the play, and its "bright decisiveness" as the dramatist's tool against the dark days of apartheid (*Notebooks*, 119–20).

Fugard's sense that Brecht's critical dramaturgy could illuminate the struggle for justice in a South Africa governed by unjust laws favoring the white minority at the expense of the majority was sharpened when Ntshinga was arrested and sentenced to five years on

[46] Mulligan Mbikwana, Letter to Athol Fugard, 18 April 1966; similar sentiments were expressed in letters by other members such as Malefetse ("Fats") Bookholane (March 1965) who went on to theatre work at Dorkay House and later at the Market Theatre. These letters form part of the Athol Fugard Collection, Lilly Library, Indiana University, Bloomington (Box 1/folder 13), hereafter AF: LL/IU; copies in the National English Literary Museum (NELM) in Grahamstown, South Africa.

Robben Island for allegedly furthering the goals of the banned ANC (*Notebooks*, 123–6). At the sentencing hearing in Cradock, another political prisoner, whom Fugard identifies only as "Number One accused" (124), gave his coat to Magada, "asking her to go to his family and tell them what had happened and give them the coat to 'use'" (125). In a series of letters to Fugard while he was awaiting trial, and afterwards while awaiting deportation to the Island, Ntshinga (Magada's husband) reiterated his sense of the capacity of theatre for making public the actions and reactions of ordinary people whose stories were repressed by the state. More specifically, he highlighted the power of objects, especially those given up or confiscated, to prisoners in solitary confinement.[47] Confronted with this "first degree experience," Fugard was tempted to dismiss his work as "second degree art," but he found in the imagined experience that the coat would give to family members receiving, touching, smelling, and using it the germ not only of an "actor's exercise" (*Notebooks*, 138), but also a way of asking questions that would provoke choices about acting on and against the given circumstances. The group used the object (in both senses) of the coat as the "mandate" (Fugard's term for the instigation of an improvised action) for a series of encounters, such as between the woman bearing the convict's message and his waiting wife, or between the latter and the rent board official threatening to evict her.

[47] Ntshinga's letters from Cradock Gaol in April and May 1965 could not mention state repression directly, but his account of relieving the distress of solitary confinement by rehearsing roles from *The Cure* and *Woyzeck*, which he performed in public, and from *Antigone*, from which he was removed by imprisonment, suggests the therapeutic value of theatre in prison (20 May 1965) and also anticipates the work Ntshinga would foster on Robben Island, such as the production of *Antigone* in which Mandela played Creon (1970). A fellow prisoner and Serpent Player, Sipho "Sharkie" Mguqulwa, also writing from Cradock, which he ironically called "Honolulu via Sing Sing," confirmed the value of rehearsing roles in solitary (2 May 1965; AF: LL/IU: 1/13). There are no letters in the collection from Robben Island; until pressure from the International Red Cross compelled the government to change prison policy in the 1970s, prisoners on the Island were permitted only one heavily censored letter every six months.

Brecht in South Africa

Fugard acted less as author than as provocateur, scribe and overall organizer.

The Coat, the play that emerged out of the "actor's exercise," combined the life-narratives of African performers with the gestic techniques honed by Brecht to show the social attitudes and interaction of characters in speech and gesture (Werke 23: 89; BoT 198).[48] It heralded a new and distinctively South African form, the workshopped testimonial play, which would educate and entertain audiences from the internationally renowned Market Theatre to schools in the townships. The text drew on Brecht both in its technique and in its critical engagement with the pedagogic imperative of "putting over certain truths to [our] people" and of the pressing contradictions between private aspiration and state repression. It also spoke directly of and to the lives of urban Africans. The manuscript initially listed actors by their own names, including experienced players such as Mbikwane, Magada, and Nomhle Nkonyeni, who had performed in The Cure, Woyzeck, The Caucasian Chalk Circle, and Antigone, as well as newcomers such as John Kani, but by the time the play reached a white Theatre Appreciation Club, in Port Elizabeth in October 1966, the players were introducing themselves using the names of characters they had played in previous Serpent productions (Kani as Haemon in Antigone, Nkonyeni as Aniko in The Caucasian Chalk Circle, Magada as Marie in Woyzeck). This strategy directed audience attention to the implications of the actions rather than the personal motivations of the characters, while also hiding the identity of the actors from the security police, who were sure to be in the audience.[49] While

---

[48] The Serpent Players, The Coat (1966), in Township Plays, ed. Dennis Walder (Oxford University Press, 1993), 122; cited as The Coat in the text. For the manuscript, see AF: LL/IU: Box 3.

[49] From the outset, members of the political police, the Security Branch, had made unannounced visits to rehearsals, starting with The Cure in July 1963. In Fugard's presence, they did not "behave offensively"; instead, the head of the Special Branch, one Officer du Plooy, "chatted" to Fugard about the London production of The Blood Knot, but the latter could not escape the thought that the officer had the power to lock him up for ninety days "without any trouble": Notebooks, 92.

243

anxiety about the police almost stymied the final rehearsal, at which several members refused to read (Fugard, *Notebooks*, 142), the actors, led by Mbikwane alias Lavrenti (his character in *The Caucasian Chalk Circle*) and a director in his own right, began the performance by presenting and analyzing their conflicting positions about the theatre and its uses prior to insisting on the priority of social reality: their performance was about the coat because it "came back" when the prisoner who had worn it could not (*The Coat*, 124).

The coolness of Brecht might at first glance seem foreign to performers and audiences accustomed to the sentiment of township melodrama, but the matter-of-fact acting favored by Brecht suited the Serpent Players. While critics like the American Russell Vandenbroucke, schooled in the emotional attachments of the Method, might find this coolness an allegedly "desperate" attempt at "objectivity" (Vandenbroucke, *Truth*, 139), black South Africans who were directly (and presumably emotionally) affected by the threat of prison were also able to present plausible reactions to this threat in a matter-of-fact manner, in contrast to the "horror and fascination" of the white club audience (Fugard, *Notebooks*, 143). It is important to remember that many members were politically active whether by inclination or necessity, and that the eastern Cape was the most politically active black community in the country: leaders of both the ANC and its rival, the Pan-African Congress, emerged here and, even after they were banned, the underground arms of both organizations continued to operate in the 1960s. An unpublished note by Fugard emphasizes that "*The Coat* must be above all for a New Brighton audience," and acknowledges the connection with the political activity of the members by quoting from Frantz Fanon's *Wretched of the Earth*: "rebellion is the most conscious act" and by documenting the trials of his colleagues.[50] The subsequent publication of the play under the name of the Serpent Players in 1967 in *The Classic*, a magazine edited initially by the black journalist Nat Nakasa and read by other

[50] Fugard, unpublished notebook no. 6; entry for 28 September 1966 (AF: LL/IU: Box 1). The reference does not appear in the published *Notebooks*.

black intellectuals, secured its identification with black theatre and made possible its performance at the short-lived South African Black Theatre Union (SABTU) festival in 1972, among other even more militant plays, including Mbikwane's staging of *The Just* by Albert Camus, and agit-prop pieces by students calling for revolution.

Also in the 1970s, black student organizations had emerged from the dormancy of the 1960s, but were subject to increasingly brutal treatment by a police force that enjoyed practical impunity due a series of "anti-terrorist" laws and so thwarted the development of new political theatre initiatives under the SABTU banner.[51] At the same time, integrated ventures led by whites began to test the "petty apartheid" laws against cultural association between black and white which had constrained Fugard's work with the Serpent Players. The Space Theatre, founded by the actress Yvonne Bryceland, her husband Brian Astbury, and her collaborator, Fugard, in 1971, was the first publicly integrated performance space to open since the Group Areas Act had closed Dorkay House in 1965.[52] It provided a venue for two key collaborations that would cement the links between Brecht and anti-apartheid theatre, in *Sizwe Bansi* and *The Island*. The latter, performed initially (July 1973) as *The Hodoshe Span* (Hodoshe's Workteam), distilled the essence of two men's lives in prison from the actual experience of Serpent Player and former political prisoner Ntshinga; the re-enactment of *Antigone* drew in part from a performance on Robben Island, in which Nelson Mandela played Creon.[53] The classical allusion as well as the resonance of its theme has earned

[51] See Kavanagh, *Theatre and Cultural Struggle*, ch. 3, and Kruger, *Drama of South Africa*, ch. 6.

[52] For the Space Theatre, see Brian Astbury, *The Space/Die Ruimte/Indawo* (Cape Town: The Space, 1979), n.p. and Kruger, *Drama of South Africa*, 154–66.

[53] In addition to the Serpent Players' production in 1965, with Nomhle Nkonyeni as Antigone and George Mnci as Creon, and the version on Robben Island in 1970, Sophocles' *Antigone* was performed by the Company (forerunner of the Market Theatre) in 1974. In 1988, Peter Se-Puma directed an adaptation called *Igazi Lam* ("My Blood"), which transposed the story into post-civil-war South Africa. For Mandela's comments, see his *Long Walk to Freedom*, 456.

The Island more international attention, but *Sizwe Bansi* offers a richer synthesis of performance forms and a more compelling engagement with South African experience.[54] The story of Sizwe Bansi ("the nation is strong"), a man from the country who comes to the city in search of work and gets it only once he appropriates the identity and the valid passbook of a dead man, Robert Zwelinzima ("weighty feeling"), with the help of Buntu ("humanity"), was prompted by a photograph of a man in his Sunday best, posing with a cigarette in one hand and a pipe in the other, and a broad smile on his face. A man with such a smile, reasoned Kani and Ntshona, had to have his pass in order. This "celebratory image of a man, affirmative, full of life" and the ambiguous tale of survival behind the picture provided the "mandate" of the drama.[55] The action was generated by the contradiction between this "dream picture" (fig. 12) and the reality of discrimination represented by the official passbook photograph and "native identification" numbers. The Space program, which listed the participants (including Fugard) by ID numbers only, emphasized this alienation as well as the collaborative creation of the play, while shielding Kani and Ntshona (temporarily) from police interference.[56]

While the play emerged out of the contradiction between an affirmative image and a sober representation of apartheid, it also

---

[54] *Sizwe Bansi* was performed in tandem with *The Island* in Cape Town, Johannesburg, London, New York, Washington, Australia, and West and East Germany and revived often in South Africa, but *The Island* was also revived on its own in Paris, Dublin, the GDR, and the United States; see John Read, *Athol Fugard: A Bibliography* (Grahamstown: National English Literary Museum, 1991), 91–117.

[55] Vanderbroucke, *Truth*, 158. Although "Bansi" has been the usual spelling and will be retained for citation here, readers should note that current isiXhosa dictionaries list only *banzi*, meaning "broad" or, by extension, "strong."

[56] The program (Fugard Collection, NELM) does not corroborate Kani's more recent claim that the Space program read "devised by Serpent Players, assisted in directing by Athol Fugard" (as cited by Vandenbroucke, *Truth*, 158). Instead, it attributes the play to Kani, Ntshona, and Fugard in equal measure, but by printing not their names but their official ID numbers.

Fig. 12. "The Dream Picture": Winston Tshona as Sizwe in *Sizwe Bansi is Dead* (London: 1972). Photograph by Donald Cooper.

negotiated the tension between different modes of performance. The balancing act between Grotowskian "poor theatre" and exuberant impersonation, Brechtian coolness and the engaging, even ingratiating, concert act corresponded to the tension, in the lives of actors and characters alike, between the matter-of-fact negotiation of absurd but painful conflicts caused by apartheid law and the energetic mockery of that absurdity. The dramatization of this tension, using props like the passbook and the social gests involved in handling them, drew on Brecht by way of *The Coat*. The pace and tone of the performance in the alternation between Kani's expansive impersonation of different characters, set off by Ntshona's straight-man portrayal of Sizwe, were also shaped by the actors' life-histories, especially Kani's seven years with Ford, and by the gags in concert sketches that toured the townships.[57] Kani's virtuoso performance as Styles, a former assembly

[57] Sipho Sepamla notes the influence of African variety concerts, and especially of the impresario Griffiths Motsieloa, who dominated the circuit from the 1920s to the 1940s, on township tyro Gibson Kente and, indirectly, on political theatre: "Towards an African Theatre,"

worker turned photographer, and his antagonists, from his boss to a horde of cheeky cockroaches, was not really a monologue, as it is often described, but a satirical concert turn. Kani's impersonation of "Baas Bradley" and his own former self at the Ford assembly plant in anticipation of the visit of Henry Ford Jr. is typical:

> "Tell the boys in your language, that this is a very big day . . ."
> "Gentlemen, the old fool says this is a hell of a big day . . ."
> "Tell the boys that Mr. Henry Ford the Second is the big
> bass, . . . the Makhulu baas . . ."
> "Mr Baas Bradley says . . . Mr Ford is the grandmother baas
> of them all"[58]

Although more subtle than much of the clowning in township concerts, Kani's comic mimicry of his boss's efforts to speak to his "boys," enhanced in performance by direct address to the audience, recalls the concert style.

This affinity with township concerts did not please everybody. Sipho Sepamla, editor of the black theatre magazine S'ketsh, criticized the ingratiating aspect of the impersonation for making black spectators "laugh too hard at the white man to see beyond that"; his scepticism was echoed in New York, where Kani's performance was compared to that staple of minstrelsy, Stephin Fetchit.[59] The published text eliminated some of the draft's satirical jabs at stupid white bosses, such as Kani's quip against "Baas van Wyk, who worked his way down through all of the departments and ended up in the general store," but audiences at the performance in St Stephen's Hall in

Rand Daily Mail (2 April 1981); for more detail on this influence see Kruger, Drama of South Africa, chapters 2 and 7. The rough draft of the play (LL/IU/Box 4) suggests that Kani's initial routine had many more gags and digressions than even the ninety-minute version at the Space; this was later cut to about half an hour.
58 Fugard, Kani and Ntshona, Sizwe Bansi [sic] Is Dead, in Fugard, Township Plays, 153; cited as Sizwe Bansi in the text.
59 See Sepamla, "Sizwe Bansi," S'ketsh (Summer 1973): 24 and M. Feingold, "Son of Stepinfetchit and a Vigorous Bolshevik," New York Village Voice (5 May 1975), 98.

New Brighton proved able to combine heartfelt laughter at situations they knew all too well with strategic intervention:[60]

> At the end of the Ford Factory story a man . . . entered the acting area and then, as if he was a referee at a boxing match, held up John's arm and announced that 'Kani has knocked out Henry Ford the Junior.'[61]

Fugard calls this intervention Brechtian and, while it corresponds to Brecht's idea of the active spectator, it also reflects a history of African vocal response to performance. As Fugard had already noted of *The Coat*, there was a significant difference between the white audience's emotional but alienated response of "horror and fascination" (*Notebooks*, 143) and the cast members' dispassionate comment on the handling of the coat and associated objects, like the *umuti* (medicine) in the pocket that allegedly lightened the convict's sentence (137). The difference between the fascination with staged suffering favored by audiences accustomed to the illusionist Anglo-American stage and an African preference for interacting with the action rather than silently watching may have been astonishing to Fugard, as his report implies, but it was, as we have seen, the common African response to stage performance.

While Kani's opening act reproduces some of the flavor of township comedy, Kani and Ntshona's attention to plot and argument in the second part of the play reflected the influence of the Serpent Players' Brechtian experiments. The invisible pass in Kani's hands (and Ntshona's meaningful stare at the object in rehearsal) conveyed the real power of this document (fig. 13). Sizwe hesitates to give up his name to acquire another man's passbook, and is persuaded only when Buntu draws him into dramatizing a series of encounters – with a policeman and a prospective employer – to bring home the urgency of the decision. While the mostly white audience in Cape Town was

---

[60] Fugard, Kani, and Ntshona, "Sizwe Bansi Is Dead" (holograph draft with notes), p. 4 (LL/IU: Box 4).
[61] See Fugard's essay "Sizwe Bansi Is Dead", in *A Night in the Theatre*, ed. Ronald Harwood (London: Methuen 1982), 30.

Fig. 13. John, Winston, Athol, and the Fictive Pass in *Sizwe Bansi is Dead* by Athol Fugard, John Kani, and Winston Ntshona (Cape Town, 1972).

touched by the bitter comedy of this predicament and if some black intellectuals in Johannesburg found the play too talky, those in New Brighton were moved to interrupt the debate. As Fugard recalls:[62]

> After watching the first few seconds of the operation [putting
> Sizwe's photograph into Zwelinzima's pass] in stunned
> silence . . . a voice shouted out from the audience: 'Don't do it
> brother . . .' Another voice responded . . . 'Go ahead and try.
> They haven't caught me yet.' That was the cue for the most
> amazing and spontaneous debate I have ever heard. As I
> stood . . . listening to it all, I realized I was watching a very

[62] For the first reaction, see Jean Marquard, "Sizwe Bansi Is Alive and Well," *To the Point* (23 December 1972); for the second, Sepamla, "Sizwe Bansi"; for Fugard's comments, "Sizwe Bansi is Dead" (essay), 31–2.

special example of one of theatre's major responsibilities in an oppressive society: to break . . . the conspiracy of silence. . . . The action of our play was being matched . . . by the action of the audience. . . . A performance on stage had provoked a political event in the auditorium.

What is noteworthy about this audience's participation in the remaking of *Sizwe Bansi* is not simply the urgent engagement with the subject matter. In contrast to the European-affiliated audience's "horror and fascination" in reaction to *The Coat*, this audience's engaged response demonstrates the remarkable convergence of Brechtian analysis and African vocal reaction to the dramatized situation.

This intervention is powerful not because it "breaks the silence" but because it acknowledges the symbolic character of the action. The audience's debate, like the show it interrupts, is a *performance*; its enactment here – in the liminal space between the familiar ground of the township outside and the occasional, unlikely character of the show inside the hall – is significant because such performance would be impossible in a public township space, since these were all controlled by the government. When Buntu and "Robert" in *Sizwe Bansi* simulate likely encounters with potential power brokers like the boss or the police, or when the prisoner John (Kani) mimes "calling home" from *The Island* – repeating the symbolic but actual acts performed by Robben Island prisoners deprived of family contact – this performance re-enacts ordinary acts in extraordinary circumstances.[63] By intervening in the play, the members of the audience do not abandon the fiction; they *use* it. This appropriation may transcend "the system of player/spectator," as in Brecht's conception of the learning play (*Werke* 21: 396), but it does so not by dissolving the realm of performance but by renegotiating the link between play and social action. This event shares some characteristics with Boal's forum

---

[63] Fugard recalls Ntshinga's account, after his release from prison, of numerous such performances, from talking into an imaginary telephone to replaying the scripts of popular (mostly American) films to telling jokes about matches between "black domination and white domination" (*Notebooks*, 151–2).

theatre in that spectators proposed an alternative "model for action" and debated the value of the alternative as an act against oppression, but it differs from Boal's scripted "rules of the game" in that spectators did not wait to be asked to intervene.[64] Many in this New Brighton audience were political actors in the most direct indicative way and were later imprisoned for their activism, but here, in the space of performance, they were able to act in ways as yet impossible in a political realm which excluded them. Their participation in a public performance re-enacts the subjunctive action of reclaiming and occupying public space and so enables the envisioning of a future public culture. In this meeting of Brecht's "pedagogics great and small" and Augusto Boal's "theatre of the oppressed," the transformation of spectator into player or spect-actor and thence to social and political actor requires play as well as politics.

It is this engagement with the critical social gest, rather than any direct quotation, that links *Sizwe Bansi* with the next generation of anti-apartheid theatre with Brecht. *Survival*, by Fana Kekana, Dan Selaelo Maredi, Themba Ntinga, and Seth Sibanda, in association with the leftist director and Witwatersrand University (Wits) academic Robert (Mshengu) MacLaren (a.k.a. Kavanagh), which opened at the Space in May 1976 and played in townships on the Witwatersrand in the wake of the student and worker uprising in June, was received by audiences and the police as part of that uprising. Before *Survival*, Workshop '71 had progressed from a workshop directed by MacLaren into a theatre company, whose *Uhlanga* (*The Reed*, 1975) by James Mthoba, a one-man Everyman, toured the country. Like *Sizwe Bansi* and *The Island*, this play grew out of the life-narratives of black male workers. But whereas *Sizwe Bansi* favored intimate talk leavened with comedy, *Survival* used dialogue chiefly to provide a functional frame for individual narratives delivered directly to the audience. Whereas *The Island* pared down the action to two individuals rather than the group of prisoners initially envisaged in the first draft of the play, *Survival* took up the challenge of using four actors to represent both

---

[64] Augusto Boal, *Games for Actors and Non-Actors*, trans. Adrian Jackson (London: Routledge, 1992), 18–21.

individual lives and the broader social conditions of apartheid, the effects of which on the lives of black people could be fully understood only collectively.[65] Performed at the Space and at Cape township venues before the uprising and then in Soweto and environs and at the Wits Box in the midst of the unrest, *Survival* was also the last production of the group, whose members went into exile when they took the show to the United States.[66] However brief its run, the performance of this play participated in a "revolutionary situation" partly by conscientizing white spectators but also by assembling township audiences as participants in defiance of laws against "riotous assembly" and "seditious speech."[67]

More than its predecessors, *Sizwe Bansi* and *The Island*, and many of its anti-apartheid successors, *Survival* draws on the analytical element of Brecht's epic theatre. It also extends Brecht's call for cultural invention in social conflict by directly engaging the response of a public that is more than an audience. Rather than a single plotline, *Survival* is structured around a place – prison – which is also an

[65] The first draft of *The Island* was called "Die Hodoshe Span" in ironic homage to the brutal prison overseer called Hodoshe (carrion-fly) by Robben Island inmates. This version opened with a work team led by Mbikwane and incorporated testimony by at least four actors; the final version included only two, Kani and Ntshona. While it is unlikely that Workshop '71 had access to Fugard's drafts or that the group prepared *Survival* as a *direct* response to Fugard, the workshop leader, MacLaren, clearly emphasized the collective focus of the work and would later launch an explicitly marxist critique of "bourgeois individualism" in Fugard's drama. For the draft of "Die Hodoshe Span" see AF: LL/IU: Box 3; for MacLaren/Kavanagh's critique of Fugard, see R. K., "The Theatre of Athol Fugard," *The African Communist* 88 (1982/83), 40–53.

[66] In 1990, the South African director Jerry Mofokeng revived the play in New York with the same actors, who had followed careers in teaching, broadcasting, and acting in the United States: see Loren Kruger "Apartheid on Display: South Africa Performs for New York," *Diaspora* 1: 2 (1991): 191–208. MacLaren/Kavanagh is now at the University of Zimbabwe.

[67] Robert Mshengu Kavanagh, ed., *South African Peoples' Plays* (London: Heinemann, 1981), 127.

occasion for four prisoners to re-enact their politicization in response to everyday life in apartheid society. Using poignant introspection reminiscent of *The Island* along with a new and militant direct address to the audience, each actor delivered a "report" in his own name, in which he re-enacted, with other actors playing roles from family members to court interpreters, the events that led to the arrest of his character. This matter-of-fact presentation, coupled with the fluid movement from one role to another, highlighted the collective impact of the action. In Themba's report, for instance, Themba Ntinga, playing Leroi Williams whose chosen American name recalls that of the black activist Leroi Jones and thus emphasizes his oft-repeated interest in international black liberation, alternates with the other characters, allowing the actors to draw from the individual stories the common social gests of oppression and resistance. As he comments, "suddenly, at obstinate moments, these circumstances come together and trap a human being so tightly that for one moment the parts become a whole."[68] Drawing on particular circumstances – Edward Nkosi kills one of his mother's clients in a revolt against the conditions that pushed her into prostitution; Vusi Mabandla kills a black policeman trying to prevent him from driving his father to hospital without a license; Slaksa Mphahlele is jailed for striking and Williams for agitation – the plot gains analytic clarity as well as militant power in generalization. As the prisoners go on hunger strike, they shout:

> Phela, phela, phela [a]malanga
> Azophela, azophela [a]malanga.
>
> [Enough, enough, enough of these days
> There will be an end to these days.]
>
> *(Survival,* 167)

Despite the (mimed) beating of the prisoners at the end of the play, the actors survive to "go forward" (168).

The reports may have seemed "strong and ugly" to some white reviewers, but the final note of anticipation of liberation struck home

---

[68] Workshop '71, *Survival*, in Kavanagh, *South African Peoples' Plays*, 160; cited as *Survival* in the text.

with whites as well as blacks.[69] In the townships, it provoked police raids as well as applause. While the relative isolation of New Brighton and the relative quiescence of 1972 had allowed the audience to play with the performance of *Sizwe Bansi Is Dead*, the explosion in Soweto and the national crisis it provoked gave *Survival* an impact that was more direct but also short-lived. Facing police at township venues such as the Dube YMCA, the players incorporated them into the show, by opening with a comic impersonation of a policeman looking for "agitators" and by encouraging audience reaction, especially in the finale, "we go forward . . ." Rather than displaying politics as a theme, the players turned threats of state violence into politically enabling performance. However brief its run, *Survival* participated in the enactment of a counter public sphere generated not only by the student rebellion in black schools and universities but also by church organizations and resurgent industrial unions. For the participants, especially director MacLaren, this enactment was transitive and indicative rather than subjunctive in the manner of the response to *Sizwe*; in his view, it "performed an effective political function" of agitation "before" the uprising.[70]

This is the public – or rather, the overlapping publics from liberal professionals through students at universities (black and white) to organic intellectuals and workers (mostly black) – that would sustain anti-apartheid theatre until 1990. Producers and engaged critics hailed this theatre as "majority theatre" and its audience as a vanguard for a future democratic South Africa.[71] The summoning of a majority or

[69] Kavanagh, *South African Peoples' Plays*, 126. Roy Christie's positive review of the "note of anticipation" in the *Star* (12 August 1976) contradicts Kavanagh's generalization about a hostile white response.

[70] Kavanagh, *South African Peoples' Plays*. On the following page of his commentary, however, Kavanagh modifies his claim for the immediate political function of the play to concede that after the uprising had begun, "conventional performances of a play, however militant, [became] anachronistic, perhaps even ridiculous" (ibid., 127). Allowing for the subjunctive force of performance might have bridged this either/or dichotomy between immediate effectiveness and ridiculousness.

[71] Kavanagh, *Theatre and Cultural Struggle*, 214–15.

even a vanguard through theatre was no easy task, to be sure. However, the Space had opened up an arena for integrated performance and social assembly that had long seemed impossible or undesirable, and the Market Theatre, founded in 1976, shortly before the uprising, would build on its example. Galvanized by the events of 1976 and sustained by the political and cultural formations that grew up in its wake to become the United Democratic Front (UDF, 1983–90), progressives, intellectuals and aspiring theatre practitioners with different racial and class identifications would, despite internal and external criticism, manage to find common ground. The mode of performance developed by *Survival*, the anti-apartheid testimonial play, presented narratives of mostly black, mostly male, individuals urgently and directly to the audience, in English, punctuated by song, usually in the vernacular. This would be the format for theatre after the Soweto uprising and in the shadow of the "emergency" in the 1980s: for plays by black men such as *Egoli* by Matsamela Manaka (YMCA, Soweto, then Space, 1979), *The Hungry Earth* by Maishe Maponya (Orlando Community Centre, Soweto, then the Market 1979), and *Asinamali* by Mbongeni Ngema (Market, 1985), as well as those produced by men and women in Market Theatre workshops, from *Call Me Woman* (1979) to *Born in the RSA* (1986), from the personal experience and public documentation of apartheid from the state's systematic oppression and collective resistance to the daily small indignities and local negotiations.

At the junction: localizing Brecht

While the Market Theatre and its signature performance form, the workshopped testimonial play, captured the attention of local and international audiences as the primary theatrical representatives of the anti-apartheid movement, and has been documented and analyzed by numerous commentators, the Junction Avenue Theatre Company, founded also in 1976, has received less attention from non-South Africans.[72] However, from the critical history play sponsored by

---

[72] For the Market Theatre, see Ian Steadman, "Drama and Social Consciousness: Themes in Black Theatre on the Witwatersrand to

Witwatersrand University's History Workshop, *Randlords and Rotgut* (1978) to the post-apartheid drama of *Love, Crime, and Johannesburg* (1999), Junction Avenue has undertaken the most sustained engagement with Brecht in South Africa. Malcolm Purkey, the founding director, has called this engagement "productive misreading," but it is perhaps better described in terms that also fit *The Coat*: the appropriation of Brecht for local stages and audience.[73] Unlike the respectful reproduction of Brecht as a European classic, this localization appropriates not only Brecht's innovations on stage but also his probing, through both historicizing and interventionist representation, of social relations in the house and beyond. Whereas the Market Theatre's reputation, at home and abroad, rested largely on its staging of immediate and urgent responses to the apartheid and anti-apartheid present, Junction Avenue instead concentrated on the critical – and playful – representation of competing South African pasts. The impact of this company may be more modest than that of the Market, where most South African plays and practitioners appeared even if not all originated there, but now, in the twenty-first century, when the anti-apartheid present is itself in the past and the Market is struggling to find a new guiding principle that might sustain a post-apartheid theatre, the value of Junction Avenue's historical project, the project to investigate not only the past but also to combine historical interpretation with, as Brecht has it, "delight in what is close and proper to ourselves" (*Werke* 23: 290; *BoT* 276) is all the more compelling.

Junction Avenue Theatre Company's first play, *The Fantastical History of a Useless Man* (September 1976), was written and performed in direct response to the Soweto Uprising, from the perspective

1984," PhD thesis, University of the Witwatersrand, 1985; Pat Schwartz, *The Best of Company: The Story of Johannesburg's Market Theatre* (Johannesburg: Ad Donker, 1988); Ann Fuchs, *Playing the Market: The Market Theatre, Johannesburg*, 2nd edn. (Amsterdam: Rodopi, 2002); Orkin, *Drama and the South African State* and Kruger, *Drama of South Africa*.

73 Malcolm Purkey, "Productive Misreadings: Brecht and the Junction Avenue Theatre Company in South Africa," *drive b: Brecht Yearbook* 23 (1998): 13–18.

of white dissidents, especially the students and recent graduates who constituted the company, who wondered, as did the character of the "useless man," whether the "the most [they could] do [would] be the least obstruction" in the struggle between the rulers and the "broad mass of the people."[74] Prefaced by "the song of the fantastical history," which satirized "sympathetic white liberals" who benefitted from the history of colonial exploitation and the present of apartheid oppression, the first act extended this satire in a vaudevillian history of imperial capital, missionary zeal, and the racist underpinnings of these and their alleged opposition in the white labor movement. This act concluded with the carnivalesque birth of the "useless man" whose arrival interrupts a genteelly neocolonial Azalea Show at which his mother quotes an actual 1950s guide on the "native garden boy" (in *Four Plays*, 46). The second focused, after an introductory list of key dates in the history of repression and resistance, on the neocolonial formation of the hero by way of Kenneth Clark's *Civilisation*, "Revolution" jeans, and other forms of "co-option" (55). Only near the end of the act does this satiric tone give way to urgent testimonial speeches, in a form borrowed from *Survival*, as individual students testify to their (mostly inadvertent) involvement in the demonstrations outside the university in the days following 16 June 1976.

This urgency, and the concluding complaint about uselessness, captured the imagination of the play's target audience of white dissidents. Students (including the author of this book) flocked to the play; the press praised "the contrast between humour and the searing indictment of contemporary South African society," and the published text sold out.[75] But, as the editor Martin Orkin noted in 1995, the play's primary subject and audience remained dissident white men.[76] Its

---

[74] *The Fantastical History of a Useless Man* was initially published in the Ravan Press Playscript series (Johannesburg Ravan, 1978). Cited here is the collection JATC, *At the Junction: Four Plays by the Junction Avenue Theatre Company*, edited and introduced by Martin Orkin (Johannesburg: Witwatersrand University Press, 1995), 60, 59. The author of all the plays in this volume is the company as a whole.
[75] *Rand Daily Mail* (22 September 1976); quoted in *At the Junction*, 22.
[76] Orkin, *At the Junction*, 23.

tone, as might be expected from a student production, was cheeky rather than analytical, in the anarchist spirit, as Purkey noted in 1978, of Alfred Jarry and Jérôme Savary's Grand Magic Circus (*At the Junction*, 62), and, I would add, Peter Brook's version of Peter Weiss's *Marat/Sade*, rather than strictly of Brecht. Although the vaudevillian history in the first act, which featured Cecil John Rhodes as a rapacious capitalist and queen, and colonial missionaries as imperial salesmen, certainly cut through liberal clichés about well-meaning British tutelage as against allegedly more racist Afrikaner oppression, the combination of introspection and nose-thumbing at bourgeois habits (including toilet habits) in the second smacked of youth rebellion against parental norms rather than socialist revolution against apartheid capitalism. Against Brecht's critical historicization, this play stuck too closely to the selves of the performers to mount a properly historicizing critique of current social relations.

Although it still featured student performers, *Randlords and Rotgut* departed from its predecessor in several ways. First, as the opening act of the second annual South African History Workshop at Witwatersrand University in February 1978, it drew more directly on the radical historiography associated with the workshop (modeled on the University of London original where many of its members trained), which had reconstructed the social life and cultural aspirations of urban blacks and demonstrated the resilience of this culture despite suppression by apartheid.[77] Second, the company absorbed black men who were members of Workshop '71 when that company disbanded in the wake of police harassment of *Survival*; the portrayal of miners by actors like Ramolao Makhene and Arthur Molepo concretized the History Workshop's emphasis on history from below, while juxtaposing that history with the contemporary anti-apartheid movement and its stage representation in the testimonial play. Like the paper by

[77] Belinda Bozzoli and Peter Delius, "Radical History and South African Society," introduction to *History from South Africa*, special issue of *Radical History* 46/47 (1990): 13–45. The play borrowed title and analysis from a chapter in Charles van Onselen's *Studies in the Social and Economic History of The Witwatersrand* (Johannesburg: Ravan, 1982).

van Onselen whose title it borrowed, *Randlords and Rotgut* exposed the hypocrisy of mining capitalists who denounced drunkenness while profiting from the sale of liquor on their property, and showed how such moralizing served to rationalize the interests of capital in a workforce that would be sober often enough to be efficient but drunk often enough to be dependent on their wages rather than any income from the land.

Randlords and Rotgut animated this materialist analysis of race and capital in South African history with techniques drawn from music hall as well as Brecht. The "dastardly" capitalists Sammy Marks, owner of the Hatherley Distillery (William Kentridge), and Sir Lionel Philips, Chairman of the Chamber of Mines (Ari Sitas), recalled – in dress, gesture, and singing delivery – the politicians and arms merchants of Theatre Workshop's *Oh, What a Lovely War!* (1963), as well as the stockbrokers in Brecht's *St Joan of the Stockyards* (1938).[78] Following Brecht, Junction Avenue attempted to demonstrate the legacy of the past in the present and thus also to remind its (predominantly white dissident) spectators that they inherited the evils as well as benefits of mining capitalism in South Africa and, whatever their liberal opinions, were thus complicit with the apartheid state's maintenance of their minority privileges through oppression of the majority. If Junction Avenue's representation of capitalists was satirical, their portrayal of workers in revolt owed more to contemporary anti-apartheid resistance, whether in the Soweto street marches or on stage in plays like *Survival*. These influences combined to produce a theatre that focused on public action rather than private emotion, social rather than personal relations, and men rather than women. Although the commentator was female (Patti Henderson), the only female character in the play was a German prostitute (played by

---

[78] Cast references are to the 1978 production, but readers should note that the published text lists collaborators without linking any individual to a particular role. The film and audio versions of *Oh What a Lovely War!* reached South Africa shortly after their London releases. Barney Simon, who worked with Littlewood in 1959, directed *Mother Courage* at the Market Theatre in 1976, and Junction Avenue members were avid readers of Brecht's writings.

Astrid von Kotze).[79] This gender imbalance may be regrettable from
the viewpoint of present-day critics, but it is an accurate representation of the overwhelmingly male population of historical Johannesburg in the two decades from the discovery of gold in 1886, and a telling
reflection of the constraints – labor, childcare, and African patriarchy –
on the present-day theatrical work of black women, ninety or so years
later, and is thus realistic in Brecht's senses of "exposing [*aufdeckend*]
society's causal network" as well as "emphasizing the dynamics of
development" (*Werke* 22: 409; *BoT* 109; trans. mod.).

Culture and working life: the long march of the cultural local
Despite intensified state repression, the years after the Soweto uprising saw an upsurge in organized opposition to apartheid, especially in
the growth of unions among black industrial workers, who had been
denied the right to organize until the 1970s.[80] This movement encouraged Junction Avenue to work more closely with workers to produce
theatre that might more directly move an audience of activists. While
Randlords and Rotgut and *The Fantastical History of a Useless Man*
satirized both the history of apartheid capitalism and the current
malaise of white liberals, *Dikitsheneng* (In the Kitchen, 1980) dramatized more immediately the plight of black domestic workers in white
kitchens but still addressed its critique primarily to white audiences.
By contrast, *Ilanga lizophumela abasebenzi* (The Sun Shall Rise for
the Workers, 1980) used the skills of Junction Avenue members, especially Makhene, Sitas, and Von Kotze, to clarify the experience and
arguments of workers who had been injured on the job or arbitrarily
dismissed, initially to their English-speaking defense lawyer and later
to fellow workers, in the languages of all concerned – Xhosa and Zulu

79 In the 1989 revival, Purkey cast women in some of the satirical male
roles (*At the Junction*, 78). While this may have drawn attention to the
performativity of gender, it masked rather than analysed the
patriarchal character of the historical period and muddled rather than
deepened analysis of a masculinist bias in the original production.
80 For a brief summary of the links and differences between union and
student mobilization in the 1970s, see Nigel Worden, *The Making of
Modern South Africa*, 3rd edn (Oxford: Blackwell, 2000), 137–53.

as well as English.[81] As Keyan Tomaselli suggests, the attempts of the workers to represent their experience underwent several degrees of mediation, from initial confrontations with management, which the latter interpreted as strikes rather than a form of communication, to a re-enactment for their defense lawyer Halton Cheadle of events and protagonists, including workers' interpretation of the roles of managers and their agents by workers, to a limited re-presentation for the court, limited in part because workers represented themselves but not the roles of their antagonists, and finally to a play performed first for a worker audience of potential actors and secondly for a mixed audience at the Wits Box, at which the representation of absent workers by Junction Avenue members signaled, in Tomaselli's view, a "dilution" of the "play's original intention."[82] While the final outcome could be described as theatre art, the autonomy of art would be achieved at the cost of the socially indicative and effective action of the performances in and for the court and in union halls for fellow workers facing similar cases. However, in retrospect, clear distinctions between art and action are somewhat blurred. Even as union militants challenging their employers at work, participants drew on skills learnt at play,

[81] The performance grew out of the experiences of three workers, Samuel Gwazilitshe, Alpheus Nhleko, and Mandlenkosi Makhoba, who worked at Rely Precision Casting in Benoni, east of Johannesburg. They represented their experience initially for the lawyer Halton Cheadle, and later, under the lawyer's direction, for the judge in court, for workers in several union assemblies, and for theatre audiences at the Wits Box Theatre, the same venue that housed Junction Avenue performances in this period. The union performances were reviewed not in the theatre pages of the mainstream press but (by M. M. Molepo) in the *South African Labour Bulletin* 6: 6 (1981), 49–51. They were analysed in the same journal by theatre and film academic Keyan Tomaselli, in "From the Laser to the Candle," *South African Labour Bulletin* 6:8 (1981), 64–70, and documented at the end of a book-length record of the oral history of one participant in *The Sun Will Rise for the Workers/ Ilanga lizophumela abasebenzi: The Story of Mandlenkosi Makhoba* (Johannesburg: Ravan Press, 1984), in Ravan's Worker Series with the Federation [now Congress] of South African Trade Unions.
[82] Tomaselli, "From the Laser to the Candle," 68–9.

from comic impersonation gleaned from the enduring "concert" to martial arts and sports, which enhanced the physical training needed to prepare for performance after a grueling work shift.

Although the initial accounts, all published in the *South African Labour Bulletin*, mentioned neither Brecht nor the long local history of labor theatre, *Ilanga lizophumela abasebenzi* established a form and mode of address that can be compared not only to the more naturalistic but less activist drama produced by earlier unionists Routh and Radebe but also to the *Lehrstück* in its abolition of the gap between actors and audience and in its transformation through performance of spectators into social actors. The title alluded obliquely to the past, especially the slogans popularized by the ANC and associated organizations during the Defiance Campaign. It also marked a road to the future and a junction in the evolution of the Junction Avenue Theatre Company. While Purkey and others continued to mine the vein of critical history plays especially on and in Johannesburg – to which we shall return – Von Kotze and Sitas moved to Durban to develop agitational and educational theatre with Zulu-speaking workers in the activist unions of Natal under the auspices of the Durban Workers' Cultural Local (DWCL). Although she posits a theoretical point of comparison with British labor theatre in the 1930s, especially Tom Thomas's "propertyless theatre for the propertyless classes," Von Kotze unwittingly erases any historical links with local labor theatre since the 1930s by opening her account of the DWCL with the claim that "there is a long history of working class struggle in South Africa [b]ut it is only over the last few years that workers have organised to fight their oppression on the cultural front."[83] Despite this historical erasure, Von Kotze, Sitas, and their associates were able to draw on the experience not only of Junction Avenue but of the integrated and multi-lingual activist theatre of Workshop '71,

[83] Von Kotze, *Organise and Act: The Natal Workers Theatre Movement 1983–1987* (Durban: Culture and Working Life Publications, 1988), 14, 8; hereafter cited in the text as *Organise and Act*. The reference to Thomas cites Raphael Samuel, Ewan McColl, and Stuart Cosgrove, *Theatres of the Left: Working Class Theatre in Britain and the United States, 1880–1935* (London: Routledge and Kegan Paul, 1985), 3–75.

to which their fellow Junction Avenue member Ramolao Makhene had belonged. This training enabled them to overcome the obstacles faced by the generation of Routh and Radebe, whose English scripts excluded Zulu and other vernacular speakers, as well as illiterate participants from the composition of the drama and its action. Many DWCL plays, especially shorter sketches addressing specific local conflicts between workers and various antagonists from sell-outs to gangsters, were developed through improvisation and rehearsal rather than from a script, and performed predominantly in Zulu, for example *Ithesho* (The Job) or *[ama]Qonda* (Vigilantes) (*Organise and Act*, 107–23). Longer pieces used more English, especially *The Dunlop Play* (1983) and *The Long March* (1985–6); these attempted to place the immediate events of workplace agitation and the intensification of the political struggle in a larger context, both of the history of the South African conflict and of the current impact of globalization on the local conditions of apartheid capitalism (*Organise and Act*, 20–40, 80–100).

The overall impact of DWCL should be measured in the conscientization and training of participants as educators and activists on issues dividing workers (such as ethnic disputes and those between urban dwellers and migrants, and the double burden of women workers) as well as the economic demands uniting them. *The Long March* stands out both as an instance of successful collaboration and performance and, as Kelwyn Sole argues in a critical review, an index of complex conflicts and allegiances that defied then (in 1988) and still do now (in the twenty-first century) any simple dramatic opposition between the state and the "oppressed."[84] The play and its performance first for the local Metal and Allied Workers Union (MAWU) and later for other unions and audiences around the country linked the immediate impact of a strike in support of more than one thousand workers fired from British Tire Regional: SARMCOL on the community of Howick/Mpophomeni, northwest of Durban with the history of apartheid capitalism in the region. The form of the play and

[84] Kelwyn Sole, Review of *Organise and Act* in *Staffrider* 8: 3–4 (1989), 204–10.

its ambitious historical reach can be fully appreciated only in their institutional context. By 1985, DWCL had spawned not only other regional cultural locals but also an educational and research arm, the Culture and Working Life project, which worked in collaboration with unions and universities to employ a new generation of cultural workers, such as Mi Hlatshwayo and, a rare woman, Nise Malange in addition to the Junction Avenue veterans, rather than relying on the limited time of industrial workers.[85] In addition the play was developed and rehearsed over a week-long retreat, which provided not only free time but "for the first time in months" regular food and rest for people who could take neither for granted (*Organise and Act*, 82). The intensive workshop was the essential element that transformed the play from a series of loosely linked satirical sketches (the standard comic concert format – albeit with political content) into a "collective story line" (89) that began with the early twentieth-century displacement of African peasants from Mpophomeni and accelerated with the industrialization of the region in the 1950s. Although the action focused primarily on the 1980s strike and its consequences, including the intervention of the international headquarters in Britain (represented by a worker impersonating Margaret Thatcher with a huge white papier-mâché head), this historical frame reminded participants of their roles in a long-term struggle and laid the groundwork for further educational performances by the SARMCOL Workers'

[85] Unlike many other DWCL members, Malange grew up in Cape Town, at the other end of the country, and was educated there and in the Transkei; she also had some secondary schooling, rare among blacks of her generation (*Organise and Act*, 44–6). As theatre activist Maishe Maponya noted in an interview with Carola Luther, African women's contribution to anti-apartheid theatre was made more difficult not only by a double labor burden, at home as well as at work, but also by the reluctance of men in their families to allow them to participate; see Maponya, "Problems and Possibilities: A Discourse on the Making of Alternative Theatre in South Africa," *English Academy Review* 2 (1984): 19–32. Despite optimistic assessments by some, such as the African American visitor Kathy Perkins, editor of *Black South African Women: An Anthology of Plays* (New York: Routledge, 1999), the marginalization of women continues to be a problem.

Cooperative (SAWCO), such as "Bambatha's Children," a play honoring the Bambatha rebellion against displacement (in 1905) and its resonances in the present.

The first performance of *The Long March*, in November 1985 for a critical audience of Mpophomeni shop stewards, who wanted to make sure the play was accountable to the community of strikers (*Organise and Act*, 92–3), can be described as forum theatre in Boal's sense but, as in the forum provoked by New Brighton audiences' reactions to *Sizwe Bansi*, the revisions were instigated by the experts in the audience rather than directed by performers or facilitators. Subsequent performances at a mass rally on May Day 1986 in Soweto and subsequently in other venues in the Johannesburg region certainly reached a broader audience beyond Zulu-speaking KwaZulu-Natal while developing the performative and political skills of the participants, individually and as members of local and national communities. In this sense, it helped to develop the burgeoning counter or proletarian public sphere as a key site in the resistance to apartheid. But the play's "affirmation" of the "struggle of the working people for their liberation" (100) had to be matched against the risks of increased publicity. In the ungovernable townships of 1986, activist theatre groups were not immune to acts of violence and theft. Several members were assassinated in late 1986 by "men in KwaZulu police uniform" and armed vigilantes associated with the exclusivist (and pro-apartheid) Zulu organization Inkatha (*Organise and Act*, 98) and, while on tour in Soweto, the *Long March* cast lost their vehicle and essential equipment to criminals who claimed to be "comrades" – in other words, activists affiliated with the unions and the umbrella anti-apartheid organization, the United Democratic Front (94–6).[86] These incidents indicate that, despite the building of solidarity between artists and activists, leaders and communities, those committed to the anti-apartheid movement and those on its margins, frictions and tensions between the self-described vanguard and a broader

---

[86] Von Kotze, "First World Industry and Third World Workers: The Struggle for Workers' Theater in South Africa," *The Brecht Yearbook* 14 (1989), 157–67, here: 163.

populace remained unresolved. Nonethelesss, the group's attempts to use their experience to forge links with unlikely allies also suggests the importance of informal and improvised contributions to the mass movement that brought about the end of apartheid.

Historicization and delight: the pleasures of past and future in Junction Avenue's Johannesburg

Written in 1985 and performed first in 1986, at a time when mass resistance to apartheid and state repression had reached a "state of emergency" (the state's term) if not civil war, from the local and ambiguous conflict sketched above to widespread state violence against civilians including children, *Sophiatown* may seem at first a retreat from the immediate urgency of the moment and the activist response of organizations like the DWCL to a nostalgic recollection of the bohemian 1950s. Sophiatown was the last integrated neighborhood to be razed by apartheid in the 1950s; it was part ghetto, part cultural bazaar, a meeting place of black radicals, bohemians of all colors, and organized and disorganized criminals.[87] It was an actual but thoroughly *imagined* place that came, despite the violence perpetuated by police as

[87] Commentary on Sophiatown varies from systematic analysis to unabashed retro-tourism. After memoirs written by exiles like Lewis Nkosi and Bloke Modisane were banned, little was written until the revival of the 1980s, which led to the republication of Modisane's *Blame Me on History* (Johannesburg: Ad Donker, 1986), new memoirs by others such as Don Mattera, *Memory is a Weapon* (published in the US as *Sophiatown* (Boston: Beacon, 1990)), photographic essays, such as Jürgen Schadeberg's *The Fifties People of Johannesburg* (Johannesburg: Baileys African Photo Archive, 1987), interviews, in particular those conducted by Junction Avenue members Pippa Stein and Ruth Jacobson, *Sophiatown Speaks* (Johannesburg: Junction Avenue Press, 1986), films, museum displays, and several plays, as well as critical analysis. Selected in chronological order: Nick Visser, "South Africa: The Renaissance that Failed," *Journal of Commonwealth Literature* 9: 1 (1976): 42–57; David Coplan, *In Township Tonight!* (London: Longman, 1985); Kavanagh, *Theatre and Cultural Struggle*; Michael Chapman, "More than a Story. *Drum* and its Significance in Black South African Writing," appendix to *The Drum Decade: Stories from the 1950s*, ed. Michael Chapman (Pietermaritzburg: University of

well as tsotsis, to symbolize a utopia of racial tolerance and cultural diversity. It was, in the words of a Sophiatown writer and later exile, Lewis Nkosi, "a new and exciting cultural Bohemia," not only for the "Sophiatown set" – writers who frequented the place even if they did not inhabit it – but also for commentators in the 1980s and 1990s, looking for evidence of an inter-cultural legacy that might nourish urban culture in a new South Africa.[88] In much of the post-apartheid treatment of Sophiatown, the place appears *merely* as a set, a backdrop to enhance the enactment of nostalgic dramas; but *Sophiatown*, which can be said to have inaugurated the 1980s revival of 1950s culture, attempts to depict it as the place and occasion of deeply felt historical experience.

The performance of the play, along with the publication of interviews collected by the company (Stein and Jacobson, *Sophiatown Speaks*), and the republication, after the performance, of banned texts like *Blame Me on History*, the memoir of actor and writer Bloke Modisane who died in exile in 1985, encouraged the rediscovery of a historical model, however flawed, of an integrated urban South Africa. The play was based on a serious prank: Nkosi and Nakasa, who were writers for *Drum* magazine, a kind of South African *Picture Post* that reached 70,000 readers in Africa by the late 1950s, advertised for a Jewish girl to come and stay with them. Out of the interaction between the visitor, Ruth in the play, and the members of a Sophiatown household – from the matriarchal owner Mamariti (Gladys Mothlale) and her daughter, Lulu (Doreen Mazibuko) to the gangster, Mingus (Arthur Molepo), and the "situation," Jakes (Patrick Shai) – Junction Avenue recreated a microcosm of the Sophiatown milieu, while also probing

Natal. 1989); Paul Gready, "The Sophiatown Writers of the 1950s: The Unreal Reality of Their World," *Journal of Southern African Studies* 10: 1 (1990): 139–64; Rob Nixon, *Homelands, Harlem, and Hollywood* (London: Routledge, 1994); Kruger, *Drama of South Africa*.

[88] Lewis Nkosi, "The Fabulous Decade: The Fifties," in *Home and Exile* (London: Longman, 1965), 24. "The Sophiatown Set" is Gready's phrase, in "The Sophiatown Writers of the 1950s," 140; examples of recovery of Sophiatown through publication include Schadeberg's *Fifties People* and Stein's and Jacobson's *Sophiatown Speaks*.

the connections and disconnections between the "bohemia" of the "fabulous fifties" and the tentative integration of the 1980s. The situation of the "situation" (township slang for intellectual) Jakes, and perhaps also Ruth (Megan Kruskal), articulated the mixture of alienation and celebration in urban life (fig. 14). As Jakes remarks after Ruth introduces the household to Jewish Sabbath wine:

> God is One and God is Three and the ancestors are many. I speak Zulu and Xhosa and Tswana and English and Afrikaans and Tsotsitaal and if I'm lucky Ruth will teach me Hebrew . . . And this Softown is a brand new generation and we are blessed with a perfect confusion.
>
> (JATC, *At the Junction*, 180)

This celebration of "perfect confusion" marks a moment suspended in time, caught in the machine of apartheid capitalism that engineered this place and will soon demolish it. Fahfee, numbers-game man and ANC activist (Ramolao Makhene), reminds the audience of the links between 1955 and 1985: "This year is the year of the Congress of the people. We won't move. What's the number? . . . It's 26. 26 June 1955" (*At the Junction*, 185). As Purkey remarks in "Sophiatown, the Play," published as an afterword to the play in *At the Junction*, the association of moments in the (anti)apartheid calendar (such as 26 June 1955, the declaration of the Freedom Charter) with the numbers game constitutes a key structuring principle of the play (*At the Junction*, 212). It also implies that the prediction of an imminent ANC victory at that time had something of a magic spell about it. Far from denigrating the Defiance Campaign and the history of struggle, this invocation bears witness to the intensity of the desire for change as well as the difficulty of achieving it.

 Sophiatown participates not only in the historical reconstruction of this period but also in contemporary debates about the legacy of the 1950s. The play engages with what might be called the partial post-colonial moment of the Defiance Campaign and the Freedom Charter (1955) in the context of the government's "emergency" measures against "ungovernable" townships in the 1980s. While

Fig. 14. The Situation of the "Situation." Patrick Shai and Megan Kruskal in
Junction Avenue Theatre Company's *Sophiatown* directed by Malcolm Purkey
(Johannesburg, 1986). Photograph by Ruphin Coudyzer FPPSA,
www.ruphin.com.

celebrating the utopian potential of Sophiatown and the "situation's" view that memorialized it in the songs and stories of the period, it also acknowledges that this utopia was at best only partially there. The mass resistance to removals never materialized, in part because Sophiatown's poorer tenants saw the Meadowlands houses as an improvement on their overpriced backyard shacks. Nonetheless, *Sophiatown* emphasizes the value of memory, not merely for healing but also for agitation. The songs that punctuate the domestic scenes in this play with comments on the struggle link the self-aware but insufficient urbanity of the *Drum* era with the militant cultural politics of the 1980s. The final song, *Izinyembezi Zabantu* (The Tears of the People), juxtaposes pathos and militancy, as the play concludes with a litany of those, such as Modisane or Matshikiza, who were to die in exile and so links the time of the plot with the time of performance:

> And out of this dust Triomf rises. What triumph is this?
> Triumph over music? Triumph over meeting? Triumph over
> the future? . . . I hope that the dust of that triumph . . . covers
> these purified suburbs with ash. Memory is a weapon. Only a
> long rain will clean away these tears.
>
> (JATC, *At the Junction*, 204–5)

Invoking Don Mattera's recollection of the Sophiatown rubble as a prediction of its revival from his memoir *Memory Is a Weapon*, the song is both a lament and a call to arms. Confronted in the turbulent 1980s with the past of Sophiatown and the present of Triomf, the Afrikaner suburb built on the ruins of Sophiatown, the ending of this play proposes an alternative history – in Brecht's terms, the "not but" of what might have happened had conditions been otherwise, and so also looks forward to the future, as yet hypothetical: to a post-apartheid era in which the false triumph of Triomf will be transformed in the image of an integrated society.

Touted by the publisher as "one of the first genuinely post-apartheid plays," *Love, Crime and Johannesburg* (first performed 1999) is also the first play by Junction Avenue that directly adapts a text by Brecht: his most popular and most imitated, *The Three-penny Opera*. Like the first localized adaptation of this play, Pioneer

Theatre's *Beggars Consolidated* (1980), *Love, Crime and Johannesburg* deals explicitly with Johannesburg's past and present notoriety as a city of crime and capitalism. Unlike its predecessor, however, it attempts to confront the present and future of one of the world's fastest-growing conurbations. It portrays not only the domestic and personal dramas of street-level denizens, but also the collective social impact of those responsible for city management and mismanagement at a time, not yet fully *post*-apartheid, when the clear political lines of the anti-apartheid movement have given way to a post-*anti*-apartheid "*im*perfect confusion" in which former leaders of the movement may be members of the new government or part of the criminal elite, while the majority remain frustrated by crime, corruption, and the apparent indifference of the new elites. While crime and criminal glamour have characterized representations of Johannesburg since Winston Churchill allegedly called the upstart city of the 1890s "Monte Carlo on top of Sodom and Gomorrah," Junction Avenue breaks new ground in depicting a criminal element in the heroic anti-apartheid movement.[89] The play was provoked by the conviction of the "people's poet" Mzwakhe Mbuli, lion of the anti-apartheid movement and official *imbongi* (praise-poet) at Nelson Mandela's inauguration in 1994, for bank robbery in 1998, and the arrest of Colin Chauke, former MK commander, for masterminding spectacular bank-heists, and inspired by Bertolt Brecht's aphorism, in the voice of Mack the Knife, "Why bother to rob a bank when you can own a bank?" Co-writers Purkey and Steinberg create a scenario that depicts not merely intrigues of "love" and "crime" but also the transformation of the anti-apartheid

---

[89] For the representation of Johannesburg crime in film and theatre, especially in the 1990s, see Loren Kruger, "Theatre, Crime, and the Edgy City in Post-apartheid Johannesburg," *Theatre Journal* 53 (2001): 223–52. Although attributed to Churchill by Richard West (*The White Tribe Revisited*, London: Deutsch, 1978, 57) and still in circulation, the description of Johannesburg as "Monte Carlo on top of Sodom and Gomorrah" actually appears in the autobiography of Churchill's contemporary William Butler, who in turn attributed it to a "well-known Cape politician." See *Sir William Butler: An Autobiography* (London: Constable, 1911), 400.

struggle for liberation into a post-apartheid scramble for money and power, about the power of capital to corrupt or confuse the governors and the governed, and about the ways in which the prize – control of Africa's richest city – dazzles and deludes even those people who think they control it.[90]

Like *Randlords and Rotgut, Love, Crime and Johannesburg* is a dramatic exploration of crime and capital in the Golden City, using tools honed by Brecht, from the use of songs to comment on the action to the critical but also playful dis-illusion of the glamorous criminal as capitalist in disguise: his two women, the "bad girl" – here Bibi Khuswayo – and the "good" – here Lulu Levine – backed, like her model, Polly Peachum, by a powerful father, here Bokkie [Buck] Levine, and assorted other players, including a female Chief of Police – former MK leader Queenie Dhlamini. Even more than *The Threepenny Opera*, however, this play emphasizes the structural as well as personal links between capitalism and crime. Brecht treats Jonathan Peachum, professional beggar, as a capitalist entrepreneur and "proprietor of the Beggars' Friend Ltd." and Brown, High Sheriff of London, as his colleague in crime and profit.[91] Macheath's link between criminal enterprise and the more efficient legal variety is left hanging at the end (to be developed in the *Threepenny Novel*, 1933); the creators of *Love, Crime and Johannesburg* highlight this connection with not one but several criminals, some but not all turned legitimate capitalists.

The play juxtaposes Jimmy "Long-Legs" Mangane, "artist, poet, soldier of the struggle" (1), and now arrested as a bank robber, with his erstwhile comrade-in-struggle, now Chairman of the Bank, Lewis Matome. "Long-Legs" is modeled on Mzwakhe Mbuli (although, in Lindani Nkosi's performance, he has the shape of a comic rather than the stature of the people's poet – Mbuli is close to seven feet) as well

[90] Purkey and Steinberg, Introduction to *Love, Crime and Johannesburg* (Johannesburg: Witwatersrand University Press, 2000), x. Subsequent citations are to this edition; comments incorporate the author's notes on the final performance at the Market (4 September 1999).

[91] Brecht, *Die Dreigroschenoper, Werke* 2: 233; *The Threepenny Opera*, trans. Ralph Manheim and John Willett (1979: New York: Arcade, 1994), 2.

as on Mack the Knife; if he lacks Mack's ruthlessness, Jimmy has his weakness for women. Matome has no immediate predecessor in *The Threepenny Opera*, but he has the ruthless business acumen of *St Joan of the Stockyards* villain Pierpont Mauler. In Arthur Molepo's performance, he is not only "dashing dangerous, and businesslike" (7), but also the post-apartheid descendant of Mingus, the no less dangerous but brash rather than businesslike 1950s gangster he played in *Sophiatown*. Although related to Mingus and his kin, Matome plays for bigger stakes – power as well as money – for which he is willing to negotiate with criminals, provided that, like capitalists and unlike small-time gangsters, they are "more organized" and therefore more efficient (9) (fig. 15). Taking up his place in the post-apartheid elite, he offers a sharp contrast to Bones (Ramolao Makhene, who played Fahfee, a numbers runner, in *Sophiatown*), Jimmy's erstwhile mentor and an old-time Sophiatown gangster. Bones's "motto" – "small amounts, pride and cleanliness in our work" (petty theft and turf wars), and an "honorable death" – marks him as an anachronism in a post-apartheid city populated, on the one hand, by "young boys who kill for nothing" (28–9), and, on the other, by ambitious dealers like Matome for whom, "there is no history, . . . no right and wrong", only "a whole new world" (25) of opportunity in the "most cosmopolitan and fastest moving metropole in the Southern hemisphere" (35).

In this promotional picture sketched by Matome, anti-apartheid guerrilla turned post-apartheid tycoon, Johannesburg may appear to fit the image of unadulterated capitalism captured by Marx and Engels in *The Communist Manifesto*: "Constant revolutionizing of production, uninterrupted disturbance of social conditions, everlasting uncertainty and agitation."[92] But, if it seems clear that, in Johannesburg, "all fixed, fast-frozen relations, with their train of ancient and venerable prejudices and opinions, are swept away" (*Manifesto*, 38) and the powerful in the play talk as though there were now "no other nexus between man and man [sic] than naked self-interest, than unfeeling cash-payment" (37; trans. mod.), it is doubtful that the "uninterrupted

---

[92] Marx and Engels, *Manifesto*, trans. Moore (1888), ed. Engels, introduction by Hobsbawm 38–9.

Fig. 15. Arthur Molepo as the guerrilla turned banker in Junction Avenue Theatre Company's *Love, Crime and Johannesburg*, directed by Malcolm Purkey (1999). Photograph by Ruphin Coudyzer FPPSA, www.ruphin.com.

275

disturbance of social conditions" constitutes a revolution or heralds the arrival of a new class capable of transforming the cash-strapped city into a productive dynamo. Instead, the play depicts characters smitten by the reigning enthusiasm for self-interest as primitive *private* accumulation. In this mania for instant wealth, it gives us a glimpse of a common African condition which Achille Mbembe has called the "post-colony." In his view, the post-colony is distinguished not by the national self-sufficiency envisaged by anti-colonial liberation movements, but by the conspicuous consumption of public assets by those with power and by a "distinctive art of improvisation" by those without; it is characterized by the violence of "subjection" as well as "indiscipline," and by the circulation of capital not according to the logic, not of efficiency, but of "indebtedness," "subordination," and patronage.[93]

The Johannesburg of the play and of lived experience seems to have little to do with the spectacular consumption of the post-colony, exemplified, for instance, by the once feted and later abandoned Pan-African National Theatre in Lagos, Nigeria, or by the grandly planned but unfinished skyscrapers in Yaounde, capital of Cameroon.[94] Nevertheless, the specter of the post-colony haunts the Golden City. The writers' misprision of Mack the Knife's aphorism – Brecht compares "burgling" to "founding" a bank, where Purkey and Steinberg have "robbing" and "owning a bank" – highlights (perhaps unintentionally) the wild capitalism of a city in which ownership of capital appears to have less to do with the productive energy that Marx

[93] The *locus classicus* of this influential argument is Mbembe, "The Banality of Power and the Aesthetics of Vulgarity in the Postcolony," trans. Janet Roitman, *Public Culture* 4: 2 (1992): 1–30; here: 2, 26.

[94] On the rise and fall of the Pan-African Theatre on the wave of Nigerian oil capital, see Andrew Apter, "The Pan-African Nation: Oil Money and the Spectacle of Culture in Nigeria," *Public Culture* 8 (1996): 441–6; on the decay of public space and conduct in Yaounde, see Mbembe and Roitman, "Figures of the Subject in Times of Crisis," in *The Geography of Identity*, ed. Patricia Yaeger (Ann Arbor: University of Michigan Press, 1996), 153–85.

associates with the rising bourgeoisie than with the *comprador* appropriation and conspicuous consumption of resources associated with
the post-colony.[95] As several South African urbanists have argued,
the Greater Johannesburg Metropolitan Council has confronted the
admittedly overwhelming problems of the city, such as maldistribu-
tion of wealth and the increasing privatization of public space and
consequent segregation of rich neighborhoods through the gating of
supposedly public streets, in an inconsistent manner, with a mixture of neoliberal restriction of public service and patronage largesse
for extravagant projects such as the new Mandela Bridge.[96] The

[95] The citation loosely follows Macheath's comment before he is taken to
the gallows (only to be reprieved at the last minute). Brecht's original
reads: "Was ist ein Einbruch in eine Bank gegen die Gründung einer
Bank?" (*Die Dreigroschenoper, Werke* 2: 305). In the definitive
translation: "What's breaking into a bank compared with founding a
bank?", *The Threepenny Opera*, trans. Manheim and Willett, 76; and
in the looser, but better-known version by Eric Bentley and Desmond
Vesey: "What is the burgling of a bank to the founding of a bank?," *The
Threepenny Opera* (New York: Grove Press, 1964), 92.

[96] See, among many articles on post-apartheid Johannesburg, plotted on
the urban grid (hence the locations rather than page numbers) in
blank __: Architecture, Apartheid and After, ed. Hilton Judin and Ivan
Vladislavić (Cape Town: David Philip, 1998), Lindsay Brenner, "Crime
and the Emerging Landscape of Post-apartheid Johannesburg," B2;
Mark Swilling, "Rival Futures: Struggle Visions, Post-Apartheid
Choices," E8; and AbdouMalique Simone, "Globalization and the
Identity of African Urban Practices," D8. For a critique of neoliberal
mismanagement, see Alan Mabin (as deputy director of the National
Planning Commission), "From Hard Top to Soft-Serve: Demarcation of
Metropolitan Government in Johannesburg," in *The Democratisation
of South African Local Government: A Tale of Three Cities*, ed. Robert
Cameron (Pretoria: van Schaik, 1999), 159–200, and for the Mandela
Bridge, opened to celebrate Mandela's eighty-fifth birthday in July
2003, see Vicki Robinson, "Bridging the Great Divide," *Johannesburg
Mail and Guardian* (18 July 2003). For the relevance of urban theory
and practice to Johannesburg theatre and further references to these
debates, see Kruger, "Theatre, Crime, and the Edgy City in
Post-apartheid Johannesburg."

contextual story of urban mismanagement casts light on an otherwise opaque scene in *Love, Crime and Johannesburg*, which seems at odds with the fast and furious double-dealing in the rest of the play but which may well foreshadow a future of fantastical and all-consuming plans for an unrealizable city. In this scene Lulu Levine (or the actor Gina Shmukler), dressed in a "beautifully cut male suit," "makes a presentation to an imaginary Greater City Council," in which she invokes "the great cities of the world. Rome, Paris, Beijing, Buenos Aires, London, New York, Johannesburg!" only to complain that "Johannesburg is the largest city in the world not built on a river! [. . .] This is why the city is crazy! We need water!"[97] Her presentation calls for a plan to "change the M1 [the north–south motorway] into a river and replace Boksburg, Benoni and Brakpan [long-depressed mining satellites east of Johannesburg] with a sea" (16). The scene sends up this plan for Johannesburg-by-the-sea by having the presenter compare it with the "man-made" but manifestly fake "sea" at the Lost City theme park (at Sun City in Mmabatho, Northwest Province, formerly in the Bophutatswana bantustan, and still part of the vast but unstable Sun Hotels and Casinos empire). Having raised audience expectations for pointed satire of one of South Africa's *comprador* capitalists, it drops the idea for a rather routine song about robbing banks, shooting people, and hijacking cars (*Love, Crime . . .* , 17), and, for most of the rest of the play, for the plot of *The Threepenny Opera*, from the hero's quarreling rivals and the scheming of the Chief of Police, to the reprieve and "general amnesty" for "all gangsters, politicians, criminals and businessmen" at the end, promulgated by an unseen, unknown but soon-to-be-inaugurated third post-apartheid president (54). The combination of an outrageous urban *anti-plan* and an apparently business-as-usual presentation to the Greater City Council could have provided an opportunity to take this drama beyond the stagy glamour of "love and crime" toward a timely critique of the much more sinister normalization of white-collar crime, corruption, and patronage schemes in which funds from

97 JATC, *Love, Crime and Johannesburg*, 16; subsequent citations in the text.

government departments, international donors and non-government foundations have been squandered for the pet projects of the well-connected rather than the truly disadvantaged; but the action returns to the safer turf of the gangster show.

A critique of corruption and grandiose planning in the 1990s would have been more difficult to render theatrically than the gangster glamour which has personified Johannesburg since the 1890s, but this scene demonstrates the potential of such a critique. The play as a whole could have encompassed, even if it did not directly address, local follies such as the Mandela Bridge, or Mbongeni Ngema's million-rand, million-error "AIDS musical" *Sarafina II*, which was without a doubt the most spectacular waste of health, education, and foundation funding in the decade.[98] The target of this critique and the protagonist of the drama would not be the fallen hero of the anti-apartheid movement or the post-anti-apartheid gangster farce of the MK bank-robbers and the city as "teenage whore" (41), but the people with capital to buy the ear, eye, and hand of government, and the representatives of government so bought. The Lewis Matomes,

---

[98] The spectacular misappropriation in 1996 of R14 million (then ca. US $3 million) out of the Health Ministry's annual total of ca. R90 million AIDS funding for *Sarafina II*, a township musical which failed as AIDS education because it promulgated dangerous errors about HIV transmission, including the presumption that AIDS causes sudden death and is caused by the alleged promiscuity of women, and because the production was too expensive to travel beyond its initial Johannesburg and Soweto venues, and led to a damning investigation by the Public Protector but left the careers of director Ngema, Health Minister Nkosazana Zuma (now Foreign Minister) and other notables intact, may be an old story to South Africans; but the damage it did to AIDS education in an accelerating crisis (current estimates place the infected at 20–25% of the population) was considerable, and it remains a spectacular object lesson in government inefficiency and impunity, if not outright corruption. See Kruger, *The Drama of South Africa*, 208–9; Zakes Mda in interview with Denis Salter, "When People Play People in Post-apartheid South Africa," *The Brecht Yearbook* 22 (1997): 283–303, and Selby Bacqua, *Investigation of the Play "Sarafina II": The Public Protector's Report* (Pretoria: Office of the Public Protector, 1996); *http://www.gov.za/reports/1996/sarafina.htm*.

Bokkie Levines, and Queenie Dhlaminis of the new South Africa are likely to be all the more dangerous when they are not "dashing" in full view but rather hedging bets, counting dividends, and distributing favors behind the scenes. It remains to be seen whether this (h)edgy dealing, rather than the old gangster show, can be the stuff of critical drama in a truly post-apartheid South Africa.

6 "Realistic engagement" and the limits of solidarity: Athol Fugard in (East) Germany

> Realistic engagement with the current condition of the world calls for dissonance rather than harmony, friction rather than confirmation. Our country lies, to be sure, neither in Africa nor in Latin America, but if today's socialism is realistic, internationalism, especially in the investigation of suffering and in the new unease with old forms of reconciliation, cannot remain outside [our borders].
>
> Robert Weimann[1]

This epigraph, by the internationally known East German Shakespeare scholar, Robert Weimann, speaks to the tradition of solidarity between socialists in the metropolitan North and anti-colonial liberation movements in the colonized South. Although this tradition is less known in the West than is Weimann's scholarship, its legacy can be traced in the cultures of socialism, including that of the theatrical avant-garde, in places apparently as far apart as the officially socialist GDR and the underground socialists working against apartheid South Africa. Against the West German tolerance of the apartheid regime, the GDR promoted a foreign policy of "solidarity and support [*solidarische Unterstützung*] for the national and social and liberation movements against imperialism, colonialism, and neocolonialism" in Asia, Africa, and Latin America, mediated in large part by its Solidarity Committee, founded in 1960 in the wake of the first decade of

---

[1] Robert Weimann, quoted from an unnamed source in the program for Athol Fugard, *Aloen*, trans. Jörn van Dyck, directed by Dietrich Körner (Deutsches Theater, East Berlin, 1985); Akademie der Künste, Berlin: Theaterdokumentation (hereafter: AdK/TD).

post-war decolonization and of GDR efforts to link its support for emerging third world nations with its commemoration of the victims of fascism.[2] The policy of international solidarity and the performance and promotion of anti-apartheid literature in the GDR, which was one of the most striking results of this policy, call attention to a barely known but nonetheless dialectical relationship between second and third world culture and politics.

This relationship and its history complement the narrative of international socialist impact on South Africa presented in the last chapter while also highlighting the ambiguities (if not downright contradictions) in GDR expressions of solidarity with liberation movements in South Africa and elsewhere. Weimann's statement appeared in the program for a 1985 revival of *A Lesson from Aloes* in the GDR's flagship Deutsches Theater in East Berlin; the play was by Athol Fugard, the South African playwright who, as witness of the social and psychological consequences of racial hatred and oppression in his country, was no socialist but a self-described "classic example of a guilt-ridden white liberal."[3] Especially after the Soweto Uprising in 1976 and the civil unrest in South Africa through the 1980s made headlines across the world, Fugard gained an international reputation. His impact in English-speaking countries, from Britain, where his work appeared from 1963, to the United States, where he became by 1990 the most performed playwright of any nationality, has been well documented but his place in the German-speaking repertoire,

[2] Gerhard Hahn *et al.*, *Außenpolitik der DDR – für Sozialismus und Frieden* (Berlin: Staatsverlag der Deutschen Demokratischen Republik, 1974), 139. As Hans-Siegfried Lamm and Siegfried Kupper note, in *DDR und Dritte Welt* (Munich: Oldenberg, 1976), although the GDR began trading with third world countries such as Egypt and India from the mid-1950s (see tables, pp. 270–1), formal diplomatic exchanges were hampered by FRG competition under the Hallstein Doctrine of a single German nation, and therefore established only in the late 1960s (53–63).

[3] Athol Fugard, Interview with Colin Smith, *London Observer* (6 January 1974), excerpted in *File on Fugard*, ed. Stephen Gray (London: Methuen, 1991), 81.

especially in the GDR, has not.[4] From *Mit Haut und Haar* (*The Blood Knot*) in Rostock in 1975 to *Ein Stall voll Schweine* (*A Place with the Pigs*) in Greifswald in 1990, German versions of Fugard's plays often premiered in the GDR, even though the West German newspaper of record published the first account of his work.[5] The production and reception of Fugard in major East German theatres suggest a perhaps surprising connection between these South African plays and the GDR theatre, despite the barriers of language, geography, and politics. While Fugard's impact on East Germany does not offer a simple parallel to the impact of Brecht on South Africa and thus of a Northern international socialism on the South, it highlights an unexpected reciprocity to the rhetoric of solidarity and dissent in both contexts and so returns the gaze from South to North.

The presence of Fugard on the GDR stage can be attributed in part to directives from the Solidarity Committee, but the repeated performance of Fugard's plays, especially ten different productions of *Die Insel* (*The Island*), and several each of *Aussagen* (*Statements*), *Aloen* (*A Lesson from Aloes*) and *Master Harold . . . and the Boys* (title in English), cannot be fully explained by them. East German directors acted in concert with this policy by including anti-apartheid materials in their programs and lobby displays, but often also used Fugard's

---

[4] Vandenbroucke, *Truths* (Johannesburg: Ad Donker, 1986), documents premieres in Britain and the United States up to 1985; Gray, *File on Fugard*, includes excerpts of reviews. Jeanne Colleran goes so far as to argue that *Master Harold and the Boys* (the first of many plays Fugard wrote in the United States) is an American play, not only because it was written for the Yale Repertory but because it conforms to American dramatic norms of treating political conflicts in terms of developmental psychology: see Colleran, "South African Theatre in the United States," in *Writing South Africa*, ed. Derek Attridge and Rosemary Jolly (Cambridge University Press, 1998), 221–36.

[5] Renate Schostack, "Antigone in Südafrika: Politische Stücke von Fugard, Griffith, und Mercer auf Londoner Bühnen," *Frankfurter Allegemeine Zeitung* (23 February 1974); this article offered the first German commentary on Fugard, by way of the Fugard season at the Royal Court Theatre in London.

treatments of political and personal betrayal under state oppression to present an oblique critique of the structures and habits of their own state. While officially sanctioned theatres stopped short of investigating the persistence of racial prejudice in an officially anti-racist society, an underground production in 1986 East Berlin of *Sizwe Bansi ist tot* (*Sizwe Bansi Is Dead*) attempted to address this issue. Performed by Afro-Germans whose existence *as* Germans or citizens of the GDR was not recognized by the state, which acknowledged only an "almost exclusively German" population, and directed by dissident Freya Klier who had been banned from state theatres after directing revisionist stagings of socialist classics, this production attempted to render visible Afro-Germans' claim to citizenship.[6] In retrospect this hidden performance can be seen to resonate with the work of other Afro-Germans, from the ground-breaking testimonies of Afro-German women collected by May Ayim and others in East and West Germany 1986 to the hardly known efforts of Miguel Hurst and other Afro-German theatre practitioners after unification to represent themselves as *black Germans,* and so to cast light not only on the legacy of racism in both Germanies but also on the global and *glocal* future of a transnational Europe and a multi-cultural Germany and multi-culturally inflected German language at its center.[7] After unification,

[6] As Marianne Krüger-Potratz notes, in *Anderssein gab es nicht: Ausländer und Minderheiten in der DDR* (Münster: Waxmann, 1991), the official GDR position was that "the German Democratic Republic population [wa]s almost exclusively German" (6). The only recognized minority were Sorbs; others, old (Roma and Sinti) or new (children of German mothers and migrant fathers), were invisible in the official census.

[7] I am following the self-definition offered first by the Afro-Germans May Opitz (later Ayim) (West) and Katherina Oguntoye (East) in *Farbe bekennen: Afro-Deutsche Frauen auf der Spuren ihrer Geschichte,* 2nd edn (Frankfurt a.M: Fischer, 1992); the first edition (1986) was translated as *Showing Our Colors* by Anne Adams (Amherst: University of Massachusetts Press, 1992). Ayim later contributed the entry on Afro-Germans to *Ethnische Minderheiten in der Bundesrepublik Deutschland: Ein Lexikon,* ed. Cornelia

under new conditions of increased migration and debates about German citizenship, a strikingly similar staging took place, in the form of a Turkish-German revival of *Hello and Goodbye* as *Merhaba und Tschüß* in 2000. Although this production had no direct connection with the legacy of the GDR, it clearly bears comparison with the earlier attempt to grapple with the racist inheritance in Germany, while offering an institutional as well as dramatic model for inter-cultural representation in the center of trans-national Europe.

By bringing to light key productions of Fugard's plays in (East) Germany, this chapter not only complements the previous chapter's account of the impact of Germany's most prominent playwright on Fugard and other South African theatre makers but also attempts to clarify a range of questions. Why did this confessed "guilt-ridden liberal" serve the purpose of mascot for the solidarity program of a socialist state, when agit-prop and forceful critiques of Fugard's liberalism by South African exiles were known to GDR directors? How did directors, actors and critics deal with this apparent paradox and with the hidden role of Fugard as the dramatist of personal betrayal in a police state? Can we reconcile their oft-expressed anti-racist convictions with the ambiguous use of racial make-up, whether in purportedly naturalistic brown or the exaggerated blackface caricatures invented by *white* American vaudeville? In what way did the tension in the GDR between solidarity and prejudice, and the desire to *see through race* to a humanist brotherhood beneath the skin, continue to inform the social and theatrical representation of Afro-Germans after unification? The reinvigoration of the historical, cultural and political exchange between second and third worlds by way of the discourse and performance of solidarity can at the very least take world literature beyond the asymmetrical dichotomy between metropolis and margins fostered by the more popular but ahistorical notion of the post-colonial by highlighting, as does Weimann's foregrounding

Schmalz-Jacobsen and Georg Hansen (Munich: C. H. Beck, 1995) but, despite recognition through readings in Europe and North America, committed suicide in 1996.

of "Africa" and "Latin America" as against his modest mention of "our country," the complexity of past and present international reciprocity rather than the binary oppositions of global domination and national liberation.

Third world theatre, second world politics

Contextualizing the stage productions of Fugard in (East) Germany calls first for an outline of the cultural policy of solidarity, defined in part by the GDR Solidarity Committee (1960–90) but also by the initiatives of other stakeholders, including South African exiles in the GDR. If the GDR used its support for third world liberation movements to support its claim for legitimacy at a time when the most powerful members of the United Nations favored West Germany, liberation movements shunned by the West, such as the African National Congress (ANC) and the South African Communist Party (SACP), could use the GDR's desire for legitimation to their own advantage. Especially after SACP and ANC delegates established a diplomatic mission-in-exile in 1972, GDR support for outlawed South African liberation movements gave the government an international occasion for proclaiming not merely solidarity with third world liberation, but also an "organic" link between the socialist tradition of proletarian internationalism and the struggle against racism, and deliberate measures to strengthen those links by training ANC and SACP cadres at GDR institutions.[8] Arguments for cultural solidarity emerged even before this political link. In 1971 a collection of essays by South African

[8] On the ANC delegation's visit to Berlin and subsequent domicile in the GDR, see the SED communiqué in *Dokumente der Sozialistischen Einheitspartei Deutschland: Beschlüße und Erklärungen des Zentralkomitees sowie seines Politbüros und seines Sekretariats* (Berlin: Dietzverlag, 1977), vol. 14: 234–7; on the claim for a link between proletarian internationalism and anti-racism, see the speech by Herman Axen (SED Central Committee Secretary) at the special anti-apartheid session of the United Nations in Berlin, 25 May 1974, *Dokumente zur Außenpolitik der DDR : 1974* (Berlin: Staastverlag der DDR, 1978), 1020–8, here: 1022. For GDR support for the Solomon Mahlanga (ANC/SACP) School and the FRELIMO school in Tanzania, see Brigitte Schultz, *East German Relations with Sub-Saharan Africa:*

exiles was published in English by the GDR Seven Seas Press, edited
by SACP member Alex la Guma. This publication highlighted the solidarity between socialism and the anti-apartheid movements, as well
as the history of this link, which dated back to the CPSA's statement
on "solidarity despite inequality" between black and white, crafted
by Sydney Bunting as early as 1922, and to the visit of Alex's father
James la Guma and other South African Communists to the Sixth
Comintern Conference in Moscow in 1928.[9] Although the national
conferences of the Theatre Workers' Union made no specific mention
of the South African struggle, they nonetheless reiterated as early as
1975, in the words of the organization's president, the link between
"national obligations" and "international activity" in the production
of socialist culture.[10] To this end the Ministry of Culture and the

Proletarian Internationalism or "Mutual Advantage" (Working Papers,
African Studies Center, no. 100) (Boston University, 1985), 8.

[9] *Apartheid*, ed. Alex la Guma (Berlin: Seven Seas Press, 1971). S. P.
Bunting, "The 'Colonial' Labour Front" (1922), in *South Africa's
Radical Tradition: A Documentary History*, 2 vols., ed. Allison Drew
(Cape Town: University of Cape Town Press, 1996), 1: 51–4. The
CPSA's visit to Moscow sparked a debate about the Comintern's
conception of an interim goal of the South African struggle in terms of
a "black republic" led by a "national bourgeoisie on the model of India
or China." For the party line on the "black republic," see "Resolution
on the 'South African Question' Adopted by the Executive Committee
of the Communist International [Comintern]" (1928), in *South African
Communists Speak: Documents from the History of the South African
Communist Party, 1915–1980* (London: Inkululeko, 1981), 91–7; for
arguments against this plan, on the grounds that dispossessed white
and black workers had more in common than black workers had with
the tiny and largely compliant black intermediate class, see the
documents reprinted in "Communists and the National Struggle: The
Native Republic Thesis," part two of *South Africa's Radical Tradition*,
1: 76–105.

[10] Walter Felsenstein, "Begrüssungswort anlässlich des 2. Kongreßes des
Verbands der Theaterschaffenden," 1 March 1971; Felsenstein Papers
no. 261 (AdK/TD), n.p. Reiterated at the third congress in November
1975 by the then president Wolfgang Heinz and the Minister of
Culture, Joachim Hoffmann; see "Gegenwartsdramatik: Zum 3.
Kongreß des Verbands der Theaterschaffenden" (AdK/TD).

Union of Theatre Workers (Verband der Theaterschaffenden) promoted translations of English-speaking socialist playwrights, such as Arnold Wesker, Edward Bond, John Arden, and Margaretta D'Arcy, as well as touring companies from socialist countries or third world liberation movements.[11]

While Fugard's apartheid-era plays are certainly anti-apartheid, they do not advocate collective political resistance or a socialist critique of apartheid capitalism in agit-prop form. Their focus on individual interiority is quite different from the agit-prop staged by ANC exiles at the Solomon Mahlanga School in Tanzania, which received support from the Solidarity Committee, or the Brechtian theatre of student–worker collaborations, like Workshop '71, whose leader, Robert MacLaren, co-creator of the influential anti-apartheid agit-prop piece *Survival* (1976), was a contributor in exile to *The African Communist* and at best a sceptical critic of Fugard. MacLaren was also the critical link between South African anti-apartheid theatre and GDR critics and theatre workers. In a polemical letter to the journal he argued that, apart from *Sizwe Bansi Is Dead* and *The Island* which was written in collaboration with John Kani and Winston Ntshona who had experienced apartheid directly, Fugard's plays were trapped by bourgeois subjectivity; they emphasized "stoic endurance" to racial oppression rather than revolt against apartheid capitalism.[12] Translated by Joachim Fiebach, the principal GDR scholar of African theatre, MacLaren's letter clearly influenced GDR engagement with

---

[11] For comment on the Tenth Weltfestspiele in 1973, the year the GDR joined the UN, which included Red Ladder from the UK and Teatro Campesino from the US under the rubric of "theatre against imperialism," see Peter Ullrich, "Theater gegen den Imperialismus," *Theater der Zeit* 10 (1973): 22–4.

[12] R. K., "Letter to the Editor," *The African Communist* 58 (1974), 122–8; trans. in *Erfahrungun mit den Werken von Athol Fugard: Materialen zum Theater 88* (Berlin: Verband der Theaterschaffenden, 1977), 70–9; subsequent citations from this text are cited in the text as *Erfahrungen mit Fugard*. MacLaren's later essays praised the political potential of *Sizwe Bansi is Dead* and *The Island* but attacked Fugard's focus on individual suffering: see R. K., "The Theatre of Athol Fugard," *The African Communist* 88 (1982/83), 40–53, here: 45.

Fugard. This engagement was highlighted by Fiebach in the introduction to *Erfahrungen mit Werken von Athol Fugard: Materialen zum Theater 88* (published by the Theatre Union in 1977), a volume which was to reappear in the archival records of several GDR productions. Responding to MacLaren's letter reprinted in this volume, Fiebach defended Fugard's focus on individual suffering rather than collective action on the grounds that this focus offers a "brutally honest" picture of the total alienation of people under apartheid and the "limitation of resistance to the individual level" and thus helped to make space for this "liberal" playwright in an officially socialist context.[13]

Although neither MacLaren nor Fiebach explicitly invokes Brecht, each draws on criteria for political theatre authorized by Brecht. MacLaren's critique of Fugard's representation of individual pathos relies implicitly on Brecht's famous critique of pathos in favor of representation of social relations and of individual fate in favor of social action (*Erfahrungen mit Fugard*, 71). Although he ultimately defends Fugard's focus on individuals, Fiebach also draws on Brecht's notion of *Verfremdung* (estrangement) as a critique of *Entfremdung* (alienation) to criticize Fugard's tendency to treat human alienation as metaphysical rather than social (*Erfahrungen mit Fugard*, 9), as well as to praise the playwright's power critically to represent both the hopeful and the illusory nature of his characters' aspirations in the specific social context of their alienation (11). Brecht's authority in this debate about an implicitly post-colonial political theatre in the third world and its place in an explicitly anti-colonial political culture in the second is all the more palpable because he does not need to be named; his implied presence on both sides of the debate serves to highlight the unresolved contradictions in his legacy as well as in the place of Fugard in this lineage. Like Brecht, Fugard's work was both an instrument of state legitimation and a "cipher for every-day life in the GDR," as a critic recalled *Die Insel* in the 1990s.[14]

---

[13] Fiebach, "Bemerkungen zu den Stücken von Athol Fugard," in *Erfahrungun mit Fugard*, 5–23, here: 9.

[14] Ingolf Kern, "Büchsenbier ist der Inbegriff des Westens," *Frankfurter Allgemeine Zeitung* (21 December 2000), B1.

The appropriation of Fugard, an author from South Africa, a nation obsessed with skin color, by theatres and audiences in a state which claimed, in the name of third world solidarity and support for the exiled cadres of the ANC and the SACP, to *see through race* to the socialist brotherhood beneath the skin, may shed some light on the cultural implication of the GDR's contradictory working-through of a long German history of racial discrimination. In the language of German nationalism ratified by the Wilhelminian Reich in 1913, well before the notorious Race Laws of the Nazis, *Blut* (blood) rather than *Boden* (ground) was the rule: German citizenship was defined by law of racial descent (*jus sanguinis*) rather than of birth (*jus soli*) and thus encouraged the alienation of outsiders rather than their integration as citizens in the making.[15] After the Second World War, hostility to actual and imagined foreigners was prevalent in West as well as East Germany.[16] Nevertheless, the contradiction between anti-racist

---

[15] Crafted in 1913 to ensure the citizenship of far-flung Germans of the Reich, the law was reinforced by the Nazis to include so-called *Volksdeutsche* in the expanded Reich (while excluding Germans of Jewish descent), and incorporated into the Western German *Grundgesetz* (Basic Law) to grant automatic citizenship to refugees from East Germany and others with claims to German ancestry going back to the eighteenth century. Only in 2000 was unified German law brought closer to *jus soli* norms: children born in Germany of at least one parent with eight years' residency can become German citizens routinely. For an English-language summary of the issues see Gerald L. Neuman, "Nationality Law in the United States and the Federal Republic of Germany," in *Paths to Inclusion: The Integration of Migrants in the United States and Germany*, ed. Peter H. Schuck and Rainer Münz (New York: Berghahn, 1998), 247–97, and Leslie Adelson, "Coordinates of Orientation; an Introduction," in Zafer Şenocak, *Atlas of a Tropical Germany*, trans. and ed. L. Adelson (Lincoln: University of Nebraska Press, 2000), xx.

[16] Popular prejudice against foreigners – as well as official denial of it – permeated the GDR, whose population was not "raised to tolerance" despite the official line of a "deep interest in the struggles of other peoples and nations" (Krüger-Potratz, *Anderssein gab es nicht*, 29). For the survey on current attitudes to perceived foreigners in Germany, conducted by the Paul Lazersfeld Society and the Free University of

solidarity abroad and the effective erasure of racialized groups as well as indigenous "dangerous elements" from the public sphere at home distinguished the paradoxical representation of racial others in the GDR from the FRG's reiteration (at least until unification) of a strict law of citizenship by descent. While the GDR distanced itself from this racialist inheritance, its official claim that "the German Democratic Republic's population is almost exclusively German" belies a link to Germany's imperial past. It also highlights unspoken tension between official anti-fascism and anti-racism, on the one hand, and the *de facto* segregation of people described officially as "migrants" from the local population and long-standing (if long-repressed) popular hostility to *Ausländer* and "half-breeds" (*Mulatten* or *Mischlinge*) on the other.[17] Despite this differentiated history, discussion of this controversy, like other social issues in Germany, tends after unification to take West German perspectives as self-evident and thus to dismiss or simply ignore the legacy of GDR policies and prejudices, particularly of the contradictions between the ideological promotion of international socialism on the one hand, and the practical encouragement of ties with "non-socialist" third world countries and the segregation of resident foreigners on the other.[18]

Berlin, see Oskar Niedemayer, "Rechtsextremismus als Orientierungsmuster," in *Sind die Deutschen ausländerfeindlich?*, ed. Ulrich Amswald, Heiner Geißler, Sabine Leuthneusser-Schnarrenberger and Wolfgang Thierse (Zürich: Pendo, 2000), 40–6.

[17] Krüger-Potratz, *Anderssein gab es nicht*, 6. The Anglo-American legal term "resident alien" is more accommodating than the German *Ausländer*, which denotes not only foreigners but also non-citizen residents of non-German extraction, but still suggests a radical separation between native and foreigner. *Mischling* was used by the Nazis to stigmatize people of "mixed" ("Aryan" and "non-Aryan") descent, and continues in current usage. Even a sympathetic observer like Klier could refer to her Afro-German collaborators as "my mulattos" in her account of life in the late GDR: *Abreiß-Kalender: ein deutsch–deutsches Tagebuch* (Munich: Kindler, 1988), 144, 155–6.

[18] From the outset, the GDR imported industrial workers from relatively poor "people's republics" such as Tanzania, Vietnam, and later Mozambique, but also encouraged trade with wealthier non-socialist

Although produced in a quite different social and cultural context, Fugard's drama engages directly with the idea of solidarity between people, and thus with the notion of seeing through race by treating it as a paradox of transparency, at once a humanist assertion of brotherhood under the skin and the misrecognition of tenacious racist habits in daily life. From *The Blood Knot* (1962) on, his plays stage social and personal identity crises as conflicts between demeaning epithets and proper names or between the power to turn people into opaque objects of power and the liberating potential of self-naming. Even if Fugard's own language dwells on the private and intimate nature of sympathy, rather than the public and political character of solidarity, his dramas of sympathy allow also for the representation of solidarity. The productions of Fugard in the GDR represent not only a critical engagement with solidarity, by way of anti-apartheid theatre and the South African liberation movements, but also with what looks like its anthithesis: the erasure, in widely differing portrayals of black South Africans by mostly white GDR actors, of the racialized subject of and in the officially anti-racist state and of self-identified socialist dissidents in the "actually existing socialist" tyranny. This equivocation between solidarity and erasure distinguishes East German practices of racial impersonation from the more ostentatiously theatrical practice in West Germany, which, especially in the last two decades, has included racial masquerade in its repertoire of ironic deconstructions of naturalistic norms.[19] Ostentatious

---

states such as Iraq. African students came from Ghana and Nigeria as well as socialist Tanzania; see Lamm and Kupper, *DDR und Dritte Welt*, 213–56. The law "on monitoring the residency of foreigners in the GDR" (*Ausländergesetz*) enacted in 1979 strictly limited their stay for study or apprenticeship: document 1 in Krüger-Potratz, *Anderssein gab es nicht*, 199–201.

[19] In *Ethnic Drag: Performing Race, Nation, Sexuality in West Germany* (Ann Arbor: University of Michigan Press, 2002), Katrin Sieg inserts racial masquerade in contemporary West German theatre in a history of ethnic drag, which begins with the caricatures of the *Judenpossen* or Jew-farces in the eighteenth century but does not draw extended comparisons with East German practices.

racial masquerade by predominantly white actors may invite comparison with Homi Bhabha's notion of "colonial mimicry" as a "strategy
of subversion that turns the gaze of the discriminated back upon the
eye of power" and thus a reflection on the ambivalence of this performance, since here the eye of power (in the form of the German theatre
institution and the wider establishment that largely avoids acknowledgment of Germany's imperial past) threatens to return and rebuff
the gaze of the discriminated.[20] The idea of solidarity promises but,
as we shall see, does not fully execute a critique of this ambivalence;
seeing through race affirms transparency but may generate opacity.

Mit Haut und Haar: unconditional solidarity in the drama of race?

Fugard wrote *The Blood Knot* in 1960 at a historical moment of white
liberal impotence in the face of the state's violent suppression of a
legitimate mass opposition. Although absent from the play, the shock
effect of the police massacre of unarmed protesters at Sharpeville in
March 1960, and subsequent banning of mass organizations such as
the ANC and the smaller, but more militant, Pan-Africanist Congress
(PAC), ripples through Fugard's work. In this play, Fugard dramatizes
the mounting tension between two brothers labeled "coloured" by
apartheid law. Zach is solidly built, dark-skinned, illiterate and apparently content to seek in drink and women solace for daily discrimination in his job as watchman; Morris (first played by Fugard himself) is
slight, fair-skinned, literate and consumed by turns by self-loathing,
the desire to pass in white society, and an envious resentment of his
brother's unreflected pleasures. Morris attempts to reform his brother,
luring him away from memories of real women with the promise of
a female penfriend. When she turns out to be white, Morris prepares
to stand in for Zach as an apparently white man, but once her visit

---

[20] Homi Bhabha, "Signs Taken for Wonders: Reflections on Ambivalence
and Authority under a Tree outside Delhi," in *"Race," Writing, and
Difference*, ed. Henry L. Gates Jnr. (Chicago: University of Chicago
Press, 1986), 173; for application of Bhabha's terms to West German
racial masquerade, see Sieg, *Ethnic Drag*, 1–23.

falls through, their rehearsals for this impersonation take a dangerous turn as Morris attacks his brother's color and their kinship. In the language of existentialism borrowed by Fugard from the humanist-marxist Jean-Paul Sartre in the 1950s, Zach exists primarily unconsciously, *in* rather than *for* himself. Morris's self-consciousness, on the other hand, is acute but, as a colonized subject in the terms developed by a Sartre reader, the Jewish-French-Tunisian Albert Memmi, he is torn by the desire for whiteness or transparency in the eyes of the dominant culture and by the hatred of his own color and cannot act as a fully conscious and sovereign individual.[21]

The play reveals its historical formation in the contradictory articulation of liberal humanism – the universal promise of self-realization regardless of race – and liberal anxiety about racial conflict. Fugard's distinctions between the articulate but impotent Morris and the angry but inarticulate Zach, as well as between the former's hatred of his body and the latter's sensuality, suggest the mutual imbrication of class and racial difference and thus the limits of liberal humanism, even if Fugard sees himself as a liberal. At a moment in South Africa when apartheid legislation had removed the veneer of liberal paternalism from South African society, Fugard attempted to render race transparent to reveal the human essence beneath. But the dramaturgical logic of the play – from Morris's overbearing speeches about kinship and its denial to the final scene which reinforces Zach's complicity in his humiliation – nonetheless encourages its target white liberal audience to see Zach's darkness through Morris's anxious eyes. This anxious fascination is captured by Nadine Gordimer: "One has merely to watch the white audiences, streaming in week after week to sit as if fascinated by a snake before Athol Fugard's *The Blood Knot*, to understand how in the theatre . . . one can bring people face to face with those things in their society or themselves which they have been long conditioned not to think about."[22] While this performance may have brought white spectators "face to face" with racial discrimination,

---

[21] Albert Memmi, *The Colonizer and the Colonized* (1957), trans. Howard Greenfeld (Boston: Beacon Press, 1965), 122–5.

[22] Nadine Gordimer, "The Blood Knot" (1965), in *File on Fugard*, 18–19.

the image of the snake suggests not that the spectators learnt from this encounter but rather that they remained in thrall to the spectacle of race. In his comments on the play, the exiled writer Lewis Nkosi argues that the portrayal of the two brothers remains under the spell of racist thinking. In his view, Zach's support of Morris's attempt to pass for white, and his capitulation to his brother's resignation to a life defined by a game of racial impersonation, suggest not merely political quietism but also an implicit concession to the rationalization of white supremacy.[23] To the extent that it invites the interpretation, favored by metropolitan observers, focusing on "human beings caught in a tragic and inevitable fate" rather than on the social and political pressures that make their fate seem inescapable, *The Blood Knot* disavows the history of those pressures and resistance to them.[24]

The Blood Knot was the first of Fugard's plays to be performed in German. Translated as *Mit Haut und Haar*, it was directed by Siegfried Böttcher at the Volkstheater Rostock in March 1975; the production reviewed in the West as the "first German production," which took place in Cologne in December 1976, was the first to use *Blutsband*, a new translation by a South African.[25] The Rostock production marked the difference between the two brothers by having Klaus Pönitz wear brown make-up. Doubtless unaware of Nkosi's sceptical response, a local critic argued that the play showed a growing "anti-colonial" attitude among blacks, while a metropolitan critic, Ingeborg Pietzsch in the Theatre Union journal *Theater der Zeit*, cites Fiebach, who argues

[23] Lewis Nkosi, "Athol Fugard: His Work and Us," in *Home and Exile and Other Selections* (London: Longman, 1983), 142–5.

[24] Ian Bannen, on his role in the first London production of *The Blood Knot* in 1963, quoted by Dennis Walder in *Athol Fugard* (London: Macmillan, 1985), 61. For a critique of this universalist reading of Fugard, see Orkin, *Drama and the South African State*, 81–107.

[25] *Mit Haut und Haar*, translated by Walter Czaschke and Frank Helgert (Frankfurt: Suhrkamp, 1970) was reprinted in the GDR in *Stücke Afrikas*, ed. Joachim Fiebach (Berlin: Henschel, 1974); *Blutsband*, trans. Allison Malherbe (Frankfurt: Fischer, 1979). For reviews of the (West) German premiere, see *Athol Fugard: A Bibliography*, compiled by John Read (Grahamstown, South Africa: National English Literary Museum, 1991), 53.

that the quarrel between the brothers should be seen as a metaphor for the "general relationship between imperialist minority and colored [sic] majority" as well as an index of the coming "transformation of the black masses' conduct towards their oppressors."[26] Read against Nkosi's comment on its obsession with whiteness, or the fact that the original performance played to integrated audiences only for a few weeks before going on a six-month whites-only tour, this counterfactual argument for the play's "revolutionary significance for African audiences" suggests rather that GDR critics wanted to shore up the power of *their* solidarity with revolution.[27] While the case for the collective political resonance of individual acts can certainly be made for South African theatre in the 1970s, a period of accelerating political and cultural resistance which would explode in 1976, this case is harder to make for *The Blood Knot*. The dramaturgy of the play pushes characterization towards abjectness and so reduces the social structure and the history of apartheid to local acts of humiliation. Furthermore, the title of this translation, *Mit Haut und Haar* (literally "with skin and hair," meaning, figuratively, "unconditionally" as in a pledge), implies an almost fiendish pact and an obsession with bodily features rather than the representation of general conditions of oppression. It prepares its audience for a fascinating but alien spectacle.

Die Insel: seeing through race?

Not all productions of Fugard's plays in the GDR served to replicate the exotic spectacle of the "snake" in blackface or to legitimate the

---

[26] Peter Kruuse, "Ich bin doch dein Bruder," *Der Demokrat* (12 March 1975); Ingeborg Pietzsch, Review of *Mit Haut und Haar*, *Theater der Zeit*, 30: 4 (1975), 33–4. The second citation is from Fiebach, *Stücke Afrikas*, 674–5. For presentation of the ANC's program as part of GDR support for "an anti-capitalist, revolutionary-democratic phase of socialism," see Joachim Fiebach, *Literatur der Befreiung in Afrika* (Berlin: Akademieverlag, 1979), 9. Rainer Arnold's afterword to his anthology of writings by South African activists, *Ich bin das Land* (Leipzig: Reclam, 1983), 281–91, published on the sixtieth anniversary of the ANC's foundation (1912), also emphasized the solidarity movement at home as well as anti-imperialist struggle abroad.

[27] Orkin, *Drama and the South African State*, 91.

state's official anti-racism. The production of *Die Insel* (*The Island*, which Fugard wrote in 1972 in collaboration with the actors John Kani and Winston Ntshona) by the flagship Deutsches Theater in Berlin in October 1976, directed by Alexander Stillmark and Klaus Erforth, with dramaturgy by Fiebach, in the (West) German translation by Eva Walch, offers a significant departure both from the "unpolitical" German-language premiere in Frankfurt am Main in January and from the orthodox solidarity politics of the GDR.[28] *The Island* follows two political prisoners (John and Winston) on Robben Island from their meaningless but exhausting labor through expressions of physical and verbal solidarity with each other, with other prisoners, and with their associates back home, to a near-breakdown of their relationship caused by the apparently arbitrary announcement that John is to be released early and Winston to remain in life imprisonment. This announcement disrupts but does not finally derail rehearsals of a version of *Antigone*. The play ends with the performance of this *Antigone* for an invisible prison audience, in which Winston speaks Antigone's appeal against the tyranny of unjust law and inflexible enforcement directly to the present audience (initially the mostly white audience at the Space, the private club in Cape Town where the play premiered) and the absent one (blacks unable to attend) as much as the fictional prison audience. This final declaration has a heroic but also tragic aspect; Winston was a freedom fighter, but in the play he is a prisoner-for-life for whom the performance of resistance is a means of survival. While this production did not address racism or anti-foreigner

---

[28] The translation was published as Fugard, Kani, and Ntshona, *Die Insel*, trans. Eva Walch, in *Aussagen: 3 Theaterstücke* (Frankfurt a.M.: Fischer, 1979), and reprinted in the GDR only after the production (Berlin: Henschel, 1979). Mechthild Lange describes the German premiere at the Thalia Theatre, Hamburg, as "a thoroughly unpolitical premiere of a very concrete play from South Africa": "Als ob nichts drinstünde", *Frankfurter Rundschau* (17 January 1976). Klaus Wagner argues in "Eingeschlossen wie Antigone," *Frankfurter Allgemeine Zeitung* (13 January 1976), that the immediate and authentic communication of Kani and Ntshona as "co-authors" of the original play could not be reproduced by "professional" actors in Germany.

feeling in the GDR, it did allow for local resonances of *The Island* and *Antigone's* treatment of the conflicting demands of conscience and unjust law and the abuse of state power in the name of national security. The GDR premiere of *Die Insel* opened on 11 October 1976 (on the official Day of Solidarity with South African political prisoners), which was three months after the Soweto Uprising but also on the eve of the *Ausbürgerung* (expatriation) in mid-November of the singer-songwriter Wolf Biermann, whose expatriation while on tour in West Germany was to re-freeze what had been a period of cultural and political thaw. In this context, it is perhaps unsurprising that the produciton was understood unofficially as an oblique comment on political imprisonment and the methods of the Stasi in the GDR.[29]

Several points lend weight to this suggestion. The statements of famous Robben Island prisoners, including Nelson Mandela, printed in the Deutsches Theater program were framed, on both covers, by a reproduction of a charge-sheet against a lesser-known prisoner for an evidently arbitrary allegation of insubordination, a procedure used against political prisoners in the GDR as in South Africa.[30] The performance took place literally "behind the iron curtain": actors and

---

[29] *Die Insel* was directed by Klaus Erforth and Alexander Stillmark and performed by Alexander Lang (later an influential director at the Deutsches Theater) and Christian Grashof (later Lang's leading actor). Fiebach, who remained in the GDR, was more circumspect, suggesting that local resonances remained indirect, but agreed that the omission of blackface, for which he was responsible, brought characters and action closer to the local audience (interview, New York, 10 November 2000). Although the review in *Theater der Zeit* makes no mention of local resonances, it does highlight the global significance of the play's appeal for human rights and justice. See Martin Linzer, "Die Insel," *Theater der Zeit* 31: 12 (1976), 27–9. My informant-spectator is Kurt Goldstein, a former BE actor who left the GDR in 1981 (interview, Berlin, 5 December 1991).

[30] See program for *Die Insel* (Berlin/GDR: Deutsches Theater, 1976). The psychological manipulation of political prisoners as well as dissidents at large by the Stasi, using methods ranging from isolation to character assassination, is now well known, as confirmed by documentation provided at the former detention center at Berlin-Hohenschönhausen; for a personal view, see Klier, *Abreiß-Kalender*, passim.

audience alike were confined to the stage space behind the fire curtain and the feeling of confinement was intensified by the loud and dissonant music accompanying the opening scene.[31] While some critics praised the noise for compelling the audience to share the pain of confinement and for bringing home the pressing actuality of the play, others, including the venerable Brecht critic Ernst Schumacher, resisted it as a meaningless "cruel theatre" trick and an attack on the audience's eardrums.[32] The opening scene departed from the South African production to return, indirectly, to Brecht: instead of miming exhausting prison labor, which Kani and Ntshona had performed with full knowledge of the experience of hard manual labor, *Die Insel* opened with the actors, Christian Grashof (John) and Alexander Lang (Winston), in street clothes rather than South African khakhi prison gear, with invisible make-up (fig. 16). Following a decision taken by Lang and endorsed by the dramaturg, Fiebach, and finally by the directors as well, the actors introduced themselves and announced that they were not impersonating black prisoners in South Africa, but rather representing their own understanding of the action. They then read the opening stage directions detailing the mimed labor over and against the insistent music, and dropped literally into their roles only when the mime was over and the two prisoners returned to the cell, designated as in South Africa by a chalk square on an empty stage.[33] In its

[31] *Eisener Vorhang* (meaning "safety curtain") appears in the rehearsal notes as well as reviews. For rehearsal notes, see "Die Insel" (AdK/TD), n.p. For the tape of sound and music used in the production, see the audio-visual archive, AdK.

[32] Christof Funke, "Erregendes Spiel der Gefangenen", *Der Morgen* (15 October 1976), v. Ernst Schumacher, "Das grausame Leben auf der Insel," *Berliner Zeitung*, 14 October 1976. "Cruel theatre" alludes to Antonin Artaud's "theatre of cruelty."

[33] This matter-of-fact report in the manner of Brecht's "street scene" should be compared with the opening description in the published text and translation, in which the sound of a siren brings John and Winston on to the stage to mime back-breaking work in the Robben Island quarry. See Fugard, Kani, and Ntshona, *The Island*, in *Statements: Three Plays* (New York: Theatre Communications Group, 1974), 47; trans. Walch, *Die Insel*, in *Aussagen*, 71–2.

Fig. 16. Prison as Brechtian street scene: Christian Grashof (John) and Alexander Lang (Winston) in *Die Insel* by Fugard, Kani, and Ntshona; trans. Eva Walch (Berlin, 1978), directed by Klaus Erforth and Alexander Stillmark. Photograph by Eva Kemlein.

economic, matter-of-fact quotation of the action, this opening demonstrated the critical as well as theatrical power of the attributes of *Kargheit* (parsimony, economy) and *Sachlichkeit* (sobriety, matter of factness), as well as in its estrangement of the audience with the aural assault of the music – despite Schumacher's objections – this opening offered a fitting tribute to the ongoing effectiveness of Brechtian techniques. Finally, Erforth's and Stillmark's subsequent work, especially Ulrich Plenzdorf's *Legende vom Glück ohne Ende* (the stage version of the film *Legende von Paul und Paula*, directed by Heiner Carow in 1973), which was written for and staged by the Deutsches Theater until canceled in 1982, confirms their willingness to provoke the state.[34]

The decision to eschew black make-up broke with the previous assertions of naturalism and the assumption of a normative triangulation of actor, character and foreign (South African) referent, brokered by official solidarity discourse, in favor of a more subtle and more transgressive triangulation in which the referent could have been the political prisoner in the GDR. Since this reference remained of necessity oblique, this *Insel* provided an instance of Brechtian "cunning" to hint at the truth by indirection rather than transparent documentary, but its revival in eleven other productions in the GDR suggests that it struck a local chord.[35] Indeed, the power of *Die Insel* rests on

[34] Ingolf Kern's review of the revival of Ulrich Plenzdorf's *Legende vom Glück ohne Ende* at the Volksbühne in December 2000 quotes Erforth on the provocation offered by the title, which suggested that happiness in the GDR was merely a legend, but suggests himself that *Die Insel* was in the mid-1970s a "Chiffre des DDR-Alltags" (code for everyday life in the GDR). See Kern, "Büchsenbier ist der Inbegriff des Westens."

[35] The Deutsches Theater production of *Die Insel* was not the first in German (the play appeared in March in the Schiller Theater workshop in West Berlin), but it heralded a series of East German runs that topped the West German competition. In addition to a guest run of the Deutsches Theater production in Leipzig in 1977, *Die Insel* was revived in Karl-Marx-Stadt (now Chemnitz; 1977), Schwedt (1978), Junges Theater, Berlin (1982), Magdeburg (1983), Halle (1984), Ernst-Busch Theatre School, Berlin (1985), Theater der Freundschaft, Berlin (1985), Junges Theater, Dresden (1985), Stendhal (1985) and Gera (1985).

what might be called the paradox of transparency. It attempts to re-envisage the official discourse of anti-racism and third world solidarity by suggesting, however obliquely, that solidarity with political prisoners begins at home, and that what director Stillmark calls the "*pose of the class warrior*" ("Klassenkämpfer-Attitude") – as, for example, assumed by Lang in the role of prisoner-for-life Winston – is more of a sustaining "life-lie" (in Stillmark's allusion to Ibsen) than an objectively determinable world-historical act in the marxist manner.[36] The force of this reinterpretation depends, however, on the audience seeing through the racial dimension of the South African drama, as well as through the minimal make-up, not merely to the universalist discourse of social justice and human rights but to the constraints on the actual application of that discourse to local conditions in the GDR, even if those constraints and the resistance to them are articulated in the *Sklavensprache* (slave language) of secret dissidence.

Statements and lessons: the critical pedagogy of *Sklavensprache*

Sklavensprache in the GDR vernacular referred to the discourse of secret dissidence hidden behind the jargon of state socialism, or in apparently unpolitical domestic speech, and its articulation in a private realm that could be a space of intimate retreat from the state; this is the idiom of the GDR's most dedicated Fugard director, Rolf Winkelgrund. Where most GDR theatres and directors took up one or at most two plays by Fugard, Winkelgrund directed five: *Buschmann und Lena* (1975: *Boesman and Lena*, 1969), *Aussagen nach einer*

---

[36] Alexander Stillmark, rehearsal notes, 3 October 1976 (TD, AdK), n.p. There is a possible link between this production's critical deployment of the "pose" and Lang's later development as a director who favored ostentatious masquerade, including the casting of white German actors in the roles of African and Arab characters in his Hamburg production of Bernard-Marie Koltès's *Le Retour du désert* in 1988, but, despite the formal comparison, the risks and critical potential of the GDR theatre's role as counter-public sphere to a repressive state had little in common with the permissive institution of West German theatre in the age of high subsidy.

Verhaftung auf Grund des Gesetzes gegen Unsittlichkeit (1978: *Statements after an Arrest under the Immorality Act*, 1972), and *Aloen* (1982: *A Lesson from Aloes*, 1980) at the Hans Otto Theater in Potsdam; and *Dimetos* (1983; 1981) and *Der Weg nach Mekka* (1986: *The Road to Mecca*, 1984) at the Maxim Gorki Theater in Berlin.[37] Citing the influence of a devout Protestant upbringing in Nazi Germany as well as the socialist idealism that led him as a young man in the Cold War of the 1950s to move from West German Bielefeld to the GDR, Winkelgrund found a kindred spirit in Fugard, whose Calvinist upbringing and later existentialist exploration of human beings in extreme situations shaped his social rather than directly political protest against the injustice of apartheid. Although Winkelgrund's productions of Fugard's plays were framed – in program notes and in foyer displays – by the official rhetoric of solidarity with South African liberation movements, the GDR director shared with the South African author a primary concern for the intimate suffering and resilience of individuals.

Winkelgrund registered his affinity with Fugard's existentialism in his recreation of intimacy in spare if not empty stage space and in his focus on individual moral dilemmas. This artistic kinship emerged already in his first production, *Buschmann und Lena* (1975: the German-language premiere), but took on a distinctive character in the productions of *Aussagen* and *Aloen* that followed. These two plays can be distinguished from *Boesman and Lena* and from *Sizwe Bansi* and *The Island* in that they depict intimate relationships between white and coloured characters, rather than between African or coloured pairs, and through these characters the difference between white and coloured daily life in South Africa is depicted in a manner potentially more accessible to a non-South African audience. Winkelgrund attempted to deepen the audience's familiarity and

---

37 First-mentioned but chronologically later dates refer to the GDR production; the following dates to the South African premiere. All of these productions used translations by the Munich-based Jörn van Dyck. Unless otherwise attributed, comments on Winkelgrund's productions are from my interview with him in Berlin, 28 September 2000.

potential identification with Fugard's characters by using overlapping casts for all three productions (Hanjürgen Hürrig as Buschmann and later as Piet Bezuidenhout in *Aloen*; Eckhard Becker as the "coloured man" Errol Philander in *Aussagen* and as Steve Daniels in *Aloen*; and Anne-Else Paetzold – Winkelgrund's wife – as the "white woman" Elsa Joubert in *Aussagen* and Gladys Bezuidenhout in *Aloen*). This technique gave audiences in Potsdam and in Berlin (at the annual Berliner Festwochen) an opportunity to reflect not only on the brutality of the apartheid state and the suffering of its victims but also on unspoken points of comparison between the surveillance and invasion of the most private spheres of life in South Africa and the pressures on dissidents enforced by the state security apparatus and its informal helpers in the GDR. Despite the lack of explicit published acknowledgment of this connection, the popularity of *Aussagen*, which went on to three other productions in the GDR, and hints in the critical response suggest that Winkelgrund was not the only one to perceive the local resonances in this South African play.[38] However, unlike the Deutsches Theater's *Insel*, which under the influence of dramaturg Fiebach had eschewed black make-up on white actors so as to make the solidarity claim all the more transparent, Winkelgrund's retention of black make-up, however naturalistically applied, sits at best uneasily with the claim to solidarity and to local impact.

The state's violation of intimate space is the central core not only of Winkelgrund's interpretation but also of Fugard's text and its original context. *Statements after an Arrest under the Immorality Act* was the first production at the Space Theatre (1972–9), itself the first integrated theatre in South Africa in almost a decade. Owned by Brian Astbury and his wife, Yvonne Bryceland, who went on to create most of Fugard's female characters, it avoided the state's prohibition of racially mixed casts and audiences by operating as a private club for members only. Like its opening production, the new theatre dramatized both the violation of the state prohibition on racial

---

[38] *Aussagen* was revived by state theatres in Dresden in October 1979 and in Greifswald in 1980 and by the amateur troupe of the Junge Garde (a youth organization) in Leipzig in 1982.

mixing and the risk of provoking state intervention, in the form of an unannounced intrusion into private space. What is striking at the outset of the play, however, is the intimate but troubled interaction between the as-yet-unnamed man and woman. Even before the rude intrusion of the policeman's flashlight reiterates the Immorality Act's prohibition of sexual intercourse between whites and members of other "races," the dialogue and gestures of the "white woman" and the "coloured man" (marked in Potsdam by black make-up on Becker's exposed skin) show not only their intimacy – although their nakedness is hidden initially by the darkness – but also the ways in which the might of the state penetrates even the most mundane moments of coloured life while affecting white lives only if they come up against it. The opening speech, the woman's account of her Saturday afternoon, focuses on the sensual pleasure of drying her hair in the sun, while the man relates how he helped a young coloured boy build an imaginary house for his family bigger than his family's reality – a two-roomed township house – would allow him to conceive, and goes on to speak in frustration of the constraints that apartheid law and custom have placed on his own capacity to better himself and his family and on the ability of the pair to love each other openly.[39]

Winkelgrund's production of *Aussagen* was not the German-language premiere, but the third after West German productions in Düsseldorf (1975) and Frankfurt am Main (1977). Nonetheless, his staging deserves attention for establishing a connection to GDR audiences which went beyond the solidarity orthodoxy. While critics responding to the Potsdam production reminded local readers first of all of the trade and tourism links between the South African regime and Western capitalist states, including West Germany, and of the peculiar power of apartheid racial laws to create a "gulf between the privileged and the utterly disenfranchised" ("völlig Rechtlosen"), while reading the "destruction of love as an indictment of state terror," they also acknowledged the importance of the intimate realm,

---

[39] Fugard, *Statements after an Arrest under the Immorality Act*, in *Statements* (New York: Theatre Communications Group, 1974), 81–2; trans. Jörn van Dyck, *Aussagen nach einer Verhaftung auf Grund des Gesetzes gegen Unsittlichkeit, Aussagen: 3 Theaterstücke*, 119–20.

of the "inner power" of the characters.[40] There is an implicit recognition of tension between the public political obligation to denounce the "reactionary" South African regime in keeping with the UN-sponsored Anti-Apartheid Year of 1978, and the private imperative to explore the SED state's intrusion into intimate relationships and even, beyond the reach of the state, of what American Fugard critic Albert Wertheim calls the "lyrical poetry of annihilation." This tension can be seen in the contrasting rhetorical strategies of the review by Klaus Hannuschka, a local Potsdam critic, and the comments in the interviews he conducted with Winkelgrund and the two actors, Eckhard Becker and Anne-Else Paetzold.[41] In the latter, interviewer and interviewees mention the political dimension of the destruction of "love between two people of a different color," but the interviewees' comments, especially those of Paetzold and Winkelgrund, highlight the contrast between the state's violation of intimacy and a general "spiritual complacency" as well as the emotional demands that the roles and the shock of nakedness to which neither actors nor audiences in the GDR were then accustomed made on the actors' capacity for "self-expression" as well as the representation of "intimate suffering," thus hinting at the local resonance of the South African play.[42]

Where *Statements* allows only indirect local allusions to state surveillance of personal intimacy, *A Lesson from Aloes* directly dramatizes the trauma of betrayal by a comrade who may or may not have been a spy. The latter thus provides a closer analogue for the manifold accounts of betrayal by and of apparent dissidents that would emerge

[40] Citations from Christof Funke's review in *Der Morgen* (20 September 1978), and Cinna Gehrke in *Brandenburgische Neue Nachrichten* (2 September 1998).

[41] Albert Wertheim, *The Dramatic Art of Athol Fugard: From South Africa to the World* (Bloomington: Indiana University Press, 2000), 78.

[42] Klaus Hannuschka, "Entwürdigung, doch Hoffnung bleibt" (review of *Aussagen*), *Märkische Volkszeitung Potsdam* (2 September 1978). Interviews with Winkelgrund, Becker, and Paetzold in the same issue. In interview (28 September 2000), Winkelgrund confirmed his sense of the shock that naked actors could still provoke in 1970s GDR (as in South Africa) and reiterated the liberating impact of that shock on prevailing sexual as well as political norms.

in Germany with the opening of the Stasi files in 1990. Although produced in South Africa in 1978 (at the Market Theatre in Johannesburg) and in the United States in 1980 (at the Yale Repertory; in a revised "definitive" version), *A Lesson from Aloes* has its origins in the political and personal desert of the early 1960s when, in the wake of the Sharpeville massacre and the banning of legitimate mass opposition to apartheid, Fugard doubted that organized resistance was still possible. Nonetheless he found some hope in the engagement of individuals, including an actual Afrikaans acquaintance called Piet, who "lost most of his money fighting court cases in the cause of freedom."[43] When the play was performed in 1978, the mood in South Africa was similarly grim, after the hopes of the Soweto Uprising had been tempered by a new round of bannings in 1977. *A Lesson from Aloes* dramatized the conflicted exchange among the bitter Steve Daniels (Bill Curry), on his way out of the country with a one-way exit permit, after doing time as a political prisoner; the stolidly hopeful Piet Bezuidenhout (Marius Weyers), whom Steve initially suspects is the informer who tipped off the Special Branch political police; and Piet's wife, Gladys, driven by police surveillance to paranoia and periodic incarceration in a mental hospital. The play certainly spoke to the gloom prevailing among white dissidents, but the "lesson" remained unclear and received mixed reviews in Britain and the United States.[44]

While West German productions (in Kiel and in Berlin) provoked negative responses including claims that "white activists [were] ridiculous," the German-language premiere in the GDR in January 1982 resonated powerfully with an audience that understood the experience of personal and political betrayal by their closest friends, even though the abbreviation of the play's title, from the published

[43] See Fugard, *Notebooks 1960–1977* (New York: Theatre Communications Group, 1984), 23–4; and Fugard's introduction to *A Lesson from Aloes* (Oxford University Press, 1981), ix–xv. Fugard's published notes identify his friend as Piet B. and record (in March 1965) that "Piet is widely suspected here in P.E. of being an informer" (*Notebooks*, 123).
[44] Vandenbroucke, *Truths*, 230–1.

Botschaft [Message] *von Aloen* to simply *Aloen* shifted attention away from any explicit political message.[45] In the recollection of Eckhard Becker, who played the role of the activist Steve, Steve's anguished cry, "I don't want to leave this country. . . . I was born here. But they won't let me live," was received in pregnant silence by the audience, whose insistent final applause suggested the resonance of the story for GDR audiences and, especially with the addition in the German of the sentence "Das ist meine Heimat," articulated the conflicted attachments of that audience.[46] As students of twentieth-century Germany well know, *meine Heimat* is only partly translated by "my home." It carries with it the history of German imperial expansion and settlers' attachment to the home country, as well as the manipulation of this attachment by Hitler's policy of "Heim ins Reich," his rationale for annexing Austria and Bohemia, and the nostalgic modulation of this attachment by Germans fleeing conceded territories after the war. In the GDR context, it invokes conflicting attachments to a range of national homes, from the GDR to an unmentionable but tenacious notion of a broader German nation. Critical response was oblique, but the *Theater der Zeit* critic's concluding attribution of "strong political impact" to the moment of denunciation and the silent farewell to the

[45] The translation was first published as Athol Fugard, *Der Weg nach Mekka und Botschaft von Aloen*, trans. Jörn van Dyck (Frankfurt a.M.: Fischer, 1984) and reprinted in the GDR as *Aloen* (Berlin: Henschel, 1985). The premiere opened at the Hans-Otto Theater in Potsdam in January 1982 and was revived in 1984 at the Maxim-Gorki Theater in Berlin, where Winkelgrund had moved, at a time marked by economic stagnation, cultural repression, and emigration of leading cultural figures. West German reactions to the play, which was not performed in West Berlin until in 1986, varied from the dismissive, as in Christian Otto, "Die weissen Kämpfer sind nur lächerlich: Athol Fugards *Aloen* in Kiel," *Die Welt* (20 March 1982) to the distantly sympathetic, Friedrich Luft, "Die innere Vergiftung: im Berliner Schlosspark-Theater," *Die Welt* (29 November, 1986), and Helmut Köpke, "Resignation nach Aufbegehen: Fugards *Aloen* im Schlosspark-Theater," *Frankfurter Rundschau* (3 December 1986).
[46] Fugard, *A Lesson from Aloes*, 77–8; trans. van Dyck, *Botschaft von Aloen*, 133.

"emigrating Steve" remains firmly on home ground, as does the title of his review, "Surviving."[47]

In this moment, the expression of solidarity turns inward, but not quite in the sense implied by Weimann's epigraph. To a degree it answers Weimann's call for linking the "investigation of suffering" internationally and at home in a "realistic engagement" with "dissonance" as well as "harmony." However, the emphasis on local resonances, especially with the ambiguous addition of "Heimat," misses other key elements of the performance, especially in the use of make-up, that disturb the "harmony" of solidarity discourse: ANC/SACP discomfort with blacking-up, picked up by Becker at the premiere, and the always ambiguous place of Fugard in the socialist repertoire.[48] Despite this background dissonance, the local sense of lost opportunity resonated in the critical response of "survival" as in Weimann's appeal to a "new unease with old forms of reconciliation." If, as Wertheim suggests, the original *Lesson from Aloes* was a *Trauerspiel*, an act of grieving for "three damaged souls and . . . the land that caused their suffering," this GDR version is also a mourning play that blocks the catharsis of tragedy – or revolution – within the prison of melancholia.[49] Unlike Freud's melancholia, however, this condition is the psychic consequence of political mourning, of grieving for a state doomed to destroy the utopia it claimed as its foundation.

Taken together, these productions highlight a complicated relationship between the rhetoric of solidarity between the "first socialist state on German soil" and South African liberation movements, and the *Sklavensprache* of secret dissidence against that state for betraying

---

[47] Dieter Kranz, "Ums Überleben," *Theater der Zeit* 12 (1985), 2.

[48] For ANC/SACP hostility to Fugard, see Gaia, "Athol Fugard," *African Communist* 58: 1 (1974), and for a more nuanced critique, R. K., "Letter to the Editor." Although Becker had only a sketchy idea of ANC/GDR relations – he thought that the ANC representative at the premiere of *Aloen* was based in West Berlin – he vividly recalled the delegate's coolness to the play as a whole and to his own blacked-up face in particular. Unless otherwise noted, references to Becker's observations are to my interview with him in Berlin, 27 October 2000.

[49] Wertheim, *Dramatic Art of Athol Fugard*, 134–5.

the human rights at home that it claimed to defend abroad. Despite the official party line that treated the protagonists as activists through and through, other directors followed Winkelgrund's insistence on "protecting the privacy" and vulnerability of these characters.[50] At the same time, the tension between the compelling urgency to "see through race" to recognize similar and familiar modes of repression and dissidence in the GDR and South Africa and the persistent denial of this similarity through the habit of racial othering through black make-up remained unresolved. Both Winkelgrund and Becker claimed in interview that the naturalistic use of dark make-up was necessary to help the audience distinguish between white and black characters, but neither had a response to the fact that Fugard himself played many coloured roles (from Morris in *The Blood Knot* to Errol in *Statements*), relying on gestural and linguistic markers, including code-switching from English to "Cape" dialect variations of Afrikaans, rather than on blacking-up; nor to the suggestion, implied by the absence of make-up in the Deutsches Theater's *Insel* and by Fugard's own insistence on human connection, that sympathy as well as solidarity might be enhanced by the elimination of racial illusionism or by the acknowledgment of the theatricality of the device of make-up.[51] While the

[50] Konstanze Lautenbach, house director at the Deutsches Theater from 2001, recalls in an interview with Hans-Dieter Schütt, in *Hinterm Vorhang das Meer* (Berlin: Das neue Berlin, 2001), 228, that, in preparing her student production of *Aussagen* at the Karl-Marx-University in Leipzig in 1981, she resisted the demand of the university's FDJ representative to sacrifice the characters' privacy to a show of activism. Although Lautenbach could be faulted for attributing the demand to the FDJ man's black South African girlfriend, whom she identifies implausibly as a member of the (American!) Black Panther Party, her insistence on the local resonance of the play is noteworthy.

[51] The GDR cast and directors may have had no access to the linguistic markers, but the fact that Grashof and Lang portrayed John and Winston in Erforth's and Stillmark's production of *Die Insel* without blacking up casts some doubt on arguments for the "realistic" defense of black make-up.

Deutsches Theater made this acknowledgment by eliminating black make-up, the explicit foregrounding of the constructed character of racial make-up marks two very different productions of Fugard's most theatrical, even vaudevillian, play, *Sizwe Bansi is Dead*.

Sizwe Bansi is alive: staging identity from blackface to black Germans?

In order to appreciate the significance of the underground production of *Sizwe Bansi ist tot*, performed by two Germans of color in June 1986, we should look first at the GDR (also the German) premiere as well as the South African original, which was first produced as a companion piece to *The Island*.[52] In the original production (1972), the performance began and ended in the photographic studio in which the photographer Styles, a lively character created and embodied by John Kani, engages his more reserved client, played by Winston Ntshona. The client is Sizwe Bansi, whose photograph in Styles's studio records his (temporary) victory over the vicious bureaucracy of South Africa's pass laws. Prevented by law from searching for work in the city, Sizwe is urged by his room-mate Buntu ("humanity") to appropriate a dead man's passbook, name, and "proper" endorsement. Sizwe Bansi hesitates to give up his name ("the nation is strong"), but is eventually persuaded that this is his only means of survival. In the South African production, Ntshona portrayed the dilemma as that of a man bitterly aware of his identity as an "undesirable" in the eyes of the law. When the play toured New Brighton, the township where Kani and Ntshona lived, the performance was interrupted by an intense debate among members of the audience about the merits and risks of Sizwe's options; the intensity of the debate, as well as the fact that it took place in a township hall rather than in parliament, testified not only to the power of the apartheid state to determine legitimate public speech, but also

---

[52] The play appeared under the names of Fugard, Kani, and Ntshona as *Sizwe Bansi Is Dead*, in *Statements*. The German translation was published as *Sizwe Bansi ist tot*, trans. Eva Walch, in *Aussagen: 3 Theaterstücke*.

to the persistence of alternative public spheres despite the power of the state.[53] The underground GDR production registered a much more modest impact. Whereas the impact of the play in South Africa was reinforced by Fugard's prestige on the one hand, and the significant, if as yet submerged, majority potential of the anti-apartheid movements on the other, its impact in the GDR was circumscribed not only by state surveillance of dissidents but by the silence of the dissidents themselves on the conditions of racialized minorities in the GDR. While dissident groups, especially the Protestant churches, protested the duplicity of official expressions of hospitality to migrant workers from the third world as "welcome guests" who were nonetheless housed in segregated institutions, they did not address the situation of GDR citizens of color.[54]

The German-language premiere of *Sizwe Bansi ist tot* at the Mecklenburgisches Landtheater in Schwerin (directed by G. Elisabeth Zillmer) opened initially in March 1976, but appeared in a revised format in October at the same Berliner Festwochen as *Die Insel*. But, while *Die Insel* attempted through the play to shine light on political repression beyond South Africa, this production of *Sizwe Bansi* appeared to vacillate between the official line of transparent solidarity with those in struggle (represented concretely by SACP exiles who acted as consultants) and experimentation with politically

53 For an account of this performance and the audience's arguments, see Fugard, "Sizwe Bansi Is Dead," in *A Night in the Theatre*, ed. Ronald Harwood (London: Methuen, 1981), 29–33; for an analysis of the event, see chapter 5.

54 Krüger-Potratz notes that the duplicity of official expressions of solidarity with migrants as "welcome guests" was first challenged by Protestant churches, who argued that "socialist society was not free from prejudice . . . against foreign fellow citizens [sic? *ausländische Mitbürger*]" or from "latent and perceptible" racism (*Anderssein gab es nicht*, 52); but even dissident publications like *Grenzfall* and *Umweltblätter* assumed that the targets of this prejudice were indeed foreigners rather than fellow citizens (ibid., 53–4). See also the decision on "ministry to foreigners" taken by the Synod of EvangelicalChurches in the GDR, document 7 in *Anderssein gab es nicht*, 209–10.

ambiguous theatrical devices, especially blackface.[55] The critical assessment of Fugard's political engagement and of the apparently petit-bourgeois aspirations of the characters, especially the photographer Styles, and the endorsement of the activist Buntu, as expressed by "R. K." (Kavanagh) in *The African Communist*, appear to have determined the position of the SACP consultants and the Solidarity Committee, who saw to it that the foyer was stocked with posters and publications promulgating ANC and SACP leaders – focusing, in the first instance, on the (white) SACP leader Bram Fischer, and only then on the ANC leaders, Nelson Mandela and others, thus reflecting the SED prioritizing of communism rather than primary support for African nationalism among dissidents in South Africa. These consultants also influenced the production in that the director edited out more of Styles's comic turns for the October revival, after the Soweto Uprising had heightened interest in South Africa.[56]

Despite this political oversight, the director's and actors' reflections on the rehearsal process suggest a more complex negotiation of the politics of form and content. Making up in full view of entering spectators, Martin Seifert (Styles/Buntu) and Günter Zschäckel (Sizwe) did not use naturalistic make-up but rather quoted a style of blackface associated in the USA and in South Africa (but not,

[55] The SACP consultants were identified as Eric Singh, Albert Ndinda, and Victor Moccho [sic?]; according to the director, Zillmer, they supplied a copy of R. K.'s letter to *The African Communist* to counter what they called Fugard's "abandonment [*Abkehr*] of the political" and to highlight the portrayal of the solidarity that Buntu shows to Sizwe; see "Sizwe Bansi ist tod," TD, file no. 164; AdK, pp. 9–11.

[56] On the reformulation of "colonialism of a special type" in the light of armed struggle by the exiled SACP in the 1960s, see *South African Communists Speak*, 280–320; for debate, see the documents in "The Turn to Armed Struggle," in *South Africa's Radical Tradition*, ed. Drew, 2: 344–92. On the foyer displays on this and related topics, see "Zur Erarbeitung der Inszenierung," TD 164, pp. 3–4; "Zum Text," 14–50; notes on the foyer exhibition, and the annotated copy of Walch's translation (TD 164; AdK).

apparently, in the GDR) with the racial stereotypes of the minstrel tradition: black face with white mouth and eyes, framed by a bowler or top hat, white coat and bow-tie for Styles and a stiffer, more formal suit for Sizwe in the photograph scene (figs. 17 and 18). Although the actors here did not use whiteface on their mouths and eyes, these photographs of their interaction clearly reiterate the broad gesticulation of minstrelsy if not Kani's bravura performance. Even if the director's notes refer only to Chaplin and Laurel and Hardy rather than to American minstrelsy, this quotation suggests at least a passing acquaintance with German copies of early twentieth-century minstrelsy in, for instance, films like *Johnny spielt auf*.[57] If the minstrelsy in the first part provoked mostly laughter and an uneven response to the comedy routine, the intimate engagement between Sizwe and Buntu, first in discovering the dead man whose passbook they take, and then in debating the pros and cons of appropriating another man's identity, appears, especially after they removed their minstrel outfits, to have rendered the "clown mask" transparent (fig. 19). Zillmer chose to edit out Buntu's actual transfer of Sizwe's photograph to Robert's pass, perhaps because tampering with an official document might have been too provocative for the Stasi; nonetheless she notes that audiences recited the new ID number along with Sizwe as he attempted to learn it, suggesting a remarkable degree of identification with his plight.[58] Although Zillmer and Zschäckel encouraged this identification by playing Sizwe as a moral man rather than a country bumpkin out of his depth in the city, the reviewers tended

---

[57] For the references to Chaplin, see TD 164, p. 5. For the influence of variety "concerts" and African-American vaudeville on South African black urban performance and on this play, see Kruger, *The Drama of South Africa*, 44–7, 139–42, 156–9.

[58] The stage directions edited out of this production call for Buntu to switch the photographs in the passbooks. They appear in Fugard, Kani, and Ntshona, *Sizwe Bansi Is Dead*, 35–6; *Sizwe Bansi ist tot*, 54. For Zillmer's comments on audience participation in Sizwe's attempt to learn his new ID number, see her "Rehearsal Notes, March 1976)" TD 164, p. 20.

Fig. 17. "A Return to Blackface?" Günther Zscäckel as Sizwe in *Sizwe Bansi ist tot* by Fugard, Kani, and Ntshona, trans. Walch. Directed by G. Elisabeth Zillmer (Schwerin, 1976).

Fig. 18. "Reframing the Dream Picture": Martin Seifert as Styles in *Sizwe Bansi ist tot* (Schwerin, 1976).

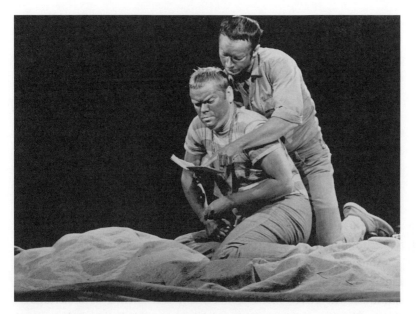

Fig. 19. Zschäckel and Seifert struggle with the pass in *Sizwe Bansi ist tot* (1976).

to treat the character as an object of pity or of political action by others.[59]

The German premiere of *Sizwe Bansi* in 1976 opened in a subsidized, if provincial, theatre with official approval; the 1986 production, however, received only four informal performances in East Berlin. It was directed by Freya Klier, whose career had begun with committed socialist training and moved through critical productions of socialist classics like Vsevolod Vishnevsky's *Optimistic Tragedy* to outright dissidence. *Optimistic Tragedy* earned the wrath of the SED when it was performed for the fortieth anniversary of the Soviet victory over Nazism in 1985, and Klier was banned from official theatres

---

[59] See Ingeborg Pietzsch, "Auf der Suche nach sich selbst. Stücke von Fugard in Potsdam und Schwerin," *Theater der Zeit* 31: 7 (1976), 39; Christof Funke, "Die Schönheit der Naïvetät," *Der Morgen* (2 April 1976); Rolf Richter, "Ein unmenschliches System ist angeklagt," *Neues Deutschland* (21 October, 1976).

for allegedly "agitating against the state."[60] Her production of *Sizwe Bansi* was unauthorized and therefore, in terms of GDR cultural policy, invisible. The performers, Rahman Satti and his partner Mario, took their official marginalization as performers and as Germans of color as the rationale for their performance, attempting to use this tale of the erasure and recovery of identity to challenge the prevailing invisibility of race in the GDR. In the post-performance discussions on "racism in the GDR," they addressed the inability of GDR audiences, even the dissident minority, to see race at home as a local problem requiring local as well as internationalist solutions. They hoped to press this audience to acknowledge the legitimate presence in the officially anti-racist state of racialized minorities, whether the first and second generation "occupation babies," former students, or long-term "economic migrants," and thus also the identity of black Germans, a category that had yet to supplant "mixed race" or "mulatto" even amongst sympathizers.[61] Klier herself remarked that she was initially unaware of Germans of color as well as their experience of racism in the GDR, and, even after her research into this phenomenon, continued to refer to the actors as "my mulattos."[62] The invisibility

[60] Klier, *Abreiß-Kalender*, 137, 155. For analysis of Klier's career in the context of GDR theatre and intellectual culture, see Kruger, "'Wir treten aus unseren Rollen heraus,'" especially 192–5.

[61] On the prejudice faced by Afro-Germans, including the persistent use of *Neger* as an allegedly neutral term, see Ayim, "Die Afro-deutsche Minderheit," and "Weiße Streß und Schwarze Nerven," in her posthumously published *Grenzenlos und unverschämt* (Berlin: Orlandaverlag, 1997), 111–32. For the experience of growing up black in the GDR, see contributions by Laura Baum, Katherina Oguntoye, and Raya Lubinetski to *Showing our Colors*, 145–63, 212–27, and for the story of a South African exile caught without appropriate identity (papers) in not-quite-unified Eastern Germany, Sithebe Nombuso, "Ost- oder West-Deutschland–für mich ist das kein großer Unterschied" in *Entfernte Verbindungen; Rassismus, Antisemitismus, und Klassenunterdrückung*, ed. Ika Hügel (Berlin: Orlandaverlag, 1999), 224–32.

[62] Klier, *Abreiß-Kalender*, 137 and personal communication, 18 January 1993.

of the performance was compounded by this persistent if unintended prejudice. Some unofficial theatre performances on issues of local concern, even when officially taboo, such as Klier's skits – *Steinschlag*, on the persistent lack of gender parity despite the official promotion of women's rights in the GDR and *Pässe Parolen*, on the problem of illegal out-migration of GDR citizens, performed with her partner Stefan Krawcyk – were housed by churches such as the Zionskirche on the border between the central Mitte district and the student and artist neighborhood of Prenzlauerberg, which also housed the dissident environmentalist and anti-nuclear publication, *Umweltblätter*. *Sizwe Bansi* did not find a home there, but was rehearsed and performed in the "Bronx," a derelict squat northeast of the Zionskirche, where Rahmann and Mario lived. This "empty apartment without windows and doors" reminded Klier of Bernard Malamud's stories.[63] This environment, and the allusion to a Jewish-American chronicler of dispossession, suggest a link, however muted, between the discourse of anti-racism and the anti-fascism promulgated internationally by many writers of Jewish descent, and that of anti-racism.[64]

---

[63] Klier, *Abreiß-Kalender*, 144, 155. Klier places the squat in Oderberg Street, now part of a rapidly gentrifying trendy area. Her claim that the churches neglected to house the play because they had "no tradition" of protesting racism in the GDR is contradicted by Krüger-Potratz in *Anderssein gab es nicht*, but it is noteworthy that those churches that supported Klier's work until her arrest in 1988 failed to house this play. In her letter of 18 January 1993, Klier recalled the production with "[her] two mulattos" as the only one of its kind, arguing that the underground theatre scene was so small that she would have known if another production of Fugard by Afro-Germans took place. Rahman Satti, who, in Klier's view, left East Berlin for Amsterdam "on account of racism," did not respond to requests for information.

[64] Klier's allusion to Malamud did not mention his Jewishness. This is not surprising, since, while the GDR had given material and ideological support to "victims of Fascism," including leftists of Jewish descent who survived Auschwitz or exile, this support, like the official commemoration of anti-Nazi resistance at concentration camps like Buchenwald, focused on their anti-fascist credentials at the expense of any official acknowledgment of their ethnicity. For official GDR

This attempt to re-envisage racialized objects of anti-racist solidarity as sovereign agents in their own right was not a success. Its very invisibility, even in the alternative public sphere of the churches and unofficial cultural groups in the GDR, prefigures the persistent reluctance of even sympathetic German intellectuals to see race in Germany in terms that went beyond abstract solidarity with beleaguered foreigners to an engagement with the multiple origins and identifications of fellow citizens and resident non-citizens.[65] The years after unification in 1990 saw immigration into Germany rival that to the United States, although changes in the *Ausländergesetz* (Aliens Act) were slow to accommodate this fact.[66] In 1993, resident aliens were granted the statutory right to naturalization, provided applicants met the same strict criteria as in the *Ausländergesetz* for residence, language competence, and financial solvency. This shift in the Basic Law from citizenship by blood towards citizenship by residency did not bring with it a corresponding change in the legal privileging of German nationals as *Staatsvolk* (people of the state) as opposed to naturalized citizens (*Staatsbürger*). At the start of the decade, even sympathetic members of the former GDR intelligentsia seemed unable to get beyond solidarity for "our foreign fellow citizens" (*ausländische Mitbürger*), despite the sharp criticism of that patronizing oxymoron

silence on the Jewish identity of "victims of Fascism," see Antonio Grunenbaum, *Antifascismus: ein deutscher Mythos* (Hamburg: Rowohlt, 1993), 120–44, and interviews with the adult children of "victims" so acknowledged, in *Zwischen Thora und Trabant: Juden in der DDR*, ed. Vincent von Wroblewsky (Berlin: Aufbau, 1993).

[65] Post-unification attempts to transcend the prejudicial dichotomy between German and *Ausländer* (foreigner) have not yet produced a standard term for long-term residents who are not ethnically German. The term favored by the German left, *ausländische Mitbürger* (foreign fellow citizen), is clearly unacceptable; "resident alien" is also prejudicial. "Resident non-citizen," suggested by David Horrocks and Eva Kolinsky in "Migrants or Citizens" in Horrocks and Kolinsky, eds., *Turkish Culture in German Society Today* (Oxford: Berghahn, 1996), xi, is more accurate.

[66] Peter H. Schuck and Rainer Münz, Introduction to *Paths to Inclusion*, vii–xxii, here: vii.

by two Turkish-German writers, Zafer Şenocak and Bülent Tulay, a generation or so younger than most of the experts.[67] In December 1991, barely a year after unification, a meeting at the Deutsches Theater advertised as *"BeFREMDet"* (alienated) allowed for a "conversation on racism, violence, and the hatred of foreigners." It was sponsored by two organizations in the soon-to-be annexed East Germany, the Academy of Arts and the Regional Office for Issues Related to Foreigners; but many of the speakers, from theatre intellectuals (such as Heiner Müller) and film-makers (Heiner Carow) to officials involved in race relations, appeared to be primarily concerned that foreigners, represented on the podium by "resident aliens" such as the Egyptian theatre director Saddek Kebir and the Vietnamese jurist Ngyen van Huong, would bear with their helplessness in the face of right-wing violence.[68] While acknowledging the limits of "socialist internationalism" in the face of "hatred of foreigners," they tended nonetheless to speak the language of commiseration and third world relief rather than that of civil rights under the law, and thus still to see Germans of color in neocolonial terms, in the sense elaborated by Memmi, as the "burden of history" rather than agents of historical change.[69]

[67] Zafer Şenocak and Bülent Tulay, "Germany – A Home for the Turks?" in Şenocak, *Atlas of a Tropical Germany*, 1–9. The essay first appeared in January 1990, before unification and the small reforms of the Aliens Law in 1991, but it anticipated the debates of the decade by arguing that social integration could only follow civil rights, including citizenship; that integration should not come at the cost of cultural and religious rights including the right to education about Islam; and, especially, that the German government and German society should be better educated about the history of Islam, including its long history in Europe, as well as its present interaction with secular culture among residents of Turkish descent. Şenocak (b. 1961) was then a Turkish national who had lived in Germany since childhood; he became a German citizen in 1992.

[68] Comments based on personal observation at the event, on 10 December 1991, and on the hand-out provided by the Deutsches Theater, which divided the proceedings into three sessions: "Internationalism and Hatred of Foreigners," "Youth and Violence," and "What is to be Done?".

[69] Memmi, *The Colonizer and the Colonized*, 92.

Despite changes to the Basic Law, *Blut* rather than *Boden* seemed still to be the defining criterion of German citizenship. While the underground adaptation of *Sizwe Bansi* to the marginal existence of blacks in the GDR went largely unnoticed, the play itself continued to capture the imagination of Afro-Germans. Miguel Hurst, an actor whose biography – born in West German Freiburg to Angolan and Guinean parents, educated in the GDR, where his student-activist father found better stipends, and later in Portugal – bears witness to the legacy of second world solidarity with the third world, claimed affinity with Fugard, whom he called a "white African," produced *Sizwe Bansi* in Krio (creolized African Portuguese) for black ghetto dwellers in Lisbon in 1995, and hoped to produce the play in Germany as well.[70] The presence of over 300,000 Afro-Germans in Germany generated more theatrical representation, from Rangi Moja (Swahili: united colors), a group of white Germans, mostly female social workers and pedagogy students, and African (mostly male) asylum-seekers engaged in intercultural theatre and social work in Hildesheim in 1997, to the Berliner Afrika-Ensemble (since 1999), whose director, Kouassi Gourgemegou (from Togo), and actors are mostly students from African countries.[71] In 2000, the latter group adapted a play by the Indian Kenyan writer Kuldip Sondhi, *Unter Vorbehalt* (original English title *With Strings*, i.e. "With Reservations," first published in 1968), about an Indian in Kenya whose parents resist his plans to marry an African woman, to conditions in Germany, where marriage with "foreigners" continues to be viewed with suspicion despite official liberalization.[72]

[70] Theo Pischke, "Weisse Afrikaner, schwarze Europäer," *die tageszeitung* (29 March, 1995); retrieved at <http://web.lexis-nexis.com/ universe/docum...lzV&_md5=fe8f]cd74a999c159bc3a3122170162e>

[71] On Rangi Moja, see Wiebke von Bernstorff and Uta Plate, *Fremd bleiben: Interkulturelle Theaterarbeit am Beispiel der afrikanischen Theatertruppe Rangi Moja* (Hamburg: IKO-Verlag für Interkulturelle Kommunikation, 1997). On the Berliner Afrika-Ensemble, see Jeannette Goddar, "Jeder ist ein Stein in einem Mosaik," *die tageszeitung* 14 July 2000; at http://www.taz.de/tpl/2000/07/14/ a0250.fr/text?re=bl

[72] *With Strings* had been published in English in 1968, in *Ten One-Act Plays*, ed. Cosmo Pieterse (London: Heinemann, 1968), but, according

By 2001, long-term residents of Germany could acquire German citizenship as a statutory right, provided they met language and economic criteria and a reduced residence requirement; but most public debates continued to focus less on questions of civil rights under law and better ways of enforcing these rights for those threatened by ongoing right-wing violence – the so-called "new intolerance" by "post-wall" youth and inadequate response by their elders in government – than on refurbished arguments about Germanness: the notion of *deutsche Leitkultur*, or German dominant culture, and the disputed corollary, argued in 1997 by Jörg Schönborn (then CDU Minister for Home Affairs in Berlin), that ethnic and religious minorities in Germany should adopt "Western" or "Christian" values and practices.[73] Reiterated regularly by the right in opposition after the Socialist Party's accession in 1998, this provocation received essentially two kinds of response from the left: many defended the "cultural richness" of a "multi-cultural society" without attending to civil rights violations, while others argued that, without enforcement of civil rights (freedom of association and equality before the law) or cultural rights (language and religious education), leftist appeals to

to Goddar, "Jeder ist ein Stein," Sondhi was "completely unknown in Germany." Another play by Sondhi, *Encounter* (about the anti-colonial struggle in Kenya), was performed by anti-apartheid groups in South Africa; see Kruger, *The Drama of South Africa*, 136.

73 Jörg Schönborn, "Integration ist keine Einbahnstraße" (*Berliner Morgenpost*, 25 April 1997) argued that state aid for minorities should be matched by integration into so-called "Christian Western" society. Although this essay provoked the immediate controversy around *deutsche Leitkultur*, Schönborn was not the first to revive a racialist definition of Germanness after unification. In 1993, the apparently apolitical writer Botho Strauss defended German nationalism against its alleged scapegoating by the left. The essay, "Anschwellender Bockgesang," appeared first in *Der Spiegel* 47: 6 (8 February 2000), and was reprinted, with endorsements by nationalists, such as the revisionist historian Ernst Nolte and the film-maker Hans-Jürgen Syberberg, director of *Our Hitler*, in *Die Selbstbewußte Nation: Anschwellender Bockgesang und weitere Beiträge zur deutschen Debatte*, ed. Heimo Schwilk and Ulrich Schacht (Berlin: Ullstein: 1994).

cultural difference are structurally similar to conservative defenses of German cultural uniqueness even if they challenge the hegemony of *deutsche Leitkultur.*[74] Members of minorities who embody the (apparently still unthinkable) combination of German identity and racial otherness have yet to be clearly envisioned as citizens, despite the negative responses of some to the question "Are the Germans hostile to foreigners [*ausländerfeindlich*]?"[75]

After unification, translation: Fugard in Turkish Berlin

Afro-Germans have been the most visible targets of extremist right-wing violence in post-unification Germany, as the high-profile murder trial of the skinheads who killed Afro-German Alberto Adriano in June 2000 shows. Nonetheless, residents of Turkish descent, at over two million people the largest minority in Germany, continue to be the primary target of attacks. In the months leading up to unification

[74] For the first position, see David Gössmann, "Kulturelles Reichtum, soziale Armut," *die tageszeitung* (11 February 1999); retrieved at <http://web.lexis-nexis.com/universe/docum ..lzV&_md5=c) b5ab5d860e091b7bdb7bdb87219096boc6. For a critique, see Richard Herzinger, "Was heißt hier deutsch? Der Irrglaube an den kulturellen Volksgeist eint Konservative und Multikulturalisten," *Die Zeit* 3 (1999); retrieved at http://www.zeit.de/1999/3/1999903_nation.html. For an account of concrete programs for education see Nicole Maschler, "Integration ist keine Einbahnstraße," *die tageszeitung* (22 January 2001); retrieved at <http://lexis-nexis.com/universe/docum ..lzV&_md5=8d2c2b5bde24f726cfb42698bb4f>, which ironically quotes Schönbohm's title in order to argue the opposite point: that the state should do more to accommodate religious and cultural needs and that these services would aid rather than thwart integration. For the political consequences of the new naturalization law, see the contributions to the section on "Possible Political Transformation" ("politische Gestaltungsmöglichkeiten") in *Sind die Deutschen ausländerfeindlich?*

[75] On citizenship used as exclusion, see Chong-Sook Kang, "Von Selbstbestimmung keine Rede: Frauen im Ausländer- und Asylrecht," and Gotlinde Magiriba Lwanga, "Deutsch? Nein, danke. Anmerkungen zu Staatsangehörigkeit, Bürgerinnenrechten und Verfassung," in Hügel, ed. *Entfernte Verbindungen*, 238–54, 260–72.

in 1990, Berliners of Turkish descent were worried that the incorporation of impoverished and allegedly intolerant East Germans would
displace resident non-citizens, especially those whose religion (especially Muslims), location (in concentrated neighborhoods), or cultural
practices (from language to food or music) allegedly place them outside
the bounds of the *Leitkultur*, whether defined by German conserva-
tives (or better, exclusivists) or by their counterparts elsewhere, such
as Samuel Huntington, the author of *The Clash of Civilizations*.[76] As
Zafer Şenocak argues in response to Huntington, the demise of Communism has seen the return of Islam as the West's favorite bogey,
"threatening Europe's borders [. . .] not with armies but with hosts
of guest workers."[77] Şenocak goes on to challenge the essentialist
presumptions of separate "German" and "Turkish" identities, which

[76] Adriano, originally from Mozambique, had lived in Dessau for twenty
years and was married to a German. His death and the conviction of
one adult and two juveniles for murder (as opposed to
homicide/manslaughter) marked a turning point in the German legal
system's treatment of right-wing violence. Although the West German
press insisted on locating this case in "East Germany," similar
assaults took place in Bochum and Bavaria, in western Germany.
"Turkish" refers here to Turkish nationals in Germany as well as
those recently naturalized as German citizens. The first generation of
"guest workers," who came to Germany from Italy, Greece, and
Yugoslavia, as well as Turkey, between 1962 and 1973, when the
government ended recruitment, are now nearing retirement; their
children and grandchildren are among those recently naturalized as
German citizens. The entries by Miram Dabag, Johannes
Meyer-Ingwesern, and Ertekin Özkan on the Armenian, Kurdish, and
Turkish minorities respectively, in *Ethnische Minderheiten in der
Bundesrepublik Deutschland*, 61–71, 310–27, and 511–27, and on Islam
and the Muslim minority (Ludwig Schlessmann and Farideh
Akashe-Böhme, ibid., 217–28) are illuminating, but it is worth noting
that neither the Turkish nor the German government treats ethnic
distinctions among Turkish nationals as relevant.
[77] Şenocak, "War and Peace in Modernity" (1994/1998), in *Atlas of a
Tropical Germany*, 83–98, here: 87. Şenocak's essay was written
initially in response to Strauss and to Samuel Huntington's article on
"The Clash of Civilizations" (1993) and revised in 1998 to include
comments on Huntington's book *The Clash of Civilizations and the*

pervade even progressive promotions of a multi-cultural society and the "foreign fellow citizen" (91), that impossible oxymoron, and insists instead that Germans acknowledge that "Germany long ago became a part of us German Turks" and thus that Turkish German identifications and practices (including Islam) be understood as part of Germany as well as Europe ("War and Peace," 98). Sanem Kleff, another second-generation Berliner of Turkish descent, concurred, arguing that "we too [resident non-citizens] are the people."[78]

The obstacles in the way of this acknowledgment at the level of daily life as well as state policy are clear not merely in the dichotomy between "German" and "Turk" in "study-groups," whose condescension Şenocak sharply criticizes, but also in the inability of the participants or institutions housing them to define their roles and thus the – social as well as theatrical – drama in which they are acting. Since these encounters take place between unequal partners in institutions shaped by the dominant culture, they are at best inter- rather

Remaking of World Order (New York: Simon and Shuster 1996), published in German the same year, in which he claimed that Western Christian civilization and contemporary European society had no room for their historic adversary, Islam. Subsequent references to Şenocak's essay are in the body of the text. For a thorough analysis of political quiescence in the face of the so-called "new intolerance," see Joyce Marie Mushaben, "What It Means to be Non-German: After Unification, the Deluge," in *From Post-War to Post-Wall Generations: Changing Attitudes towards the National Question and NATO in the Federal Republic of Germany* (Boulder: Westview Press, 1998), 315–59. For an analysis of Şenocak's "transnational way of thinking," see Hans-Peter Waldhoff, "Ein Übersetzer: über die sozio-biographische Genese eines transnationalen Denkstils," in *Brücken zwischen Zivilizationen. Zur Zivilisierung ethnisch-kultureller Differenzen und Machtungleicheiten: Das türkisch-deutsche Beispiel*, ed. Hans-Peter Waldhoff, Dursun Tan, and Elcin Kürsat-Ahlers (Frankfurt a.M.: IKO-Verlag für interkulturelle Kommunikation, 1997), 323–64.

[78] Sanem Kleff, "'Wir sind auch das Volk!' Die letzten zwölf Monate des geteilten Berlin aus der Sicht nicht-deutscher Berlinerinnen," in *BRD-DDR: Alte und neue Rassismen im Zuge der deutsch–deutschen Einigung*, ed. Sanem Klett et al. (Frankfurt a.M.: Verlag für interkulturelle Kommunikation, 1990), 3–17.

than multi-cultural, in that they posit a binary opposition between two distinct cultures rather than allowing for the possibility that these cultures have already undergone syncretic transformation.[79] Although these terms and the debates around them have yet to penetrate German culture to the degree they have American, several bicultural playwrights have begun to explore the possibilities of syncretic theatre. Emine Sevgi Özdamar, a Turkish-German writer a generation older than Şenocak, noted in her account of the production of her play about Turkish migration to and settlement in Germany, *Karagöz in Alamania/Schwarzauge in Deutschland* (Black Eye in Germany, produced 1986), that Turkish and German and Turkish-German participants in this drama continually come up against stereotyping on all sides. She went on to engage in a critical mimicry of these stereotypes in her next play, *Keloglan in Alamania* (1991).[80] The parabolic element of both plays draws not only on Anatolian folk tales of migration but

---

[79] For this distinction, see Patrice Pavis, "Introduction: Towards a Theory of Interculturalism in Theatre?" in *The Intercultural Performance Reader*, ed. Patrice Pavis (London: Routledge, 1996), 1–25, here: 8. For a compelling argument for the greater theoretical flexibility and empirical validity of syncretism in the theatre, which allows for the agency of the parties as well as the complexity of the influences to a greater degree than the binary "interculturalism" or the biologistic "hybridization," see Christopher Balme, *Decolonising the Stage* (Oxford University Press, 1999), 63–6, 93–8.

[80] Emine Sevgi Özdamar (b. 1946) wrote *Karagöz in Alamania* in 1982. The play was inspired by a letter written by a "guest worker" in Germany to his wife in their home village in Turkey. Although the play premiered at the prestigious Frankfurt Schauspielhaus in 1986, it was not revived or published as a play, but appears instead in parable form in Özdamar's short-story collection *Mutterzunge* (1992), which won the prestigious Ingeborg Bachmann prize. Although initially published in 1991, *Keloglan in Alamania* had its premiere only in 2000. Özdamar's parabolic account of the first play, "Black Eye and his Donkey: A Multi-Cultural Experience," is in Horrocks and Kolisnky, eds., *Turkish Culture in German Society Today*, 54–70. Özdamar's parable was originally published in *Die Zeit*, 25 February 1992, and appears in this collection in parallel German text and English translation. Subsequent citations are in the body of the text.

also on Özdamar's work in 1976 as a director's assistant to two of Brecht's students, Benno Besson and Matthias Langhoff, at the East Berlin Volksbühne, which was at that time a more compelling heir to Brecht than the Berliner Ensemble, bound by Brecht's heirs to a faithful reproduction of his model books. Özdamar presented her observations on the 1986 production of *Karagöz* in the form of an ironic parable about explaining her play to Turkish and German actors in the Frankfurt Schauspielhaus, the prestigious state theatre that produced it in 1986. She charts the fall from the "almost sacred atmosphere" that pervaded the stage at the start of this "special" experiment – "a play about Turks. For the first time!" ("Black-Eye and his Donkey," 59) to the mutual insults, such as the spat between the "SS-Man" and the "caraway-chewing Turk," to the management's distribution of explanatory pamphlets to the audience – without consultation with the author (63). In *Keloglan in Alamania*, this ironic mimicry of stereotypes drives the drama as Özdamar undercuts and overlays the pathos of Anatolian parable with quotations, in plot and in gest, from German folk sources, especially *Rotkäppchen* (Little Red Riding Hood), and, more noticeably, from the already syncretic form of operas, from *Die Zauberflöte* (*The Magic Flute*) to *Madame Butterfly* to *The Bartered Bride* to dramatize in comic form the serious situation of a German-speaking "blond Turk" threatened with deportation if he does not immediately find a job or a German wife.[81]

Özdamar thus challenges not only persistent German prejudices against Turks, but also the tendency, common on the German left, to treat German–Turkish interaction as an encounter with the exotic rather than as an acknowledgment of the quotidian presence in Germany of citizens and residents with multiple identifications. Although clearly drawing on Brecht, she also highlights the limits of Brecht's own relatively unreflected use of racial, especially orientalized, stereotypes in characters from Schlink in *Jungle of Cities*

---

[81] The most accessible publication of the play is the reprint published at the time of the premiere at the regional Oldenburgische Staatstheater in *Die Deutsche Bühne* 10 (2000), 30–7. For a discussion of this production, see Sieg, *Ethnic Drag*, 233–53.

to *The Good Person of Setzuan.* Her ironic, but no less serious, attempt to overcome the alienating effects of such stereotypes on both the subjects and objects of this prejudice recontextualized and revitalized Brechtian *Verfremdung* as a way of critically estranging assumptions about racial or cultural essences to highlight their character as *gests*, social attitudes and the actions embodying them. Özdamar's commentary shares with other commentators cast in the role of "native informants," such as the Indian theatre activist Rustom Bharucha, a skeptical view of the dominant culture's understanding of the "other," but her participation in the experiment and her ironic rather than dismissive commentary confirm her sense that the "other" culture should be understood as part of the landscape of the "home" culture.[82]

In the post-unification (and post-apartheid) period, the drama of South Africa has faded from international stages and Fugard's plays appear no longer to hold the fascination they did in the apartheid era. The last production of Fugard in the GDR had been *A Place with the Pigs*, his meditation on a story in *The New York Times* about a Soviet deserter in the Second World War who emerges into an incomprehensible world after forty years in hiding. The play clearly had allegorical significance for GDR audiences facing the consequences of decades of stagnation.[83] Most post-unification productions revived the standard

---

[82] Rustom Bharucha's attack on Western orientalism is compelling, but he shares with orientalism a belief in a distinct and separate "Indian" culture, as the first chapter of his book makes clear: see "Collision of Cultures," in *Theatre and the World: Performance and the Politics of Culture,* 2nd edn (London: Routledge, 1993), 14–41. Nigerian theater scholar Biodun Jeyifo provides a more useful map for the German–Turkish terrain in his argument that syncretic theatre necessarily involves the "reinvention of tradition" rather than the interaction of distinct received traditions: see Biodun Jeyifo, "The Reinvention of Theatrical Tradition: Critical Discourses on Interculturalism in the African Theatre," in *The Intercultural Performance Reader,* 149–61.

[83] In Jörn van Dyck's translation, *Ein Stall voll Schweine* (A Sty Full of Pigs), this story of a Soviet deserter of the Second World War, holed up in a pigsty that is cleaned by a woman whom he persuades to collect a hero's pension on his behalf who is unable to leave his self-imposed

"poor white" *Hallo und Adieu* (*Hello and Goodbye*), as in the Pasinger Fabrik in Munich in 1993 and the Heidelberg City Theatre in 1996, but some theatres produced German versions of later plays, such as the post-apartheid *Valley Song* at Grips-Theater, Berlin's best-known youth-oriented house, in 1997, which portrays a young rural colored girl determined to become a singing sensation in Johannesburg. But, while the revivals of *Hallo und Adieu* did not appear to depart radically from the pattern of highlighting the difference between audience and story, Germany and South Africa, which had characterized the first German productions of this play in the mid-1970s, *Merhaba und Tschüß*, a Turkish–German adaptation that transported Fugard's 1965 play set in a "poor white" Afrikaner household in Port Elizabeth, South Africa, to Kreuzberg, Berlin, in 2000, suggests that Fugard's project of dramatizing oppression through the intimate interactions of everyday life remains relevant to the contemporary representation of minorities in Germany.[84]

Adapted (by Hülya Karcı and Yüksel Yolcu, and directed by Yolcu) from Fugard's play about a woman who returns to her

> prison even when the Soviet Union collapses, clearly spoke to a population alternately inebriated and numbed by the prospect of unification. Winkelgrund had wanted to put on the play at the Deutsches Theater, but the play's explicit allusion to the end of the Soviet Union and its implicit commentary on the GDR made it too awkward for the capital. Instead, the play opened on 4 April 1990, barely six months before the GDR officially dissolved on 3 October, under the direction of Thomas Roth in the north-eastern city of Greifswald. This production took contemporary conditions as its point of departure; the poster featured a shadow portrait of Stalin behind the image of the pigsty, and the director's notes highlighted the prevailing state of "denial, failure, and social collapse" in the Eastern German population, which he saw as the inevitable "hangover" after the first "intoxicating taste of freedom." See "Ein Stall voll Schweine," AdK: TD 729, n.p.
>
> [84] The German premiere, in the translation by Jan Lustig, *Athol Fugard: Drei Theaterstücke* (Frankfurt: Fischer, 1979), took place in "der Keller" (cellar) in Cologne in January 1975, followed by the Werkstatt at the subsidized Schiller Theatre in West Berlin. The GDR premiere took place at the Brandenburg Theatre in September 1976.

childhood home in inner-city Port Elizabeth after twelve years to confront the legacy of a strict father whose house and faith she abandoned
for a precarious life as a prostitute, and the brother who remained to
look after him, *Merhaba und Tschüß* premiered in July 2000. It was
produced by the Tiyatrom, Berlin's subsidized theatre for the Turkish-
German community in central Kreuzberg (formerly Kreuzberg 61),
whose program has served first-, second- and third-generation Berliners of Turkish descent since 1973 with a mix of Turkish folk-drama,
children's plays, and the occasional cabaret show addressing Turkish
life in Berlin, where thirteen percent of the population is estimated to
be of Turkish descent.[85] The Tiyatrom is not the only theatre targeting
Turkish Berliners, but it is currently the only subsidized institution in
this category. Its longevity is testimony to the permanent residence of
its audience and to their diversity; Turkish Berliners include not only
migrant workers and their families but also intellectuals and political
exiles, such as the actor, Cetin Ipekkayan, who helped to spearhead
the subsidy drive of the theatre in 1984.

The title of the adaptation, *Merhaba und Tschüß*, highlights
the syncretic culture of its characters and their counterparts in the
audience who typically use the Turkish *merhaba* for "hello" and the
casual German *tschüß* for "goodbye."[86] As in Fugard's play, the scene
opens with the brother, here Mahmut (Celâl Bozat), living alone after
the death of his father, who had been a forbidding figure despite being
crippled by a work injury. Whereas Fugard places the house in a poor

---

[85] The Tiyatrom was founded by its current manager, Yekta Arman, in
1973 as an amateur group playing with and for Turkish-speaking
friends. Thanks in part to Peter Stein, then the world-renowned
director of the Schaubühne, Tiyatrom received Berlin Senate subsidy
in 1984. It remains the only subsidized theatre in Germany performing
in Turkish, but has been criticized by younger directors, such as Talcin
Baykul of the unsubsidized and experimental Theater Tiyatroia, for its
"amateurish" folkish program and for neglecting younger
German-speaking audiences of Turkish descent. See Oliver Kranz,
"Babylonische Bühne Berlin," *die tageszeitung* (23 October 1998).

[86] Dursun Tan and Hans-Peter Waldhoff, "Turkish Everyday Culture in
Germany," in Horrocks and Kolinsky, eds., *Turkish Culture in German
Society Today*, 137–56, here: 146.

white neighborhood of his native Port Elizabeth, and makes its inhabitant an odd young man living off his father's pension and filling his days with trips to the local beach, the adaptors create a vividly realized equivalent in the cramped apartment in eastern Kreuzberg (formerly Kreuzberg 36) which remains, despite post-unification gentrification elsewhere in the city, the largest concentration of people of Turkish descent outside Turkey, as well as in the limited outing options available to those on public assistance like Mahmut, such as the Turkish market along the neighboring Landwehr Canal.[87] In addition to the precisely realized set, the live music (by Mustafa Sarışın and Bülent Tezcanlı) highlighted not so much the clash of cultures as the creative potential of their syncretic encounter.

This is more than a mere adaptation, however. Like most Turks who came to Berlin in the 1960s, this family is Muslim but, as children of "guest workers," Mahmut and his sister Filiz (Dilruba Saatçi) speak both German and Turkish and appear to be acclimatized to life in Berlin. The contrast between acculturation and attachment is established by the decorations on the wall – a velvet painting of Mecca and an embroidered reproduction of the Arabic exordium that opens the Qu'ran, "In the name of God, the compassionate, the merciful" (common in Muslim homes around the world, including in South Africa) – on the one hand, and Mahmut's obsession with Batman comics on the other.[88] However, this obsession, as well as his retreat from the world after giving up an apprenticeship at Siemens to care for his

---

[87] Although this area is often labeled a "Turkish ghetto," Şenocak points out that its population is more German than otherwise. The inhabitants of the "so-called ghetto" are linked by their underemployment and "exclusion from consumer society" despite attempts by the "political elite" to appeal to German ethnic exclusiveness: see Şenocak, "In den sogenannten Ghettos landen die Verlierer der Konsumgesellschaft – unabhängig von ihrer ethnischen Zugehörigkeit," *die tageszeitung* (28 November 1997).

[88] The cultural resonance of Arabic script, as the script of Islam and of transnational Arabic literacy, generations after the romanization of Turkish by the modernizing leader of Turkey, Mustafa Kamal, a.k.a Ataturk in 1928, remains considerable, even among secular Turks outside Turkey. For a literary meditation on the power of what

father, suggests not only personal limits but also social constraints on assimilation. In Bozat's portrayal, Mahmut matches the eccentricity of Fugard's Johnny, who takes refuge from the world in finicky rearrangement of the few items in the kitchen and, finally, in the role of cripple, as he leans on the crutches left by his dead father, but adds a new dimension to the original character in his old-fashioned Muslim house-clothes; apart from the Muslim cap, the slippers and too-short pants look as though borrowed from an older – and shorter – man (set and costume were by Dieter Rinke). Unlike Fugard's Hester, who in Yvonne Bryceland's signature performance (in 1974 at the Space Theatre) was a cynical streetwalker, old before her time, Filiz appears at the outset to be a feisty and confident young woman. Dressed in modern but not immodest clothing, she demands – in aggressively fluent German against her brother's linguistic mixture – her share of her father's inheritance almost immediately after she walks into the apartment and, at the end, tries to persuade her brother to come away with her to start a new life. This association of the dominant language with escape into the wider world and the family language with imprisonment by religion and custom corresponds to the association, in Fugard's original, of English with escape but also with corruption, and of Afrikaans with the constraints of the patriarchal Calvinist family. But in Saatçi's performance, Filiz's retreat into Turkish increases as the play progresses, and this is more ambiguous than Bryceland's expletive use of Afrikaans. Filiz's fear of reprisals from her father (who, according to her brother, is still bedridden in the next room), and of being trapped like her mother as an oppressed Muslim wife and household drudge, go beyond Hester's resistance to her Calvinist father to highlight in this instance the specific ways in which immigrant patriarchs use religion, here Islam, to enforce female compliance with "family honor"[89] (fig. 20). The code-switching between German and Turkish designates an intimate space in which Filiz and Mahmut

Özdamar calls her "grand-father tongue," see her "Mutterzunge," the title story in *Mutterzunge*.
[89] Yasemin Karakasoglu, "Turkish Cultural Orientations in Germany and the Role of Islam," in Horrocks and Kolinsky, eds., *Turkish Culture in German Society Today*, 157–90, here: 161–3.

Fig. 20. "Sister and brother in Turkish Berlin." Dilruba Saatçi as Filiz and Celâl Bozat as Mahmut in *Merhaba und Tschüß*, an adaptation in Turkish and German of Athol Fugard's *Hello and Goodbye* (1965), adapted and directed by Yüksel Yolcu (Berlin, 2000). Photograph by Jörg Metzger.

can recreate family ties, while also highlighting the tension between a pathologically defined, limited and limiting, incomplete bilingualism or *Halbsprachigkeit* (half-speech) and what a Turkish-German feminist prefers to call the "cultural innovation" of speakers between two languages.[90]

Although Filiz departs decisively once she has confirmed her father's death and searched his suitcases in vain for the pension, the audience is left with the sense that Filiz, like Mahmut, has not quite escaped the effects of her parents' poverty and isolation. Although the play was performed in an institution whose relatively solid appointments (and well-stocked bar) contrasted with the continuing marginalization of the mostly Muslim residents of surrounding high-rise projects, the audience (on 13 October 2000, but according to the managing director, Yekta Arman, it was a general trend) was composed of mostly second- and third-generation Turkish-German young people, with only a few non-Turkish speakers whether German or other, although Arman argued elsewhere that the audience was on average twenty percent "German."[91] The leftist Berlin paper *die*

90 Umut Erel, "Grenzüberschreitungen und kulturelle Mischformen als anti-rassistischer Widerstand?" in Cathy Galvin, Käthe Kossik, and Peggy Piesche, eds., *Aufbrüche: Kulturelle Produktion von Migrantinnen, Schwarzen und jüdischen Frauen in Deutschland* (Königstein: Ulrike Helmer Verlag, 1999), 182. This optimistic view of bilingual innovation is controversial; in an essentially monolingual dominant culture, which grants only German higher-status functions while downgrading Turkish and its speakers to marginality, Turkish-German children are no more likely to grant their home language high status than are the children of immigrants to the Anglo-dominant United States. For a brief account of debates about language and migration in the German context, see Ingrid Gogolin's entry on "Sprache und Migration" in *Ethnische Minderheiten in der Bundesrepublik Deutschland*, 481–90, and, for an English-language discussion, see Tan and Waldhoff, "Turkish Everyday Culture in Germany," 142–50.
91 Arman's comments in Kranz, "Babylonische Bühne Berlin" were reiterated to me on the night of the performance. "German" is a difficult category to assess, since it could include Germans of Turkish descent as well as members of the German majority.

tageszeitung the only non-Turkish paper to review the production, highlighted a local project to use this play as a means of raising consciousness through gender role-playing among high school students and other young people in Turkish Berlin, in order to help other young women to better negotiate the conflicting pressures of family and society, Islam and *deutsche Leitkultur*, in Berlin.[92]

The social as well as cultural value of this role-play and the play that inspired it is potentially considerable, since both take as their point of departure the fact that young people in Turkish Berlin identify in different measures with the emancipatory promise of general education and with Islam. It is however striking that the cultural pages of the mainstream press remain more likely to carry stories about international theatre touring companies from Asia or the Americas than detailed accounts of this and other syncretic productions at home. Much has been made of the globalization of Europe and of the transformation of Berlin from the twin frontier posts of the American and the Soviet empires into the capital city of Europe's most formidable economic power in the late twentieth century, but, if German culture is to be truly post-imperial, it is the glocalization of Berlin, the reformation of this German city in the image of its newly naturalized citizens, that deserves full attention in the twenty-first.

---

[92] For an account of this project led by a feminist theatre-in-education activist, Simin Turgay, see Tom Mustroph, "Fremd im eigenen land: Die Verhältnisse haben sich geändert: "Merhaba und Tschüss" im Tiyatrom," *die tageszeitung* (7 July 2000).

7 Truth, reconciliation, and the ends of political performance

In the wake of Brecht, political performance occupies a liminal space between what he called the "smaller pedagogics" of a critical theatre and the "greater pedagogics" of political transformation, between what Raymond Williams called subjunctive and indicative acts, or between what we might simply, perhaps too simply, call art and action. In the long years of anti-apartheid struggle in South Africa, this threshold became blurred as theatre and other arts practitioners called themselves "cultural workers" and acted in the firm belief that their work would not only bear witness to the atrocities of apartheid but also bring it down by beating artistic forms into cultural weapons with which to lead the Struggle.[1] In a country in which civil society and legitimate dissent had been uncivilly suppressed, performance and other arts provided an alternative public sphere in which those excluded from legitimate publicity and political representation might

[1] When Barbara Masakela, secretary for culture for the ANC in exile in the 1980s, used the terms "people's culture" and "cultural weapon" as synonyms at the Conference for Another South Africa in Amsterdam in 1989, this normative collocation of culture and agit-prop in the service of the Struggle (often capitalized) was ANC policy as well as the practice of anti-apartheid cultural workers in South Africa. Later that year, however, Albie Sachs, also of the ANC, delivered a speech in Lusaka that challenged the authority and the effectiveness of agit-prop. See Masakela's keynote address in *Culture in Another South Africa*, ed. Willem Campschreur and Joost Divendal (New York: Olive Branch Press, 1989); for Sachs's speech and a sample of South African responses, see *Spring is Rebellious: Arguments about Cultural Freedom by Albie Sachs and Respondents*, ed. Ingrid de Kok and Karen Press (Cape Town: Buchu Books, 1990).

represent themselves. Further, the urgency of this representation in the face of massive state violence diverted attention from tensions between assertions of political effectiveness and the unpredictable play of a performance on its participants and audiences. Instead, anti-apartheid activists, from Mulligan Mbikwana in the 1960s to the worker-poets and performers of the Culture and Working Life Project (CWLP) in the 1980s, argued that theirs was the art of "putting certain truths across to [the] people" or of making sense of the struggle "as it starts *coming* to you" when you wake up, "if it has let you sleep at all."[2]

Even at moments of great urgency, however, cultural organizations like CWLP paused to ponder the question of the art required to re-member the experience of struggle. Writing in 1990, as South Africa entered an interregnum between apartheid and the first democratically elected government which came to power in 1994, Nise Malange and CWLP colleagues returned by way of the "issue of quality" to the question of art:

> The issue of quality is important – what we need to be asking
> ourselves is . . . will these times we are living through be
> *remembered* through our work? . . . Will 1984–86 [the
> emergency] be remembered better, its tensions shown clearer,
> its darkness illuminated through our plays? Or will [they] be
> surface statements that need to be understood as poor
> products of the time?
>
> (Malange, 102)

Although this statement does not directly quote Brecht, its authors call for an acknowledgment of diverse and not always compatible popular traditions (Malange, 101) in language that echoes Brecht's call for popular practices that "make lively use of all means, old and new, tried and untried, deriving from art and from other sources, in order to put

---

[2] Mulligan Mbikwana, Letter to Athol Fugard, 18 April 1966 (AF: LL/IU: 1/13); Nise Malange and other members of the Culture and Working Life Group, "Albie Sachs Must Not Worry," in *Spring is Rebellious*, 99 [–106]; hereafter cited as Malange in the text.

reality in the hands of living people in a way in which it can be mastered."[3] Their rehabilitation of "quality" as part of the value of the cultural weapon also evokes Brecht's suggestion in the *Messingkauf Dialogues* that, if art is an instrument to right a world out of joint, it should be a delicate instrument, "a small knife" (*Werke* 22: 817), rather than a sword or the hammer that is often figuratively associated with proletarian culture.[4] As their figuration of the struggle suggests, CWLP members shared with Brecht and with other practitioners of critical theatre of instruction, argument, and social action such as Augusto Boal the long-standing Enlightenment conviction that culture should be part of the process not only of labor *working* life but also part of *waking* life, the activity of conscious, active, engaged individuals. However playful, theirs is a theatre of instruction that presupposes the capacity of actors to gain awareness of themselves as conscious agents of transformation, whether small changes of role or greater transformations of social structures, and thus also the transitive connection between the "subjunctive enactment" of theatre and the "indicative" effectiveness of social action.[5]

The impact of Brecht on theatres of instruction and social action in interregnum and post-apartheid South Africa has been more indirect than it was in the anti-apartheid years. Nonetheless theatre practitioners dedicated to enlightening actors and audiences about social ills, from the acute AIDS crisis to chronic but no less disruptive patterns of domestic violence, have continued in the belief, inherited from the Enlightenment tradition to which Brecht also belongs, that theatre and other forms of testimony necessarily enlighten participants and transform spectators into social actors.[6] In post-apartheid

---

[3] Brecht, "Volkstümlichkeit und Realismus," *Werke* 22: 410; "On the Popular and the Realistic," *BoT*, 110.

[4] Brecht, *The Messingkauf Dialogues*, trans. John Willett (London: Methuen, 1965), 94, has "scalpel," but Brecht has "kleines Messer."

[5] This articulation of the subjunctive action of socially critical fictions and the indicative action that its producers hope to provoke in actual practice draws on Raymond Williams's analysis of critical theater and media, in "Brecht and Beyond," 214–34.

[6] Whether under the rubric of activist theatre or, more recently, that of theatre in education (TIE) or theatre for development (TfD), theatre for

South Africa, however, especially in the wake of the Truth and Reconciliation Commission (TRC, 1996–2000), this belief has been challenged by traumatic testimony whose silences block the Enlightenment project of illumination through rational speech.[7] The accounts

social action in South Africa deals with pressing issues, from the
domestic abuse of children and women to the imposition of
fundamentalist religion to prejudice against foreigners to the
overwhelming AIDS crisis, as well as issues more conventionally
associated with TIE (education, socialization, the interpretation of the
past and present) or TfD (distribution of resources, including clinical
and social resources needed to tackle AIDS and other public health
problems). The influence of Brecht has made itself felt through
instruction, as many theatre activists received training from formal
programs at universities or non-formal instruction from institutions
like the Market Theatre Laboratory, whose organizers, such as
Malcolm Purkey or Ramolao Makhene, had worked with Brechtian
techniques and principles, as well as syncretic local workshop forms
developed at the Market Theatre and elsewhere. Since the 1990s this
influence has been leavened by interest in the work of Augusto Boal,
whose forum theatre and theatre therapy techniques have been
modified for local conditions. See Loren Kruger and Patricia Watson
Shariff, "'Shoo – this book makes me to think!': Education,
Entertainment, and 'Life-Skills Comics' in South Africa," *Poetics
Today* 22 (2001), 475–513; Gay Morris, "Reconsidering Theatre Making
in South Africa: A Study of Theatre in Education in Cape Schools,"
Theatre Research International, 289–305; Stephanie Marlin-Curiel,
"Long Road to Healing: From the TRC to TfD," *Theatre Research
International* 27: 3 (2002); and Zakes Mda, "South African Theatre in
an Era of Reconciliation," in *The Performance Arts in Africa*, ed.
Frances Harding (London: Routledge, 2002), 279–89.

7 The TRC hearings opened in 1996 and ended after an extension of the
deadline for amnesty applications in 2000. The official Final Report,
published before the conclusion of the amnesty hearings in South
Africa in 1998 and abroad in 1999, thus reflects the findings of the
Human Rights Violation Committee, which heard the testimony of
victims, but does not take full account of the findings of the Amnesty
Committee, which concluded its deliberations only in May 2001, well
after the hearings had ended. Hearings were led by seventeen
commissioners who represented diverse ethnic groups and political
positions, including those within the old regime and those

of more than seven thousand perpetrators to the Amnesty Committee, the testimony of more than twenty thousand survivors to the Human Rights Violations (HRV) Committee, and the trauma relived by many survivors during and after their testimony have challenged experts and activists, from the clergymen who chaired the TRC, Archbishop Desmond Tutu and the Rev. Alex Boraine, to therapists working with survivors and perpetrators, to theatre groups collaborating with survivors, with or without contributions from such experts, to review the presumption that testimony necessarily empowers its subjects, enlightens its audiences, or regenerates the capacity of either or both to act as whole persons or social agents. Therapists working with survivors of physical and psychic trauma, particularly those who have been called upon publicly to testify about their experiences after years of silence, have argued that "the price of speaking [may be] *re-living*; not relief but further retraumatization," unless the survivor can externalize and *narrativize* the event by bearing witness to attentive listeners, and the listener in turn does not block the process of reciprocal attention by succumbing to the defenses of withdrawal or hyper-emotionality.[8] All stakeholders have thus had to revise received anti-apartheid practices of testimonial performance that were conceived as the conscious expression of waking life so as better to represent and to transform the return of the repressed.

Theatre practitioners attempting to make theatre out of such testimony have had to tackle the moral ambiguity, the phenomenological difficulty, and the artistic limitations of making a witness into a performer. The moral problem is clear in the risk of exposing witnesses to retraumatization or exploitation or that of inflating the notoriety of perpetrators by reiterating their sensational accounts.

representing the new. Although the group included human rights lawyers, its chair and vice-chair were clergymen: Desmond Tutu, former Anglican Archbishop of Cape Town and Nobel Peace Prize laureate and the Rev. Alex Boraine, now with the Institute for Transitional Justice in New York.

[8] Dori Laub, "Bearing Witness," in Shoshana Felman and Dori Laub, *Testimony: Crises of Witnessing in Literature, Psychoanalysis, and History* (New York: Routledge, 1992), 57–74; here: 67 and 72.

The phenomenological problem emerges out of the incommunicable character of suffering. As Elaine Scarry reminds us, pain is the most unshareable of sensations: "what pain achieves, it achieves in part through its unshareability, and it ensures its unshareability in part through its resistance to language," including, I would add, to the physical and gestural language of performance.[9] A related epistemological problem comes out of the difficulty of adjudicating the truth of the most seemingly sincere perpetrator's expression of remorse. As philosopher Antony Holiday suggests, the "sincerity test" presumes that intimate emotional states can be directly translated into public declarations without taking the deliberate impersonation of remorse into account.[10] The artistic problem lies in the tension between the writer's or director's desire for authentic expression by real survivors and the recognition that these subjects do not necessarily make good interpreters of their experience, whether (as in the case of survivors) they are retraumatized by the act of retelling or (in the case of perpetrators) because their testimony may already be theatrical (sensational as well as possibly deceptive) enough to overwhelm the more subdued representation of suffering.

Making sense of the sensation and the memory of pain and of witnesses' difficulty in conveying its meaning constitutes the challenge for those who would perform it. Drawing from her work creating performances out of testimony by refugees from conflicts in the Balkans, Julie Salverson has argued that the experience of telling "stories of emergency and violation" can reiterate and reawaken the teller's repressed experience of violation while displaying an "erotics of injury" that may titillate rather than enlighten audiences who have not personally experienced comparable violation.[11] Even in the

---

9 Elaine Scarry, *The Body in Pain: The Making and Unmaking of the World* (New York: Oxford University Press, 1985), 4.

10 Antony Holiday, "Forgiving and Forgetting: The Truth and Reconciliation Commission," in *Negotiating the Past: The Making of Memory in South Africa*, ed. Sarah Nuttall and Carli Coetzee (Cape Town: Oxford University Press, 1998), 47–56; here: 52–4.

11 Julie Salverson, "Change on Whose Terms? Testimony and an Erotics of Injury," *Theater* 31: 3 (2001), 119–25.

hands of an experienced practitioner, anti-apartheid forms of emphatic testimony that invite similarly emphatic vocal solidarity from audiences have proved inadequate vessels for containing and processing retraumatization. Bongani Linda, a former student of Malcolm Purkey, Barney Simon, and other practitioners of Brechtian pedagogy, made this discovery as director of the Victory/Sonqoba Theatre, a community theatre with aspirations to tackle popular responses to the TRC, when his actors proved unable to impersonate dead and "disappeared" comrades in the face of retraumatized family members of the deceased.[12] Confronting the eruption of trauma into the waking life of survivors – and also the risk that the listener will withdraw in defense or reduce the testimony to a spectacle – demands forms and skills of performance and witnessing that have so far only haunted the dreams of practitioners of enlightened pedagogy through theatre.

The breakdown of an authoritative anti-apartheid pedagogy of the oppressed and the uncertain steps towards an art of witnessing that might deal delicately with apartheid trauma are themselves testimony to South Africa's incomplete liberation from the past and to its citizens' hesitation in the antechamber to the future. In order to understand the structuring absences of this state of uncertainty, and thus also the challenges confronted by actors who attempt both to perform fictions and to act in and on society, this final chapter shifts ground from the mobilizing and educational (or, in the historical

[12] For Linda's training and early work, including the dramatization of assigned public school texts such as Alan Paton's rather sentimental and, for many black intellectuals, patronizing novel *Cry the Beloved Country* (1948), see David le Page, "The Play's the Thing," *Johannesburg Mail and Guardian* (hereafter *M and G*) (26 May 1995); accessed 13 April 2003, http://archive.mg.co.za; for his ongoing work with community theatre, especially in Alexandra, a slum close to Johannesburg's wealthiest areas, see Reggy Moalusi, "Back to Basics," *M and G* (20 March 2003); accessed 13 April 2003, http://www.chico.mweb.co.za/art/2003/2003mar/030314-basics.html; confirmed by his teacher Malcolm Purkey on November 19, 2002. For commentary on Linda'a dramatization of responses to the TRC, *Thetha ngikhulume* (Speak that I may speak), see Marlin-Curiel, "Long Road to Healing," 282–5.

terms of political theatre, agitational and pedagogic) performances that characterized the anti-apartheid movement in South Africa as well as dramatizations of solidarity with that movement in apparently unlikely contexts such as East Germany. It focuses instead on the troubled intersections between theatre and testimony, actors and witnesses, spectators and collaborators, in the proceedings of the TRC hearings, and in performances around and about the TRC. This shift risks undermining the authority of Brecht's pedagogical enterprise or what I have called the *theatre of waking life*, but it is a risk that must be taken. We can evaluate the power of Brecht's project of enlightenment through theatre only if we appreciate its limits. A theatre of waking life may not fully illuminate the shadowy performances of apartheid's perpetrators or give those who survived infallible means to act, but attending to both the potential and the pitfalls of such a theatre should highlight the value of working the frontier between the speech of survivors and the speech of perpetrators.

The TRC as moral institution or theatre of national instruction

To compare the TRC with theatre, even with the dignified "moral institution" which Friedrich Schiller hoped would assemble (summon and create) the nation under its "mild rays," might seem to confirm the attacks of those who argued at the time that the public display of fake remorse by unrepentant perpetrators circumvented, if it did not utterly travesty, justice that might have come through prosecution.[13]

---

[13] Friedrich Schiller, "Was kann eine stehende Bühne eigentlich wirken? Das Theater als moralische Anstalt," in *Werke* (Munich: Hanser, 1984), 1: 694–729; trans. "What can a Stable Theatre Actually Achieve? Theatre as Moral Institution," in *German and Dutch Theatre: 1660–1848*, ed. George Brandt (Cambridge University Press, 1991), 200–22. Among the most vocal opponents of amnesty were the families of activists such as Stephen Biko and Griffiths and Victoria Mxenge, who were brutally murdered by the apartheid security forces. In "Amnesty and Denial," in *Looking Back, Reaching Forward: Reflections on the Truth and Reconciliation Commission of South Africa*, ed. Charles Villa-Vincencio and Wilhelm Verwoerd (Cape

Nonetheless, the TRC had both dramatic and theatrical elements that contributed to the power of its revelation and representation of pasts and presents repressed. Before the TRC began its public proceedings in mid-1996, debates about the staging of the hearings, from their geographical location to the placement of commissioners relative to the designated witness and of both to the professional observers from the media as well as onlookers, viewers or listeners variously constituted as "the public," implicitly acknowledged the theatrical dimension of the event. Although the hearings drew on established rituals – from the courtroom procedures for cross-examining witnesses to the Christian custom of consecrating the space through prayer, they also invented others, such as placing the commissioners at the same level as their interlocutors, allowing victims to cross-examine their tormentors, and praising both testifying victims and confessing perpetrators for their sincerity and courage.[14] Further, the commission's commitment to public airing of the voices of victims as well as perpetrators required the engagement of translators, who had to perform

Town: University of Cape Town Press, 2000), 193–8, Nkosinathi Biko argued that the contempt shown the TRC by high-ranking apartheid officials such as the former president. P. W. Botha, who refused to respond to subpoenas, and the indifference to the victims' testimony by many white South Africans, cast doubt on the TRC's execution of its mandate to facilitate understanding and reconciliation.

[14] A photograph of the first hearing on 15 April 1996, in East London, main city of the so-called Border region, site since the eighteenth century of clashes between colonizers and indigenous peoples, shows the seventeen commissioners seated in a crescent-shaped formation in front of a stage and facing in the first instance a witness seated at a table on the same level, with some other observers just visible behind her. See Truth and Reconciliation Commission of South Africa, *TRC Report* (London: Macmillan, 1999), vol. 1, between pp. 44 and 45. The *TRC Report* refers to witnesses who survived human rights violations as victims rather than survivors in order to highlight the "intention and action of the perpetrators" that created victims (1, ch. 4, para. 38), but witness organizations prefer the term "survivor." To facilitate access to both printed and CD-Rom editions of the *TRC Report*, citations refer to paragraph rather than page numbers.

the role of each speaker by representing his or her words in the first person albeit in a second language.

This syncretic assemblage from different rituals had thus to be continually reformed. The attempt to invent a new kind of truth commission was a source of the TRC's legitimacy, but also of its unpredictability. Unlike the limited truth commissions of Chile and Guatemala, which acted in secret and left the impunity of perpetrators largely intact, the South African TRC used its authority first to subpoena perpetrators publicly to answer their victims as well as the appointed representatives of the post-apartheid government, and finally to deny amnesty to more than ninety percent of applicants.[15] Rather than the settled character of church, especially Anglican, liturgy or established legal procedure in which the outcome, as in a trial, may be unknown but the arc of the event from the hearing of evidence to the weighing of that evidence in judgment is predictable, the TRC hearings had more of the risky character of an experimental theatre in which participants might at any time break the rules. Speakers could and did depart from prepared scripts (statements submitted to the TRC), by drawing in interrogators, whether commissioners or survivors, to rehearse roles from their pasts. The most notorious case was a Terrorism Detection Unit officer, Jeffrey Benzien, who replayed his torture methods on unnamed volunteers in front of named victims and

---

[15] The Amnesty Committee granted amnesty to 849 perpetrators and denied amnesty to 5392; see the Amnesty Index page at the Truth and Reconciliation Commission website at http://www.doj.gov.za/trc/ amntrans/index.htm, retrieved 31 March 2003. For comparisons between the South African TRC and truth commissions in Latin America and elsewhere, see Priscilla Hayner, "Same Species, Different Animal: How the TRC Compares to Truth Commissions Worldwide," in Looking Back, Reaching Forward, 32–41; Robert I. Rotberg, "Truth Commissions and the Provision of Truth, Justice, and Reconciliation"; Amy Gutmann and Dennis Thompson, "The Moral Foundations of Truth Commissions"; and David A. Crocker, "Truth Commissions, Transitional Justice, and Civil Society," in Truth v. Justice: The Morality of Truth Commissions, ed. R. I. Rotberg and D. Thompson (Princeton University Press, 2000), 3–21, 22–44, and 99–121.

members of the commission at his hearing before the Amnesty Committee. In many cases victims recounting their experiences before the Human Rights Committee broke down into speechlessness that the hearing and the commissioners' expressions of sympathy could not easily overcome.

Complicating the theatricality of unpredictable forms, improvised departure from prepared scripts, and unexpected denouements was a certain dramatic element in the conflict between guiding concepts of truth, especially between the singular forensic truth of the law and a multitude of subjective truths invoked by the TRC. The Final Report invokes a singular idea of "the truth" when arguing for the efficacy of the commission: "the Commission was founded . . . in the belief that . . . telling the truth about past gross human rights violations, as viewed from different perspectives, facilitates the process of understanding our divided pasts, while the public acknowledgment of 'untold suffering and injustice' . . . helps to restore the dignity of victims and afford perpetrators the opportunity to come to terms with their own past." It goes on, however, to describe the Commission's mandate in terms that highlight potential conflict among multiple truths, from forensic truth, through personal and narrative truth, to an ideal but as yet unrealized consensual social truth, as well as the "healing potential of telling stories."[16] This argument concedes the relative (if not the fictional) character of personal truths, but also emphasizes the dramatic power of storytelling. Testimony could involve not only the revelation of facts – deaths, disappearances, acts of betrayal – suppressed above all by the apartheid state and its agents and to a lesser extent by the liberation movements, but also a cathartic resolution for individuals, families and political associates – the clarification and closure of life-histories left unfinished by disappearance or unexplained death. Although the Commission initially hoped that this resolution would provide the basis for reconciliation on the national level, it acknowledged the concerns of those who regarded the Christian notion of reconciliation "associated with contrition, confession, forgiveness, and restitution" as an imposition on a "diverse

[16] *TRC Report*, vol. I, ch. 4, para. 3, and ch. 5, paras. 29–45.

and divided society" and revised the report to call more modestly for "respect for human dignity and shared citizenship."[17]

The TRC Report made no explicit comparison between the Commission's proceedings and those of theatre. Indeed, its mission to reveal the truth about victims' suffering and the enormity of perpetrators' atrocities could not countenance an association with the make-believe associated with the stage. Nonetheless, a number of elements invite theatrical analysis. Although the official transcripts present all testimony in English, regardless of the many languages used by the witnesses, observations by and about translators highlight their difficult role as impersonators. In Tutu's account, translators may have been physically separated from their subjects, as they spoke in a glass booth on the edge of the hearing space, but they were nonetheless overwhelmed by the conflicting demands of "switching identities, speaking now for a victim, then for a perpetrator, and for both in the first person."[18] Translators were well aware that their

[17] *TRC Report*, vol. 1, ch. 4, para. 4; ch. 5, paras. 16–28. Skepticism about the transformation of individual acts of forgiveness into a national project of reconciliation was raised early – not only by those who, like the Biko and Mxenge families, wanted perpetrators to face cross-examination and criminal penalties in a court of law, but also by those who had moral as well as political objections to the imposition of a theology of individual forgiveness on collective action and national policy. For the defense of forgiveness as a national goal if not national policy, see Desmond Mpilo Tutu, *No Future without Forgiveness* (New York: Doubleday, 1999); for a philosophical critique of the slippage between forgiving and forgetting, see Holiday, "Forgiving and Forgetting," 47–56; for a liberal political critique of the capacity for reconciliation to deal with deep divisions exacerbated by the revelations, see Frederick van Zyl Slabbert, "Truth without Reconciliation: Reconciliation without Truth," in *After the TRC: Reflections on Truth and Reconciliation in South Africa* (Cape Town: David Philip, 2000), 62–72; for an ANC defense of the struggle as a just war, see Kadar Asmal, Louise Asmal, and Robert Suresh Roberts, "When the Assassin Cries Foul: The Modern Just War Doctrine," in *Looking Back, Reaching Forward*, 86–98.

[18] Tutu, *No Future*, 286. Witnesses used all the official languages of South Africa: in alphabetical order, Afrikaans, English, Ndebele, North

work involved not only impersonation but also sympathetic reflexes. As Lebohang Matibela noted, "it's quite interesting to sit in that booth. You're aware that you're becoming an actor but . . . unconsciously you end up throwing up your hands as he throws his; you end up nodding as he nods." At the same time, they could not forget the difficulty of making sense of another's sensation: "it becomes difficult to interpret when they are crying."[19] The smoothly edited English dialogue of the transcripts omits not only the nuances of other languages but also a range of interruptions, from throat-clearing to complete collapse, and thus occludes aural and visual signs that contributed in the live hearings, as well as radio and television broadcasts, to the meaning and significance of testimony.[20]

Sotho, South Sotho, Pedi, Tsonga, Tswana, Venda, and Zulu – in addition to sign language, and Polish in the single case of Janusz Walus, the assassin hired to kill SACP leader Chris Hani.

[19] Lebohang Matibela, quoted in Antjie Krog, *Country of My Skull: Guilt, Sorrow, and the Limits of Forgiveness in the New South Africa* (Johannesburg: Random House S.A., 1998), 290.

[20] Heidi Grunebaum and Steve Robins provide a rare glimpse into the mediation of embodied testimomy by way of radio in their analysis of the testimony of Zahrah Narkedien: see their "Crossing the Colour(ed) Line: Mediating the Ambiguities of Belonging and Identity," in *Coloured by History, Shaped by Place*, ed. Zimitri Erasmus (Cape Town: Kwela Press, 2001), 159–72. Narkedien (formerly Greta Appelgren) was detained and tortured under Section 29 of the Internal Security Act, and sentenced to nine years in prison on five counts of alleged terrorism. While in prison, she was the object of sexual aggression by a fellow prisoner and former comrade who, once rejected, denounced Narkedien as a "gangster" and trouble-maker to prison guards, who sent her into solitary confinement for seven months. At the hearing, Narkedien punctuated this account of the collusion between black prisoner and white guard against herself as "coloured" with intense emotion: "I was so disturbed but I would never, never let the wardresses know [breaks down and cries]": quoted by Grunebaum and Robins, "Crossing," 165. The printed transcript acknowledges the witness's tears only through chairperson Mdu Dhlamini's interjection "Take it easy, Zahrah," but it does retain the emphatic second "never" in the foregoing sentence: see Truth and

The gest of disclosure: on the power and power failure of testimonial performance

The impact of the hearings, and more broadly of the process and procedures of the TRC on a still divided nation, emerged not only out of this documentation but also out of the power – and the *power failures* – of the performances whose traces are invisible but still palpable in the official print and electronic record. As Peggy Phelan writes, "performance disappears into memory" even as it "plunges into visibility."[21] In the TRC hearings, witnesses "plunged" into public audibility as well as visibility; individual speakers came to embody typical, even stereotypical, roles, as imposed on them by the media. At one extreme, the most notorious death squad commander, Eugene de Kock, was dubbed "Prime Evil" in a South African Broadcasting Company documentary – allegedly by his cronies invoking the *Ninja Turtles*, and thereafter by journalists reporting on his criminal trial and subsequent TRC hearing.[22] At the other, a sheep farmer and rural patriarch,

Reconciliation Commission, *Special Hearings: Prisons: Mrs Zahrah Narkedien; case #JB04418*; accessed 13 April 2003 at http://www. doj.gov.za/trc/special/prison/narkedie.htm.

[21] Peggy Phelan, *Unmarked: The Politics of Performance* (New York: Routledge, 1993), 148.

[22] From 1986 to 1993, de Kock ran the security force's most notorious death squad, based at Vlakplaas. The squad tortured and killed not only anti-apartheid activists but also their own black subordinates who knew of the white officers' fraudulent deals and assaults on bystanders in the conflict. After a long trial lasting from February 1995 to October 1996, de Kock was sentenced initially to 212 years, but later received a partial amnesty for conspiring to bomb the SACP London office and for the so-called Parker Pen Bomb Incident – but not for the torture, executions, and gun running out of Vlakplaas. For the trial and de Kock's revelations, see Martin Meredith, *Coming to Terms: South Africa's Search for Truth* (New York: Public Affairs, 1999), 27–72; for the amnesty application and results, see Truth and Reconciliation Commission, *Amnesty Decisions 1999b; Case no. ac990292*; http://www.doj.gov.za/trc/decisions/1999/ac990292.htm and TRC, *Amnesty Decisions 2001; Case no. ac21002*; http://www.doj.gov.za/trc/decisions/2001/ac21002.htm, accessed

Lekotse, who survived the assault of security police investigating his
son's alleged association with the African Peoples' Liberation Army,
appears in journalist and poet Antjie Krog's vivid, moving, and controversial reflection on the experience of reporting the TRC hearings as
the narrator of a "Shepherd's Tale," an epic verse rendering in English
of Matibela's translation of Lekotse's Sotho account of the police violation of his house, his dignity, and the integrity of his person.[23] Some-
where in between, Owen McGregor, a young white man, presented a
statement in the voice of his brother, who died in unexplained circumstances as a conscript in the South African Army's assault on alleged
terrorists in Namibia.[24] These and other embodiments almost vanished, leaving minimal traces in the TRC transcripts, however, since
the texts, translated into a neutral English, erased the pauses, hesita-
tions, and outright breakdowns that punctuated, if they did not completely puncture, the hearings. Further, witnesses who contested the
roles assigned to them in media reports had no public stage equivalent
to the hearings on which to enact alternative roles, but had instead to
resort to print and thus to a delayed and disembodied rejoinder to this
public characterization.

1 April 2001. Jacques Pauw's documentary *Prime Evil* was aired on
SABC 1 in October 1996, just before de Kock's sentencing and well
before he appeared before the TRC in 1999. Miki Flockemann quotes
the connection to the *Ninja Turtles* in "White Men with Weapons;
Black Women with Dresses: The TRC and Refashioning Myths of
Identity," *Journal of Theatre and Drama* 4 (1998): 7–22, here: 14.

[23] Krog, *Country of My Skull*, 278–85. Krog's account was controversial
in part because she equipped witnesses with personas like this one and
because she edited testimony gathered during her tenure as TRC
reporter for SABC Radio to highlight what she perceived to be the
witness's emotional state. For a witness's critique of this editorial
intervention, see Yazir Henry, "Where Healing Begins," in *Looking
Back, Reaching Forward*, 163–83.

[24] For an extract from this statement and an account of its presentation,
see comments by a former HRV committee member and practicing
psychotherapist, Pumla Gobodo-Madikizela: *A Human Being Died
That Night: A South African Story of Forgiveness* (Boston: Houghton
Mifflin, 2003), 111–13.

At issue here is not merely the effacement of emotion or of the presumably sincere expression of feeling, whether remorse on the part of the perpetrator or pain on the part of the survivor, but also the erasure of the *gestic* dimension of testimony. "Gestic" here ought to mean not only Brecht's Enlightenment sense of the conscious purpose and point of view (*Absicht* and *Ansicht, Werke* 23: 86) of the speaker towards her testimony but also the anti-Enlightenment gest of deception, especially of faked remorse. It might also be extended to include expressions that elude the clear articulation of the enlightened consciousness: the gest of an inchoate or blocked recollection of experience or that of an account of experience that the speaker insistently repeats, even after witnesses challenge this version of events. This extension brings with it the difficult adjudication between competing gests, between contrition and deception, inadvertent betrayal under torture or unforgivable disloyalty to the cause. While the testimony of victims certainly raised political questions about the new state's responsibilities vis-à-vis nation building and reparations and moral questions about the responsibilities of South Africans who might not have perpetrated violence but who benefitted from apartheid, it did not raise difficulties of belief. With very few exceptions, the testimony of victims and survivors could be taken as sincere, their gests as the transparent expression of suffering. In contrast, perpetrators' testimony raised precisely this difficulty of belief. While the problem of perpetrators' sincerity or fakery did not undo the TRC's fundamental distinction between perpetrators (especially those representing the apartheid state) and victims of human rights violations, especially those suffering violations at the hands of state operatives, it casts a shadow on the Commission's faith, Enlightened and Christian, in the power of full disclosure in combination with sincere remorse to constitute the testimony of waking life, to reveal the truth and provide resolution if not reconciliation.

Among the perpetrators, the case of Jeffrey Benzien presents an exception to the anger of many petitioners, such as de Kock, who called down blame on the highest apartheid officers, such as the former president, F. W. de Klerk, who denied knowing anything of the death squads.[25] Benzien's conduct also offers the most telling instance of the difficult discrimination between this testimony of waking life, the enlightened and enlightening act of full disclosure, and the expression of its shadow, in the blocked and fragmented recollection attributed to post-traumatic memory. Benzien followed the requirements of the TRC Act by basing his claim for amnesty on an assertion of full disclosure and sincere remorse for acts of torture and other violations that he committed as an officer in the Terrorism Detection Unit in the Cape Peninsula from 1986 to 1990. After the Internal Security Act of 1982 permitted detention for an indefinite period or until the "Commissioner of Police determine[d] that the detainee ha[d] satisfactorily replied to all questions at the interrogation and that no useful purpose w[ould] be served by his [sic] detention," women as well as men were routinely subjected to physical trauma, from electric shocks to near-suffocation, and to psychological torture such as threats to their families.[26] Benzien claimed himself to be suffering from flashbacks, dissociation, and other symptoms of post-traumatic stress, but both disclosure and amnesty were challenged not only by victims, who testified to suffering torture at Benzien's hands that he did not recall perpetrating against them, but also by inconsistencies in Benzien's own testimony. On some occasions, he asserted that he did not remember using a specific device on a particular individual; on others, he denied that the event ever took place. In contrast, he sometimes conceded that, despite his own lack of recall, his challenger's account of the experience of torture was probably right. His apparent inability

---

[25] De Kock's revelations implicated many more security policemen who had hitherto refused to testify. By compelling his colleagues to apply for amnesty, de Kock helped to expose the truth about hundreds of victims. In prison, de Kock's anger has evolved into remorse, expressed in contact with the widows of some of the men he tortured and killed and in extended conversations with Pumla Gobodo-Madikizela (documented in *A Human Being Died That Night*).

[26] Internal Security Act 74 of 1982, s.29(1)(i). For further analysis of this legislation, see Stephen Ellman, *In a Time of Trouble: Law and Liberty in South Africa's State of Emergency* (Oxford: Clarendon Press, 1992), 15.

to remember acts of torture experienced by witnesses was interpreted by his attending psychologist as a symptom of post-traumatic stress disorder (PTSD), but this was contested by the attorneys for survivors and for the family of an activist killed by Benzien's gun, who argued that Benzien's behavior could be seen as deliberate malingering rather than as the involuntary manifestation of post-traumatic stress.[27]

The intervention of Benzien's psychologist, Ria Kotzé, cut across this conflict between the truth or falsehood of Benzien's statement but did not resolve it. In her view, Benzien's PTSD was manifested in involuntary memory blockage in general – "when confronted with severe trauma, patients block out negative experiences . . . in an unconscious effort to forget unpleasant detail" – and "tunnel memory" in particular – "he could remember certain aspects of the situation and had no recollection of others . . . specifically . . . his memories regarding the interrogation of people."[28] Noting in

[27] Before 1986 Benzien had been a member of the Murder and Robbery squad and commended for his investigative skill; he was not introduced to torture as a means of extracting information until he joined the Anti-Terrorist Unit. For Benzien's testimony and cross-examination by victims – Anwar Dramat, Ashley Forbes, Peter Jacobs, Nico Pedro, Tony Yengeni, and Gary Kruse – and victims' counsel, including counsel for the family of Ashley Kriel, whom Benzien killed while arresting him, see Truth and Reconciliation Commission, *Amnesty Hearing: Jeffrey Benzien*, 14–16 July 1997; accessed on 26 March 2003 at http://www.doj.gov.za/trc/amntrans/ct3/benzien.htm. These men represented a fraction of those who were tortured at the Culemborg Police Station.

[28] At the hearing (see TRC, *Amnesty Hearing: Jeffrey Benzien*, 20 October 1997; accessed on 13 April 2003 at http://www.doj.gov.za/trc/amntrans/ct4/benzien3.htm), the psychologist Sarah Maria Kotzé cited her own report as well as the standard *Diagnostic and Statistical Manual of Mental Disorders (DSM)*, 4th edn (Washington: American Psychiatric Association, 1994), 424–9. Symptoms referenced in the manual included the "avoidance of stimuli associated with the trauma" and "numbing of responses," including the "inability to recall important aspects of the trauma" and avoiding "places or people that arouse recollections of the trauma" (*DSM*, 428). The literature on PTSD and torture deals exclusively with victims. While this priority

cross-examination that the standard diagnosis is applied to victims, to people who have both (1) "experienced, witnessed or confronted . . . actual or threatened death . . . or a threat to the physical integrity" and (2) responded with "intense fear, helplessness, or horror" (*DSM*, 427–8) and that "malingering should be ruled out in those situations in which . . . forensic determinations play a role" (427), the advocate Michael Donan, who represented two of Benzien's victims, argued for a fundamental distinction between "helpless victims" of torture and a perpetrator who was not under immediate threat but who "might stop at any time." Donan argued that there were several levels of contradiction in Benzien's testimony. He argued first that there were local contradictions between Benzien's emphatic denial that he had assaulted particular individuals and his claim at other moments that he could not remember one way or the other, and secondly that there were discrepancies over the long term between Benzien's apparently firm loyalty to the Security Forces in his perjured statements at key trials of alleged terrorists in the 1980s and the "onset" of symptoms – from flashbacks to self-loathing – much later in 1994. The second point led in turn to the implication that Benzien's anxiety or, less generously, malingering, could have been triggered by the threat of investigation in

makes sense from a therapeutic as well as moral standpoint, it does not provide resources for analyzing either the pathological effects of torture on torturers or the differential structure of *social* repression. These structures might include normative taboos that allowed remembrance and the public mention of certain kinds of torture but not others, such as the use of a cattle prod for anal penetration, which Benzien repeatedly denied using on all but one of his detainees, or the unacknowledged influence of Afrikaner ethnic loyalty, especially under threat by the TRC, on Kotzé's defense of Benzien. Although dealing with the very different case of Argentina, Diana Taylor's *Disappearing Acts: Spectacles of Gender and Nationalism in Argentina's Dirty War* (Durham, NC: Duke University Press, 1997), 151–57, marshals the resources of gender and performance studies to show how the hyper-masculinity of Argentinian military culture made the brutal feminization of male detainees into an essential step in the validation of the torturer's identity, not only as a masculine agent but also as a legitimate national subject.

the new South Africa.[29] Despite these arguments and despite Benzien's acknowledgment that he had committed perjury by denying claims of torture at the 1988 terrorism trial of a key detainee who was ironically to become Benzien's superior in the post-apartheid police force, the Amnesty Committee accepted his assertion of "full disclosure" and read his conduct as the execution of the "political objective" of "defending the state against its enemies" and duly granted him amnesty in 1999.[30]

Making and defending a distinction between the sanctioned performance of disclosure and remorse and an ineffable authenticity of expression will not reconcile opposing views on Benzien or other perpetrators, but it may provide a provisional frame for evaluating

[29] Donan quoted directly from the *Diagnostic and Statistical Manual* during cross-examination of Kotzé on 20 October 1997. Although officially he represented only Dramat and Pedro, Donan's closing argument that Benzien's violations of human rights constituted an international crime in terms of the UN Convention on Cruel and Inhuman Punishment (1984) applied to his conduct towards all detainees. This argument was granted general validity in the amnesty decision, which acknowledged the description of Benzien's conduct as "gross violations of human rights" under the Convention but still concluded on the imperative to grant amnesty to those offering full disclosure of violations with political objectives. See TRC, *Amnesty Decisions 1999: AC/99/0027*, at http://www.doj.gov.za/trc/decisions/1999/99Benzien.html.

[30] Ibid. Benzien received amnesty for Kriel's death, for the torture of Dramat, Forbes, Jacobs, Pedro, Yengeni, and Kruse, and for his perjury in disavowing torture at Kruse's terrorism trial and at the inquest into Kriel's death. At the time of the hearings, Kruse had become a director in the police force and thus Benzien's superior officer; Benzien acknowledged on the first day of his TRC testimony (14 July, p.m.) that he perjured himself at Gary Kruse's terrorism trial by denying to the court that he used torture to extract information. The amnesty decision recapitulates Benzien's known and alleged acts for which he claimed amnesty, but concludes that Benzien acted as part of the anti-terrorist unit, which was itself "part of the machinery of state" and thus that his actions "related to a political objective." Discrepancies between victims' assertions in particular cases were mentioned but not adjudicated.

356

this testimony. Any replay of Benzien's testimony has to deal with its most spectacular and disturbing aspect: on the one hand, his re-enactment at the public hearing of the so-called wet-bag method, the near-suffocation of a prisoner by pulling a wet canvas bag over the head for the stated purpose of extracting information; and on the other, his disavowal of the anal prod, which raised questions about sexual degradation that neither male witnesses nor commissioners confronted directly.[31] Benzien denied using the latter instrument on victims who nonetheless claimed to have suffered by it, and in so denying also disavowed the sexual element, not only in the act of torture but also in the hyper-masculine conditioning that reinforced demands for displays of toughness and loyalty among members of the terrorism unit, which was rewarded in the case of Benzien with medals hitherto reserved for soldiers in combat against guerrillas beyond South Africa's borders.[32] He nonetheless avowed to Tony Yengeni, the first victim

---

[31] Special hearings for women and the gendered specificity of human rights violations experienced by them did take place at the urging of two researchers at the Centre for Applied Legal Studies in Johannesburg, Beth Goldblatt and Sheila Meintjies, who submitted a report to the Commission on Gender and the Truth and Reconciliation Commission in May 1996, *in advance* of the general hearings. Despite this official sanction of gender specificity, witnesses and commissioners alike were unwilling to deal with charges of rape and sexual abuse outside the narrow purview of anti-apartheid activists abused in prison by agents of the apartheid state. On the one hand, women were extremely reluctant to testify to rape by fellow activists in exile or in the townships; on the other, men proved unable to describe assault by anal prods as rape, possibly because to do so would risk emasculation and thus loss of status in the still highly macho culture of the "comrades." See Beth Goldblatt and Sheila Meintjies, *Gender and the Truth and Reconciliation Commission* (May 1996), at http://www.doj.gov.za/trc/submit/gender.htm and Krog, *Country of My Skull*, 233–50.

[32] Benzien admitted using this instrument on Peter Jacobs only, but Forbes, Yengeni, and Jonas all claimed that he had used it on them as well. Taylor's analysis of the conditioning of hitherto untrained soldiers in the arts of torture in the Argentinian "Dirty War," as the affirmation of the military male as the sole "legitimate national

to cross-examine him, that the wet-bag method was his acknowledged specialty, the use of which enabled him to extract information from detainees in less than thirty minutes. Benzien also agreed, under duress, to demonstrate the procedure: he straddled a volunteer who was lying on his stomach, covered the latter's head with the bag, and explained but did not execute the pattern of tightening and loosening the cord in full view of observers at the hearing and the television audience nationwide.

Although this demonstration followed an exchange in which Yengeni posed the question "What does this torture do to you as a human being?" and Benzien replied that he had asked himself that question because he was "losing his mind," Yengeni's submission that "it would be in the interests of the public and the Commission for you to demonstrate the use of this bag" and implication that it might reveal something about "the man behind the wet bag" was not in any simple way confirmed by the re-enactment itself.[33] The official transcript records the dialogue around the act, from the chairman's injunction that commissioners and others would "have to stand and have a look," to questions from several sources about Benzien's manipulation

protagonist" in a war against feminized "subversives" coded as "weak" as well as devious and dissembling, and the construction of the torture unit as the "elite corps" in this war (*Disappearing Acts*, 152–3), is illuminating here. The difference between an explicit celebration of military masculinity as an "aura of carnal exhalations" (ibid., 156) in the Argentine case and the reticence of both witnesses and examiners in the South African case is however also noteworthy; Calvinist strictures on public discussion of any sexual matters, and especially of anything coded as deviant, offer a sharp contrast to the macho transference of deviance solely to the subversive as proto-invert or *invertido*.

[33] Citations from the afternoon session of day one of Benzien's amnesty hearing, 14 July 1997, at http://www.doj.gov.za/trc/amntrans/ct3/benzien.htm. The historical import of this event has been complicated by Yengeni's subsequent career. A prominent ANC MP at the time of the TRC hearings, he was subsequently indicted for accepting bribes from arms dealers keen to influence parliament and was sentenced to four years in prison.

of near-suffocation to extract information about hidden weapons and comrades, to Yengeni's probing of the line of command and account-ability from the anti-terrorism unit to the cabinet level State Security Council. But it remains silent about the theatrical aspects of this dis-play, from Benzien's limited imitation of the actions prior to actual torture to the noise of commissioners, press, photographers, and others scrambling "so as not to miss the spectacle."[34] It includes Benzien's reply to Yengeni's question "How did I respond to you at the bag?", which foregrounded the ends of torture rather than suffering by it: "I cannot say how you reacted. I know that after the method was applied . . . you told us where your weaponry was," but not Yengeni's "choked voice" (Krog, *Country of My Skull*, 93). It also omits the reac-tion of the next witness, Ashley Forbes, who was allegedly "biting his upper lip" (*Country of My Skull*, 94) as Benzien answered his ques-tions about acts of torture repeated over several months to the point of attempted suicide by "conceding things [he] cannot remember," such as assaulting Forbes especially on the sixteenth of each month, the day of his arrest, and by remembering instead Forbes "playing in the snow on the N1" during a trip Benzien took him on to uncover arms caches.[35] It documents Benzien's verbal concessions to victims' mem-ories during the hearing but not his handshake with Forbes and his wife beforehand or his appearance in the same grey suit for three days and his tendency to remain alone in the chair during breaks. While Krog calls these instances of performance Benzien's "techniques" to "manipulate most of his victims back into their previous relation-ships" (*Country of My Skull*, 95), Albie Sachs, a Constitutional Court judge, anti-apartheid activist and victim of an apartheid government bomb, reads Benzien's "crying" during the wet-bag demonstration as sincere shame.[36] While commentators as authoritative as Sachs were moved by Benzien's "shame," those who had suffered at his hands did not see convincing evidence in this apparently "evident" outburst

[34] Krog, *Country of My Skull*, 93.
[35] Forbes's questions followed Yengeni's on 14 July 1997.
[36] Albie Sachs, "His Name Was Henry," in *After the TRC*, 94–100, here: 98; see also Van Zyl Slabbert, "Truth without Reconciliation," 69.

and opposed his amnesty on the grounds that, as Yazir Henry, former ANC activist, victim of Benzien's regime of torture, and now a docent (instructor) with the survivor-run Direct Action Centre for Peace and Memory in Cape Town, put it, his "actions were disproportionate to his political motivation."[37]

As these contradictory moments suggest, calling Benzien's appearance a performance does not automatically entail a set evaluation of its effects. The characterization itself implies neither that it was a malingering counterfeit of remorse nor, on the contrary, that it was a sincere expression of Benzien's true belief. Rather it highlights, in the first instance the amnesty committee's interpretation of his testimony as a *performative utterance*, not merely an expression of remorse or description of his state of mind but an act, in J. L. Austin's sense of an utterance that entails a transaction (in this case), of contrition that bound the Committee to grant amnesty, even though his disclosure did not match the accusations of victims; and in the second instance, the unresolved question of the truth or fiction of his enactment. The lack of resolution was registered in the skeptical responses of the legal advocates, who accused Benzien of malingering, and in the challenges voiced by the survivors, who argued that the memory loss was faked and thus the expression of remorse, in Austin's language,

[37] The Henry in Albie Sachs's title is the first name of an Afrikaner policeman from Potchefstroom, *not* the surname of Yazir Henry. Yazir Henry testified to torture by Benzien and his superiors at his own hearing before the HRV Committee but did not pose questions at Benzien's amnesty hearing the following year. For Henry's testimony, see TRC, *University of Western Cape Hearings. Case no. CT00405*, 14 August 1996, accessed on 1 April 2003 at http://www.doj.gov.za/trc/hrvtrans/henry/ct00405.htm. For his reasons for testifying on this occasion but not at Benzien's hearing, and for the cited comment on Benzien's case, see Y. Henry, "Where Healing Begins," in *Looking Back, Reaching Forward*, 170–1. As a docent with the Direct Action Centre, Henry works with other survivors to educate South Africans and others about the contradictory legacies and experiences of anti-apartheid struggles, including the experience of solidarity and its limits while in exile in sites from the Soviet Union and Eastern Europe to ANC camps in countries bordering South Africa.

was no more than an "insincere" or "impure" performative.[38] In this light, Benzien appeared to be merely an actor and a bad one at that. In contrast, the psychologist read Benzien's conduct, from his incomplete recall to his bouts of weeping, not as acting but as *acting out*, as the uncontrolled expression of the intrusive past erupting in the present.[39] In this light, Benzien's most truthful disclosure appears to be his exposure of the failure to disclose: the truth of his pathology lay in his simultaneous avowal and disavowal of his perpetration of the violence experienced by his victims. But this truth, like Benzien's unconscious, is inaccessible. If, as Cathy Caruth suggests, "PTSD is not so much a symptom of the unconscious as a symptom of history" because the traumatized "become symptoms of a history they cannot possess," we can argue that the radical loss of the history of power and of control over a present now beholden to the history of the formerly powerless provides the impulse that compels a man like Jeffrey Benzien to see himself, however incoherently and intermittently, as the monster his victims encountered.[40] The latter's objections notwithstanding, it may be the evidence of this radical recasting that brought the Amnesty Committee to acknowledge the *legitimacy* of his performance as a reason for amnesty, even if they could not adjudicate the authenticity of his trauma.

Confronted with the persistent ambiguity of offenders' testimony, we should not find it surprising that the first theatrical

[38] J. L. Austin posits a "performative utterance" as an utterance which performs an act or effects a transaction: see his *How to Do Things with Words* (Cambridge, MA: Harvard University Press, 1962), 6–7. Although he goes on to assert a distinction between true performatives and "impure" performatives or "part descriptions" such as "I am sorry" (83–5), he leaves untouched the problem of adjudicating between insincere expression and a performative utterance of contrition compelling enough to effect a binding transaction, in this case amnesty.

[39] See Bessel van der Kolk and Otto van der Hart, "The Intrusive Past: The Flexibility of Memory and the Engraving of Trauma," in *Trauma: Explorations in Memory*, ed. Cathy Caruth (Baltimore: Johns Hopkins University Press, 1995), 158–82.

[40] Caruth, Introduction to *Trauma*, 5.

responses to the TRC drew inspiration (if only in part) from the sensational exposés of the perpetrators. Well before Benzien's testimony, the high-profile shows of *Truth Omissions* (1996), satirist Pieter-Dirk Uys's updated imitation of key Afrikaner politicians in denial, and *Ubu and the Truth Commission* (1997), a multi-media collage of elements from Alfred Jarry's *Ubu* and the early TRC hearings by the Handspring Puppet Company, William Kentridge, and Jane Taylor, tackled ambiguously the ambiguous power and power failures of that notorious criminal, since Ubu was seen by many critics and spectators watching the play in 1997 as a stand-in for one of the most infamous perpetrators, Eugene de Kock, who was then on trial. In the latter, two actors played Ubu and his bully wife, and attacked with farcical but compelling violence the wooden puppets who, with their visible human handlers, represented victims and witnesses.[41] To a degree, as Kentridge, the director, argues, using puppets as a "medium through which the testimony c[ould] be heard" provided a way to represent witnesses without mimicking their pain and thus relieved the audience of the tension between "believing the actor for the sake of the story" and "not believing the actor for the sake of the actual witness" whose words were borrowed for the performance.[42] The figuration of testimony and suffering in the puppets and animations undeniably avoided what Kentridge described as the "awkwardness" of having actors play witnesses and so also mitigated, if it did not quite dispel, what Salverson calls the "lie of the literal," the assumption that testimony can be authentically and compellingly delivered only by the sufferer; but the

---

[41] See Jane Taylor *et al.*, *Ubu and the Truth Commission. From the production by William Kentridge and the Handspring Puppet Company* (Cape Town: University of Cape Town Press, 1998); for commentary on the puppets, see Yvette Coetzee, "Visibly Invisible: How shifting the conventions of the traditionally invisible puppeteer allows for more dimensions in both the puppeteer–puppet relationship and the creation of theatrical meaning in *Ubu and the Truth Commission*," *South African Theatre Journal* 12: 1–2 (1999): 35–51 and Kruger, "Making Sense of Sensation," especially 556–61.

[42] William Kentridge, "Director's Note," *Ubu and the Truth Commission*, xi.

puppets' moving depiction of suffering and testifying victims could not offset the stage dominance of the two human actors who not only played Pa and Ma Ubu but also impersonated unnamed perpetrators at the TRC.[43] Despite the absence of names from the TRC record, Dawid Minaar's Ubu was shadowed by de Kock's Prime Evil, whose combination of bravado and sullen blame of the higher-ups at his trial found its way into Ubu's repertoire. Amplified by media commentary on this association between Ubu and "Prime Evil," Minaar's stage persona threatened to overshadow the puppets and thus the play's answer to the director's ethical question "What is our responsibility to the people whose stories we are using?" Especially after Ubu's desultory confession "Remorse, I assure you, a helluva lot" and his departure into a sunset figured by a great animated eye on the horizon were followed by the national anthem and the familiar film footage of the Struggle, the ambiguous and fascinating figure of perpetrator in dirty underwear lapsed into cliché.[44] Instead of a Brechtian moment of "thinking behavior" that might have showed the "not/but" or a more probing treatment of the contradictions in the perpetrator's charisma (and especially in his sexual swagger highlighted by the dirty underwear), the play ended rather by letting Prime Evil drift into Banal Evil.[45] In

---

[43] Julie Salverson, "Performing Emergency: Popular Theatre and the Life of the Literal," *Theatre Topics* 6 (1996), 184. Even though Busi Zokufa also spoke the words of TRC translators on more than one occasion, she did so while still in her "Queen Ubu" costume and burlesque white face, and while speaking from a booth whose previous function as Ubu's shower and torture chamber interfered with the untroubled transmission of testimony.

[44] Kentridge, "Director's Note"; Taylor *et al.*, *Ubu and the Truth Commission*, 69–73.

[45] For "Banal Evil," see Hazal Friedman, "The Horror," *M and G* (8 August 1997). Although *Ubu and the Truth Commission* appeared on stage before Benzien's testimony and should not in any case be expected to depict the figures of Benzien, de Kock, or any other actual perpetrator, allusions to de Kock were picked up by local critics, who noted that de Kock himself presented an unexpected face (perhaps his "not/but") when he met with Jan Turner, the daughter of one of his high-profile victims, Professor Richard Turner.

retrospect, the most powerful element of this production appears to be not so much the opportunistic textual collage of Ubu and TRC testimony as the compelling images of suffering in Kentridge's animations and the creations of puppeteers Basil Jones and Adrian Kohler.

Sharing the unshareable: towards a survivors' theatre of waking life

Although *Ubu and the Truth Commission* challenged the "lie of the literal," especially with its creative attention (by way of the puppets) to the necessary mediation of testimony in performance, it did not fully respond to the ethical question of usurping the presence of witnesses. In Kentridge's own acknowledgment, this question was answered incompletely by a decision that was at the outset a matter of "performance style."[46] This professional production of fictions based on TRC testimony in the full public scrutiny of a formal theatre could not but run the risk of turning the experience of witnesses into an accessible but exploitative spectacle. This risk is all the greater when the performance includes the dramatization of perpetrators in which the charisma of the lead actor combines to disturbing effect with that of the notorious criminal. In other words, art, however arresting, addressed primarily an international audience of connoisseurs rather than South Africans seeking a forum for reconciliation or, more modestly, for understanding, if not resolving, conflicting experiences of apartheid. The immediate expression of survivors themselves is, however, no more guaranteed to generate resolution. Survivors re-enacting their own experience, even if doing so exclusively in the company of other survivors and trained mediators, run the risk of reliving rather than re-presenting and processing experience, but may also gain social as well as performative agency through the process of representation. Impersonators, especially those such as translators or actors performing for survivors, may be overwhelmed by the reaction of these witnesses and by the enormousness of their task, but their ability as performers to shape what Salverson calls the "subtleties of damage, hope and the 'not-nameable'" (or, in Scarry's terms, the

---

[46] Kentridge, "Director's Note," xi.

"unshareable") may help to make sense out of the raw sensation of experience.[47]

The difficulty of transforming testimony into resolution is acknowledged in the Commission's own retrospective distinction between the clarifying outcome of resolution and the impossible, and possibly dangerous, appeal to transcendent unity in an emerging democracy that must honor difference and dispute if it is to thrive.[48] The call for national reconciliation in the wake of the revelation of gross human rights violations invokes the notion of catharsis, and, in contrast, skepticism about the relevance of catharsis in national policy invites comparison with philosopher G. W. F. Hegel's distinction between *Schlichtung* (resolution in the sense of legal settlement of discord or debt) and *Versöhnung* (reconciliation in a metaphysical transcendent sense).[49] Both hopeful appeal and skeptical response resonate in the tension between translations. In Afrikaans, formerly the language of apartheid power and still the third most widely spoken mother tongue in the country, *versoening*, like *Versöhnung*, invokes metaphysical reconciliation, while the English "reconciliation" contains both the theological resonance and the connotations of settlement or canceled debt. Xhosa, by contrast, draws on *uxolo* (peace) to create *uxolelwano* (coming to peace), which highlights the process of reconciliation in the spirit of *ubuntu* (common humanity).

The concept of "coming to peace" by acknowledging common humanity alongside persistent differences and disputes about the truth may provide a more effective guide for the ongoing journey of survivors and bystanders (and possibly also perpetrators) than appeals to the drama of cathartic reconciliation. Coming to peace may be a more

---

47 Salverson, "Performing Emergency," 184.
48 *TRC Report*, vol. 1, ch. 5, paras. 19–28.
49 G. W. F. Hegel, *Vorlesungen über die Ästhetik* (Frankfurt a.M.: Suhrkamp, 1970), 3: 475; trans. T. M. Knox as *Aesthetics* (Oxford: Clarendon Press, 1998), 2: 1159. For analysis of Hegel's theoretical categories and their powerful if not fully acknowledged influence on common-sense ideas about drama in general and the representation of sense perception in particular, see Kruger, "Making Sense of Sensation," 543–54.

modest goal than the TRC's conception of restorative justice, which called, as the Report had it, for "offender accountability" and "reparation" as well as the more abstract "restoration of all concerned," victims and offenders, to the "larger community."[50] The national and regional hearings of the TRC performed the important function of publicly acknowledging not only individual wrongs but also systematic human rights violations mandated by the apartheid state; but this public disclosure also exacerbated abiding differences of experience and belief.[51] Whereas this national exposure had the value of reminding South Africans that the persistence of deep economic, social, and cultural divisions, rather than any immediate reconciliation, was indeed the truth of South Africa, the processes of individual and community restoration has taken place in the more intimate settings of survivor groups and supporting non-government organizations (NGOs). In other words, while the publication of the truth, and with it the correction of the historical record, required the authority vested in the state, the processes of resolution and healing depended in contrast on more intimate encounters between witnesses and sympathetic listeners in order, as human rights scholar Martha Minow put it, to translate truth-telling about "shame and humiliation" into a "portrayal of

---

[50] *TRC Report*, vol. 1, ch. 5, paras. 80–100; here: para. 82. Critics such as the Asmals and the Biko family regarded restorative justice as at best a poor substitute for sentencing in a court of law and at worst no justice at all, but a range of commentators, theologians, political philosophers, and human rights lawyers have defended both the concept and its imperfect but far-reaching practice in South Africa. See citations in notes 14 and 16; also Elizabeth Kiss, "Moral Ambitions within and beyond Political Constraints: Reflections on Restorative Justice," and Martha Minow, "Hope for Healing: What Can Truth Commissions Do?" in *Truth v. Justice*, 68–98, and 235–60.

[51] This exacerbation can be seen in the "register of reconciliation" posted on the TRC's website while it was in session. Although statements of contrition and regret from private individuals appeared at the outset, these were quickly overwhelmed by a much larger number of angry and vindictive statements, above all by those whites who felt that the TRC was a witch-hunt against them.

dignity and virtue."[52] This small-scale resolution between individuals should not be automatically favored over the national exposure of the truth merely because the former promises healing while the latter appears to highlight conflict, but rather because these small-scale re-presentations recognize the fundamentally social character of coming to peace, based as it is on the concept of *ubuntu* or common humanity.[53]

Highlighting the social dimension of the process of resolution entails an understanding of the dynamic and often conflictual character of narrativizing trauma. The re-presentation of acts of witnessing on small stages, to sympathetic listeners in workshops, therapy sessions, and theatrical re-enactments has enabled many survivors to translate their experiences into manageable narratives, while also allowing a smaller number of bystanders and beneficiaries of apartheid to examine their own acts and omissions in past and present South Africa. But such acts and activities have not and, one could argue, could not have produced a cathartic reconciliation but should strive rather, to recall Caruth's idea, for an understanding of trauma as a historical as much as a psychological symptom.[54] Although groups such as the Khulumani (Speak (Out)!) Survivors' Support Group and the

---

[52] Minow, "Hope for Healing," 243.

[53] Overseas interest in this African (or more precisely South Bantu) concept has led to complicated translations of the form "being a person through other people," but as the abstract concept-noun derived from the common noun *umuntu* (Zulu) or *umntu* (Xhosa), meaning "person," *ubuntu* can be succinctly translated as "common humanity." As such, it reminds Westerners, especially individualists and sentimentalists, that healing in the wake of the apartheid is necessarily social.

[54] Survivors' support groups set up by NGOs, such as the Khulumani group established by the Centre for the Study of Violence and Reconciliation, were supplemented by others which attempted to bring together South Africans from different groups, such as the Institute for the Healing of Memories (HOM), which operates under the auspices of a broadly Christian program of healing and forgiveness and employs a theatre group called Mina naWe (Me and You) to open workshops with a performance on these themes, as well as informal attempts by community theatre organizations, such as Linda's Victory/Sonqoba, to

Institute for the Healing of Memories have attempted, as their names imply, to enable survivors to heal themselves and each other through mutual testimony to listeners who suffered as they did, we should not assume at the outset that this commonality always means that "the individual account of a single person will *immediately* be pluralized: so the oppression of one is the oppression of all" (emphasis added).[55] This assertion comes from Augusto Boal, a world-renowned theorist and practitioner of theatre of the oppressed and, in this context, also of theatre as therapy, who has been cited as a model for theatre after the TRC.[56] Nonetheless, Boal's claim that the act of testimony translates directly into the gest of witnessing – in other words, into a clearly shared communication – invites a measure of skepticism in the face of ongoing difficulties of translation. This skepticism, however tempered by sympathy, should accompany even this incomplete account of the healing potential of theatrical enactments of apartheid trauma, since even well-conceived and well-executed experiments highlight the irresolute nature of such performances.

Even before the TRC began hearings in 1996, organizations from community theatres to NGOs dedicated to conflict resolution attempted to harness theatre to the treatment of trauma as well as the defusion of political tension. Some institutions, such as the Centre for the Study of Violence and Reconciliation (CSVR), which began

tackle the themes of violence and reconciliation. For a brief account of Mina naWe's *That Spirit*, see Marlin-Curiel, "Long Road to Healing," 279–81. Organizations like these have had some success in giving survivors a safe place to speak, but have not been able to deal with charges that particular religious, especially Christian, practices may alienate others, such as Muslims, even though an imam now sits on HOM's board. This point has been acknowledged even by participant observers, such as the anthropologist Undine Kayser, who comments on HOM workshops she attended: "Creating a Space for Encounter and Remembrance: The Healing of Memories Process," CSVR (Centre for Violence and Reconciliation) website at http://www.csvr.org.za/ papers/paphom.htm, accessed 2 April 2003.

[55] Augusto Boal, *The Rainbow of Desire: The Boal Method of Theatre and Therapy*, trans. Adrian Jackson (London: Routledge, 1995), 45.

[56] Citation in Marlin-Curiel, "Long Road to Healing," 277.

as the Project for the Study of Violence at Witwatersrand University as early as 1989, drew on the anti-apartheid repertoire of cultural as well as social work to examine the broadly social impact, as well as the specific consequences for therapy or criminology, of the endemic and politically ambiguous violence that plagued South Africa in the interregnum and continued into the post-apartheid period.[57] The persistence of the CSVR and related associations across the academic/popular divide, such as the History Workshop, formerly a key collaborator with the Junction Avenue Theatre Company, highlights an important element of continuity between anti-apartheid and post-apartheid NGO work which is often ignored by newcomers to South Africa. Founded under CSVR auspices in 1995, the Khulumani Survivors' Support Network provided survivors of apartheid an opportunity to speak out before the TRC convened and later to re-present their TRC testimony to sympathetic listeners like them. Initially this forum included only other survivors and therapists, to create what the psychiatrist Dori Laub identifies as a dynamic that allows the listener

[57] Founded, like many research and intervention organizations in the anti-apartheid era, under the auspices of a liberal university, the CSVR was by the mid-1990s conducting research and intervention into a range of areas from police violence against criminal suspects to the social and other causes of the escalating rape rate, as well as providing therapy for TRC witnesses and others in its trauma center. In keeping with its engagement with grassroots organization, the central Transition and Reconciliation Unit is now called Themba leSizwe (Hope for the Nation). For further information see the CSVR website at http://www/csvr.org.za. After 2000 and the end of the TRC process, Khulumani turned to skills development and advocacy for communities beset by poverty and the AIDS epidemic. Since November 2002, however, these community-based activities have been overshadowed by the group's involvement in a high-profile lawsuit in the US federal court against Barclays Bank and other multi-nationals based in South Africa. The case for monetary compensation for individuals' pain and suffering allegedly caused by such companies' business with the apartheid government borrows from successful suits brought against US multi-nationals with war-time ties to Nazi Germany, but its application to a very large and broadly defined class of plaintiffs in South Africa remains controversial.

"to be a witness to the trauma witness and a witness to himself [sic]."[58] Unlike Jewish Holocaust survivors, many of whom, in Laub's view, "preferred silence" for fear of not being listened to, several Khulumani members broke silence publicly by appearing in a 1995 video, *Khulumani!*, before the TRC had officially convened to hear testimony, while others came to the organization after testifying at the TRC.[59] Although they found that national public exposure unsettling, they were nonetheless willing to risk contributing not only their stories but also their embodiment of that experience to the creation of a play, *The Story I Am About to Tell.*[60]

In collaboration with Ramolao Makhene, a veteran performer of anti-apartheid and Brechtian history plays with JATC, and Bobby Rodwell at the Market Laboratory, a community theatre, sister organization to the high-profile Market Theatre, the testimony of three witnesses – Duma Khumalo, who spent three years on death row for a crime he did not commit; Caroline Mlangeni, whose son was killed by a booby-trapped personal cassette player; and Thandi Shezi, an ANC activist tortured and raped in prison – who appeared at the TRC in mid-1997 was recontextualized within a fictional frame of a taxi ride. Makhene played the driver as a kind of catalyst, asking questions that allowed the survivors to re-present their stories in the company of actors playing a former freedom fighter and a former SADF soldier. This fictional encounter was not entirely convincing, since the last-mentioned characters would be unlikely to share a taxi with the others. Nonetheless, this contrivance enhanced rather

[58] Laub, "Bearing Witness," 58.

[59] *Khulumani!* was directed by Henion Han and produced by Lauren Segal for CSVR and was followed in 1997 by a second video, *Sisakhuluma* (We are Still Speaking (Out)), which documented the views of witnesses after they had testified at the TRC.

[60] Comments based on observation of the performance at the National Arts Festival in Grahamstown, 5 July 1999, as well as accounts of earlier community performances in 1997, such as the one in Duma Khumalo's home town of Sharpeville. For more information, consult the interview with the founder, Shirley Gunn, on Radio Netherlands' "A Good Life," broadcast on WBEZ-Chicago, 91.5 FM, Sunday 29 April 2001, and Marlin-Curiel, "Long Road to Healing," 281–2.

than undermined the performance of the witnesses. Makhene's professional collegiality (in his double role as fictional taxi driver and actual workshop animator) provided the ground against which the witnesses' embodiment of as-yet-incompletely mediated trauma stood out sharply: Khumalo wrung his hands as though still chafed by the chains he wore on death row, while Shezi covered her face as she spoke of her experience of repeated rape in prison.[61]

The evolution of the play, from post-traumatic inarticulacy to the processing of trauma in narrative and gesture in therapeutic setting to the representation of this embodied narrative at the national fora of the TRC and, differently, for audiences in the home communities of the witness-performers such as Khumalo's Sharpeville in 1997, to its performance for unrelated audiences at theatrical venues, formal and otherwise, from the National Arts Festival in Grahamstown to venues overseas such as Germany (in 1999), may suggest a movement from authenticity to artificiality. This initial impression is subject to challenge on several fronts, however. Most immediately, the gestures of the witnesses did not dissolve the symptoms of trauma into the sovereign gest of the actor, but rather highlighted the still painful gap between trauma and performance. Moreover, the title invoked the conventional rubric of TV docudrama: "The story I am about to tell is true; only names have been changed to protect . . ." and thus highlighted, whether intentionally or not, the mediation of the true stories by the forms and conventions of fictional representation. This mediation and the re-presentation of the performance in a venue dedicated to "national art" did not, however, prevent commentators from treating it as a contribution to national healing.[62]

---

[61] I am using the term "animator" in the sense borrowed by Boal from the French *animateur*, the person who provokes as well as enlivens performance, part *raisonneur*, part joker. See Boal, *Theatre of the Oppressed*, trans. Robert McBride and Maria-Odilia Leal McBride (New York: Urizen, 1979), 182.

[62] See Alex Dodd's response to the 1999 Grahamstown performance, "Face up to Honest Reality," *Johannesburg Mail and Guardian* (11 June 1999), http://www.sn.apc.org/wmail/issues/990611/ARTS21.html, retrieved 21 March 2000.

The national dimension of the *Story* was both highlighted and complicated by the witnesses' choice of languages. Mhlangeni, the oldest, had delivered her brief account of her son's death in English in the *Khulumani!* video, but preferred to speak primarily in Zulu in the play. Although also a Zulu speaker, the younger Shezi chose to speak in English as a member of the ANC women's league at the TRC and in the play. Even if witnesses themselves reiterated in interviews a distinction between English as a political language and vernaculars as intimate and by implication less political, this is a conventional opposition inherited from anti-apartheid lore that should not be used to reinforce the assumption that emotional self-expression, especially to an outside observer, is more authentically truthful than public political speech to fellow citizens.[63] Khumalo's Sesotho performance in his home town of Sharpeville may have created an intimate connection to the Sesotho speakers among speakers of other languages in the community, but his turn to English when reiterating his innocence of the legal charges against him suggests a pointed shift to national address that was repeated by other witnesses, who often punctuated narratives in the vernacular with English words, especially when naming techniques of torture. Moreover, the group's choice of Sharpeville was dictated not only by one member's origin but by the historical and present significance of Sharpeville as the place where the killing of unarmed demonstrators by the police took place in March 1960, the moment that marked the apartheid government's move towards a police state and the outlawed ANC and others towards armed resistance, and thus the inauguration of the period officially covered by the TRC's investigation into gross human rights violations.

Shezi's case is particularly interesting, not so much because she was an ANC activist, but rather because her stated commitment to English was framed in a way that complicated the political claims routinely made for English and for the more dominant

[63] Marlin-Curiel, "Long Road to Healing," 282, reiterates this assumption when she glosses Shezi's defense of English in interview as primarily "emotional," as a way of "controlling her tears," without returning to Shezi's reason for avoiding tears: she wanted to speak clearly to other women.

voices of male activists. Whereas most witnesses at the HRV hearings spoke directly in response to prompting from the commissioners, testimony at the special women's hearings opened with a statement by Thenjiwe Mtintso, Chair of the Commission on Gender Equality, who used the occasion to criticize not only the TRC but also the new government as a whole. She argued that the mostly male executive branch was not fully attending to the extent to which the bodies of women in South Africa (as in the former Yugoslavia) became a "terrain of struggle" violated by men on all sides of the conflict, and, in immediate terms, that these former guerrillas were not fighting escalating violence against women and children in the post-apartheid period with the same vigor as they had fought the war against apartheid. After Mtintso's bracing commentary, Gcina Mhlophe, a well-known storyteller, poet, and cultural animator, introduced each witness's testimony with one or more poems, most of which were more conciliatory than combative.[64] Shezi's testimony was prefaced by two poems by Mhlophe. The first, "The Wedding Dancer," was a praise poem (*izibongo*) in Zulu, directed in the first instance to her own mother and more generally to all mothers of the nation, and to those women whom the struggle compelled to be dancers at funerals rather than at weddings; the second, in English, called "Leader, Remember," exhorted an unnamed post-apartheid leader to remember "the promises you made, the hope you represent."[65] Listeners familiar with Mhlophe's earlier work, especially her autobiographical play *Have You Seen Zandile?* (1986), would have had a sense not only of the personal story behind her elliptical comment, "My mother did not like the fact that I ended up in show business," but also of the collective experience of women

---

[64] The proceedings of the Women's Hearing of the HRV Committee on 28 and 29 July 1997 opened with a prayer to "God our Father and God our Mother" by the Rev. Vanessa McKenzie, and continued with the first of many poems by Gcina Mhlophe and a statement by Mtintso, followed by the first witness, a senior activist, Sheila Masote. See http://www.doj.gov.za/trc/special/women.

[65] Mhlophe, "The Wedding Dancer" and "Leader, Remember," http://www.doj.gov.za/trc/special/women/shezi,htm. Subsequent citations of Mhlophe and Shezi in the text are from this site.

subject not only to explicitly "politically motivated" violence but also to rape and abuse, as well as more subtle kinds of patriarchal coercion, in the heart of their communities.[66] Unlike Mtintso's explicit indictment and Mhlophe's implicit critique of patriarchies African as well as Afrikaner, Shezi's testimony at the TRC and in *The Story I Am About to Tell* focused for the most part on her contribution to the anti-apartheid struggle and on her effort to overcome her sense of worthlessness after being raped by four white policemen in prison. The struggle narrative underwent an unexpected twist, however, when Shezi described her endeavor in (anti) theatrical terms. She describes her post-traumatic struggle as an effort to avoid "falling into a role" like an "actor" whose identification with a character (whom we could describe as *abject*) might encourage people to treat her as an object of pity rather than as the "strong person," as the social agent she had been and desired to be again.[67]

In this apparently anti-theatrical gesture, Shezi nonetheless highlighted the theatrical (in the sense of imagined and imaginatively performed) character of social agency *as gest*, in terms that Brecht and Boal would read as an act of analysis as well as potential transformation but that her male companions in struggle had yet to perform

---

[66] *Have You Seen Zandile?* (Portsmouth, NH: Heinemann, 1986) was written and initially also performed by Mhlophe in collaboration with the actor Thembi Mtshali and the writer Marilin van Renen. The play followed a young girl who lives with her grandmother in the city of Durban until her hitherto absent mother abducts her from her grandmother's house to prepare for a traditional Xhosa marriage in rural Transkei, and the girl's rebellion against this lot. Mhlophe herself lived through this experience and went on to begin writing while working as a domestic servant for white householders in Johannesburg. Autobiographical information confirmed by an audiotape letter to the author, December 1994; see also Kruger, *Drama of South Africa*, 181–4.

[67] Julia Kristéva describes the experience of abjectness in opposition to an object that the subject can master: "the adject is an object abandoned [*objet chu*], a radically excluded other that draws me to the point where meaning collapses." See *Pouvoirs de l'horreur: essai sur l'abjection* (Paris: Seuil, 1980), 9; trans. Leon S. Roudiez as *Powers of Horror* (New York: Columbia University Press, 1982), 2 (trans. modified).

completely. In her closing affirmation that, unlike many witnesses
who remained unemployed and unmoored after the TRC, she was
employed as a field worker for Khulumani, she emphasized her reintegration as an effective social agent, if not as the "hero" that her TRC
interlocutor, Commissioner Hlengiwe Mkhize, dubbed her. Although
Shezi's TRC testimony and performance in *The Story I Am About to
Tell* revealed the ongoing power of post-traumatic stress symptoms –
from flashbacks to unpredictable aggression against family members
to fear of intimacy – to interrupt this process of reintegration, these
symptoms did not betray her. Rather, in the process of restoring her
agency, they became no longer entirely "symptoms of a history [she
could] not entirely possess," to rephrase Caruth, but rather gestic signs
of a national, local, and personal history that she was learning to
repossess.

Shezi's case is not unique, but she does offer a heartening example of the power of performance in this process of repossessing the past
and sustaining hope for the future. Although her symptoms may not
have completely vanished at the time of this performance in 1999, her
re-entry on to the stage of waking life by way of the space of therapeutic expression, the theatrical platform, and the social activity of
working life demonstrates that the power of *ubuntu* and *uxolweno*
rests not on abstract principles but on the processes of social action,
and the shaping of those processes in the dialectic between the subjunctive action of imaginative rehearsal on stages and other virtual
public spheres and the indicative performance in the public sphere of
society. While post-traumatic symptoms, and their power to interrupt
or silence enlightened and enlightening speech, complicate any simple assertion of the translation of subjunctive into indicative action,
the examples of Thandi Shezi, Yazir Henry, and many others at and
after the TRC affirm the capacity of enactment, as the opening declaration of Culture and Working Life had it in an acknowledged allusion
to Brecht, to "illuminate the darkness of those times" and to offer a
guiding light amidst the shadows of these.

Coda

I began this book by suggesting that Brecht's legacy should not be mapped only on the Cold War axis of West to East or only on the post-colonial axis of North to South, but rather that Brecht and his legacies, including those traces attributed to him after the fact, should be plotted within multiple lines of force, so as to highlight the intersection and interference of these axes. By highlighting East and South, as against their usually dominant opposites West and North, I aimed in the first instance to document, in the connection and opposition of East Germany and South Africa, the intersection of performance and politics in the name of Brecht and his associates, from the immediate, such as Heiner Müller, to the mediated, such as Athol Fugard. Despite apparently disjunct trajectories, these dramatists, their translators, and their interpreters from actors through directors to audiences and critics highlight in converging themes and forms a tradition of political performance, especially of a theatre of dissidence against ideological tyranny, which allow us to make unexpected connections, locally between the liberal disquiet of Fugard and the explicit if ambivalent commitment of Brecht, or, much more broadly, between the familiar but fuzzy terrain of the "third world" and the unfamiliar and likewise ambiguously located "second world," and thus establish points of cultural contact across great chasms of ideological conflict.

I hope that mapping this documentary project on an East/South axis and extending this map across the temporal frame of a post-imperial era provides terms for critical re-examination of the conventionally distinct North/South and West/East coordinates of geographical, historical, and theoretical orientation and for an interrogation of the commonplace (but still problematic) boundary invoked but never quite specified by the "post-colonial." As the texts and performances here demonstrate, the post-imperial rubric allows us to see Cold War battles between capitalism and communism anew when juxtaposed with competing discourses of imperialism and anti-imperialism, while also reviewing the anti-apartheid struggle in the light of overlapping narratives of international socialism. Looking back over the particular forms and languages of Brecht, Fugard, Müller, the Junction Avenue Theatre, and the testimonies of and around the TRC, this book cautions against the habitual monolingualism of global (usually English) studies and against the premature assumption that all cultural practices can be equally mapped on a global scale. Looking forward beyond the well-known icons of Brecht and Fugard, and working through the lesser-known but compelling performances of the directors, actors, and dramatists in the preceding chapters, it also invites readers to explore other histories that challenge the ingrained separation between Western and third world culture, European and African theatres, metropolitan and (post) colonial literatures, so as to weave without obliterating the irreducibly multiple strands of truly "worldly" cultures.

Index

Index

Index

psychology 87–8; v. subjectivity 92

solidarity, as principle of international socialism 8–12, 220–7, 286–93; anti-capitalist 97–8; v. egoist 136–7, 159–64; v. interiority 309; in South Africa 226–31, 241–5, 261–7; limits of 281; v. racial prejudice 285–91, 293, 296, 312; "seeing through race" 290–3, 302, 310–11; v. tribal affiliations 266–7

Solidarity Committee (GDR) 9, 281–3, 286–91; and GDR promotion of Fugard 286–91, 312–13

South Africa 6, 215, 216–79, 304–5, 306–7; Jewish population 224; truth and reconciliation in 337–74

Soviet Union and Bolshevik revolution 21, 26–8, 152–3; and GDR 49–52, 63, 69, 83; and GDR reparations 90; and German exiles 39–41

Soviet allies: and destalinization 102; and *glasnost* 123; underdevelopment of 132; Czechoslovakia 49, 123; and Soviet invasion 50; Hungary 50, 123; and uprising 94; Poland 49, 50, 69; resistance to collectivization 69–70

SPD (*Sozialistiche Partei Deutschlands*: Socialist Party of Germany) 3, 21, 22–3, 103; v. KPD

Spur der Steine (Neutsch) 82, 103, 109; see also films

stage design: *Bau* (Müller) 118–19; *Island* (Fugard) 298–301; *Lohndrücker* (Müller) 126–8;

Massnahme (Brecht) 201–6; v. radio space 166

Stalin (Josif Vissaronovitch Dzhugashvili) 10; image on program 182; image on stage 126

Stalinism 21, 34–5; and the "Moscow group" of German exiles 40–1, 47, 49; in the GDR 81–2, 100–1; Gorbachev's critique of 123

Stalinallee (later Karl-Marx-Allee, now Frankfurter Allee; Berlin) 88, 178–82, 211; see also Berlin; modern architecture

Stasi (Ministry of State Security: GDR) 50, 88, 128, 306; and Müller 138–9; and Wekwerth 137–8; v. BOSS 11

Strittmatter, Erwin 61; and defense of collectivization 71; *Szenen aus dem Bauernleben* 66–9, 74

subjectivity: allegedly bourgeois in Fugard 288–9; critiqued by socialization 92; disengaged 153–4; and GDR modernity 118–19; proletarian 73–4

subjunctive, as index of utopian possibility 27, 375; v. indicative fact 337–9; opposition defined 339

Survival (Workshop' 71) 218, 236, 288; and creating a majority public sphere 255–6; v. *The Island* 254; v. *Sizwe Bansi* 255

syncretic theatre (in South Africa) 219, 222, 243–4; see also genre; *Lehrstück*; testimonial performance

Szondi, Peter 90–1

testimony 18; disclosure v. acting out 361; as deception 351–64; as enlightenment 339; gestic 352;

395